FOODS THAT HEAL

Dr. G.N. Chauhan retired from Rajasthan University as Senior Professor of Homeopathy. He enjoys a countrywide reputation as an expert naturopath, homeopath and a prolific writer. His well-researched articles on nature cure, health, nutrition and herbs appear regularly in various newspapers and magazines and bear the stamp of authority.

FOODS THAT HEAL

A Handy Reference of Herbal Cures for Common Ailments

Dr. G.N. Chauhan

P·B·D

POPULAR BOOK DEPOT

Popular Book Depot G-15, Dhamani Street, Chaura Rasta, Jaipur-3. India.
Phone:91-141-2325965, 0-98290-89555
email:pbdjpr@rediffmail.com • www.pbdbooks.com

Fifth Edition published by Popular Book Depot, 2015

10 9 8 7 6 5

Typset in AGaramond

Preface

India has always been a treasure trove of herbs. There is hardly any traditional Indian cuisine which is considered complete without the use of herbal spices. The herbs are seen as agents of taste, satisfaction and well being. Indian herbalism was developed by the ancient seers, sages, wanderers and tribals, who through intution and observation discovered the many properties of plants and their products.

This book deals with various herbs, fruits and vegetables, etc. commonly found in the markets of subcontinent. Most of them are familiar kitchen and spice box staples having therapeutic properties. Dealing with each herb or fruit, the author has recorded its traditional use alongwith its efficacy as a drug. The book has several herbal and alternative medicine remedies.

The ailments have been arranged in groups under the system of related organs, however, the contents in the beginning of the book have been listed in the alphabetical order of the diseases and their remedies for easy reference. The glossary of English Terms, Non-English Terms and Plants and other Ingredients have been appended separately for the benefit of the readers. The extensive index given at the back of the book allows the quick location of the multiple remedial properties of a particular herb or fruit with respect to the diseases listed beneath it. The index facilitates easy location of herbs or fruits by their Hindi names. The diagramatic representation of few plants and their parts etc. has been given in the last few pages.

This book is an attempt by the author to contribute by documenting and making available to a larger public what he has practised during the long course of his research and practice. We sincerely hope that this version of the book will facilitate an informed understanding among the readers regarding herbalism and alternative medicine and will help to reinforce the therapeutic value of the foods that we generally consume daily.

—Publishers

Contents

Of Related Interest

- Ayurvedic Cures for Common Diseases
- Homeopathic Remedies
- Health and Harmony through Ayurveda

- *Bhojan Ke Dwara Chikitsa*
- *Shaktivardhak Bhojan*
- *Kya Khayen aur Kyon?*
- *Swadeshi Chikitsa Saar*

FOODS THAT HEAL

NOURISHMENT

Life is a divine gift, and a disease-free sound health is a great blessing. Nourishing food is essential for a sound health. We need to know what to eat and when to eat, so that the food consumed may not only satisfy our hunger, but also keep us healthy through its medicinal effects.

Food provides a base to live a healthy life. If food is to our taste and easy to digest, it surely keeps us healthy. A number of health food charts based on modern scientific studies are available that prescribe the quantities of carbohydrates, proteins and vitamins, etc., to be taken daily through various items of food according to the calorie requirement of our body. But because of defective digestive system, our body is not able to burn fully all the calories we consume, as a result we fall sick. Therefore, we should pay due attention to food and consume such things as would provide nourishment to our body acting as medicines and keep us disease-free. The present book prescribes 'treatment through food' based on this very principle.

A patient is better treated in a kitchen than in a hospital. In our daily life we take almost dead or nutrition-less food. We can certainly increase our life-span to a hundred years if we improve our food habits and observe restraint in our life. Gita says *satvik* food and frugal eating increases our longevity. You can even realize God by observing a fast. Howsoever tasty the food may be, it should be chewed properly. More men die of over-eating than from hunger. Eat less so that your digestive system can work better. Keep yourself cheerful. Medicines would not work if you do not follow the dictum of 'prevention is better than cure'.

It is, therefore, better to eat wholesome food because health and beauty are better preserved by eating according to your need only. Follow nature, the closer you are to nature, the healthier and longer your life will be.

Pure food is endowed with the quality of *Sattva. Satvikta* makes the memory retentive. Retentive memory in turn helps in the attainment of knowledge which unfolds the knots of one's heart. In other words, ignorance vanishes and all doubts are cleared. Thus pure food ensures one's total well-being.

The most beneficial food is the one, which is in its natural form or which has been the least tempered with (reformed).

Naturopathy favours only *Satvik* foods. According to Naturopaths food is medicine and medicine is food. Natural food activates the inner resistance power or the immune system in such a way that it is able to fight all infectious diseases. Therefore, treatment through food is a part of Naturopathy.

People who feel sick most of the time, should consume only vegetables, salad and fruits for some time. It is beneficial in a great number of diseases. If the food items stated in this book are taken together in as large a number as possible, relief will come promptly.

It is imperative to improve your style of eating if you want to keep healthy. Fruits, vegetables, etc., should be taken regularly because they provide all the vitamins required by our body. To keep healthy treat your food as medicine. According to Socrates, health lies in wholesome food, and wholesome food is medicine. Food should be taken for nutrition when healthy and as medicine when sick.

Proper food is as vital as medicine for prompt relief and healing. Vitamins are also in a way food items; they help us in keeping healthy. Their deficiency can cause certain diseases. The vegetables, fruits and spices described in the following pages not only help in curing diseases, but also work as a healthy diet for the patient. Any alternate medicine, if necessary, can also be taken with this diet. They should be prescribed according to the nature and condition of the patient. If in any way they cause trouble or problem, their use should be discontinued. Vitamin C has been discussed below. Its appraisal will help us understand how useful some of the particular substances are in maintaining a sound health and combating disease.

DISEASES CAUSED BY THE DEFICIENCY OF VITAMIN C

Paleness of face, debility, body ache, swollen gums, bleeding gums, loose teeth, foul breath, bleeding from skin and phlegmatic sources are the diseases caused by the deficiency of Vitamin C. Teeth become irregular and defective. The patient suffers from pyorrhoea. He loses appetite and does not get full nourishment.

Bones, cells and arteries get damaged or the wounds do not heal easily and even small hurts and slips cause fractures in the bones. The deficiency of Vitamin C causes the terrible disease 'scurvy'. One becomes debilitated and irritable. One can also suffer from anaemia. Red blood corpuscles become weak and deficient. The blood vessels contract and the heart also becomes weak. The immune system too gets weakened. As a result, the patient is unable to fight infectious diseases. Common cold or severe cold, pneumonia, etc., afflict the body frequently. One suffers from lack of stamina and gets tired easily and even in youth looks like an old man.

Benefits of Vitamin C : It is essential for pregnant and suckling mothers. It is useful in several diseases of the stomach, intestines and liver. It accelerates the growth of the body, increases the weight, sharpens the appetite and helps in the formation of blood. It is an essential part of the diet for growing children and is an established cure for scurvy.

Sources of Vitamin C : It is found in abundance in oranges, lime, *mausambi* and other juicy fruits. It is also found in *chaulai,* cabbage, small carrots, onions, tomatoes, radish, coriander leaves, spinach, beet root, pears, berries, pineapple and guava. *Amla* is full of Vitamin C. It does not lose the vitamin even after it has been cooked. *Amla* enhances the formation of semen and destroys '*pitta*' in blood. Dried *amla* powder sieved through muslin cloth taken daily (3 gms.) with honey for four months can bring about a transformation in the body *(Kayakalpa).* It sharpens the appetite, induces good sleep, gives a boost to mental powers, strengthens the heart, makes hair black, splendid and cures headaches. Sometimes it works better than powerful patent medicines. Take 6 tablets made out of *amla* powder, thrice a day. (Refer the chapter on *amla* in the present author's book entitled '*Bhojan ke Dwara Chikitsa*'). The green vegetables mentioned above can be taken raw or you may take them in the form of juice; they will enhance your longevity and you will retain the vigour of a young man even in old age.

Vitamin A : If your eyesight has gone weak, you cannot see clearly in the dark or suffer from night-blindness; if the eyes suffer from dryness, irritation or a burning sensation, they cannot stand light, have lost lustre, have developed cataract in old age, the eyesight has become dim; if stones are frequently formed in the kidney and teeth become loose, the symptoms indicate that there is a deficiency of Vitamin A. You can get rid of these symptoms by consuming fresh green *chaulai,* cabbage, coriander leaves, green mint leaves, fenugreek leaves, spinach, carrots, papaya, mangoes and home-made fresh butter. The vegetables and fruits can be consumed raw or in the form of *chutney* or you could have them by way of juice. If taken for three to four months, they will help in curing the above mentioned diseases.

USE OF FRUITS AND VEGETABLES

People with poor digestion should dilute fruit and vegetable juices with water. Diluted juices are easy to digest. Taking them on an empty stomach is highly beneficial.

Fruit and vegetable juices should be taken raw and fresh. The treatment with juices is slow and complete cure takes a long time. Other things can also be taken as supplementary treatment. Juices should be taken in the morning and in the afternoon. 16 Ounces of juice can be taken at a time. Seasonal fruits and vegetables should be used. As far as possible, sugar should be consumed in small quantities. Human body is capable of synthesizing sugar from the foods we eat.

SKIN/RIND

When the skin of a vegetable is not too hard it should be cooked without removing the skin. The skin is a source of energy. It relieves constipation and clears the bowels. Use whole pulses. Eat fruits with the skin on.

The food items mentioned here are beneficial if taken by a patient as an auxiliary treatment alongwith regular medicines according to the nature and the stage of the disease. If these food items cause any problem their use should be discontinued.

Vegetarian diet : India is a tropical country. Summers are long and hot here. Therefore you need such food which can keep you cool and vegetarian diet is very good in this regard. Alcohol is highly injurious to health in a climate like ours.

ILLNESS AND DIET

Three sips of water before meals will cool down the heat in the esophagus and stomach. The ill effects of the heat in the food and the pungency of spices will also subside. The mental state in which we eat affects our thinking also. While eating, our thoughts should be pious and *Satvik*. The food we eat shapes our mind. Every man has in him a bio-clock which plays an important role in controlling his physical activities. That is how we have a cycle of eating, sleeping and waking up.

Foods That Heal

These days man has alienated himself from nature. Human body has a built-in mechanism to keep itself healthy but the man's alienation from nature has a damaging effect on this mechanism.

A disease cannot be totally cured with the help of medicines. But those who exercise and restraint in matters of food do not fall sick. If you have wrong food habits no treatment can keep you fit. Food and health are closely related. The more a man knows about foods the healthier he will be. You can keep yourself disease-free if you take food as per your need. Thus, your health with sweetness of life is in your own hands. Your food will affect your nature or behaviour. Food goes into the making of blood in the body. Defective blood is responsible for several illnesses. Therefore, to keep ourselves healthy we should include those diet items that can purify blood. When fallen sick, read the present book and the other title *Bhojan ke Dwara Chikitsa* by the same author for treatment and to know about the virtues of health foods.

Proper care about food brings an improvement in health. In case you fall ill take great care regarding your food for quick recovery or consult a doctor. Healthy diet, rather than medicine, is of special importance. Unless you have a serious illness, you can solve most of the problems with the help of food.

Total health : Take raw foods whether your ailment is old or new. Do away with salt and intoxicants. Take only seasonal fruits and vegetables which are within the reach of your pocket. You have to have patience with this method to feel fully healthy.

Wind (*Vata*), Bile (*Pitta*), Phlegm (*Kafa*) are Bodily Humours :

(1) Clear eyes indicate the dominating presence of wind in the body.

(2) Reddishness in the eyes shows bile.

(3) Earth-coloured eyes show phlegm.

It is advisable that : (1) a man with *vata* should take sweet, sour, and salty foods, (2) in case of *pitta*, he should take sweet, hot and bitter foods, and (3) in case of *kafa*, bitter and pungent foods should be taken.

WHEN TO EAT WHAT?

A patient suffering from Malaria should be given milk and the juice of *mausambi*, oranges and sugarcane. After recovery from fever he should be given thin soup of pulses and porridge. He should not be given solid food for few days.

For swollen and painful tonsils, put some common salt and alum into lukewarm water and gargle for a few seconds. Gargling with water boiled with tea-leaves is also useful.

Diarrhoea : Curd, rice, *khichadi*, butter milk, ripe bananas and apples should be given. Milk should be avoided.

Nutmeg scoured with water and given thrice a day cures diarrhoea.

Jaundice : Sugarcane juice, juicy fruits or their juice and glucose should be given.

Warts : Warts can grow anywhere on the body. If you take homeopathic medicine they dry up and fall. Take four parts of lime used by *paanwala* and one part of washing soda and put in a glass bottle. Seal the bottle with a cork and shake well. It should be a plastic or glass cork and not of iron. After some days the ingredients will dissolve and blend. Put a little of this mixture on a cotton wad and apply twice a day on the wart. Care should be taken so that it does not touch the skin. It is injurious to the skin. The wart will dry up in a day or two and come off. The mixture does cure the warts but they grow again. Therefore, it is advisable to use the homeopathic medicine Thuja-200 for twenty days, taking a dose every third day.

Prickly heat, eczema, ringworm, shingles, itching, ulcer, tumour, boil : Don't take oily and fried food and tea. The patient should eat spinach, radish leaves, onions, tomatoes, carrots, guavas and papaya. Apply *mitti* on the stomach.

Weak eyesight : Don't consume vegetable *ghee*.

Diabetes : Don't take bananas, sugar, jaggery and sweets.

Rheumatism : Don't take spinach, bananas and potatoes.

Acidity : Don't take pickles.

Paralysis : Don't take sweets.

Ulcer : Don't take lemons, oranges and sour fruits.

Liver : Don't take alcohol, sugar, biscuits, *ghee*, oily and fried food.

Chicken pox : The meal should include milk, grapes, pomegranate, *mausambi*, etc.

Wound : Reduce your salt-intake.

Sciatica : Curd, bananas, rice, radish, tomatoes, potatoes, sour things like tamarind, pickles, *urad*, gram *daal* and cold drinks are harmful.

Stones : Eat plenty of fruits and seasonal vegetables in summer.

Cough, asthma, cancer, T.B. : Don't smoke or don't use tobacco and avoid worries and anxiety.

Hypertension and hypotension : Don't take salt in hypertension, but use salt in hypotension.

Catarrh : Don't take milk, *ghee*, oil and their products.

Itch : Application of lemon juice mixed with jasmine oil in equal quantities cures dry and seasonal itch during rains.

Reduce your intake of salt when suffering from skin diseases.

CHARACTERISTICS OF GOOD HEALTH

The main characteristics of good health are : cheerful appearance, slim and straight waist, firm body, clean and white teeth, sharp appetite, good digestive system, capacity to do hard work without exhaustion, a zest for work, stamina to face hot and cold weather, healthy parts of the body, soft skin, no dryness on the face, no cracking of the lips, bright eyes, sharp eyesight, clean pink tongue, broad chest, no bulging stomach, soft hair, deep breath free from foul smell, dreamless sleep, odourless sweat, refreshed mouth, no frequent spitting or coughing, regular stool, feeling of freshness in the morning, agility, warm stomach, cool head, pinkish nails, etc. Good health is essential to life because only a healthy person can enjoy the blessings of life.

RULES FOR HEALTH PROTECTION

After you wake up in the morning rinse your mouth and drink fresh water. Get up before Sunrise, get yourself free and sit down quietly and meditate. This way you will lead a cheerful day. To continue sleeping even after Sunrise is not good for health.

Take your meals before sunset : Food is digested by the heat from the Sun. While you are asleep the digestive system gets weakened. Therefore, you should not go to sleep at least before three hours after the meals during the day or at night. People from *Jain* community and some others take their meals before sunset. This way food gets digested before you go to sleep. It is indeed a good practice. Eating late at night does not allow the food to be properly digested. If you have to eat late at night, take some fruits and milk. Sexual intercourse should be avoided at least for three hours after the meals. If you indulge in it before that, it upsets the stomach. Before going to sleep, offer joint prayers and worship God. Do not sleep straight on your back. During summers, wash your hands and feet with cool water before going to bed. It will induce good sleep and you will not have a nocturnal emission. You should go to bed when you feel sleepy.

Before the meals : Drink a glass of water an hour before the meals. It would be better to squeeze half a lemon in a glass of water and then drink it. Before you begin the meals take a sip of water. Also, before taking meals wash your hands, feet and face. Washing the feet stimulates the fire of the stomach which helps in digesting the food.

During the meals : Take your meals in a cheerful mood. Don't drink water during the meals. If necessary, take a sip or two. Drink water an hour after the meals. At the end of the meals take a glass of butter milk. Laugh open-heartedly after the meals, it will help in the early digestion of the food and you will not suffer from constipation. Include five basil leaves in your daily diet. Taking these regularly saves you from malaria. Milk should be taken after half an hour of the meals. Don't gorge on food. Eat a little less than your appetite. In old age digestive power weakens and you don't do much physical labour. Therefore, in old age you should eat frugal meals.

After the meals : A leisured stroll of a hundred steps after the meals helps in digesting the food properly. After the walk lie straight and breathe eight times, turn right and breathe sixteen times, then turn left and breathe thirty two times. After that you can do whatever work you have to do. Above the navel lies the seat of *agni* (fire, digestion), therefore, to facilitate digestion of food one should always sleep on the left side (*Bhaav Prakash*). If you keep sitting after meals it makes you lazy and dull. Sleep makes the body strong. While washing your face, fill your mouth with a draught of water, then splash water on your eyes. It improves your eyesight. Blocking your left nostril after the meals strengthens your digestive system. Drink a little water before going to bed. Filtered water is good for health. Rest for half an hour after the meals is good because when food reaches the stomach, nature gets involved in the job of digestion and more blood starts flowing towards the stomach so that more digestive juices can be produced.

Therefore, if immediately after meals we do something that involves physical or mental exertion, take bath or indulge in sex or eat our meals immediately after the above activities, the stomach gets less blood because the flow of blood is diverted towards other parts of the body. As a result, there is lesser secretion of digestive juices and the digestive system gets weakened. Persons who are weak or have a defective digestive system should take rest or a stroll after meals.

It is the disciplined life of a mother that keeps a child fit. A woman should not feed her child soon after sexual intercourse. Heat gets transferred to the body of the child if she does so. At least once in a week you should massage your body with mustard oil. Keep yourself free from worries. Anxiety is more harmful to human health than anything else. Those who keep themselves tension-free even when they are sick, recover soon. Auto-suggestion that you are getting better is quite helpful. If you press your teeth tight while easing your bowels, your teeth will not get loose all your life and you will not get a stroke of paralysis. If a diabetic jogs for a sufficiently long distance in the morning and evening he will stop passing sugar in the urine without taking medicines. The Institute of Gerontology in Russia has found out that old age does not need rest but hard work to keep health in good shape.

Sitting with bent back is an early invitation to old age. If you press your left foot while easing your bowels, you do not get piles and the bowel movement gets facilitated. Mahatma Buddha says, "One who takes a light frugal meal once a day is a Mahatma, one who eats twice in a controlled manner is a wiseman and one who eats more than that, is a big fool."

Dr. D.G. Patwardhan of Maharashtra Ophthalmologists Association says that indiscriminate use of sunglasses is injurious to eyes. It destroys the natural power of the eyes to cope up with bright light.

Laughter : Laughter is the best medicine. It strengthens the muscles of the stomach, stimulates blood circulation and gives exercise to the body.

Indigestion is the cause of pain.

Treatment is not for the disease but for the patient, not for the body but for the vital force that keeps the body going.

—*Organ of Homeo*

The light of the inner mind is reflected in the outer world. Those who want the outer world to be better should purge their inner soul.

—*C.H. Keyserling*

The greatest healers are : Time, Nature and Patience.

The secret of fitness : A person who does his job with faith in God and renders all his deeds unto Him, conquers all diseases, maladies and miseries of the world and all his wishes are fulfilled. A person who begins to hate himself, undoubtedly comes close to self-destruction.

TAKE A COLD BATH

Doctors suggest that we should not take a hot bath even in winters. We should bathe everyday in winter with cold water, i.e. ordinary tap water. It is not necessary that the water should be ice cold. We can see that most of our fairs and holy bathing festivals fall in winter. In the beginning, most of us would begin to shiver at the very sight of cold water but once you take to bathing with cold water you would overcome the fear.

How to bathe : The easier way to take a cold bath is first to pour water on the head. You might have watched that people first immerse their head in water while bathing in a river. If you wet your head, while taking a bath the heat from the head travels down the body and escapes through the feet. But if you wet your feet and legs or the lower portion of the body first, the body heat escapes through the head. This should not be allowed to happen from health point of view.

You should not hurry through your bath. Rub with your palms the different parts of the body. This way you can fully enjoy your bath. Rubbing opens the pores of the body and activates them. A great deal of sweat and filth is excreted through these pores.

After rubbing your body with your hands, rub it with a dry towel. Rubbing with a towel does not mean only wiping the water off your body but also giving a good rubbing to the skin.

After a cold bath you should immediately put on warm clothes because the body generates heat after a cold bath, otherwise a cold breeze may do you a great harm.

Benefits : A cold bath has various benefits which a hot bath lacks. A hot bath is not completely satisfying. We start shivering soon after the hot bath. With a hot bath the blood circulation does not reach the uppermost layer of the skin. Besides, the blood cells near the outer skin become weak, whereas a cold bath strengthens them. When our skin comes in contact with cold water, it contracts. The contractions caused by the loss in temperature provide relief to the body. It creates an effect equal to that of body massage. It is good to take a bath with lukewarm water occasionally but it should not become a regular habit.

When we use cold water for a bath it accelerates the blood circulation; we can feel it while bathing. The interesting thing is that when we take a cold bath the body experiences a sort of inner warmth. It happens because of the rapid flow of blood.

People who take a cold bath seldom fall sick. A cold bath does not make you sick but it could be harmful to a person who is already sick. Generally speaking, people who bathe themselves with cold water or in a river enjoy better health than others.

WHAT TO EAT

(Health Bulletin No.23 Published by Govt. of India)

In order to keep our body healthy and strong we should eat things which contain the following elements :

1. Protein : It builds the body, imparts agility, vigour and energy. It compensates the body losses. It is found aplenty in pulses, cereals, gram, peas, milk, butter milk, cottage cheese, fatless milk, fruits, dry fruits, etc. Protein is responsible for the production of new cells and regeneration of dead cells in the body. Protein also provides energy like carbohydrates. Pulses contain about 20-25 per cent protein.

2. Fat : It gives heat and energy to the body. It is found in milk, curd, *ghee*, butter, oil, almonds, walnuts, cashewnuts, ground nuts, etc. The oiliness in things indicates the presence of fat. Oils and vegetable *ghee* are the food stuffs full of fat.

3. Mineral salts : Minerals preserve the body, strengthen the bones and protect the body from disease. They are found in fresh vegetables, fruits, wheat, rice, milk, etc.

4. Carbohydrates : They impart energy and heat to the body. They are especially found in rice, wheat, maize, different kinds of millet, sugarcane, dates, sweet fruits, bananas, etc.

5. Water : It cleans the body and helps in the excretion of sweat, stool, urine, etc., from the body. It helps in the digestion of food and blood circulation. It maintains the temperature of the body at the required level.

6. Calcium : It strengthens the body and the teeth, makes the skin fair and gives the hair bounce and richness. It is found in green vegetables, milk, curd, butter milk, cottage cheese, etc.

7. Iron : Its deficiency reduces the red blood cells. Without its help the blood cannot take oxygen to each tissue of the body, which causes anaemia. It is found in green vegetables, cereals, bread (*roti*), beans, peas, green pods, fresh leafy vegetables, non-leafy vegetables, dry fruits, etc.

8. Vitamins : They keep the body healthy and free from disease. They are found in rice, wheat, milk products, butter, fruits, fresh leafy vegetables, lemon, tomatoes, peas, beans, pulses, etc.

9. Calories : They work as a scale for measuring energy and heat of the body. Just as burning coal provides heat and driving power to an engine, similarly heat and power is supplied by food to the body which is known as calories. One gram of protein contains about four calories, one gram of fat contains about nine calories and one gram of carbohydrates contains four calories.

10. Carbohydrates : The sweetness in eatables indicates the presence of carbohydrates. Carbohydrates are found aplenty in jaggery and its powder and are easily digestible and energy giving. An adult needs 40 gms. of jaggery and its powder daily.

—*Nutrition and Balanced Diet* - *Rajamal P. Devdas*

11. Iron : It makes blood. Iron deficiency leads to anaemia.

Women generally suffer from iron deficiency. A large number of Indians suffer from anaemia.

Symptoms of anaemia : Due to the deficiency of blood the liver is not able to digest food properly. It causes flatulence. The eyes below the eyeball turn white, the skin becomes pale, one feels exhausted and sometimes loses consciousness, the stomach is upset and one feels utterly debilitated.

Sources of iorn : Iron cannot be eaten directly. It is to be obtained from food. Tomatoes, spinach and honey contain it in plenty. The following items contain iron as indicated below :

chaulai (1.4 mg per gm.), green coriander leaves (10 mg per gm.) dry soyabean (8 mg per gm.), dry pulses (7.4 mg per gm.), peas (5 mg per gm.) and boiled *bathua* (5 mg per gm.). Our intake of iron should be 15 to 20 mg per day which can be obtained from the items mentioned above.

The daily requirement of food for a healthy man to remain fit can be judged from the following table:

The daily requirement of food for a healthy and strong body	
Rice, wheat, maize, millet, etc.	450 gms.
Milk, curd, butter milk, etc.	250 gms.
Green gram, black gram, gram, *masoor*, etc.	100 gms.
Bottle gourd, *tinda, torai, parwal* and other non-leafy vegetables	200 gms.
Fat from *ghee*, butter, oil, etc.	50 gms.
Mango, melon, orange, banana, guava, etc.	175 gms.
Total	**1225 gms.**

CONSTIPATION

Constipation is a more common problem than any other disease among the intellectuals. Constipation means not being able to ease the bowels at fixed hours, insufficient evacuation of the bowels, hardening of stool, persistent non-clearing of bowels, not passing the stool daily, non-clearance of digested food, not feeling relieved after visiting the toilet, etc.

What causes constipation : Frequent meals eaten at different times do not facilitate assimilation of food, as a result there is no full clearance of bowels in a single visit to the toilet. After partial clearance of the bowels the remaining faeces get deposited in the intestines. In this way there is a lot of retention in the bowels. Even though there should be no formation of mucus during a fast, but there is lot of excretion during the usual call of nature or when enema is taken after the fast.

Diseases caused by constipation : The stool deposited in the stomach rots because of the heat and moisture in the intestines and generates foul wind. The filthy secretions from the deposits are absorbed by the intestines and get mixed with blood and make it impure. This leads to filth, flatulence and germs which cause a number of diseases. Just as the foul smell of the shit lying along the road causes heaviness of the head of a passer-by and makes breathing difficult, in the same way, the foul smell of the rotten deposits in the intestines destroys the cheer and vigour of the body. Several symptoms like cheerlessness, lethargy, dripping of saliva and foul smell from the mouth, feverishness, lack of appetite and headache appear. Persistent constipation causes piles and sciatica.

Causes of constipation

1. Spoilt food habits : Feasts are common in India and the food at a feast is usually hot and tasty. Consequently, people overeat because it feels good. However, the more you eat, the hungrier you are and the more you sleep, the more sleepy you feel. Therefore, while enjoying a feast you should keep in mind that you are spoiling your own stomach even though the food is free and tasteful. Not taking care of your stomach, eating hot and spicy food without appetite, over-eating and taking cold drinks after meals, eating hastily without chewing the food properly and irregular food habits cause constipation. It is advisable to exercise self-control while eating. There is a popular saying that "one should eat according to his own will and wear clothes of others' choice."

2. The habit of holding back the pressure : One should visit the toilet as soon as one feels the pressure. Mothers often produce *cee-cee* sound to encourage children to pass the stool. The child responds to it. This is a device to build pressure.

People usually answer the call of nature in the morning, but after that their busy schedule and other activities during the day prompt them to hold back the pressure. But holding back the pressure causes constipation and flatulence.

3. Lack of physical exertion : The rich and the intellectuals do not exert themselves physically. Therefore, they suffer from constipation.

4. Lack of rest : The busy run-on life-style of today does not allow the inner organs of the body to function properly. This leads to constipation. There are people who do not have time to rest, but whenever they visit the toilet after getting up from sleep their bowels clear a lot of stool. Getting enough sleep at proper time makes you strong. It also adds to beauty and strength, sharpens the appetite, shakes off lethargy and equalizes the elements.

5. Tension : Anxiety, unhappy thoughts, obsession with sex and brooding all the time cause tension of the inner organs leading to constipation.

6. Intestinal weakness : The frequent use of laxatives is habit- forming and harmful in the long run. It hampers the natural functioning of intestines. The intestines become sluggish, weak and dry. Laxatives are hot and stimulating. Their use causes piles and nocturnal emission.

7. Hurried evacuation of bowels : Once you are seated on the pot, you quickly pass the stool but it takes time to evacuate the remainder. If you wait and try for sometime, press the stomach on the left side, you can evacuate the bowels fully. Therefore, you should not pass the stool hurriedly.

8. Lack of enough water in the body : Not taking enough water causes constipation. Everybody takes water when thirsty but taking water before going to the toilet, at 4 o' clock early in the morning, an hour before lunch, two hours after lunch and before going to sleep at night is quite helpful.

9. Cleanliness of the toilet : Even a dog sits at a clean place. If the toilet is dirty and stinking it hampers the smooth movement of the bowels. It is easy to evacuate the bowels at a clean place.

10. Use of intoxicants : The use of intoxicants like tobacco, *bidi*, tea, opium, alcohol, etc. weakens the nerves which lead to constipation. The food eaten is not digested.

How to relieve constipation

Constipation is not a disease in itself, but a consequence of disorganized life-style, when the bowels are not fully evacuated. Laxatives should not be used to cure it. First of all, you should not be obsessed with the idea of constipation. One should consume raw vegetables and fruits in plenty. You should visit the toilet as many times as you eat, even if you don't feel like it. If you follow this routine regularly, it will relieve you of constipation. Those who do not get a chance for physical labour should go for a walk and exercise regularly. You should get up before sunrise and relax and entertain yourself for sometime after meals. You should eat in a cheerful mood. You should also cultivate the habit of evacuating the bowels regularly at the proper time. Once in a week, you should take only fruits and juices. It gives relief to intestines. If intellectuals develop an attitude for walking, yoga, exercise in routine, it could have a favourable impact on them and they could be relieved of constipation.

Treatment through food in constipation

Food occupies a primary position in any treatment. Through dietary regime you can cure all sort of diseases. Therefore, food is the chief medicine. Gita says, "Wholesome food keeps the disease away." One should eat food items that stimulate the bowel action in a natural way, for example, sprouted beans, cooked pulses, boiled vegetables and leafy green vegetables regularly. Drink plenty of water. Spinach juice, white-gourd-melon juice, *bel* syrup, oranges, *mausambi*, lemon, mangoes, papaya and guava should be a part of the diet. These fruits naturally relieve constipation.

Harad : (1) It is said that to keep fit, "the healthy should take *harad* and the sick should observe a fast." Take a spoonful of *harad* powder with warm water in winter and with fresh water in summer before going to bed at night. It relieves constipation. *Harad* is not a laxative; it is a part of the diet. It is a chemical which clears the bowels and prevents skin diseases. You will not suffer from prickly heat in summer. Take *harad* powder without any hesitation and be free from constipation.

(2) Eat a piece of *harad* preserve at night with milk. The following morning you will have a clear motion.

Mustard oil : Massaging the belly with mustard oil, in the morning and before going to the bed at night, relieves constipation.

Carrots : Eat and chew properly 250 gms. of raw carrots daily on empty stomach. It will relieve you of constipation and sharpen your appetite.

Lemon : (1) Lemon juice taken with warm water at night helps in clearing the bowels fully.

(2) 12 gms. each of lemon juice and jaggery powder taken with a glass of water at night for few days cures chronic constipation.

Orange : Orange juice taken with breakfast for a number of days creates a natural urge to evacuate the bowels. It also helps digestion.

Fenugreek leaves : Taken as a vegetable it relieves constipation. You can take two spoonfuls of fenugreek seeds powder with warm water in the morning and evening. This will keep the stomach in order, sharpen the appetite and you will never suffer from constipation.

Wheat : The juice of wheat grass relieves constipation.

Aniseed : Taking half a spoonful of aniseed powder with warm water proves to be useful.

Ginger : Mix spoonful beaten ginger in a cup of water. Boil it for 5 minutes. Drinking the filtered water relieves constipation.

A little cinnamon, dried ginger, cardamom seeds taken together is also useful.

Tomato : They act as a remarkable agent for relieving constipation. They expel the deposits in the stomach and intestines and help in the revitalization of different organs. They also activate the inner parts of the body.

***Amla* :** Taking a spoonful of *amla* powder with warm water or milk helps in clearing the bowels and relieving the constipation. Intestines and the stomach remain clear.

Spinach : The juice of raw spinach in the morning relieves constipation within a few days. Spinach and *bathua* taken with meals also help in clearing bowels.

Bitter gourd : 5 to 10 drops of homeopathic medicine Momradica Charantia Q based on bitter gourd taken four times daily relieve constipation. Bitter gourd curry with very little oil and spices taken for a full week cures dyspepsia, maladies of the stomach, constipation, flatulence, etc.

Turnip : Eaten raw, they clear the bowels.

Apple : If taken on empty stomach, it cures constipation. If eaten after the meals it causes constipation. The skin of the apple works as a laxative. If you are constipated you should eat apples with the skin on. When suffering from diarrhoea take it after removing the skin.

Large raisins : (1) It is useful for relieving constipation if it is taken after boiling it in milk.

(2) Soak overnight 20 gms. of raisins, three large raisins and one fig in 250 ml. of water. In the morning mash all these

and mix a little water and strain. Then squeeze a lemon into it and mix two tea-spoonfuls of honey and slowly sip the concoction. Repeat it for a few days. It will relieve constipation.

Guava : Eating a guava gives freshness to the intestines and cures constipation. It should be eaten before meals because if taken after meals it causes constipation. Constipated persons should take guavas with breakfast. Chronic patients should take guavas in the morning and evening. It will clear the bowels.

Papaya : Ripe papaya is useful in curing constipation. When you feel constipated, take papaya before going to bed. The following morning your bowels will be cleared.

Dried dates : Soak two dried dates in water in the morning and have them at night. Chew them properly. Take a frugal evening meal. You can also take two dried dates boiled in milk. It relieves constipation.

Onion : One raw onion taken with meals cures constipation.

Radish : Take it regularly with salt and black pepper powder with meals for two months. It will relieve constipation.

Rice : Eating *khichadi* prepared with one part rice and two parts green gram boiled together and mixed with *ghee* relieves constipation.

Tamarind : Boil tamarind pulp in water and mix sugar. Its use will relieve flatulence and constipation.

Milk : Take 2 tsp. of *gulkand* made of roses or husk of *isabgol* with hot milk at night. It will relieve constipation.

Clarified butter : Take it with black pepper for three days. It softens the intestines and allows the stool to swell. Also take it with hot milk. It will also soften the stool and facilitate easing of the bowels.

Fig : If the constipation is chronic, eating figs will relieve it. Eat ripe figs or take five dried figs boiled in milk before going to bed.

Cauliflower : Taking half a glass of cauliflower juice at bed-time is quite helpful.

Melon : Eating ripe melon relieves constipation.

Cabbage : Regular use of cabbage leaves relieves even chronic constipation. It expels foreign elements and toxins from the body.

Bathua **:** (1) It strengthens the stomach and relieves constipation. Those suffering from constipation should use it regularly. Its regular use for a few weeks helps in relieving chronic constipation. It gives energy and agility to the body.

(2) Boil *bathua* in water, strain it, add sugar to it to taste. Drink a glassful daily in the morning and evening. It will relieve constipation.

Chaulai **:** It is beneficial to eat *chaulai* as a cooked vegetable for relieving constipation.

Green gram : Eating green gram with rice as *khichadi* relieves constipation. Prepare *khichadi* with two parts of green gram and one part of rice. You may add some salt. Eat it after adding some *ghee* to it. It will solve the problem of constipation and help in easing the bowels.

Masoor daal **:** Eating it is beneficial in constipation.

Butter milk : It relieves constipation. Mix caraway seeds with it.

Neem **:** Make powder of dried *neem* blossom. Take a pinch of it daily at night with hot water. It is beneficial in constipation.

Soap : If you are not able to pass the stool at all, insert a piece of soap with a little oil or grease into the rectum. It will facilitate the passing of the stool.

Water-melon : Eating water-melon regularly for a few days helps in relieving constipation.

Water : (1) Drinking hot water regularly, as hot as you can drink, after meals relieves constipation.

(2) Those suffering from constipation should keep sipping water alongwith meals. A glass of water should also be taken after getting up in the morning.

(3) In case of constipation put a piece of wet cloth on the abdomen. It will energise the intestines and sharpen the appetite.

Sesame seeds : Mix equal quantity of jaggery with 62 gms. of pounded sesame seeds and eat it. It will relieve constipation. *Khichadi* prepared with sesame seeds, rice and green gram also relieves constipation.

Castor oil : Taking 2 tsp. of castor oil at bed time relieves constipation. You can take it mixed with milk also.

Honey : It is a natural mild laxative. Take 50 gms. of honey mixed in fresh water or milk in the morning and before bed time.

Clay : Spread a piece of wet cloth on the stomach. Put a layer of wet clay on it. Wrap it with another piece of cloth. Overnight treatment with wet clay will relieve constipation, regulate the stool and evacuation will be easy.

The use of *chaulai*, *masoor ki daal*, water-melon, dry fruits, butter milk, etc. also relieves constipation. Use these foods as much as possible. They will solve the problem of constipation. Treatment with these items is easy and beneficial.

One should not take medicines to treat constipation. If medicine is essential in some cases, treatment with homeopathic medicines will be specially helpful. In this connection, reading the present author's book *Bhojan ke Dwara Chikitsa* about homeopathic treatment of stomach diseases and further details about the recommended food items will be of special help.

DIARRHOEA

When the stool is very thin and watery and there are frequent visits to the toilet though there are no spasms, it is known as diarrhoea or dysentery. It is not a disease in itself but a symptom of other diseases. Diarrhoea is more common during the summer season.

Causes

Heavy fried or oily food, over-eating, dirty toxic food, the use of laxatives, consumption of ice, worms, hot spices, keeping awake during the night, constipation, etc. are the major factors that cause diarrhoea. Nature does not allow the body to retain certain foods in the stomach or intestines, therefore, it results in diarrhoea. Other causes that lead to diarrhoea are eating either raw or over-ripe fruits, sudden fear, sorrow or terror, mental agony, disorders of the digestive system because of sudden changes in the weather, paucity or overflow of bile in the intestines, etc.

There is a thin film of mucus on the intestines, which constantly secretes a kind of juice. This is the juice that facilitates the digestion of food. If the food is not digested properly and there is indigestion, it may result in diarrhoea. During the process of digestion, the thin membrane over the intestines reabsorbs the juice secreted by it. But sometimes, due to certain reasons, the membrane cannot reabsorb the juice and one suffers from diarrhoea. Due to stimulation created by food, the intestines release a lot of water, for example, the use of red chilli stimulates them to release excessive water. There are several other factors which cause secretion from the intestines leading to diarrhoea. During the treatment, the patient should try to avoid such situations which may aggravate the problem. Diarrhoea may lead to Gastritis, Enteritis or a combination of both called Gastroenteritis.

Preventive Measures

Water : Boil 1 litre of water. When it is reduced to one-fourth, strain it using a piece of clean cloth. Drink it when it is lukewarm. It will check diarrhoea, sharpen the appetite, provide relief from flatulence, stomachache, constipation, hiccups and vomiting.

In diarrhoea one has mostly frequent loose watery stools. Whatever the colour and cause of diarrhoea, it is usually a signal of a serious danger. It is a fatal disease which especially affects young children. Some of the following preventive measures can be of great help :

1. As far as possible, mother should breast-feed her child.
2. Instead of using a feeding bottle, use a bowl and a spoon to feed milk to the child.
3. Keep the drinking water covered in a clean pot. Use a mug with a handle to take water out of it.
4. Get drinking water from a clean source.
5. Keep food items covered and protect them from flies.
6. Don't eat stale food. Also don't take cut and rotten fruit infested with flies.
7. Wash the hands well before taking your meals.
8. The toilet should be away from the living place.

How to Cure Diarrhoea?

As soon as you realize you are suffering from diarrhoea you should go in for home remedies. Diarrhoea reduces the level of water and salt in the body, therefore ORS should be administered immediately to the patient. This solution can be prepared easily in the following manner :

1. Take a glass or 200 ml. of clean drinking water.
2. Pour the water in a clean bigger utensil.
3. Add a pinch of salt with clean hands.
4. Stir with a clean spoon so that salt gets fully dissolved in the water.
5. Taste the solution to ascertain that it is no more salty than tears.
6. Now mix a tsp. of sugar in the water.
7. Stir with a spoon to dissolve the sugar. If sugar is not available, you may use jaggery.
8. After every loose motion, give a half to one glass of it to the patient to be sipped slowly. ORS is available in readymade packets also. The contents of one packet are to be dissolved in one litre of water.

During diarrhoea special care should be taken of the patient's diet. Infants should be fed on mother's milk. Besides, the patient should be given sufficient quantity of other liquids such as lemon water, rice gruel, *kanji*, etc. The patient can be given soft foods like *khichadi*, mashed banana, curd, etc.

In case diarrhoea is not cured within two days and the child feels weak, consult a doctor.

Treatment Through Food

If the diarrhoea has been caused by indigestion or dyspepsia, the patient should go without food. Taking butter-milk is beneficial. Use the following food items in as much quantity as you can. They will not only meet the requirement of food but also cure the disease.

For the treatment of diarrhoea, give *lassi* made of plain curd, butter milk or 2 tsp. of *isabgol* husk in butter milk. As regards fruits, you can give apples and pomegranate juice and *khichadi* with curd.

Lemon : Squeeze a lemon in milk and drink it. It will be beneficial. If the diarrhoea is spasmodic or amoebic, the use of lemon is helpful. Squeeze one lemon in a cup of water and drink it. Take it five times a day. It checks diarrhoea.

Mango : Mix ½ cup of sweet mango juice with 25 gms. of curd and 1 tsp. of ginger juice. It cures chronic diarrhoea, dyspeptic residue in diarrhoea and piles.

Amla **:** Taking ½ tsp. of *amla* powder mixed with little quantity of black salt with water provides relief from diarrhoea.

Rose apple : Take two and a half leaves of a rose apple tree (the leaves should neither be too hard nor too soft) and grind them into a paste, add a little rock salt and make pills. Take a pill each in the morning and evening to get immediate relief from diarrhoea.

Pomegranate : (1) Put a layer of clay around a pomegranate and roast it. After roasting, take out the seeds and extract their juice. Mix some honey with it. It can cure all types of diarrhoea.

(2) Grind 15 gms. of dried rind of pomegranate with two cloves and boil in a glass of water. When it is reduced to half the quantity, strain it and divide it into three doses. Take the doses at an interval of three hours each. It will be beneficial in diarrhoea and dysentery. To the persons who suffer from amoebic condition or irregularity of the bowels, its regular use will be beneficial.

Bottle gourd : The use of bottle gourd in the form of **raita** (mixed with curd) is beneficial in diarrhoea.

Mint leaves : Take ½ cup of the juice of mint leaves every two hours.

Rice : After cooking rice, usually we throw away the boiled rice water, known as *maand*. This *maand* is quite useful for patients of diarrhoea. Children should be given ½ cup and grown-ups one cup every hour. It will cure diarrhoea. Little kids can be given a small quantity. If a little bit of salt is added, it will increase its taste and nutrition value and it will be easily digestible. If you keep it long, it begins to smell. Therefore, do not keep it for more than six hours. There is a simple way to prepare *maand.* Grind 100 gms. of rice into fine powder. Boil it in 1 litre of water. When it is fully boiled, strain it and mix salt to taste. Take it as mentioned above. You will find it useful in diarrhoea. Rice is a good diet in diarrhoea. It should be taken mixed with curd.

Poppy seeds : Take 2 tsp. of poppy-seeds, mix a little water and ¼ cup of curd and take it twice daily at an interval of six hours. It provides relief from dysentery, spasms and diarrhoea. Eating poppy-seeds *kheer* is also beneficial.

Coriander : (1) Grind green coriander leaves mixed with black salt and black pepper into chutney. Take a little at a time. It is easily digestible. Heat coriander powder and take a tsp. at a time with water. It controls diarrhoea. If diarrhoea is accompanied by amoebae and spasms, mix sugar candy in the concoction of coriander. If loose motions occur after meals, mix black salt to taste with coriander powder and take a tsp. with cold water twice daily after meals.

(2) Mix black salt with coriander powder and take it after meals. It will provide relief from the habit of passing stool after meals. Coriander powder is effective in curing diarrhoea.

Water : Thousands of children die because of diarrhoea every year. This happens because of dehydration. As soon as a child has three or four loose motions, give him the following solution which can be prepared at home. The child will recover soon if he takes plenty of water. Give him the usual food to eat. Infants should be fed on mother's milk also. This prescription has been successfully used in several countries :

Clean Water	-	1 Litre
Sugar	-	40 gms. or 8 tsp.
Salt	-	5 gms. or 1 tsp.

If the water is not clean, boil it and let it cool down. Mix salt and sugar in it. The solution is ready. Feed the small kids with a spoon and older children may use a glass tumbler. It should be given at small intervals. The child will recover in two to four days. Remember, a little bit of common sense can save the life of your child.

***Peepal*:** The leaves of *peepal* tree can cure diarrhoea. Chew five leaves or boil them in a glass of water and then drink the boiled water.

***Bel* :** (1) Mash *bel* pulp in water, mix sugar and prepare syrup. Take a cup of it thrice daily for a few days regularly.

(2) Grind the sun-dried slices or pulp of *bel* into a fine powder and take a tsp. of it mixed with curd or 250 ml. of butter milk twice daily in the morning and evening. It will control diarrhoea.

Banana : It is a constipative. Taking two bananas with 125 gms. of curd daily for a few days provides relief from diarrhoea, dysentery and irregularity of the bowels.

Plum : It is a constipant but still does not cause constipation.

Guava : Boil the tender leaves of guava in water. It can cure even chronic diarrhoea.

Papaya : Boil raw papaya in water. It can also cure chronic diarrhoea.

Carrots : It cures chronic diarrhoea as well as the diarrhoea caused by dyspepsia.

Onion : (1) Grind onions and apply the paste on the navel. It will provide relief from diarrhoea.

(2) Mix opium to the weight of a mustard seed in onion juice and drink it. It provides immediate relief from diarrhoea and spasms.

***Masoor daal* and Rice :** It makes a good diet for the patients of diarrhoea or dysentery.

Wheat : Grind aniseed into a fine powder. Soak it in water. Knead wheat flour using this water and prepare *chapatis*. Eating these *chapatis* will be beneficial in diarrhoea or dysentery.

Butter milk : Taking 125 ml. of butter milk mixed with 12 gms. of honey will provide relief from diarrhoea.

Clarified butter : To get relief from diarrhoea take a tsp. of clarified butter in half a glass of hot water twice daily in the morning and evening. For children reduce the quantity as per their age. This recipe has been tried by several families for generations.

Aniseed : Grind 3 gms. of roasted aniseed with 3 gms. of unroasted aniseed and add ground sugar candy to it. Its use is beneficial in diarrhoea. If the patient is a little child, boil 6 gms. of aniseed in 82 ml. of water. When the water is reduced to half the quantity, add 1 gm. black salt to it. Give 12 ml. of it to the child thrice a day. It will be very beneficial.

Nutmeg : Grate dried ginger and nutmeg with a little water and give it to the patient thrice a day. It is very useful for children.

Cinnamon : Take two gms. of cinnamon powder with water. It checks diarrhoea.

Basil : (1) The decoction of basil leaves is beneficial in diarrhoea. Taking 10 gms. juice of basil leaves is highly useful in spasms and other disorders of the stomach.

(2) Mix in equal quantity the juice of basil leaves and *pan*, heat it and give it to the child suffering from diarrhoea. It provides relief from flatulence and distension.

***Isabgol*:** Take a tsp. of *isabgol* husk in hot milk at bedtime. The following morning mix *isabgol* husk in curd and eat it after adding salt, dried ginger powder and cumin seeds. Its regular use for a few days will effectively check amoebic dysentery.

Alum salt : Grind 20 gms. of alum salt and 3 gms. of opium and mix them. Give a minute quantity equal to the weight of a grain to the patient twice a day with water. It is beneficial in diarrhoea.

Cumin seeds : When the stool is watery thin, roast cumin-seeds, mix with ½ tsp. honey and take it four times a day. Take butter milk with roasted cumin-seeds and black salt added to it after meals. It will provide relief from diarrhoea.

Ginger : Take half a cup of hot boiled water. Mix a tsp. of ginger juice in it. Sip as hot as you can. Repeat it after every hour. It will cure diarrhoea.

Sugar : Boil water, allow it to cool down and fill a glass tumbler. Add a little bit of salt and sugar to taste. Give it to the patient frequently. Keep giving some or the other kind of liquid to the patient and ask him to take meals regularly. The patient will not feel debilitated.

Neem **:** Grind 1 gm. of the kernel of *neem* seeds alongwith a little sugar and take it with water. Take only rice for meals.

Walnut : If the diarrhoea is spasmodic, grind two walnuts mixed with water and apply it on the navel. It will provide relief from spasms.

Orange : Orange juice mixed with milk is beneficial in curbing diarrhoea in children.

Apple : If a child cannot digest milk or vomits and suffers from diarrhoea after taking milk, stop giving him milk and feed him with apple juice at short intervals. It will provide relief from diarrhoea.

Apple juice is beneficial in chronic cases also. It is useful in cases of spasmodic diarrhoea among grown-ups. Apple juice also cures diarrhoea attended with bloody stools. Patients of diarrhoea should take peeled apples. The apple preserve is also beneficial in diarrhoea.

Diarrhoea Attended with Blood in the Stools

Mango : Grind the mango kernel and take it mixed in butter milk. It is beneficial for patients suffering from diarrhoea attended with blood in the stools.

Rose apple : Grind 20 gms. of the kernel of rose apple in water and give it to the patient twice daily in the morning and evening. It will be beneficial.

Ber**:** It helps in the healing of wounds caused in the intestines by dysentery attended with blood.

Onion : Eating cut and washed onions with fresh curd is beneficial in amoebic and bloody stools.

Sugarcane : Taking sugarcane juice mixed with pomegranate juice cures the problem of bloody stools.

Coriander : Grind 15 gms. of Coriander seeds and add 12 gms. sugarcandy powder to it, mix in water and drink it. It checks the flux of blood in stools.

The patient who suffers from flatulence, should use pure *desi ghee* or oil for meals. Reduce the use of red-chilli and pulses to the minimum. Don't consume alcohol.

DYSENTERY

Dysentery is a disease of the intestines attended with frequent bloody and mucous stools. The patient does not feel hungry and feels weak. In the beginning, there are frequent stools marked by spasmodic pain in the stomach and passing of a white oily substance called mucous, but gradually the frequency of diarrhoeic stools increases. There is a bloody flux also. While passing the stool, one feels pain in the stomach. The dysenteric patient should take plenty of rest. The chief reason for dysentery is an inflammation in the lower part of Ileum and the large intestine. There are two types of dysentery.

1. Bacillary Dysentery : The patient feels the urge for passing the stools frequently. The stools are marked by a bloody flux. Sometimes he feels he has passed only blood. The frequency sometimes ranges between 20-30 times in a day and the patient sometimes develops fever. But the patient recovers soon. For prompt relief suck 10 globules of homeopathic medicine Merk Cor five times a day.

2. Amoebic Dysentery : It is caused by the germ Entamoeba Histolytia. It gets into the intestines with dirty food and causes inflammation. It gradually becomes chronic and then it is difficult to treat. But treatment through food proves effective. The frequency of stools is 2-4 to 8-10 times in 24 hours. The stools are large and loose and are marked by an urgency. This type of dysentery is attended with frequent bloody and mucous stools. Because of the presence of blood, the stools are thin and loose. In some cases Melaena is the major symptom and in others it is constipation. Because of the loose motions, the patient develops distaste for food, flatulence, stomachache or restlessness. If the patient works hard, he feels tired and giddy. Dysentery can lead to Asthma, Eczema, Inflammation of the liver and also Ulceration.

Treatment Through Food

The patients of dysentery should not be given anti-diarrhoea drugs. The stool is attended with mucous, which is a kind of toxin. If the mucous is allowed to remain in the stomach it can lead to serious problems like swelling on hands, feet and face and jaundice, hepatitis, disorders of the spleen, leprosy, loss of appetite, low fever, dropsy, etc. The physician treating the patients of dysentery should first ask about the history of mucous and diarrhoea and if mucous has been restrained, treatment should be given to expel it. Dysentery is also caused because of accumulation of too much of stool in the intestines. Nature tends to expel it and clean the stomach. We should therefore, assist nature in this respect.

Castor oil : Take 2 tsp. of castor oil mixed in hot milk as soon as you notice mucous in the stool. It will give prompt relief. Castor oil is beneficial in dysentery attended with both mucous and blood.

***Bel* :** Ripe *bel* syrup provides a successful treatment for dysentery with mucous. It clears the bowels effectively.

Water : A glass of hot water taken regularly after meals is good for patients of amoebiasis.

***Isabgol*:** It is very beneficial in amoebic dysentery. It expels amoebae and checks its formation.

(1) Put a tsp. of *isabgol* in hot milk, let it swell, then take it at bed time. Next morning mix *isabgol* in curd, let it swell, mix salt, dried ginger powder, cumin seeds and then eat it.

(2) Take 4 parts of *isabgol*, one part aniseed of which half should be roasted and one part sugar-candy—grind them and take 2 tsp. of the powder with water twice daily.

(3) Soak a tsp. of *isabgol* in a cup of water for at least six hours. Take it at the end of the meals. Soak another tsp. of *isabgol* for six hours and take it after the second meal.

(4) If it is not possible to take it as prescribed above in number 3, grind 75 gms. *isabgol*, 25 gms. roasted aniseed and 25 gms. raw aniseed and take a tsp. of the powder daily after meals. It will make life comfortable. It should be taken over a long period.

(5) Take aniseed half of which should be roasted, coriander seeds, sugar candy, sun-dried slices of *bel*—all in equal quantity, mix with them one-fourth quantity of dried ginger powder and grind them together into a fine powder. Take 2 tsp. with cold water twice daily. It will provide relief from dysentery, diarrhoea and bloody-flux. It is also beneficial in amoebiasis.

Lemon : Lemon juice in a cup of fresh water thrice a day is helpful in dysentery. Taking lemon in milk is also useful.

Fenugreek : (1) Eating fenugreek leaves fried in *ghee* cures dysentery.

(2) Take 60 gms. juice of fenugreek leaves with 6 gms. sugar mixed in it. A tsp. of the powder of fenugreek seeds can be taken mixed in curd.

Rice : For patients of dysentery, rice is a good diet.

Wheat : Grind aniseed, mix the powder in water, strain it and use it to knead wheat flour. Prepare *chapatis* (a thin cake or bread) and eat them during meals. It will be beneficial in diarrhoea and dysentery.

Aniseed : Boil 6 gms. aniseed in 82 ml. of water. When the water is reduced to half the quantity, mix 1 gm. black salt and give to the patient. If the patient is a little child, give 12 ml. of it, thrice a day. It is highly beneficial.

Black pepper : Taking black pepper is useful for patients of dysentery.

Basil : The use of basil leaves mixed with sugar cures dysentery.

Pomegranate : Boil 15 gms. dried rind of pomegranate alongwith 2 ground cloves, strain it and drink half a cup of it thrice daily. Those who suffer from amoebiasis or dysentery or stomach cramps should use it regularly. It will be quite beneficial.

Dates : Taking dates with curd is beneficial.

Lady finger : Eating lady finger as a cooked vegetable is useful in dysentery. It removes friction in the intestines.

Gram : Soak two handful of gram husk overnight in water in a new clay pot, strain it the following morning and drink the water. If the blood in the stool follows burning and heat, the above treatment will provide relief.

Poppy seeds : Mix 2 tsp. of poppy seeds with a little water, grind it into a paste and mix in ¼ cup of curd. Eat it twice daily at an interval of six hours. It will cure dysentery, diarrhoea and spasms. Eating the *Kheer* made with poppy seeds is also beneficial.

Alum salt : Grind and mix 20 gms. alum salt and 3 gms. opium. Take small quantity (approx. 2 gms.) of it twice daily with 2 tsp. of water. It is beneficial in diarrhoea. Afterwards take it with *isabgol* husk. It will cure dysentery attended with blood.

Cumin seeds : Grind roasted cumin seeds, mix a tsp. of it with honey and take it daily after meals. Take butter milk with cumin seeds powder added to it. It is beneficial in chronic dysentery and disorders of the stomach.

Tea : Tea contains polyphenol which destroys the germs causing dysentery. The patients of dysentery can take tea. It will be beneficial.

***Harad*:** Fry small *harad* and aniseed in clarified butter, grind it, mix sugar candy powder and take a tsp. daily with hot water. It will be useful.

DYSPEPSIA

(DYS = HARD, PEPSIN = DIGEST)

Weakness of digestion or indigestion leads to pain in the parts related to digestive system and there is flatulence which causes heaviness, restlessness, nausea and vomiting. Loss of appetite, indigestion, feeling of surfeit and stomach derangement all mean that the food eaten is not being digested. The diarrhoea caused by dyspepsia is known as sprue.

Lemon : (1) Cut a slice of a lemon, heat it, sprinkle salt on it and suck on it to get relief from indigestion. It will improve the digestive system. Lemon is useful in all ailments of the liver.

(2) Take half a glass of lemon water with sugar daily in case of loss of appetite, indigestion and sour burps.

(3) Squeeze a lemon in a glass of water, add salt and a tsp. of ginger juice to it and drink it.

Guava : It is a good medicine for dyspepsia, loss of appetite and flatulence. The patient should eat 250 gms. of guava fruit after meals. Others should eat it before meals.

Cauliflower : Taking mixed juice of cauliflower and carrots in equal quantity is beneficial in joint pains, dyspepsia and weakness of eyesight.

***Bathua* :** Take it as a cooked vegetable or drink its juice. It cures all sorts of ailments of the stomach, liver, spleen, indigestion, flatulence, worms, piles and stones.

Curd : Eating curd regularly with roasted cumin seeds, salt and black pepper cures dyspepsia and improves digestion.

Cloves : Grind two cloves and put in half cup of boiling water, let it cool a little, then drink it. Take it thrice a day. It provides relief from dyspepsia.

Asafoetida : (1) Grind asafoetida, small *harad*, rock salt, caraway seeds in equal quantity. Take a spoonful thrice daily with hot water. It will cure dyspepsia.

(2) Ten drops of homeopathic mother tincture of asafoetida mixed in a tsp. of water cures dyspepsia.

Cumin seeds : (1) Mix cumin seeds, dried ginger powder, rock salt, long pepper, black pepper in equal quantity and grind. Take a spoonful after meals with water. It facilitates digestion of the food.

(2) Boil 2 tsp. cumin seeds in a glass of water, when it cools down, strain it and take ½ cup thrice a day.

(3) Mix a tsp. of roasted cumin seeds powder with a tsp. of honey and eat it twice daily after meals. It cures dyspepsia.

Coriander : If it is difficult to digest food and you have the urge to pass stools immediately after meals, take 60 gms. of dry coriander powder, 25 gms. black pepper, 5 gms. of salt, mix and grind them. Take ½ tsp. of the powder after meals daily.

Caraway seeds : (1) Grind Caraway seeds and small *harad* and mix asafoetida and salt to taste. Take a tsp. of the powder after meals with hot water.

(2) Taking a tsp. of ground caraway seeds mixed with rock salt to taste with water on empty stomach in the morning is beneficial.

***Neem* :** Grind 25 gms. of dry *neem* leaves, three cloves, three black pepper and mix a little water and sugar. Eat it twice daily in the morning and evening.

Water : If you suffer from dyspepsia and it is difficult to digest food, don't eat anything for a day, take only water. If you suffer from constipation, keep sipping water with meals. Take a glass of water in the morning as soon as you get up.

Radish : The patients of dyspepsia should eat radish with salt and black pepper powder daily for two months.

Pineapple : Eating a slice of pineapple with salt and black pepper powder gives relief from indigestion.

Papaya : If you cannot digest food, it would be better to eat papaya. If you suffer from loss of appetite, dyspepsia, indigestion, stomachache and sour burps, eat papaya continuously in breakfast in the morning for twenty days.

Carrots : If you cannot digest clarified butter, oil or oily things, take 310 gms. carrot juice mixed with 185 ml. of spinach juice.

Onion : Cut an onion into pieces, squeeze a lemon on it and eat it with meals. It will provide relief from indigestion. If the patient is a child, give him five drops of onion juice. It will be beneficial.

Butter milk : If the indigestion is because of clarified butter, oil or groundnuts, taking butter milk will be beneficial.

Mustard : To cure indigestion take 3 gms. of mustard seeds powder in water.

Salt : (1) If the digestive system is not working properly, even eating light meals causes diarrhoea, dysentery or constipation and the body becomes weak, take 5 gms. of black salt dissolved in hot water. Children should take it once in a month or two. Mix one part of rock salt and four parts of *desi* sugar and grind. Taking ½ tsp. of it with water ten minutes after meals will cure indigestion and loss of appetite.

(2) Some people suffer from the problem of sour burps after meals. Acids come upto the throat. All the symptoms of indigestion appear. In such cases, giving up salt altogether or taking very little of it provides relief from indigestion. The reason is that there is already a lot of hydrochloric acid, which is sour, in the digestive juices of the stomach. This acid is generated by salt. If you don't take salt, the excessive acids in the stomach are reduced to the normal level and you get quite a bit of relief from stomach-related problems.

Ginger : (1) Mix ginger juice with lemon juice and rock salt and take it twice, before meals and after meals. It will provide relief from indigestion. It will improve digestion.

(2) Mix ½ tsp. of dried ginger powder with a little jaggery and take it after meals for a few days. It sharpens the appetite, tones up the digestive system and cures stomach ailments.

(3) Eating a guava fruit with dried ginger powder helps in the digestion of food and improves the appetite. Take it atleast for ten days regularly.

Basil : Chewing basil leaves with black pepper provides relief from indigestion and loss of appetite.

Coffee : Taking coffee after meals makes you feel cheerful and light as if you had not eaten anything. Strong coffee provides agility and relief from stomachache after meals or indigestion caused by opium eating.

Red chilli : 5 drops of the homeopathic mother tincture *Capsicum Anum* made of red chilli taken in a tsp. of water before meals also cures dyspepsia.

Cinnamon : Frequent eating of a little bit of cinnamon, dried ginger and cardamom provides relief from indigestion.

FLATULENCE

Accumulation of wind or gas in the stomach and the resultant distension is known as flatulence. The wind or gas is generated in the stomach and gets accumulated there. It is generated both in the intestines and stomach because of dyspepsia and constipation. The air that we gulp down and which gets accumulated in the stomach is known as ligamentary flatulence. Flatulence during pregnancy causes a lot of uneasiness.

As a result of excessive accumulation of wind, the stomach gets distended. Sometimes there is a fluttering in the heart and people think it is related to heart problem. It is actually because of the disorders of the stomach. Sometimes the stomach gets very tense.

To keep healthy it is necessary to include spices in your diet. Usually, turmeric, coriander, salt and chilli are used as spices. The use of roasted asafoetida is good for people with *vata* tendency. Cumin seeds are useful for those with *pitta* tendency and hot spices for those with *kafa* tendency.

Fatless foods generate too much of gas in the stomach. If there is too much of gas-formation, it is advisable to take fats in food like oil, *ghee*, etc. Meat-eaters usually take fatless food because there is a lot of fat in meat. If your diet includes spices, vegetables, *ghee*, milk, curd, and sweets, it is considered to be good food.

Treatment Through Food

Radish : Eating radish with salt and black pepper for two months regularly will provide relief from wind in the stomach, gas and flatulence.

Jaggery : Eating jaggery after meals checks the formation of gas in the stomach.

Orange : It cures the ailments of the liver. Those who suffer from dyspepsia or flatulence because of gas or any other reason or have a feeling of fullness should take oranges. If you take a glass of orange juice in the morning, it clears the intestines and relieves constipation.

Guava : It provides relief from gas. It improves digestive system if taken with rock salt in the morning and evening.

Cauliflower : Take mixed juice of raw cauliflower and carrots in equal quantity. It will check the formation of gas.

Potato : The juice of raw potatoes is helpful in relieving flatulence.

***Bathua* :** You can take *bathua* as a cooked vegetable or take its juice or boil and strain it and drink the water. It will relieve flatulence.

Bitter gourd : Eating it as a cooked vegetable and taking its juice is highly beneficial in flatulence.

***Arhar*:** It generates gas in the stomach. Patients of flatulence should not take it.

Cumin seeds : Grind roasted cumin seeds and mix a tsp. of the powder with a tsp. of honey and take it after meals daily.

Coriander seeds : Boil 2 tsp. of coriander seeds in a glass of water, strain it and divide it into three equal doses. Take it for a few days.

Cinnamon : It provides relief from stomachache caused by flatulence. Take only a small quantity. **An overdose can be harmful.**

***Sahjan* :** The flowers or pods of *sahjan* taken as a cooked vegetable are useful in relieving accumulated gas in the stomach.

Breathing : Lie down straight on your back after meals and breathe deeply eight times. Turn to the right and breathe sixteen times, then turn to the left and breathe thirty-two times. This exercise will enable the food to find its proper place in the stomach. The gas in the stomach will be expelled through the mouth as burps or through the anus. Write down this recipe and place it near your pillow. It will save you from flatulence.

Cloves : Grind 5 cloves and mix in ½ cup boiling water. Drink it when it cools down a bit. Repeat it thrice daily. It will expel gas from the stomach.

Asafoetida : Dissolve asafoetida in hot water and apply on the stomach around the navel. Also eat 1 gm. of roasted asafoetida with any eatable thing you like. It will be beneficial. If the pain in the stomach is due to flatulence, boil 2 gms. of asafoetida in ½ litre water. When the water gets reduced to one-fourth, drink it when it is bearably hot.

Caraway seeds : Mix 1.5 gms. black salt with 6 gms. powder of caraway seeds. Take it with hot water after meals. It will relieve flatulence. Caraway seeds expel the gas in the stomach. You can use caraway seeds with meals in any form you like.

Brinjal : If you suffer from flatulence or the stomach gets distended when you drink water as if it were a football, eat fresh long brinjals as a cooked vegetable daily as long as they are available during the season. It will cure flatulence.

Mint leaves : Taking 25 ml. of mint juice mixed with 31 gms. of honey in a glass of water in the morning is especially beneficial for patients of flatulence.

Fenugreek : Fenugreek leaves cooked as a vegetable are beneficial in flatulence. Grind fenugreek seeds, *arjun ki chhal, kair,* dried *amla i*n equal quantity and take 1 tsp. daily on empty stomach in the morning with cool water. It provides relief from flatulence and a feeling of heaviness in the stomach, sharpens the appetite and gives a feeling of lightness in the body.

Milk : Add a long pepper to milk when you boil it and drink it when it is bearably hot. It checks the formation of gas in the stomach.

Ginger : Cut 6 gms. of ginger into fine pieces, add a little salt and eat it once daily before meals for ten days. It will relieve flatulence.

Mustard oil : In case of displacement or disorders of the navel, there is usually gas formation or pain in the stomach and loss of appetite also takes place. To cure it, the position of the navel needs to be set right. The application of mustard oil on the navel is helpful. If the problem is acute, take a cotton swab soaked in mustard oil and place it on the navel and wrap it with a bandage.

Nutmeg : Scour nutmeg in lemon juice and lick it. It will clear the bowels and cure flatulence.

Salt : Grind one part of rock salt and four parts of *boora.* Take ½ tsp. thrice daily with hot water. It will provide relief from flatulence and wind in the stomach.

Water : Sipping a glass of hot water, as hot as you can sip, after meals for a few weeks will cure flatulence.

Aniseed : Eating aniseed soaked in lemon juice after meals provides relief from heaviness of the stomach, expels gas and clears the bowels.

Apple : Apple juice forms a thin layer on the digestive organs which protects them from infection and foul smell. It also checks gas-formation. The lower intestines and the rectum do not get infected.

Turmeric : When gas accumulates in the stomach it causes a lot of pain. To get relief, take 5 gms. each of turmeric powder and salt with hot water. It will give quick relief.

Black pepper : (1) Taking the powder of ten black pepper corns with hot lemon water in the morning and evening will prevent gas-formation in the stomach.

(2) Boil 6 corns of black pepper and 3 cloves in a cup of water, add common salt to taste and drink it. It provides relief from flatulence.

APPETITE

A man with good appetite enjoys good health. If one wants to live long, one should not eat anything unless there is a strong urge for eating. Usually there are three complaints regarding appetite—

(1) Loss of appetite,

(2) Excessive urge to eat, and

(3) Urge to eat certain unusual things like clay and coal.

Causes for loss of Appetite : There is a loss of appetite when one falls sick. Constipation, lack of exercise, excessive drinking and smoking are the other reasons. If you take a brisk walk before meals, it sharpens the appetite and the food tastes better.

Take 10 globules of homeopathic medicine 'Vanadium 6' five times a day. It will sharpen the appetite. Buy one dram of this medicine from any homeopathic doctor. It does not cost much. This is the medicine I prescribe first of all for loss of appetite. To cure loss of appetite and the problems of digestion, a patient should be given a medicine to strengthen the digestive system first. Vanadium is a medicine which energises the digestive system.

Lemon : (1) Mix a tsp. of ginger juice in a glass of water, squeeze a lemon into it, add salt to taste and drink it. It will sharpen the appetite.

(2) Eat ginger *chutney* with lemon juice added to it. Also use coriander leaves when they are available. It sharpens the appetite and you feel like eating.

(3) Cut a lemon into four pieces without separating them. Put salt, black pepper powder, dried ginger powder and sugar into them, respectively, and keep it overnight covered in a saucer. In the morning roast it slightly on a hot plate and suck on it. It will sharpen the appetite and improve the functioning of the liver.

Orange : Sprinkle some dried ginger powder and black salt on the slices of an orange and then eat it. It will sharpen the appetite within a week.

***Ber* :** Eating *ber* is good for appetite.

Wheat : Drinking the juice of 5-inch high tender wheat grass daily induces a good appetite. To know more about the merits of wheat grass, consult the present author's book *Bhojan Ke Dwara Chikitsa.*

Coriander : In case of loss of appetite, take 30 gms. juice of coriander leaves daily to sharpen the appetite.

Salt : Grind one part of rock salt with four parts of unrefined sugar powder (*boora*). Take it with hot water ten minutes after meals. It will enhance the appetite.

Ice : If you do not feel like eating because of summer heat, taking a glass of iced water an hour before meals will be beneficial.

Apple : (1) Taking a glass of the juice of sour apples with sugar added to taste daily for a few days gives you a feeling of good appetite.

(2) Knead wheat flour in the juice of sour apples and prepare *chapatis* and eat them daily.

Large raisins : Eat large raisins with salt and black pepper. It will sharpen the appetite. This prescription is really beneficial in cases of loss of appetite due to chronic fever.

Guava : Eat daily 250 gms. of guava fruit after meals. It will sharpen the appetite.

***Chaulai*, Bitter gourd, Fenugreek :** Eating them as a cooked vegetable daily is helpful. It sharpens the appetite.

Ginger : Grate 500 gms. of ginger and soak well in lemon juice, add black pepper powder and rock salt and stir well. After twenty four hours spread it for drying on a clean cloth in the Sun. Suck on one piece at a time. You will find it to be very tasty and pleasant. It is beneficial for hoarse throat, cough and kindles the appetite, improves digestion and is good for the gums.

Tomato : Tomatoes sharpen the appetite. Use them as much as you can.

Tamarind : Soak it in a glass of water, mash and strain it. Add salt and black pepper powder to taste and drink it. It will sharpen the appetite.

Caraway seeds : Roast caraway seeds and grind them. Add salt to taste. Take ½ tsp. After meals with water.

Gram : Boil a cup of black gram in 3 glasses of water. Strain and drink the water. This helps in subsiding hunger.

Red chilli : The homeopathic mother Tincture Capsicum kindles the appetite very well. Take 5 drops in a tsp. of water before meals.

Tea : Tea helps to subside hunger.

EATING CLAY

Mango : If a child has taken to eating clay, grind mango kernel in fresh water and give it to him. The child will give up the habit of eating clay.

Banana : Give mashed banana mixed with honey to the child to eat. He will stop eating clay.

VOMITING

Banana : Eating ripe bananas checks bloody vomiting.

Pistachio : Eating four pistachios will check vomiting and nausea.

Cauliflower : It contains substances which are alkaline. It purifies blood. Eating cooked or raw cauliflower is beneficial in bloody vomiting. The patients of T.B. should definitely take it.

Mint leaves : Take half a cup of the juice of mint leaves at an interval of every two hours. You can add lemon juice to it.

Frequent use of the *chutney* of green coriander leaves and mint leaves is quite beneficial.

Coriander : (1) Boiled coriander water with sugar candy is beneficial.

(2) 33 ml. of the juice of green coriander leaves checks vomiting. Vomiting during pregnancy can also be checked. It should be taken frequently.

Harad **:** Taking *harad* powder mixed with honey controls vomiting.

Cumin seeds : Soak 125 gms. of cumin seeds and 50 gms. of rock salt in the juice of four lemons. When the juice evaporates and the cumin seeds are dry, store it in a glass bottle. Take ½ tsp. of it thrice daily. It checks vomiting during pregnancy.

Ginger : (1) It is very helpful in controlling vomiting. Lick a tsp. of ginger juice with a little rock salt and black pepper powder. If required, take another dose after three hours.

(2) Mix 1 tsp. each of ginger juice, onion juice and water. It will check vomiting.

Honey : Taking onion juice mixed with honey checks vomiting.

Onion : Taking 2 tsp. of the mixed juice of ginger and onion can control vomiting.

Basil : The juice of basil leaves checks vomiting. Taking honey mixed with the juice of basil leaves provides relief from vomiting and nausea.

Neem **:** Grind 25 gms. of *neem* leaves, mix with water, strain and drink. It can check all types of vomiting.

Water-melon : In case of heart burn after meals and yellowish vomit, take water-melon juice with sugar candy in the morning.

Rice : Vomiting during pregnancy—soak 50 gms. rice in 250 ml. water. After half an hour put 5 gms. coriander seeds in it. Then after ten minutes stir and strain. Divide it into four parts and take them as four doses in one day. It will provide relief to the pregnant woman from vomiting.

Cloves : (1) Grind two cloves and give it with honey to the pregnant woman, in case of vomiting. Sucking a roasted clove checks vomiting. Whenever vomiting takes place, suck a roasted clove.

(2) Crush four cloves and boil in a cup of water. When it is reduced to half cup, add some sugar and drink it and go to sleep on one side. It will check vomiting.

(3) Boil two cloves and a little bit of cinnamon in a cup of water. When the water is reduced to half, strain and drink it. Whenever vomiting takes place, repeat the above prescription. It will check vomiting.

Amla **:** In case of retching and vomiting during pregnancy, take two pieces of *amla* preserve four times daily to get relief from the problem.

Lemon : As soon as you feel nausea, use lemon. It will check vomiting. You may put sugar and black pepper powder on a piece of lemon and suck it. It will provide relief from vomiting. When you mix lemon juice and sugar with cold water you get lemonade. It is good for nausea and vomiting. If you give a few drops of lemon juice in water to the infant, it will not throw out the milk. Mint leaves and lemon together are effective in preventing vomiting. It is beneficial to suck a lemon with cardamom powder on it. For the treatment of vomiting do not take heated lemon.

Orange : (1) The use of oranges is beneficial in retching and vomiting. While travelling by bus or a motor vehicle, keep eating oranges at short intervals.

(2) Grind dried orange peel, add double the quantity of sugar and again grind. Take 2 tsp. of it every two hours with cool water. It will provide relief from vomiting.

Tamarind : Soak ripe tamarind in water, then mash, strain and drink it. It will check vomiting.

Gram : Soak gram in water at night. Take the water next morning. In case of vomiting in pregnancy, the woman should be given *sattu* made of roasted gram.

Sugarcane : In case of bilious vomiting, taking sugarcane juice mixed with honey will be beneficial.

Cinnamon : Take cinnamon powder mixed with honey to get relief from bilious vomiting.

Mustard : To treat vomiting which is difficult to cure, mustard liniment is wonderfully effective. Grind mustard seeds, put a wet muslin cloth on the stomach and use the ground mustard seeds for embrocation. Let it remain there for 15 minutes. Then remove it. It will put an end to vomiting. This prescription is based on experience.

Ice : Sucking a piece of ice checks frequent vomiting. To treat all types of diseases with various food items, see the present author's book *Bhojan ke Dwara Chikitsa.*

ACIDITY

Blood is 20% acid and 80% alkali. When the proportion of acid in the blood increases, it affects the digestive system in the body and gives rise to the ailment of acidity.

Acidity is usually known as heartache, acidic pain and heart-burn. When the acid in the stomach travels with saliva to the throat, there is a burning sensation and sourness in the stomach. When the patient says that he has a heart-burn and sourness has come upto the throat, he should be given treatment for acidity. Loss of appetite, indigestion and dyspepsia also have similar symptoms. Therefore, one should be able to differentiate between the two. Acidity is caused by hasty eating or taking improper food. The use of alkali food is beneficial in it. The symptoms of this disease include vomiting of sour undigested food, one or two hours after meals, burning in the throat and the chest, constipation, stomachache, sickness of stomach, etc. The chief symptoms, however, are burning in the chest and throat after meals and feeling of sour water in the mouth and sour vomit. This disease is quite prevalent in Bihar and Bengal.

Food : The patients of acidity should be careful about the food they take. The patient should be given dry, tasty and spicy food though several scholars do not subscribe to this theory. But you can yourself experiment with this kind of food and see the result. According to my experience the above type of food is beneficial. The use of liquids should be restricted but milk can be taken frequently. Pickles and tea are harmful.

***Phalsa* :** The use of *phalsa* provides relief to the patients of gas and acidity.

***Amla* :** Take 2 tsp. of *amla* juice mixed with equal quantity of sugarcandy powder or take dried *amla* powder mixed with sugarcandy powder with water.

Potato : Potato is naturally alkaline. It contains potassium salt which restricts acidity. The patients of acidity can reduce their problem by taking potatoes regularly with meals. Take roasted or boiled potatoes only.

Tea : Tea is harmful for the patients of acidity.

Carrots : Carrot juice cures acidosis.

Cloves : Eating a clove after meals in the morning and evening is beneficial.

Radish : In case of sour burps because of heat, drinking radish juice mixed with sugar candy powder will be beneficial.

***Petha* :** If the patient takes two pieces of *petha* (sweet) regularly, it will cure the problem of acidity.

Banana : Eating a banana with sugar and cardamom powder is beneficial.

Lemon : The patient should take a glass of hot water with lemon forty-five minutes before meals. It will help in the digestion of the food. The potassium in lemon neutralizes the acid.

Taking a glass of hot lemon water in the evening is also useful. Dr. Albert in his book, **Fruits for Health** has written that people have a wrong notion that lemon is acidic. As a result, because of ignorance about its medicinal effects the patients of acidity do not use it. They should know that lemon neutralizes acids.

Lemon juice cures acidosis. You can take lemon juice in water several times in a day. To improve the taste, you can mix honey; do not add salt to it. If you are suffering from hyper-acidity, do not eat food for 2-4 days. Take only the juice of such items as lemon, orange, *mausambi*, pineapple, carrots, pumpkin, cucumber, bottle gourd, etc.

Milk : Taking a little quantity of cold milk thrice a day is beneficial for patients of acidity.

Coconut : Drinking the milk of raw coconuts is highly beneficial in acidity.

Onion : Mix 60 gms. of onion pieces in 30 gms. of curd and take it thrice daily. To derive maximum benefit take it at least for a week.

Cumin seeds : Mix and grind equal quantity of cumin seeds, coriander seeds and sugar candy. Take 2 tsp. of it with cool water twice daily in the morning and evening after meals. It will provide relief from acidity.

Black pepper : Grind black pepper, mix rock salt to taste and take ½ tsp. with water after meals in the morning and evening. It is beneficial for patients of acidity.

Caraway seeds : Mix a tsp. of the powder of caraway seeds and the juice of a lemon in a glass of water and drink it. It will be beneficial.

Take only light food items like rice, *moong daal* and vegetables like bottle gourd, ridged gourd, *parwal, tinda,* etc. Also make use of green coriander leaves with meals.

WORMS

Worms are found in intestines. Sometimes they come close to the rectum, can be seen or come out with the stools. This disease is quite prevalent. When you take some medicine they get expelled but their recurrence is not checked. By modifying your food habits you can save yourself from this disease.

Treatment Through Food

It will be helpful if the patient is given mash in the evening and a laxative the following morning. Worms are caused by the accumulation of stools in the intestines. It is, therefore, essential to keep the bowels clear. Sometimes, enema can be taken. Worms are also caused by eating too much of sugar or sweets; the intake of sugar should therefore be restricted. First of all, take clarified butter mixed with black pepper powder. It allows the stools to swell and makes the intestines soft. Then take one of the items prescribed for constipation. It will clear the bowels. The entire accumulated stools will be expelled. Then take only jaggery for one day. The worms in the stomach will come to one point. At this stage take some medicine to expel worms. The worms will come out. If you take the food items mentioned below regularly for a few weeks, you will be able to get rid of worms.

Harad : Grind *harad* and *wybidang* in equal quantity and give ¼ tsp. to children and 1 tsp. to grown ups with hot water twice daily in the morning and evening after meals. It will kill the worms.

Papaya : Grind ten papaya seeds in water, mix in ¼ cup of water and drink it. It will kill the worms. Take it regularly for seven days.

Garlic : Eating five cloves of garlic with large raisins or honey thrice daily will enable you to get rid of worms. If you take it for two to three months it will improve your health. Eating raw garlic after meals also kills worms.

Bitter gourd : It is good to take the juice of bitter gourd for patients who have worms.

Butter milk : Butter milk taken with salt in the morning destroys worms.

Basil : The juice of basil leaves will destroy worms in the stomach.

Neem **:** Upto 5 drops of *neem* oil given to children according to their age will destroy worms in the stomach.

Honey : Taking honey in the morning and evening is beneficial—*E.F. Farrington* : **Therapeutic Pointers and Laser Writings**. Taking two parts of curd and one part of honey will kill the worms and expel them from the stomach.

Pomegranate : The juice of pomegranate, if taken regularly, will destroy worms.

Coconut : Take coconut milk and then eat raw coconut. It will expel worms.

Petha **:** Its use can kill worms.

Bathua : Taking a cup of *bathua* juice with salt once daily will provide relief from the problem of worms. A tsp. of the powder of *bathua* seeds mixed with honey is also beneficial.

Parwal **:** It also destroys worms.

Mint leaves : In case of worms in the intestines, take ½ cup of the juice of mint leaves daily.

Jaggery : It destroys worms. The patient should eat jaggery before taking the medicine. The worms sticking to the walls of intestines will move to one point to eat jaggery. If it is followed by a wormicidal medicine, they will be expelled from the stomach. Taking a tsp. of ground caraway seeds with jaggery thrice daily will expel worms.

Asafoetida : Sometimes worms can be seen crawling in the rectum of a child. Soak a little bit of cotton in the solution of asafoetida and place it on the anus. It will destroy the worms. Eating a minute quantity of asafoetida will prevent the occurrence of worms in the stomach of a child.

Tomato : Red tomatoes taken with black pepper powder and salt in the morning on empty stomach destroys worms.

Lemon : Grind lemon seeds into a fine powder and take it with water. It will destroy worms in the stomach.

Apple : Eating two apples for a few days at night expels the worms with stools. Do not take water during the night after taking apples.

Mango : Two gms. of the powder of mango kernel with hot water kills the worms in the stomach.

***Amla* :** Taking one oz. of fresh *amla* juice daily for five days will destroy worms.

Pineapple : It destroys worms.

Mulberry : The fruit and its syrup both kill worms.

Carrots : 125 ml. of carrot juice taken daily on empty stomach for two weeks expels worms from the stomach. Eating raw carrots is also beneficial.

Walnut : Drinking milk after eating a walnut for a few days is helpful. It is specially beneficial for children.

Black pepper : 1 gm. black pepper powder in butter milk to eat. They eliminates worms.

Caraway seeds : 4 gms. of the powder of caraway seeds in butter milk will kill worms. 7 drops of caraway oil will eliminate worms.

Water : Take hot water, as hot as you can, regularly after meals. It will destroy worms.

Salt : Take ½ tsp. of salt with hot water daily for ten days before meals in the morning and evening. It will expel the worms from the stomach and will check their recurrence. Even worms like earthworm will be expelled from the stomach.

***Masoor daal*:** The use of *masoor daal* is beneficial for patients who have worms.

JAUNDICE

The red cells in the blood have a life of 120 days. If their life span is reduced or if their generation occurs in large numbers, it leads to Jaundice. There is a yellow substance in the blood known as bilirubin. This appears in the blood when red blood cells get degenerated. It gives the body a yellow appearance. Jaundice is also caused by the malfunctioning of the liver.

Bile is secreted in the liver. Stones or tumours develop in the tubes carrying bile from the liver to the intestines or some defect occurs in the cells of the liver because of some virus or chemical substance. As a result, bile gets mixed with blood and it makes the skin yellowish. The yellowishness of the skin is a symptom of jaundice.

In most cases, it is catarrhal jaundice. It causes nausea for a few days and one feels depressed. Eyes and the skin become yellow. The tongue appears unclean and the patient's temperature fluctuates between 99 and 100. When you touch the liver and the gall bladder, they appear to be soft. The urine becomes dark, the stools are foul smelling, bulky and yellow.

Symptoms : The pulse rate in jaundice is reduced to around 45 per minute and it is difficult to digest clarified butter, oil and oily substances; the liver becomes hard and painful; the body, the eyes, the nails and the urine all look yellowish. There appears an itching over the body. Lot of bleeding occurs when the patient gets hurt and starts bleeding. The eyes become dry and the visibility at night is reduced. Everything seems to be yellow. Its important symptoms include reduction in weight, loss of appetite, flatulence, bitterness in the mouth, weakness in the body and feverishness.

Treatment Through Food

Give the patient a laxative first, then start the treatment. Usually, the patients become healthy by taking a laxative. The patient should be allowed complete rest. It is beneficial to give him liquid diet like gruel, *khichadi*, boiled old rice, cooked green vegetables, milk boiled in an iron pan and butter milk with salt. He should not eat meat, fish, clarified butter, oil, fried items or oily food. If necessary, he should take enema to move the bowels. At the initial stages, glucose and sugarcane juice should be given to the patient. The use of the following items regularly for a few days will cure the ailment.

Almonds : Soak overnight 8 almonds, 5 small cardamoms, two dried dates in a new clay pot. Grind them the following morning, mix 70 gms. each of sugar candy and butter. The patient will begin to pass clear urine on the fourth day itself. I have experienced it myself.

Eating plums, water-melons, tomatoes, melons and oranges is beneficial for patients of jaundice.

Tamarind : Soak tamarind in water, mash it well, strain and drink it. It will be beneficial.

Bottle gourd : Roast a bottle gourd in embers and mash it, squeeze the juice out of it, add a little sugar candy and drink it. It is beneficial in jaundice.

Bitter gourd : Grind a bitter gourd, add water and give it to the patient twice daily in the morning and evening.

Alum salt : Add a pinch of alum salt to 200 gms. of curd and eat it. If the patient is a child, reduce the quantity proportionately. Eat only curd and nothing else. It will promptly cure jaundice. There should be no cause for worry if a patient vomits. *—Sh. Gopal Chand Jaju, Bundi*

Gram : Soak gram *daal* in water. Then remove the water and mix jaggery in equal quantity with the *daal* and eat it for three days. If you feel thirsty, drink the water in which the *daal* was soaked.

Amla **:** Taking 60 ml. of fresh *amla* juice, mixed with 23 gms. of honey provides relief.

Long pepper : It is blackish in colour. It is available with an apothecary. Soak 3 pieces of long pepper in 3 tsp. of butter milk. After 24 hours, grind the long pepper, add a little bit of salt and take it with water. Each day increase the number of long peppers by one.

When you reach ten, start decreasing them one by one per day. Its use solves the problems of jaundice, liver, chronic fever, loss of appetite, diarrhoea caused by indigestion, etc. It is highly beneficial in chronic fever. This recipe is based on experience.

Onion : (1) Cut an onion into small pieces and put them in lemon juice. Add salt and black pepper powder. In this way eat an onion twice daily in the morning and evening.

(2) Taking the juice of white onions mixed with turmeric powder and jaggery is beneficial.

Garlic : Grind 4 cloves of garlic, mix in milk and drink it. Then take some more milk. Take this treatment for four days. It will be beneficial.

Dried ginger powder : Taking 12 gms. of dried ginger powder with jaggery is good for patients of jaundice.

Carrots : Carrots are a natural medicine for jaundice. In Europe, they give carrot juice, carrot soup and hot carrot to the patients of jaundice.

Cauliflower : Taking mix juice of cauliflower and carrots in equal quantity is beneficial.

Radish : (1) Eating raw a radish early in the morning provides relief from jaundice within a few days.

(2) Mix 30 gms. of sugar in 125 ml. of the juice of radish leaves and drink it in the morning. It will provide prompt relief. It is beneficial in all types of jaundice.

Wheat : Rinse ½ cup of wheat and soak it in two cups of water. After twelve hours drink the water in the morning and evening.

You can eat the soaked wheat by adding salt and chillies or by making *halwa* after grinding then.

Sugarcane : Eat some barley *sattu* and then drink sugarcan juice. It will cure jaundice within a week. Take sugarcan juice several times a day. Take mostly liquid diet.

Honey : Taking a tsp. of honey in a glass of water thrice a day is beneficial.

Papaya : Grind finely 75 gms. of raw papaya with the skin on and dissolve it in ¼ litre of water. Mix sugar or glucose to taste and give it to the patient of jaundice thrice a day regularly. It will cure jaundice within a few days. To make it tastier, you may add lemon and black pepper to taste. If the patient is a child, reduce the quantity as per requirement. The papaya syrup cures jaundice. The papaya should be raw and fresh. The milk in the papaya is beneficial.

Butter milk : Mix the powder of ten black pepper corns in a glass of butter milk and take it daily, till jaundice lasts.

Mint leaves : Eating the *chutney* of mint leaves with meals is beneficial for patients of jaundice.

PAIN IN ABDOMEN

Pain in abdomen is quite a common ailment. There are several causes which lead to this pain. Usually the pain is because of indigestion. Fomentation with a hot water bottle is beneficial in all types of pains in the abdomen. Don't eat anything unless the pain has fully subsided. It is good to drink sodawater. The treatment should be in keeping with the cause of the pain.

Treatment Through Food

Fenugreek seeds : Take 2 tsp. of the powder of fenugreek seeds mixed with salt with hot water in the morning and evening. It will provide relief from pain in the abdomen.

Aniseed : Grind aniseed, mix a little rock salt and take 2 tsp. with hot water.

Black pepper : Grind black pepper, asafoetida and dried ginger in equal quantity and take ½ tsp. with hot water in the morning and evening.

Red chilli : Eating red chilli powder mixed with jaggery is beneficial in pain in abdomen.

Salt : Mix ½ tsp. of salt in a glass of water and drink it. It will provide relief from pain in abdomen. Taking salt in hot water expels the unwanted elements from the body.

Cardamom : Taking cardamom powder mixed with honey provides relief.

Cinnamon : It relieves the pain caused by flatulence. It should be taken in a small quantity. Its over use is harmful.

Coffee : Drinking coffee will relieve the pain caused by opium eating.

Water : Taking a glass of hot water, as hot as tea, in the morning provides relief from constipation and dyspepsia. If you take lemon juice in it, it will remove gas and foul smell from the stomach. It will also relieve pain in the abdomen.

Pomegranate : Suck pomegranate seeds after adding salt and black pepper powder to them. It checks pain in the abdomen.

Butter milk : If the pain has been caused by hunger, taking butter milk is beneficial.

Honey : If the pain has been caused by eating (usually the patients say that the pain increases when they eat something) taking honey for a few days will be beneficial.

Lemon : (1) Mix 12 ml. of lemon juice, 6 ml. of ginger juice and 6 gms. honey and take it. It will provide relief from the pain.

(2) Put black salt, black pepper powder and cumin seeds powder into a slice of lemon, heat it and suck on it. It will relieve pain in the abdomen and destroy worms in the intestines.

Ginger : (1) Taking 1 gm. dry ginger powder, a little bit of asafoetida and rock salt with hot water relieves pain in the abdomen.

(2) Mix ginger powder and rock salt in a glass of water, heat it and drink it. It will provide relief from pain, constipation and dyspepsia.

Harad**:** Taking a tsp. of *harad* powder with hot water relieves pain in the abdomen. The use of *harad* in this way twice a week will keep the digestive system in order.

Guava : Grind tender leaves of guava tree, mix in water and drink. It will provide relief.

Garlic : Taking garlic juice with salt relieves pain in the abdomen.

Coriander : (1) Coriander Syrup is beneficial. Take 2 tsp. of it mixed in a cup of hot water.

(2) In case a child is suffering from stomach ache, amoebiasis, indigestion, boil a tsp. of coriander seeds and 1/4 tsp. of ginger powder in a cup of water and give it to him to drink.

Mint leaves : (1) Grind 3 gms. of mint leaves, with a little bit of cumin seeds, asafoetida, black pepper and salt and take it with hot water. It will provide relief from the pain.

(2) Mix mint powder and sugar in equal quantity and take 2 tsp. of it with hot water. It relieves the pain.

Asafoetida : Dissolve asafoetida in hot water and apply around the navel. Also eat a minute quantity of roasted asafoetida with some eatable. It provides relief from pain in the abdomen. If the pain is because of flatulence, boil 2 gms. of asafoetida in 1/2 litre water. When it is reduced to one-fourth quantity, drink it hot. Taking ten drops of asafoetida mother tincture mixed in a tsp. of water is also beneficial.

Radish : Taking radish juice mixed with salt and black pepper powder relieves pain in the abdomen.

Mustard : Grind mustard seeds in a little water, put muslin cloth on the abdomen and spread the paste on it. Remove after ten minutes. It will provide miraculous relief from pain in the abdomen.

Cumin seeds : Taking cumin seeds powder mixed with honey is helpful in relieving pain.

Caraway seeds : (1) Two gms. of caraway seeds and 1 gm. of salt taken with hot water will provide relief from pain in the abdomen.

(2) Grind 15 gms. of caraway seeds, 5 gms. of black salt and 1/2 gm. of asafoetida into a fine powder and store in a bottle. Whenever you feel pain in the abdomen, take 1 gm. of it with hot water twice a day.

(3) Grind 2 tsp. of caraway seeds, 8 tsp. of cumin seeds and 2 tsp. of black salt and store in a bottle. When in pain, mix 2 tsp.

of it in a glass of water, add a few drops of lemon juice and drink it. It will provide relief from pain in the abdomen. It is beneficial in dyspepsia, flatulence and the resultant pain in the stomach.

—Dr. Poddar Jalendra Maharathi

Basil : Mix the juices of basil leaves and ginger in equal quantity, heat it and drink it. It will be beneficial. Taking 12 ml. of the juice of basil leaves will provide relief from spasms.

BILIARY DISORDERS

***Phalsa*:** Mix water, ginger powder and sugar with ripe *phalsa* juice and drink it. It will provide relief.

Mulberry : Eat mulberry fruit in the afternoon during the summer season. It will cure biliary disorders.

Cloves : Grind four cloves, mix in water and drink it. It reduces the severity of high fever and bilious fever.

BILIARY COLIC AND GALL BLADDER STONES

One of the tubes of the liver goes to the stomach. Through this tube the bile from the liver gets into the stomach and helps in digesting the food. Sometimes the bile dries up and becomes hard like stone and gets stuck at the mouth of the liver or in the tube and causes a severe pain. There is a bilious vomit or nausea. This condition is known as biliary colic. This pain usually occurs either above or to the right side of the navel. This kind of pain is caused by gall bladder stones also.

Carrots : Taking 250 gms. juice each of carrots and salad leaves expels gall bladder stones.

Dried ginger powder : 6 gms. of dried ginger powder mixed with 1 gm. salt and taken with hot water is wonderfully effective in relieving biliary colic. It is as effective as an injection of morphia.

—Vaidyaraj Pt. Ram Narain Sharma :
Arogya Prakash Shri Vaidyanath

Radish : The use of radish juice prevents the formation of gall stones. Refer to "Stones".

APPENDICITIS

Red tomatoes eaten with rock salt and ginger before meals are helpful in appendicitis. During pain take only liquid diet. Do not eat bread.

Carrots : Carrot juice is beneficial in appendicitis. It is very useful for the disorders of the stomach.

PEPTIC ULCER

The patient of peptic ulcer requires physical and mental rest. He should eat food at short intervals. The diet should be liquid, especially milk to which clarified butter may be added. The patients of peptic ulcer should take foods which do not allow high rate of secretion in the stomach.

Peptic Ulcer : The foods recommended under 'Acidity' are beneficial for it.

Orange : If there is peptic or gastric ulceration, orange juice is very useful.

Cabbage : Its juice can cure peptic ulcers. Take a cup of cabbage juice thrice daily for two weeks. Only fresh juice is beneficial. You can eat raw cabbage leaves also.

Milk : The patient should live on milk diet, that is, he should take milk frequently. He should also take pomegranate juice and *amla* preserve.

Tea : It is extremely harmful to the patients of peptic ulcers.

ASCITES

It is a condition in which fluids accumulate in the abdominal cavity. The stomach of the patient gets swollen; he has a feeling of heaviness and uneasiness. The legs also get swollen, breathing becomes difficult, the palpitation becomes rapid. The patient should not be given salt as far as possible. He should be given diuretic medicines. It is caused by diseases such as those of the heart, kidney, liver, and T.B., cancer, aneurysm and thrombosis, etc.

Treatment Through Food

Garlic : Half tsp. of garlic juice taken in 125 ml. of water cures Ascites. It should be taken regularly for some days.

Mango : Eating mangoes is beneficial in Ascites. Eat two mangoes at a time thrice a day.

Gram : Boil 25 gms. of gram in ¼ litre of water. When the water is reduced to half the quantity, strain and drink it. Take it regularly for three weeks.

Onion : Eating onions frequently proves to be diuretic and is a good medicine for ascites.

Bitter gourd : Taking 25 gms. of bitter gourd juice mixed with water thrice daily provides relief from ascites.

Radish : ½ cup of the juice of radish leaves mixed with a little water daily is beneficial for patients of ascites.

Fenugreek seeds : Take cooked fenugreek seeds or soak them overnight in water, strain and drink it. It is beneficial in ascites.

Carrot juice, butter milk and melon are useful for patients of ascites.

HICCOUGH

Because of a certain excitement in the sinews a condition arises in which a diaphragmatic spasm causes a sudden inhalation which is interrupted by a spasmodic closure of the glottis. This condition is known as hiccough.

Hiccough occurs because of dyspepsia but sometimes it may be a symptom of a serious disease. In case of sinewy disorders it may be symptom of diseases like epilepsy, brain oedema, encephalitis lethargica and hysteria. Hiccoughs are common if the patient suffers from nephrites and uraemia. They disappear in tetanus, hydrophobia and strychnine poisoning.

Treatment Through Food

If hiccoughs have been caused by dyspepsia, taking baking powder in a glass of water provides relief. The patient suffering from hiccoughs should not be given to eat anything except hot water and hot milk. When the excitement in the stomach subsides, hiccoughs will also subside. The water or milk should not be very hot. The patient should not eat to his fill. Hold your breath as long as you can. It will provide relief. If you divert the attention of the patient, it will stop hiccoughs. If the hiccoughs have been caused by an adverse circumstance, taking a sedative medicine will be helpful. Sucking on sugar or a piece of sugar candy stops hiccoughs. Eating radish leaves also stops hiccoughs. Sucking mint leaves or a piece of lemon is quite beneficial. You can chew mint leaves with some sugar.

Lemon : Mix a tsp. each of lemon juice and honey and add black salt to taste. Take it every twenty minutes till you get relief from hiccoughs.

Onion : Eating sliced onion with salt provides relief from hiccoughs.

Black gram : Put whole black gram on burning coal and fire and inhale the fumes. It will put an end to hiccoughs.

Salt : (1) Grind rock salt, black salt and common salt in equal quantity. Take ½ tsp. of it mixed in hot water. It will provide relief from hiccoughs. Do not take it if you have been advised not to take salt because of other ailments.

(2) Boil 60 gms. mustard powder in ½ litre of water. When it is reduced to one-fourth quantity, add rock salt to taste and drink it. It will provide relief from hiccoughs.

(3) Dissolve rock salt in water. Put a few drops in the nostrils. It will put an end to hiccoughs.

Radish : Eating four radish leaves stops hiccoughs.

Mint leaves : If hiccoughs do not stop, suck on mint leaves or a piece of lemon. You may chew a few mint leaves with some sugar.

Jaggery : Grind old jaggery, mix ginger powder and inhale the smell. It will put an end to hiccoughs.

Soda water : Drinking a bottle of soda water will provide relief from hiccoughs.

Milk : Drinking hot milk puts an end to hiccough.

Ginger : (1) Grind dried ginger in water and inhale the smell. It will stop hiccoughs.

(2) Grind dried ginger, *amla*, long pepper and sugar candy and take 3 gms. of it with honey. It will be beneficial.

(3) Sucking on small ginger pieces provides immediate relief from hiccoughs.

Clarified butter : Drinking a little bit of hot clarified butter puts an end to hiccoughs. Mix rock salt in clarified butter or water and inhale the smell. It will stop hiccoughs.

Sugarcane : Drinking sugar cane juice provides relief from hiccoughs.

Black-pepper : Pierce a black-peppercorn with a needle and burn it. Then inhale the fumes. It puts an end to hiccoughs.

Cinnamon : Chew some Cinnamon. It will stop hiccoughs.

Cardamom : Chewing Cardamom puts an end to hiccoughs.

Honey : Mix honey with onion juice and lick it.

Licking only honey will also provide the necessary relief.

Mustard : Boil 10 gms. mustard seeds in ¼ litre of water, strain and drink it when it is lukewarm. It will provide relief from all types of hiccoughs.

Asafoetida : If it is a severe problem, take a minute quantity of asafoetida with jaggery or a banana.

Basil Leaves : Mix 12 ml. of the juice of basil leaves with 6 gms. of honey and take it. It will stop hiccoughs.

Holding the breath, sudden fear, anger or joy are usually effective in controlling hiccoughs.

LIVER DISEASES

Liver is situated under the ribs on the right side. At the initial stage of a liver disease, the patient develops fever with shivering. Later, the temperature subsides but the liver disease remains uncured. When the problem gradually becomes chronic, the liver gets hardened and enlarged. If you press the spot where liver is situated, you feel pain there. Hard work also proves to be painful for the liver. Sometimes, there is pain in the liver even if you are not working. Whiteness of the tongue, headache, weakness, anemia, dyspepsia, pain on the back side of the right shoulder, amoebic stools like mud and bad taste in the mouth are its symptoms. Constipation and flatulence are its major symptoms. It gets fatal if it is not controlled because ultimately the liver shrinks and the patient dies. It is caused by the amoeba of chronic dysentery which affect the liver or by chronic Malarial fever, or as a result of the reaction of quinine or mercury, excessive drinking, living in a hot place or eating too much of sweets, etc. Till a few years back the incidence of liver diseases was common among children as a consequence of which they could not become physically strong. The eyes and face of the patient suffering from a liver disease appear to be pale and bloodless.

CIRRHOSIS OF THE LIVER

'Cirrhosis' means brown. In cirrhosis of the liver, the liver becomes hard and smaller in size. Because of the impaired functioning of the liver, the patient develops, fever, pain in the liver region, aversion for cereals, nausea, debility, a tendency for plethora, etc. The patient becomes week and pale with prominent blue veins and protruding face. The proteins from the intestines get mixed with the poisoned blood due to toxins and cause the death of the patient. It is, therefore, a fatal disease. But when some external or internal toxins keep entering the liver in small quantity continuously, excessive generation of cells occurs in place of some dead cells or there is an infiltration of fibrous tissue, which results in the increase of the size and hardening of the liver. It is called acute enlargement of the liver. Its incidence is higher among men between the ages of 40 and 50.

Treatment Through Food

It is beneficial for a patient of cirrhosis to take fruit juice, salad, juice of green vegetables, citrus fruit, pineapple, *mausambi*, oranges, sweet items—arum, potatoes, carrots, beetroot, dates, figs, raisins, mango, papaya, honey, etc. The patient should stop the use of fried food, coffee, strong spices and tobacco. Alcohol is just like poison for such a patient. It should be stopped altogether.

The patient should reduce the intake of clarified butter and sugar to the minimum. The use of items prescribed for patients of dyspepsia is also beneficial for patients of liver diseases. The use of longpepper as mentioned under the heading 'Jaundice' is also beneficial. The patient should take *lychee*, beetroot, bottle gourd, *bathua* and butter milk. They are highly useful and provide strength to the liver.

Lemon : Cut a lemon into four parts without separating them. Fill one of them with salt, the other with black pepper powder, the third with dried ginger powder and the fourth with sugar or sugar candy powder.

Keep it overnight covered in a plate. The following morning heat it on a hot plate and suck it. It will cure the liver problem and sharpen the appetite. There cannot be a more effective medicine for such a patient.

—As tried by Sh. Hukumatrai, Ajmer

Coriander : Prepare a powder (*churan*) of coriander seeds, dried ginger and black salt and take it thrice a day. It provides relief from the problem of loss of appetite and strong and energy to the liver. It enhances the appetite.

Apple : It is beneficial in liver ailments. It provides strength to the liver.

Other things which give strength to the liver are—butter milk, *bathua*, *lychee*, pomegranate, rose apple, beetroot and plums. They provide relief from flatulence and constipation. Their regular use is advisable.

Bottle gourd : Roast a bottle gourd on fire, mash it and squeeze out the juice, mix sugar candy and drink it. It is beneficial for patients suffering from liver diseases.

Rice : Get up before sunrise, rinse your mouth and chew a few grains of rice. This recipe is very useful in strengthening the liver. Those who have taken rice like this have benefited from it.

Salt : Grind ½ tsp. salt and 4 tsp. of mustard seeds and prepare a paste; apply it on the liver area for five minutes, wash it and then apply clarified butter there. It is beneficial in relieving pain in the liver.

Betel leaf : Apply oil on the smooth side of a betel leaf, heat it and put it on the liver area and wrap it with a piece of cloth. It will relieve pain in the liver.

Long pepper : Grind four pieces of long pepper, mix with honey and lick. It is beneficial in cases of enlargement of the liver.

Papaya : It cleanses the bowels and energizes the liver. Little children who have liver problems should be given papaya to eat.

Carrots : People with liver ailments and bilious problems should eat carrots frequently. In France, they consider carrots to be beneficial for patients suffering from the above problems.

Melon : It alleviates swelling of the liver.

Bitter gourd : ½ tsp. of the juice of bitter gourd given to children between the age of 3 and 8 keeps their livers fit. It cleanses the bowels. If the liver is enlarged, the patients should be given 50 ml. of the juice of bitter gourd mixed in water. It will be beneficial.

Brinjal : It provides relief to patients with enlarged livers.

Caraway seeds : Soak 15 gms. of caraway seeds in water in the morning in a clay pot. During the day put it in a room and during the night put in an open place under the dewy sky. The following day strain it and drink the water. Take this treatment for 15 days. It cures the problem of enlargement of the liver and kindles the appetite.

Basil Leaves : Boil 12 gms. of basil leaves in a glass of water. When it is reduced to one fourth, strain it and drink it. It cures the problems of the liver including enlargement.

DIET DURING WINTER

Of the three seasons, it is only the winter season which provides natural nourishment to the body and helps in keeping it healthy and increases physical strength and potency. The energy we store in winter is of use throughout the remaining part of the year.

During this season, the human body, in order to keep itself warm, generates a lot of energy as a protection against the cold weather and chilly winds. This warmth intensifies the fire of the stomach which helps to digest the food and strengthens the digestive system of a healthy and strong person. It is then able to digest heavier food taken in large quantity. Therefore, during the winter season nutritious food can be taken.

We should include such items in our diet which contain fat or sweet, salty, citrus, nutritious and which provide strength to the body.

Wheat, millet, maize, gram, *moong, moth*, black gram, *masoor*, etc. are especially beneficial. Besides, milk, clarified butter, *mawa, rabri, kheer*, cream, sweets, etc., are foods that provide energy. During winter, one likes to take carrot *halwa* and preparations of sesame seeds and jaggery. Other food items like groundnuts, dates, papaya, banana, apple, pomegranate and cheeku are also beneficial. It is good to eat dates boiled in milk two hours after the evening meals. The use of garlic is also beneficial. It is not necessary to take costly nutritious food items in winter. You should also take carrots, radish, tomatoes and cucumber in the form of salad. The juice of *amla*, carrots and tomatoes is also highly beneficial. Therefore, you can get good nutrition at a low cost. (See—'Food during Winter' at *pg.365*)

CATARRH, CORYZA

In medical books, there is no treatment for catarrh or coryza. The medicines prescribed by a doctor simply give you a feeling of relief but they do not shorten the duration of the disease. They suppress the disease temporarily but it appears again at any time. Catarrh is marked by inflammation of the mucous membrane. It is not advisable to use inhalers or nasal drops to open up a blocked nose. It increases the blood pressure and there is a narrowing of blood vessels.

Catarrh is a common problem. Given below are a few food items which can cure catarrh. If you are taking some other treatment, even then you can use them. An analysis of these items will show that treatment through food is easy and harmless.

Causes

(1) Accumulated Disorders : Breathing disorders, constipation, tonsillitis, nasal problem, debility and sensitivity to cold.

(2) Immediate stimulating Causes : Getting drenched in the rain, catching cold, walking in the hot Sun and immediately afterwards drinking cold water, keeping awake at night, dyspepsia, sudden stopping of perspiration, too much of sexual intercourse, lack of clean air, taking hot water baths, being scared of cold, use of cold drinks and foods.

Prohibited Food Items : The patient of catarrh should not take milk and curd. If you have to take milk, take it only after boiling one of the following in it : a large cardamom, two pieces of long pepper, two dried dates or four dates. The use of large raisins as mentioned in the foregoing chapter "Energy Foods" is highly beneficial.

To cure catarrh and coryza the use of Vitamin 'C' is most helpful. Please consult the present author's book "*Shaktivardhak Bhojan*" for details on the use of Vitamin 'C'. But besides Vitamin 'C' there are some other traditional ways which provide relief from catarrh, as gargling, the use of ginger and honey and steam inhaling, etc. However, people do not seem to be interested in old recipes. Unless they give up this kind of attitude, it will not be easy to get rid of the problem.

Water : If the catarrh is due to an immediate stimulating cause, take hot water and do not eat food. It will cure catarrh. This kind of catarrh is common. One catches a cold on a day, the next day one has a running nose and the third day it matures and one is on the way to recovery. If the cold is treated with medicines instead of through food, it may become worse and lead to several other diseases.

Jaggery : (1) The use of *laddoos* made of jaggery and black sesame prevents the occurrence of catarrh.

(2) If the cold has gone bad, to eat 30 gms. of jaggery and 6 gms. of black pepper powder mixed in 60 gms. of curd is the first thing in the morning after you get up and again in the evening for five days. It will be beneficial. It is also a preventive treatment. When the Catarrh goes bad, the patient develops low fever, a distaste for food, *Kaf*, cough mucous, foul smell emanates from the nose and there are foul smelling secretions, headache, etc.

Orange : The patient suffering from coryza and cough should take orange juice with cold water in summer and hot water in winter. It is beneficial. Cut the peel of an orange into small pieces and boil it in a glass of water. When the water is reduced to half, strain and take it twice in the morning and evening. The orange peel can be dried in the Sun and stored for this purpose. Use it as and when required.

Apple : Catarrh is common among persons with a weak brain. Such people do not benefit from medicines. Such persons should eat an apple without peeling it before meals. It will provide strength to the brain.

***Amla* :** People suffering from frequent attacks of catarrh should use *amla* regularly.

Grapes : Eating at least 50 gms. of grapes daily prevents the occurrence of catarrh.

Fig : Boil five figs in water, strain and drink the water twice daily in the morning and evening.

Garlic : If the patient sneezes 5 to 7 times continuously, give him garlic to eat. It will provide relief from sneezing.

Maize : Burn a cob of maize and grind it into powder. Add salt to taste. Take ¼ tsp. four times daily with hot water. It will be beneficial.

Milk : Put 5 pieces of long pepper in milk and boil it. Add sugar and drink it twice daily in the morning and evening.

Tea : If the catarrh is because of cold, there is sneezing and secretion from the eyes and the nose, taking tea will be helpful. It gives warmth and causes sweating. In this way it provides relief from cold. If the catarrh is dry and the mucous is thick, yellow and foul swelling and if there is headache and sinusitis, taking tea is harmful.

Betel leaf : Eating a betel leaf with a clove is beneficial in catarrh.

Coriander : Boil 125 gms. of Coriander powder in ½ litre of water. When the water is reduced to one-fourth quantity, strain it and mix 125 gms. sugar candy and heat it once again. When it thickens, lick 10 gms. of it every day. It will cure the catarrh caused by the weakness of the brain. It will also provide energy to the brain.

Mulberry : It is beneficial for patients suffering from catarrh and throat ailments.

Carrots : Mix 310 ml. of carrot juice and 125 ml. of spinach juice and drink it. It will provide relief from cold and coryza.

Aniseed : Boil 15 gms. of aniseed and 7 cloves in ½ litre of water; when it is reduced to one-fourth drink it sip by sip after adding sugar or loaf sugar to it.

Turmeric : (1) If you have the problem of mucous because of catarrh or asthma, take a tsp. of turmeric powder thrice daily with hot water.

(2) Inhaling the fumes of turmeric acts as an expectorant of *Kafa*.

(3) Mix the powder of 10 black pepper corns and ½ tsp. of turmeric powder in a cup of hot milk and drink it. It is beneficial in catarrh and fever.

Salt : Grind one part of rock salt with four parts of sugar. Take ½ tsp. of it thrice a day with hot milk. It will cure catarrh.

Lemon : Drinking lemon juice in lukewarm water cures coryza. If the problem is severe, squeeze a lemon in a glass of boiling hot water, mix honey and drink at night.

***Mausambi* :** Those who suffer from frequent attacks of catarrh and coryza, they can get relief by taking *mausambi* juice for some days.

Large raisins : (1) Large raisins are beneficial in coryza. If you suffer from frequent attacks of cold or if it is difficult to cure, soak 11 large raisins, 11 black pepper corns and 5 almonds and peel them. Grind them together, mix 25 gms. of butter and eat before going to bed. Next morning boil long pepper, black pepper and dried ginger powder in milk and drink it hot. Continue with the treatment for a few months. It will provide a permanent cure.

(2) Soak 6 almonds, 6 large raisins, 6 pistachios, one clove, one cardamom and 2 tsp. of poppy seeds in water in the morning. Use minimum quantity of water to soak them. In the evening,

peel the almonds, remove seeds from the raisins, grind all of them and put the paste in a piece of thick cloth and tie it to make a little bundle, heat it on a hot plate. Eat it before bed-time. Do not take water after that during the night. It will cure coryza.

(3) Eating large raisins with hot water provides relief from catarrh.

Mustard oil : Mix 15 drops of mustard oil with 7 drops of water, stir it well till there is frothing, smell it and also apply few drops in the nostrils before bed-time. It is beneficial if the catarrh is chronic, foul smell emanates from the nose or if there is expectoration of bloody or bloodless phlegm.

Asafoetida : Smelling the solution of asafoetida is helpful in removing phlegm deposits and foul smell from the nose.

Guava : You can cure chronic catarrh and coryza by eating guavas only for three days.

Onion : Eating raw onions cures catarrh. It is beneficial in cold related ailments. If you have a running nose, smelling at onion juice is beneficial.

Mint leaves : Boil mint leaves in water, add a little salt and sip it like tea. It is beneficial for patients of coryza and cough.

Gram : Smell at hot roasted grams tied in a piece of cloth. They can also be eaten. It cures coryza. Boil gram, strain and drink the boiled water. Eat boiled gram. To enhance the taste add some salt and black pepper powder. Gram is very beneficial for patients of catarrh.

Caraway seeds : (1) Smoking caraway seeds the way you smoke a cigarette or **bidi,** is beneficial in coryza.

(2) Tie 6 gms. of caraway seeds in a piece of muslin, rub it on your palm and smell it frequently. It will provide relief from catarrh.

Ginger : Boil dried ginger and Jaggery or sugar in water. When it is reduced to one-fourth quantity, strain it and drink it when it is pleasantly hot. Take it thrice a day. It will prove to be beneficial.

Basil : Boil 10 basil leaves and five corns of black pepper just as you boil tea. Add a little jaggery and clarified butter or rock salt and drink it. It is beneficial in coryza. Little children should be given basil leaves boiled in water.

Honey : (1) Mix 2 tsp. of honey and ½ tsp. of baking powder with 200 ml. of mildly hot milk and drink it twice daily in the morning and evening. It will cause a great deal of sweating. Do not expose yourself to open air while you are sweating. It will cure coryza and flue.

(2) Mix 30 gms. honey and 2 tsp. of ginger juice in hot water and drink it. It will cure coryza.

Nutmeg : Scour nutmeg with a little water, mix honey and give it to the patient if it is a child to lick twice daily in the morning and evening. It will provide relief from frequent attacks of catarrh.

Sugar : Inhaling the fumes of sugar put on burning coal clears the blocked nose.

Mustard : Smelling mustard seeds powder mixed with honey in summer provides relief from catarrh.

Black pepper : Chew ten corns of black pepper followed by a glass of hot milk; it will be beneficial in catarrh.

COUGH

Cough in itself is not a disease. It is only a symptom of other ailments. But if it persists it can cause other problems. Besides catarrh and coryza, the disease of the breathing tubes, lungs and heart are other causes of cough. It is also a symptom of T.B. and asthma. You cannot cure cough unless you take the treatment for the disease causing cough. The patent medicines for cough provide only temporary relief. There are two types of cough—(1) dry and (2) phlegmatic. Dry cough is usually not old and expectoration of mucous is difficult and not much in quantity while in phlegmatic cough, the mucous comes out easily without much effort. Chronic cough is usually phlegmatic. Eating hot things can usually control cough. Catarrh is the major cause of cough. Therefore, the food items prescribed for catarrh can be used for cough also. Use the following food items to cure cough.

Lemon : It will be beneficial for patients of cough and asthma to suck on a piece of lemon filled with black pepper powder and salt.

Orange : Taking orange juice mixed with hot water in winter and cold water in summer is quite beneficial.

Apple : Taking the juice of ripe apples mixed with sugar candy in the morning provides relief from chronic cough.

***Amla* :** (1) Prepare a paste with *amla* powder and a tsp. of honey and lick it twice daily.

(2) For dry cough use the *chutney* of green or dry *amla* ground with green coriander leaves. It will provide much relief from cough and help in the expectoration of mucous.

Grapes : Eating grapes provides strength to the lungs. It helps in the expectoration of mucous. Do not drink water after eating grapes.

Spinach : Gargling with lukewarm spinach juice is beneficial in relieving cough.

Turnip : Boil it in water, strain, mix sugar and drink it. It will be beneficial.

Fenugreek seeds : Boil 4 tsp. of fenugreek seeds in a glass of water. When it is reduced to half, strain it and drink it hot.

Fig : It is beneficial for patients of chronic cough because it dilutes the mucous and helps in its expectoration.

Milk : Boil five pieces of long pepper in milk, add sugar and drink it twice daily in the morning and evening for a few months.

Sesame seeds : If the cough has been caused by cold, boil 4 tsp. each of sesame seeds and sugar candy in a glass of water, when it is reduced to half, drink it. Take it thrice daily.

Cinnamon : Suck on pieces of cinnamon to control cough.

Cloves : Grind one part of cloves and two parts of pomegranate rind. Mix ¼ tsp. of it with ½ tsp. of honey and lick it thrice daily. It will cure the problem of cough.

Aniseed : Boil 2 tsp. each of aniseed and caraway seeds in ½ litre of water, mix 2 tsp. of honey and give three tsp. of it to the child every hour.

Black pepper : (1) Suck on black pepper and sugar candy. It is soothing for the throat.

(2) Mix the powder of five corns of black pepper and ½ tsp. of dried ginger powder with a tsp. of honey and lick it twice daily in the morning and evening. It cures phlegmatic cough.

(3) Mix a tsp. of black pepper powder with 60 gms. of jaggery and roll into pills. Suck on half a pill twice daily in the morning and evening. It cures all types of cough.

(4) Grind black pepper and sugar candy in equal quantity. Mix a little clarified butter so that you can make pills. Suck on one pill at a time. It will cure all types of cough.

(5) Grind ten corns of black pepper and mix with honey. Lick it twice daily in the morning and evening.

(6) Licking the powder of ten black pepper corns mixed with hot clarified butter provides relief from dry cough.

(7) Boil 10 corns of black pepper in water and drink it.

Coriander : Grind coriander and sugar candy in equal quantity and take 1 tsp. of it with a cup of rice soaked water. It will be beneficial.

Sugar candy : In case there are frequent bouts of cough, suck on a piece of sugar candy.

Coffee : If the cough is severe, take hot black coffee without milk.

Betel leaf : In case of frequent bouts of cough chew a roasted piece of turmeric with a betel leaf. If the cough occurs at night, chew caraway seeds with a betel leaf and do not spit it out.

Pomegranate : Grind eight parts of pomegranate rind and mix one part of rock salt, mix a little water and roll into pills. Suck on a pill thrice a day. It will provide relief from cough.

Cardamom : Eating small cardamoms provides relief from cough.

Garlic : (1) Boil a garlic bulb in 62 ml. of mustard oil. Massage the chest and the throat with this oil. Eat garlic with large raisins thrice a day. Do not take sour food.

(2) Mix 20 drops of garlic juice with pomegranate juice and drink it. It is beneficial in all types of cough.

Water : Drinking hot water before bedtime provides relief from cough.

Mint leaves : Drinking mint tea with a little salt is beneficial in cough.

Wheat : Boil 20 gms. of wheat and 9 gms. of rock salt in a glass of water. When it is reduced to one-third, strain and drink it. The treatment should continue for seven days.

Clarified butter : Heat some jaggery with clarified butter and eat it when comfortably hot. Massage the chest with a mixture of clarified butter and rock salt. It cures chronic cough.

Mustard oil : If the patient is a child, massage the chest with mustard oil. Also apply oil to the rectum. If the patient is asthmatic and has a congested chest massage it with mustard oil mixed with rock salt. It will be beneficial.

Jaggery : Eating black sesame and jaggery in the form of *laddoos* in winter provides relief from cough, asthma and bronchitis.

Turmeric : If you have cough, soar throat and a congested chest, take hot water with salt in it. Suck on a piece of turmeric. It will provide relief.

***Mausambi*:** Those who frequently suffer from cough, coryza and cold, can get lasting relief from these problems by taking *mausambi* juice for some days.

Large raisins : It is beneficial in cough. If you suffer from cold frequently and it is difficult to cure, soak 11 large raisins, 11 corns of black pepper and 5 almonds. Peel the almonds. Grind them all together, mix with 25 gms. of butter and eat before bed-time. The following morning boil long pepper, black pepper and dried ginger powder in milk and drink it. Continue the treatment for 2 or 3 months. It will provide lasting relief from coryza and cough.

Alum salt : Licking ½ gm. of alum salt mixed with honey will provide relief from asthma and cough.

Honey (1) Boil a lemon in water, then squeeze it into a glass tumbler. Mix one oz. glycerine and three oz. honey and stir well. Take a tsp. of it four times a day. It will provide relief from cough.

(2) Honey provides relief from cough. Licking 12 gms. of honey thrice a day expels the phlegm and cures cough.

Red chilli : There is a homeopathic medicine called Capsicum Annum which is made of red chilli. Take five drops of the mother tincture of this medicine with hot water thrice a day. It is beneficial in phlegmatic cough.

Caraway seeds : Eating caraway seeds followed by a drink of hot water provides relief from cough.

Ginger : Heat ginger juice (30 gms. at a time) and drink it thrice daily. It is very useful in cough and asthma. Do not take curd and sour things. Slice 12 gms. of ginger into small pieces, boil it in water mixed with milk and sugar and drink it hot like tea. It will provide relief from cough and coryza. Heat jaggery with clarified butter. Mix 12 gms. of dried ginger powder. It will make one dose. Take it daily in the morning empty stomach. It will cure cough and coryza. Boil 8 corns of black pepper in a glass of water, add ¼ dried ginger powder, salt and jaggery to taste. When it is reduced to half the quantity, drink it when it is pleasantly hot. It will cure cough. Cut 10 gms. ginger into fine pieces and put it in a bowl, add 20 gms. jaggery and heat it. When the jaggery melts, stir it with a spoon. When they get properly mixed, remove it from the stove. Lick one or 2 tsp. of it when it is pleasantly hot. It provides relief from phlegmatic cough. Do not take water for an hour after eating it or you could take it before bedtime. Rinse your mouth with lukewarm water before going to bed. It is a highly beneficial treatment.

Basil : If the patient feels pain in the chest or has developed fever, it will be helpful to take the juice of basil leaves mixed with sugar candy.

(1) Roast five cloves and chew them with basil leaves. It provides relief from all types of cough. Eating dry basil leaves with sugar candy (One dose = 4 gms) cures cough and ailments of the chest.

(2) Grind basil leaves and black pepper in equal quantity and make pills. Take a pill four times a day. It also cures whooping cough.

(3) It is beneficial to take the juice of basil leaves, ginger and onions mixed with honey in cough. It facilitates expectoration.

(4) Taking the decoction of 12 gms. of green basil leaves mixed with milk and sugar provides relief from cough and pain in the chest.
(5) Taking the juice of basil leaves mixed with honey is beneficial in cough.
(6) Taking 3 ml. of the juice of basil leaves mixed with 6 gms. of sugar candy and 3 corns of black pepper provides relief from congestion in the chest, chronic fever and cough.
(7) Mix 3 gms. each of the juice of basil leaves and ginger with 5 gms. of honey and lick it twice daily in the morning and evening. It is useful in fever, cough and asthma.
(8) Grind dry basil leaves, catechu, camphor and cardamom in equal quantity and mix with 9 parts of sugar and make a fine powder. It is helpful in coryza, cough, sore throat and congestion of lungs. In homeopathy it is known as 11X Trituration. Take a pinch of it in the morning and evening. It facilitates expectoration.

Coconut : Grate a dry coconut. Soak ¼ cup of it in a cup of water for two hours. Strain and grind the grated coconut. When it turns into a paste, dissolve it in the water in which it was soaked and drink it. Take it thrice a day. It will be helpful in cough, diseases of the lungs and T.B. It strengthens the body. Also take coconut with it.

DRY COUGH

Jaggery : Mix 15 gms. of jaggery with 15 ml. of mustard oil and lick it. It is beneficial in dry cough.

Water-melon : It is useful to eat water-melon in dry cough.

Mango : Roast a ripe mango in hot ashes. Eat it when it is cool. It cures dry cough.

Dates : Dates provide relief from dry cough.

Sugarcane : Drinking sugar cane juice is beneficial in dry cough. It provides relief from whizzing in the chest.

Black pepper : (1) Suck on black pepper and sugar candy in dry cough. It opens up the throat.

(2) Grind black pepper and sugar candy in equal quantity.

Mix clarified butter and make pills. Suck on a pill at a time. It will cure all types of cough.

(3) Grind 10 corns of black pepper, mix with honey and lick twice daily in the morning and evening. Take hot milk mixed with black pepper at bed time.

Carrots : Taking 310 ml. of carrot juice mixed with 125 gms. spinach juice provides relief from bronchitis.

In dry cough, sucking on an almond keeps the throat wet and provides relief from cough.

WHOOPING COUGH

It is an infectious disease. If a child catches it, other children get the infection from him. It is also called Pertussis. The literal meaning of Pertussis is too much cough. The patient first develops low fever. The intensity of cough gradually increases. Day and night there are recurrent bouts of cough. The cough seems to be uncontrollable and one bout of cough lasts from 30 seconds to a minute. There seems to be suffocation, the eyes become red and the constant coughing leads to vomiting. The cough produces a whooping sound. That is why it is known as whooping cough. It is a very painful diseases for children and it lasts quite long. Various medical systems believe that it takes 4-6 weeks to cure but it gets cured in a short time if treated through food and with homeopathic medicines. For homeopathic treatment of whooping cough please read the present author's book "*Homeopathic Vyavaharik Chikitsa Saar.*"

Coconut : Give 4 ml. of pure coconut oil without any fragrance to one year old child four times daily. It will be beneficial.

Garlic : (1) Soak overnight 5 almonds in water. Peel them the following morning and grind them alongwith some sugar candy and a clove of garlic and give it to the child to eat. It will cure the whooping cough in two or three days. Make the child wear a garland of garlic cloves and massage his chest with garlic oil. It will be helpful.

(2) Mix 10 drops of fresh garlic juice with four gms. each of honey and water. Give such a dose to the child four times a day.

Sugarcane : Taking 62 ml. of radish juice mixed in sugarcane juice is beneficial in whooping cough.

Alum salt : Taking 1 gm. of alum salt with hot water daily provides relief from whooping cough.

Cloves : Roast cloves, mix with honey and eat them. It will cure whooping cough.

Basil Leaves : Grind basil leaves and black pepper in equal quantity. Make very small pills. Suck a pill at a time four times a day. It will cure whooping cough.

Guava : Roast a guava in hot sand or ashes and eat it. It is beneficial in whooping cough.

Maize : Burn a maize cob and grind it into a fine powder. Add rock salt to taste. Take ¼ tsp. of it four times daily with hot water. It will be beneficial.

BRONCHITIS

Ginger : Grind 15 gms. ginger, 4 almonds, 8 large raisins and eat it twice daily, followed by drinking hot water.

ASTHMA AND ALLERGY

Asthma

Causes : It is caused by such microbic elements which cannot be seen with the eyes, for example, the pollen of a flower. Some people may get this disease in the bathroom or bedroom where minute microbes prosper, such as dust-mite, dust particles found in blankets, curtains and carpets. It has often been noticed that asthma patients cannot live with hairy pets such as dogs, cats, rabbits, etc. Spores found in mould, and fungi can also cause the problem of asthma.

Some asthma patients are allergic to food items such as milk, eggs, fish, yeast and certain preservatives (such as sulphur-dioxide). Sometime they get sick simply by smelling such foods or by eating them. There are people who get asthmatic by wet colours, vehicular exhaust, cigarette smoke and some medicines. Some elements which stimulate the respiratory system can cause allergic reaction in it. The changes in temperature due to seasonal variations, excessive physical labour, emotional setbacks or too much of laughter can cause asthmatic attacks.

Allergy

The substances which are capable of causing allergy are known as allergen. A healthy body has a special mechanism to check this reaction and is called immune system. The chief element of this mechanism is the White Blood Cells (W.B.C.) in the body. These cells keep often prepared to tackle all the allergen entering the body from outside (or bacteria attacking the body) and produce a protein like substance which is called anti-body. This antibody is helpful in tackling the antigen. Our body has a large number of antibodies which neutralize the ill-effects of the foreign elements.

For example, once a patient has had measles, a viral disease, his body will develop anti-bodies which do not allow the recurrence of that disease. But there are diseases like flu and coryza whose viruses undergo transformation frequently. Therefore, the antibodies already existing are not effective and flu and coryza keep recurring.

Asthma is a kind of allergic reaction. When it happens in the skin it is called eczema. The allergic condition of the eyes and the nose is called hay-fever and when it affects the respiratory system it is known as asthma. In fact, the above parts of the body react in a similar way. When the allergy becomes serious it is known as anaphylaxis. This condition poses a threat to life because it not only causes narrowing of the respiratory system but also swelling in it. The blood pressure also drops and the patient begins to lose consciousness.

Often those people are allergic who have a hereditary factor of diseases such as asthma, eczema and hay-fever. Such type of asthma can occur at any age and due to any reason and may be curable. It sometimes happens due to hormonal imbalance. Emotional problems such as excessive fear of examination, excessive labour, etc. can turn asthma into a serious problem.

The respiratory tubes connected with the lungs are covered with a layer of very small muscles. When their movement is hindered, breathing becomes difficult and there is a wheezing sound. This condition is known as asthma. At the initial stage, asthmatic attacks are not so frequent and do not last long. But gradually it becomes chronic and one suffers from daily asthmatic attacks. It is a very painful disease. When there is an attack of asthma, it should be allowed to subside first; then the treatment should be started. Steps should be taken to check its recurrence. It is a mistake to expect that asthma can be cured with medicines. For a permanent cure it is necessary to be careful about your food, life-style and observance of rules of nature. Fomentation of the chest of an asthmatic patient provides him relief. The increase of isonophelia in the blood causes dry asthma.

Prevention : Avoid constipation and keep the bowels clear. Protect yourself from cold. Do not eat food which takes long or is hard to digest. The evening meal should be taken before sunset, take a small quantity and it should be easy to digest. Drink hot water. Go for a walk in the fresh air. The regular use of the following food items for a few months is beneficial for patients of asthma. They will be helpful in curing asthma. If asthma is accompanied by cough, you may use the food items mentioned under the title 'Cough'.

Vitamin 'E' : It is essential for the treatment of asthma. It helps in the production of blood cells. It also helps in reducing the effect of harmful toxic reactions in the body due to pollution. Its daily dose is 15-20 mg.

It can be obtained from wheat sprouts, pistachio, soyabean, saffola oil, coconut, *ghee*, fresh butter, tomatoes, grapes and dry fruits, etc.

Calcium : Calcium-rich food is useful for patients of asthma. Its daily dose is 0.8 gm. but can be taken in higher doses if required. The requirement of calcium by the body can be met by eating 50 gms. of sesame seeds. It is also found in milk, spinach, *chaulai*, soyabean, dry fruits, *amla*, carrots and cheese.

Dried dates : Dried dates are hot by nature. It provides strength to lungs and chest. It is beneficial in phlegmatic condition and cold.

Lemon : During an attack of asthma it is beneficial to take lemon juice in hot water. It will be very useful if the patient regularly takes a tsp. of lemon juice with 2 tsp. of honey and a tsp. of ginger juice mixed in a cup of hot water. It can be taken during an attack of asthma also. It is also beneficial for heart patients and for those who suffer from the problem of blood pressure and digestive system and also for maintaining good health. Licking lemon juice mixed with honey provides relief to a child from the problem of breathlessness.

Dates : Dates are useful for patients of asthma.

Carrots : Carrots or their juice is beneficial in treating asthma. To derive the maximum benefit take mixed juice of carrots (185 gms.), beetroot (150 gms.) and cucumber (125 gms.).

Grapes : Eating grapes is highly beneficial. If the patients spits blood with the phlegm, even then eating grapes will be helpful.

Fig : Figs are useful if the asthma is phlegmatic. They facilitate expectoration and the patient gets prompt relief.

Fenugreek : Boil 4 tsp. of fenugreek seeds in a glass of water. When it is reduced to half the quantity, strain and drink it hot.

Banana : Asthma patients should avoid eating bananas. They should bear in mind that if the problem gets worse after eating it, it should not be eaten at all. Usually asthma patients are allergic to bananas.

Bitter gourd : Eating cooked bitter gourd is useful for asthmatic patients.

Mint leaves : Taking ¼ cup of the juice of mint leaves mixed with water in equal quantity thrice daily is beneficial.

Mint leaves are good and effective in cough, asthma, etc. because they are an expectorant. The extract of mint leaves is especially effective in these diseases.

Milk : Boil five pieces of long pepper in milk and drink it twice daily in the morning and evening.

Coriander : Grind coriander and sugar candy and take it with the water in which rice has been soaked. It will be beneficial.

Water-melon : Asthmatic patients should not take the juice of water-melon.

Infrared rays : These rays are beneficial in asthma.

Garlic : It is mentioned in the book *Therapeutic Byways* written by the homeopath, Dr. E.P. Andrews that garlic is useful for patients of asthma. Taking garlic juice with hot water is beneficial in breathing problems and asthma. It will be helpful if the patient takes ten drops of garlic juice and 2 tsp. of honey in a cup of hot water daily in the morning. It can be taken during an asthmatic attack also.

Onion : Smelling a crushed onion provides relief from cough, throat problems, tonsillitis and lung ailments. Smelling onion juice mixed with honey is also useful.

Turnip : Taking mixed juice of turnips, cabbage, carrots and kidney-beans twice daily in the morning and evening for two weeks is beneficial.

Wheat : The eminent Physician, *Dr. N. Vigmore* has successfully treated even chronic patients of asthma by asking them to take wheat grass juice. Read the present author's book '*Bhojan ke Dwara Chikitsa*' for details for preparing the wheat grass juice.

Jaggery : Eating jaggery and black sesame seeds in the form of *laddoos* during winter is beneficial.

Turmeric : If the asthma is phlegmatic, take 5 gms. of turmeric powder with hot water thrice daily. It is highly beneficial in allergic asthmatic conditions. Roast turmeric in hot sand, grind it and take a tsp. of it twice daily with hot water. Turmeric is beneficial in all types of asthmatic conditions.

Rock salt : Grind one part of rock salt and four parts of *desi* sugar into a fine powder. Taking ½ tsp. of it with 100 ml. of hot water thrice daily will be beneficial.

***Peepal* :** Pick dark green leaves of a *peepal* tree and allow them to dry in the shade. Then grind them into a fine powder. Take a tsp. of it with water twice daily in the morning and evening. If there is cough, lick 1 tsp. of the above powder mixed with 2 tsp. of honey twice daily. It will provide relief from cough.

***Kulthi* :** Taking *kulthi ki daal* twice daily provides unexpectedly great benefit. Continue with the treatment at least for three months.

Cardamom : Eating it is useful in asthma.

***Isabgol* :** Taking *isabgol* regularly twice daily for 6 months or a year provides relief from all types of breathing problems. It can cure even two-year old asthma.

***Mausambi* :** Take *mausambi* juice mixed with half quantity of water and a little bit of the powder of cumin seeds and dried ginger.

Alum salt : Licking ½ gm. alum salt mixed with honey provides relief from asthma and cough.

Honey : For phlegmatic and weak persons whose lungs are congested because of phlegm, there is a very old recipe. They should take onion juice or paste mixed with honey. The use of honey provides relief from asthma and other diseases of the lungs. Honey gives strength to the lungs. It solves problems of cough, dry throat and sinews. It removes whizziness of the chest. You can take only honey also.

Barley : Grind 6 gms. of barley ash with 6 gms. of sugar candy and take it with hot water twice daily in the morning and evening.

Mustard oil : Massage the body with mustard oil mixed with rock salt. It will provide relief from cough, asthma and phlegmatic condition.

Gram : Eat hot roasted gram at bedtime and then take hot milk. It will facilitate the expectoration of phlegm in the respiratory tubes.

Basil : During an asthmatic attack efforts should be made to facilitate expectoration by weakening the phlegm. The patient will feel relieved only when phlegm is expectorated. The juice of basil leaves can liquefy the phlegm and it acts as an expectorant. The juice of basil leaves mixed with honey, ginger juice and onion juice is highly beneficial in asthma. If the patient is a child give the juice of basil leaves mixed with honey.

Cloves : Sucking on a clove acts as an expectorant, and it also curbs the foul smell of the phlegm. It checks the foul smell emanating with the breath or coming from the mouth.

Coffee : Taking a hot cup of Coffee without milk and sugar provides relief at the time of an asthmatic attack.

Water : During an asthmatic attack immerse your hands and feet in hot water for ten minutes. It provides immense relief.

Mulberry : Mulberry fruit and its syrup are both expectorants.

PNEUMONIA

Pneumonia is inflammation of the lungs. Its incidence is higher in children. Once stricken by the disease, the patient becomes prone to frequent relapses.

Garlic : It is beneficial to take five drops of garlic juice in 2 tsp. of hot water.

Asafoetida : If the child is suffering from pneumonia or asthma, give him a minute quantity of asafoetida dissolved in water. It will help in the dilution of phlegm and expectoration. It destroys germs and eliminates foul smell.

Basil Leaves : Grind 20 green basil leaves alongwith 5 corns of black pepper, mix in hot water and drink it. It will prove to be beneficial in pneumonia.

Honey : The digestive system in pneumonia is unable to function properly. Mix honey in warm water and drink it hot. It will have a soothing effect on the intestines. The patient does not feel debilitated. Honey not only energizes but also treats the problem.

Salt : Heat salt, put it in a piece of cloth, tie it and foment the chest with it.

Black pepper : If there is a great deal of whizzing in the chest, the phlegm produces a whirring sound, grind 6 corns of black pepper and 5 large raisins in two cups of water. When the water is reduced to half the quantity, strain it and drink it thrice. It will act as an effective expectorant.

DISEASES OF CHILDREN

If the food requirements of children are taken proper care of at the initial stages, they will remain healthy throughout life. We have to take care of a child's diet from the time of a mother's pregnancy. That is the right time to begin caring for a child's diet.

DIET DURING PREGNANCY

Orange : If a pregnant mother takes two oranges daily throughout the period of pregnancy, the child will be beautiful.

***Mausambi*:** It contains calcium in a large quantity. Its juice provides energy both to the pregnant mother and the infant in the womb.

Coconut : Eating coconut with sugar candy eliminates the chances of pain during delivery. The offspring is also healthy.

Honey : During pregnancy women develop deficiency of blood. During this period they should eat things which lead to an increase in blood. Taking 2 tsp. of honey daily prevents deficiency of blood and provides energy to a pregnant woman. The infant also becomes healthy. If a pregnant woman is given honey mixed in milk from the very beginning or during the last three months of the pregnancy, the child will be healthy and beautiful.

CHILD CARE AND DIET

Newborn Infants : Give the decoction of caraway seeds and *harad* in a small quantity with lukewarm water.

Constipation : Scour a little bit of large *harad* with water and add a minute quantity of black salt and give it to the child, mixed in hot water to relieve constipation. It is a good digestive as well.

Digestion of Milk by Children : Mother's milk is the best for an infant. It is disease-resistant and energizing; it protects the child from infectious diseases and makes his body beautiful. Mother's disciplined life can keep the child healthy. A woman should not breast-feed her child immediately before or after sexual intercourse. It imparts heat into the body of the infant. Similarly, when she is angry, she should not breast-feed her child. If the mother takes a glass of water before breast feeding her child, it helps the child to digest the milk easily and he does not develop diarrhoea.

Vomiting : Give a few drops of lemon juice mixed in water and the infant will not throw up milk.

Diarrhoea : Give the child a pinch of cinnamon powder mixed in hot milk if he has developed diarrhoea.

Aversion to Milk : If the child does not drink milk do not force him to do so. You can give him other milk foods like curd, butter milk, *kheer* and *sooji*, etc. in place of milk. After a few weeks the child will start taking milk. Keep changing the menu of his diet every now and then. You can mash a banana and give it to him mixed with milk.

Diseases of Children : Children usually have the problem of distension of stomach, diarrhoea, cough, cold, catarrh and throwing up milk. Make a syrup by mixing the juice of basil leaves, sugar and water. Give a small spoonful of it to the child. It will provide relief from the above problems. Its regular use will ensure good health for the child. There is another recipe to keep a child healthy. Heat the mixed juice of basil leaves and ginger and allow it to cool down. Then mix honey with it and give it to the child to drink.

NAPKIN RASH

Napkin rashes are common in the first year of the child's birth. The child develops whelks on the rectum because of defects in mother's milk, or not cleaning it properly after passing the urine and stools or leaving it wet after a bath. The whelks are red in colour. In an aggravated condition, ulceration and bleeding take place. Apply the following paste on the affected part:

1. Grind basil leaves and make the paste.
2. Mix turmeric powder with butter and prepare the paste.
3. Grind green grass and apply the paste.

ENERGY FOODS FOR CHILDREN

Orange : You can feed fruit and vegetable juice, soup to the infant when he has reached the age of six weeks. Orange juice makes an infant bony and healthy within a short time and they get quick nourishment. It strengthens the bones and removes their crookedness. Children are able to walk at an early age. Children who are fed on tinned milk or cow's milk should be regularly given orange juice. This juice can even cure atrophy in children and make them healthy. It accelerates the functioning of the intestines.

Carrots : Giving carrot juice to weak children thrice daily makes them healthy. Healthy children become healthier by taking it. If the mother that breast-feeds the child also takes carrot juice, it will have a salutary effect.

The children who are given carrot juice since birth do not fall sick. Carrot juice mixed with milk facilitates a speedier growth of children.

Mustard oil : Give a massage to the child with mustard oil and let him have a sun-bath.

Potato : Potato juice given to infants and grown up children makes them healthy and strong.

Garlic : Mix a drop of garlic juice with 2 tsp. of water and ¼ tsp. of honey and feed it to the child. It will strengthen his body.

Almonds : Almonds contain lime, iron and phosphorus in plenty. These make the bones of children strong. Soak an almond overnight for a suckling child. Grind it the following morning, mix in milk and feed it to the child.

As far as possible, do not give medicines to children. They should be treated with common food items. homeopathic treatment is safe for children.

DISEASES OF THE HAIR

To keep the hair healthy it will be beneficial to take protein-rich diet. Milk, cheese, fresh fruit, green vegetables and salads are useful. To know more about it, read the present author's book *Shaktivardhak Bhojan*.

DANDRUFF

Dandruff leads to falling of hair. It is caused when hair is not kept clean or soap is not fully washed off. This disease causes small husk-like white particles in the hair. When the hair is combed or the head is scratched these particles scatter all over in the head and begin to multiply quickly. Dandruff causes intense itching. Frequent indiscriminate itching prompts a person to scratch consistently and the affected part of the scalp becomes hot. As a result, the hair at that spot becomes thin, dry and weak and falls off.

Dandruff is the biggest enemy of healthy hair. It not only weakens the roots of the hair but also causes skin related diseases. The process of the degeneration and regeneration of the skin cells goes on constantly inside our body. This process goes on in the scalp as well and the dead cells keep on falling off periodically. But if too many cells die and fall off, it becomes a disease and needs to be treated.

There are two types of dandruff—*(i)* dry, which falls off when scratched, and *(ii)* oily, which sticks to the scalp.

When it forms a layer on the scalp, the roots of the hair are deprived of oxygen and the hair become weak and fall off.

Causes : Dandruff is caused by dirty hair, irregular blood circulation, infection and lack of balanced diet, etc.

Prevention : Since it is an infectious disease, people suffering from it should have their own separate combs, hair brushes, towels and pillows etc. At an advanced stage, it spreads to the face, eye-brows and even eye-lashes.

Dettol : Taking bath with a few drops of dettol added to the water helps in checking the infection.

Poppy seeds : Grind 4 tsp. of poppy seeds with milk and apply the paste to hair roots and wash off after half an hour. You may use shampoo or soap to wash the hair. Wash the hair twice a week in this way and you will get rid of dandruff.

Gram : Mix four tsp. of *besan* in a glass of water and rub it into the hair. Wash it off after some time.

***Arhar* :** Soak overnight a cup of *arhar* (whole) in water. In the morning, grind it into a paste and rub it on the scalp. Wash it off after half an hour and comb the wet hair. It will clear the dandruff.

Curd : Mix salt in a cup of curd, churn or batter it. Rub it into the hair and wash it off after some time. It will clear the dandruff.

***Amla* :** Soak overnight 5 tsp. of *amla* powder in half cup of water. In the morning, rub it into the hair and wash it off. It will clear the dandruff cast sticking to the scalp.

Beet root : Boil beet root leaves in water and wash the hair with that water. It will clear the dandruff and kill lice as well.

Sesame seeds : Massage the scalp and hair with sesame oil. After half an hour, rinse a towel in hot water and wrap it around the head. When it gets cold, again rinse it in hot water and wrap it around the head. After five minutes wash your hair with cold water. It will clear the dandruff.

Soap nut : Washing the hair with soap nut also clears the dandruff.

LICE

Lice weaken the hair. Lice is caused by the lack of proper cleanliness. While lice weaken the hair, it also causes itching which leads to hair-loss because of constant scratching and dandruff.

Black pepper : (1) Mix the powder of 6 corns of black pepper with a cup of curd, squeeze the juice of a lemon in it and rub it into the hair. Wash off after 20 minutes. It will provide relief from lice and dandruff and give nourishment to the hair. Take care that it does not get into the eyes. While washing the hair, be quick, use a lot of water and keep the eyes close.

(2) Grind 6 corns of black pepper and four seeds of custard apple with water and mix with a tsp. of *ghee* and rub it on the scalp. Wash it off after two hours. It will kill the lice. Keep the eyes closed while washing the hair and use plenty of water.

Lemon : Rub a slice of lemon on to the scalp and wash the head after half an hour. It will remove the oil from the scalp and kill the lice. Mix lemon juice with coconut oil and apply it on the scalp. Washing the hair with water mixed with lemon juice makes it soft.

Garlic : Mix lemon juice with ground garlic. Rub it on the scalp before going to bed. Wash it with soap and water the following morning. Repeat it for five days regularly. It will provide relief from lice.

***Neem* :** Boil ground *neem* leaves in water and wash the hair with it. It will kill the lice.

Beet root : Boil beet root leaves in water and wash the hair with it. It will kill the lice.

***Bathua* :** Boil *bathua* leaves in water and wash the head with it. It will kill the lice and clean the hair.

PEDICULUS CORPORIS (BODY LICE)

It is found on the skin, eye lashes, eye brows and hair on the body.

Mustard oil : Mix 20 ml. of mustard oil with 25 ml. of lemon juice and rub it on the body. It will kill the body lice.

BALDNESS, ALOPECIA

Alopecia causes loss of hair. The disease is commonly known as baldness. When afflicted with this disease one suffers from rapid loss of hair and there is no growth of new hair at the bald spot. The pores in the skin at that spot get blocked and the skin also becomes oily and smooth. This hairless condition of the scalp is known as baldness.

There are no specific causes of this disease. However, blood disorders, toxins, syphilis, ring worms and eczema may be its probable causes. But those persons who do a great deal of mental work or are of advanced age get baldness.

Banana : Grind banana pulp with lemon juice and apply it on the scalp. It will prove beneficial.

Pomegranate : Grind pomegranate leaves with water and rub on the scalp. It will be useful.

Lemon : Rubbing a slice of lemon on the bald patches for a month or two will restore the growth of hair.

Salt : Excessive use of salt causes baldness. Mix a tsp. each of salt and black pepper powder with 5 tsp. of coconut oil and apply it to the bald patches. It will restore the growth of hair.

Onion : Round patches of baldness appear on the scalp when hair fall off in bunches. Onion juice should be rubbed into such bald patches regularly for some time. It will help the hair to grow again.

***Neem* :** Application of *neem* oil regularly for two-three months at the bald spots helps the hair to grow again.

Garlic : Eating garlic is beneficial for hair growth.

***Arhar*:** Rub the bald spots with a piece of rough cloth and apply the paste of ground *arhar* thrice a day. Apply mustard oil the following day and sit in the Sun. Again apply the *arhar* paste after four hours. Repeat this treatment for a few days. It will help in the regrowth of hair at the bald spots.

Black gram : Boil black gram and grind it. Apply the paste on the bald patches before going to bed. It helps hair to grow again.

Coriander : Application of green coriander juice on the bald patches helps the hair to grow again.

Jasmine oil : Jasmine oil provides relief from headache. Jasmine, Coconut and *amla* oil—all are beneficial for the hair.

GREY HAIR

Hair is made of epidermis cells. An oily substance called sebum is secreted from sebaceous glands in the skin at the roots of the hair which determines the colour of the hair and also provides nutrition to it. Hair does not receive nutrition from external resources. It gets it only through blood.

Melanin is a natural substance in the body. When due to known or unknown reasons there is a decay in it, the hair roots and cells do not get enough of it or if the root cells become weak, there is a premature greying of the hair. The following reasons are considered to be the causes of premature greying :

(1) Decay of melanin, (2) Anxiety, sorrow etc., (3) Keeping

late nights, (4) Excessive, untimely sex or sex in a standing position, (5) Hereditary factors, (6) Chronic cold, (7) Use of very hot or immature spices, (8) Frustration or dejection in love, (9) Use of inedible oils, (10) Faulty circulation of blood in the head, (11) Secretion of oil or sweat from the scalp, (12) The damage caused by syphilis, (13) Excessive exposure to the Sun, (14) To remain hungry for long periods or excessive fasting, (15) Excessive secretions from thyroid gland in tall persons, (16) Too much eating of foods cooked in mixed oils, (17) Appearance of white spots on the scalp, (18) Burns, (19) Frequent use of hydrogen peroxide in the hair, (20) Mental shock, (21) Eating hot food, excessive physical labour, anger, fear, jealousy and failure, (22) Lack of Vitamin B, iron, zinc and iodine in the food, (23) Washing the hair with hot water and the use of a dryer for drying it, (24) Constipation, (25) Heavily scented hair oils, (26) Refined sugar and sugary products such as tea, coffee, soft drinks, pastries, jam and jelly. One should avoid eating these things because they lead to the depletion of energy, cause wrinkles in the skin and untimely greying of the hair.

(The hair of princess Marry of Philippines turned grey overnight all of sudden at the age of 21 when she heard of the shocking news of the death of her husband in an accident.)

COLOURING THE HAIR BLACK

Herbal Mustard oil : Take 100 gms. each of *ratanjyot,* henna leaves, *jal bhangra* leaves, mango kernel, pound them, grind them with a little water and make a paste, then soak it in water for two days. Use only as much water as is sufficient to immerse the paste. After two days, drain the water and also squeeze the paste. Mix this water with 1 litre of mustard oil and then boil it till all the water evaporates and only oil is left. Sieve it and apply it daily to the hair.

Perform *Shirshasana* in the morning and drink 250 ml. of milk twice daily in the morning and evening.

Lemon : Application of lemon juice into the hair stops greying and falling of hair. Mix dried *amla* powder with lemon juice and apply it to the grey hair to make it black. It will also provide relief from several other problems of the hair.

Clarified butter : Eating clarified butter is beneficial. Also rub some of it in the roots of the hair.

Ridged gourd : Cut ridged gourd into small pieces, allow them to dry in the shade, pound them and soak them in coconut oil. Use only as much oil as is sufficient for the immersion of the pieces in it. Soak them for four days, then boil, sieve and store in a bottle. Use this oil for regular application into the hair. It will make the hair soft and black.

Carrots : Taking carrot juice regularly makes the hair healthy.

Onion : Grind onions and apply the paste to the hair. It will help in the growth of black hair.

Curd : Mix black pepper powder of 10 corns with half cup of curd and squeeze a lemon into it. Apply it into the hair and wait for 20 minutes. Then wash the hair. It will make the hair soft and black.

Sesame seeds : Eating sesame seeds regularly checks greying and falling of hair and makes it long, soft and black.

Anger : Too much of anger and anxiety turn the hair grey. Therefore, avoid worries and keep cool.

Fenugreek : Eating fenugreek checks greying of hair. Therefore, eat it and also apply it into the hair with oil.

Wheat : Drinking the juice of wheat grass turns the hair black after some time. To know about the method of preparation of this juice, please read the chapter on "Cancer".

Black pepper : Coryza turns the hair grey. If coryza is the cause of grey hair, chew 10 corns of black pepper on empty stomach twice daily in the morning and evening. It will check the disorder of *kafa* and help in the growth of black hair once again. Continue with this treatment atleast for a year. Application of sesame oil mixed with blackpepper powder is very beneficial.

Amla **:** Mix five tsp. of henna and *amla* powder with a tsp. of coffee and ¼ tsp. of catechu and soak in water in an iron pan. The following day apply it to the hair. Wait for 20 minutes. Then wash it off. Apply *amla* hair oil afterwards.

FALLING OF HAIR

Falling of hair is natural and is common to everyone. Hair tend to fall after gaining full length and new ones grow. But excessive hair-loss is a real problem.

It is natural for hair to stop growing after a certain period. Depending on the conditions of an individual, the lower part of the hair gland gets withers or dries up, the old strand of hair is severed from the pore. This process of severance from the pores is known as falling of hair but the fallen hair is replaced by the growth of new hair.

Usually the hair grow by one centimetre in a month. The falling of upto 100 hair in a day is considered normal because the head can grow this much of hair again. Usually, there is a cycle according to which every strand of hair falls within 3-4 years and new growth takes place. Physicians, generally prescribe iron capsules and vitamin tablets to check the falling of hair but it does not seem to be necessary. One should consult a physician only if the hair-loss is more than 100 per day.

The main causes for the falling of hair are anaemia, disease affected roots of the hair, the diseases caused by heat in the body, dandruff, lack of nutrition or too much exposure of the hair to the Sun.

There is hereditary factor also—if the hair of the mother had a tendency to fall prematurely, the daughter may have the same tendency.

It also happens when one develops leucoderm in the scalp.

Hair-loss also occurs as an after effect of the use of medicines for cancer, e.g., the women who are given pills or injections for the treatment of breast or uterus cancer suffer from hairloss.

There is a gland of internal secretion situated in the lower front region of the neck which is known as thyroid gland. The secretions from it keep the chemical process in the body in order. It ensures a balanced growth and strengthening of the human body. If the secretions from it are deficient or irregular in some way, it directly affects the hair as well. In case of hyper-thyroidism, the hair become relatively thin and soft but hypo-thyroidism makes the hair thick and dry.

In both the conditions, hair becomes weak and hair-loss occurs. Therefore, it is important that the gland should function properly not only for healthy hair but also for a healthy body. If the hair is not properly cleaned and if you suffer from the problem of worms and fungus, it may cause new problems like whelks, ulcers, eczema, ring-worms and itching, etc. They infect the pores and the loss of hair occurs. Mental tension is also responsible for it.

Other diseases also lead to loss of hair. Dum-dum fever (*kala-azar*) destroys the natural shine of the hair; they become weak and dry and begin to fall. But as one recovers from the fever, the hair naturally stop falling. New hair begin to grow in place of the lost hair. Similarly some chronic diseases or typhoid also cause hair-loss. The main reason is that like other parts of the body, the pores in the scalp are also affected by the disease. In the beginning the loss of hair occurs but as the patient recovers and gains strength, the pores also get strengthened. That is why, new hair begin to grow in place of the lost ones. Therefore, it is better to pay attention to the restoration of one's health after recovery from such a disease and not worry about hair-loss.

Excessive hair-loss occurs because of long-lasting illnesses such as typhoid or during pregnancy, as a reaction to drugs, the use of highly-scented oils or cheap and inferior quality shampoos or as a result of imbalanced diet, etc.

One of the reasons for hair-loss is lack of proper nutrients in the food. It is, therefore, advisable to take protein-rich diet.

Gram, soyabean and rajma are rich in protein. The use of milk and milk products is also beneficial.

There are glands in the human body which secrete oily substances which provide nutrition to the hair and make it soft and also facilitate its growth. Hair also get nutrition through blood circulation. If the blood circulation is proper, the growth of hair is rapid and it becomes soft and bright. Any flaw in the above two systems can cause hair-loss.

Oil : Application of oil is necessary for the health and beauty of the hair. These days most people prefer dry hair. But the roots of dry hair become weak and it leads to hair-loss. Besides application of oil, it is also necessary to brush the hair briskly for some time to give it exercise. Brushing also improves blood circulation in the scalp and makes the hair roots strong and prevents hair-loss.

First of all, massage your scalp softly with a good oil like coconut oil or almond oil. Rub the oil into the hair gently with the pores of your fingers. Avoid scented oils as far as possible because they make the hair weak and cause premature greying.

Steam : Steaming keeps the hair soft like silk and healthy. It prevents hair-loss. Take some hot water in a pan, dip a towel in it, squeeze it lightly and wrap it around the head. When it gets cold, use another towel in the similar way. In this manner, steam your hair for ten minutes. Apply oil into the hair a day before steaming.

Washing : In case of excessive hair-loss frequent washing of the head is recommended. Do not comb the wet hair because the wet hair are weak and fragile and can break easily. Allow the hair to dry for some time before combing.

Do not use a hair dryer daily for drying the hair because it weakens the hair roots. When using a hair dryer, keep it at a distance of 6-8 inches away from the hair. Do not leave the hair spray in the hair for long because it contains severe harmful chemicals which can cause damage to the hair.

Tea : After a headwash, rinse the hair with tea liquor (without sugar and milk) to give it shine and bounce.

***Neem* :** In case the hair-loss has just started, boil *neem* and *ber* leaves in water and wash the hair with this water. It will prevent hair-loss. It will keep the hair black and facilitate its growth. It will also kill lice. But be careful, while washing the head the water should not get into the eyes. Keep the eyes closed during the head wash.

Lemon : (1) Rub lemon juice into the hair; wash it off after some time. It checks hair-loss.

(2) Boil 2 tsp. of tea leaves in a glass of water and allow it to cool down, strain it and squeeze a lemon into it. After having hair wash and thorough cleaning of the hair, give a wash to the hair with the above mentioned tea and lemon water. Finally, again wash it with clean water. It will make the hair bright, soft like silk and check hair-loss.

***Amla* :** Soak dry *amla* overnight in water. Next morning wash your hair with it. It will strengthen the hair roots and enhance their natural beauty. It is also beneficial for the brain and eyes.

Coconut : Application of coconut oil checks hair-loss and facilitates hair growth.

Long cucumber : The juice of long cucumber facilitates thick growth of hair. It contains silicon and sulphur in plenty. Taking mixed juice of cucumber, carrot, lettuce and spinach also helps in the growth of hair. If any one of these foods is not available, you may take the juice of the items readily available during the season.

Beet root : Grind beet root leaves alongwith henna into a paste and apply on the hair. It checks hair-loss, facilitates hair growth and new hair also grow.

Cabbage : Eating 50 gms. of cabbage leaves daily helps in the growth of new hair.

Wheat : Taking the juice of wheat grass daily for forty days checks hair-loss.

Chaulai **:** Eating *chaulai* as a vegetable is beneficial and prevents hair-loss.

Basil : In case of hair-loss and greying of hair, mix the powder of dry *amla* and basil leaves with water and rub into the scalp. Wash it off after ten minutes. It will check hair-loss. The hair will retain its natural black colour. It will also kill the lice.

UNWANTED HAIR

Turmeric : Unwanted hair on the face or any other part of the body can be removed by using a face pack prepared with turmeric powder.

TUBERCULOSIS (T.B.)

What is Tuberculosis? Any infection with the tubercle bacillus is called tuberculosis. It sets in decay. Whatever part of the body is affected, decays gradually.

Symptoms of the Disease : The patient suffers from constant cough, chronic fever in which the temperature is higher in the evenings, lack of appetite, pain in the chest, problem in breathing, weakness and gradual enervation of the body, excessive mucus of yellowish colour, occasional blood in the mucus, soreness in the larynx because of constant coughing and the resultant hoarseness and sweating at night, etc.

This disease is more common among children than in adults. The germs of T.B. find an easy shelter in the delicate lungs and wind-pipe of a child. The symptoms of T.B. are the same in children and adults. Sometimes lack of appetite, weight-loss, exhaustion, light fever and lack of stamina are main symptoms of T.B. Children suffering from frequent cold, cough and breathing problems should be pathologically checked up for T.B. Tubercles on the neck are a special symptom of T.B. in children.

Affected Organs of the Body by T.B.

The most affected part of the body by T.B. is the lungs.

Other parts which are usually affected include bones, intestines, tonsils, skin, kidneys and reproductive parts.

Whichever part may be affected, the symptoms are usually similar. Feverishness, light fever in the evening, loss of appetite, loss of weight are the common symptoms of T.B. In pulmonary T.B. the prominent symptoms are cough, phlegm, pain in the chest, breathing problem, blood in the mucus, etc. The Chief symptoms of intestinal T.B. are flatulence, indigestion, distension of the stomach, etc. Infertility is usually the result of indigestion, flatulence and the T.B. of uterus. The T.B. of kidneys is indicated by the presence of blood in the urine and swelling of the kidneys.

B.C.G. inoculation protects one against T.B. throughout life. One can be inoculated with this vaccine a day after birth or at any stage in life.

In Hindi, Tuberculosis is also known as *yakshma*, *rajyakshma*, *tapedik*, *kshaya*, etc. When it becomes chronic, the patient gradually turns into a bundle of bones and if he does not respond to treatment, he dies. This disease can be diagnosed through X-Ray.

Causes : The germs of T.B. (Tubercle Bacillus) are formed in the mucous or spit of the patient and they spread through air, water, milk, etc. The disease spreads from one patient to another through polluted air, wet places, breathing filthy air, too much indulgence in sex, unhealthy diet, too much of labour beyond one's stamina, birth of more children, drinking, sexual relations with a T.B. patient, etc.

Treatment : The most important factor in the treatment of T.B. is that the patient should not stop treatment or taking medicines even for a day. Most of the patients stop taking medicines when they get symptomatic relief. That is why such patients develop so many complications and sometimes the disease proves to be fatal. If the treatment is taken properly for the prescribed period as per the directions of the physician, one can fully recover from it and root out the disease altogether.

Special attention should be paid to the diet of a T.B. patient, rather food should be considered as a medicine. It is essential that the patient gets Sun-light, clean air, nutritious diet and complete rest. He should strictly avoid smoking and sex. Temperance is necessary for a healthy life. The following food items are beneficial for the patients of T.B. :

Sugar : According to American scientist Tilbert, the germs of T.B., Cholera and smallpox can be destroyed by burning sugar.

Milk : Boil a glass of milk with 5 pieces of long pepper in it, add sugar and give it to the patient to drink twice daily in the morning and evening. It provides relief from cough, cold, asthma, weakness of the lungs and T.B. at the initial stages.

Butter : Taking butter with sugar candy and *ghee* cures T.B. and provides strength.

Lemon : T.B. patients suffering from chronic fever should drink a glass of warm water with 11 leaves of basil, salt, cumin seeds and asafoetida thrice daily for a few days.

*—Swami Sadhanand-**Bhojan Dwara Swasthya***

Apple : Eating apples is beneficial for patients of T.B. It is useful for intestines, liver and brain.

Mango : Mix 60 gms. of honey in a cup of mango juice and take it twice daily in the morning and evening. Also take cow milk thrice daily. Taking this treatment for 21 days will prove to be quite beneficial.

Grapes : One should eat grapes for food for the cure of T.B.

Large raisins : Grind large raisins, long pepper and *desi* sugar in equal quantity and take a tsp. of it twice daily in the morning and evening. It will cure T.B., asthma and cough.

Coconut : Eating 25 gms. of fresh or ground coconut kills the germs of T.B. and provides strength to the lungs.

Dates : Eating dates is beneficial for patient of T.B.

Cloves : Cloves are an effective cure for T.B.

Carrots : Taking carrot juice is beneficial in T.B. It contains nutrients in a balanced form.

Banana : Fresh juice of a banana tree or raw bananas used as a vegetable are a sure cure for T.B. A T.B. patient who suffers from severe cough, is highly phlegmatic, sweats so heavily at night that his clothes get wet and also suffers from high fever, diarrhoea, loss of appetite and weight should take a cup or two of the juice extracted from a piece of banana tree trunk every two hours. It should be sipped slowly. This treatment, if taken for two months, can cure T.B. altogether. The juice should be prepared afresh every 24 hours. Soak 8-10 banana leaves in 200 ml water. Strain it and give a tablespoon of it thrice daily to the patient. It expels the phlegm from the chest. Giving the juice of banana leaves mixed with honey to the patient heals the wounds in the lungs. It also reduces the quantity of phlegm in the chest and checks bleeding. If banana trunk is not available use banana leaves for this purpose.

Onion : Many years ago, Dr. Pearse of England used to prescribe raw onions for T.B. Dr. C. Minchen says that onion juice enables the patient to fight against the germs of T.B. Eating raw onions is also equally effective. It is healthful and germicidal. Eating raw onions with salt is beneficial in T.B.

A ¼ cup of onion juice mixed with equal amount of water provides relief from the problem of phlegm in T.B. Cut an onion into five pieces and boil in a glass of water. When the water is reduced to half the quantity, strain it and drink it. It will provide relief from phlegm.

Garlic : Dr. E.P. Andrews, a homeopath, is of the opinion that people who eat garlic do not suffer from T.B. Its use destroys the germs of T.B. Garlic is a boon for the patients of T.B. It is a sure cure for all types of T.B. Garlic contains a large quantity of sulphuric acid which can destroy the germs of T.B.

In pulmonary T.B., the use of garlic reduces the severity of phlegm, checks sweating at night, sharpens the appetite and gives good sleep. The patients of pulmonary T.B. should soak a little cotton in garlic juice and inhale the smell so that it reaches the lungs with the breath. The patient should keep inhaling the smell for a long time. Its sharp smell can destroy the strongest bacteria and worms and cure even incurable diseases. Garlic should be eaten after meals as well.

For intestinal T.B., the juice of one bulb of garlic should be taken mixed with 12 ml. of water.

Cauliflower : Eating raw cauliflower or as a cooked vegetable checks vomiting with blood. T.B. patients should eat it regularly.

Bottle gourd : Plaster a fresh bottle gourd with barley flour, wrap it with a piece of cloth and roast it by inserting it in burning coals. When it becomes tender, squeeze the juice out of it and give it to the patient to drink in several doses. This treatment for a month will cure T.B.

Maize : At early stages of T.B. the patient should eat maize flour *rotis*.

Walnut : Grind walnut and garlic in equal quantity and saute in cow's *ghee*. Its use is beneficial in T.B.

Honey : Take 25 gms. of honey mixed with 100 gms. of butter.

FEVER

Symptoms : Sudden increase in body temperature is called fever. Feeling tired, out of sorts, bad taste in the month, water running from eyes, yawning, heaviness in the body, feeling of unhappiness, feeling cold, rise in body temperature and body-aches are the common symptoms of fever.

Causes of Fever

Fever is usually caused by infectious and harmful bacteria. These bacteria produce a toxin named pyrogen in the cells which disturbs the temperature control system in the brain and the patient develops fever. In fact, the rise in temperature helps the patient to fight and destroy the harmful bacteria. During this period, several bio-activities take place in the body at a fast pace. The growth of blood cells, enzymes and hormones suddenly goes up in order to destroy the harmful bacteria. But it is dangerous for the body if the fever continues for a long period because the body gets dehydrated because of rise in temperature. Consequently, the blood and urinary cells begin to contract and the protein in the cells also gets exhausted, which in turn affects the brain in several ways.

When you develop fever, do not get nervous and rush to doctors for treatment and medicines. It is a common problem and needs to be tackled with patience.

There are several types of fever. Whatever type of fever it may be, do not eat regular food during the fever. Simple and light food such as milk, green gram soup, large raisins, *saboodana*, glucose, *mausambi*, liquids, vegetable broth, juicy fruits and hot water can be taken. When the fever is under control even then very light food should be taken at least for three-four days. Fried and heavy food, sweets and sexual activity should be stopped altogether. The use of cucumber and fenugreek leaves is useful in fever.

When the fever is high, lots of calories are burnt, therefore calories need to be replenished though when the fever is high the patient does not feel like eating anything. Therefore, as and when the fever is under control, the patient should be given something to eat at regular intervals.

As the fever destroys body tissues, the patient should be given food rich in protein. He needs at least 50 per cent more protein during this period than in an ordinary situation. But keep in mind that the protein consumed by the patient should be easily digestible. Heavy protein, such as meat, should not be given to the patient.

Protein in the form of milk can be given. Soyabean can also be given.

Carbohydrates should always be taken in the form of glucose. It is easily digestible. It is better to give the patient only milk and juices during the fever.

The patient should not take fat in the form of butter, *ghee*, oil, etc. Fat can be consumed after recovery from fever.

Lemon : Whenever the patient feels thirsty, squeeze a lemon in boiling water and give it to the patient to drink. It will reduce the temperature. Fill a slice of lemon with rocksalt and black-pepper, heat it and ask the patient to suck it.

Large raisins : Take the seeds out of 20 large raisins and soak them overnight in ¼ litre of water. The following morning, boil them using the same water and eat the raisins and drink the water. It will provide relief from the fever.

Tamarind : If the fever is caused by heat, taking tamarind water is beneficial.

Coriander : The kernel of coriander seeds reduces fever. The use of the kernel of coriander seeds is especially useful in the fever caused by heat.

Tomato : During fever, there is an increase in toxic elements in the blood. Tomato soup expels them. It provides relief to the patient. Tomato juice is beneficial in all types of fever and has a cooling effect and removes restlessness. It quenches the thirst. It does not let the body become weak. It rather activates it.

Coconut : Tender coconut water reduces the temperature and lessens the severity of the fever.

***Tinda* :** It cures light fever. Boil it and eat it after adding the usual spices to it.

***Parwal* :** It is beneficial for patients of chronic fever.

Fenugreek : It cures fever. Application of the paste of ground fenugreek leaves on external parts relieves burning sensation, pain and hot flushes.

Cloves : Grind a clove and take it with hot water, thrice a day. It will provide relief from common fever.

Barley : Boil a cup of barley in 1 litre of water, let it cool down and then drink it. It will be beneficial.

Tea : It is useful if fever is due to cold and catarrh.

Water : Naturopathy believes that it is the colon or intestines where rotting of waste matter takes place and toxins are generated, which lead to a rise in temperature of our body or causes fever. That is why they insist on putting a wet pad on the belly and clearing of the intestines and the bowel. It also reduces the temperature.

Sponging the body with cold water is beneficial in high fever. A towel dipped in cold water should be put on the head and the entire body should be sponged with a piece of wet cloth. While sponging, the body should not be exposed to air. Keep the body covered.

Carrots : Carrot juice expels the toxic elements from the body. Take mixed juice of carrots (185 gms.), beetroot (150 gms.) and cucumber (125 gms.)

Garlic : In case of high fever, pound garlic cloves, mix with a little water, put in a piece of cloth and ask the patient to inhale the smell. It will reduce the severity of the fever. Give the patient 6 ml. of garlic juice thrice daily in the morning, afternoon and evening. The fever will subside.

Aniseed : If the fever is high, boil aniseed in water and give 2 tsp. of it frequently to the patient. It will help in containing the fever.

Black pepper : Pound 20 corns of black pepper and boil in water and when the water is reduced to one-fourth, give it to the patient to drink twice daily in the morning and evening. It provides relief from the fever and is beneficial in yawning, body-ache, weakness and shivering.

Mint : Taking mint tea with a little salt is beneficial in fever. If the patient feels thirsty frequently, give him mint juice immediately.

Green gram : It is very beneficial in fever. It should be taken whole or with the skin.

Salt : Grind finely one part of rock salt and four parts of *boora.* Take ½ tsp. of it thrice daily with hot water. It is beneficial in seasonal fever.

Ginger : If the fever has been caused by cold or cold and heat and is quite high, mix 6 gms. juice each of ginger, betel leaves and honey and ask the patient to lick it. It will prove to be beneficial.

Basil : (1) In case of chronic fever and cough that causes pain in the chest, take the juice of basil leaves mixed with sugar candy. It is beneficial in chronic fever.

(2) It is beneficial to take three ml. of juice of basil leaves mixed with 6 gms. of sugar candy and three corns of black pepper.

(3) Boil ten basil leaves along with three gms. of dried ginger powder, five cloves, 22 corns of black pepper and sugar to taste. When the water is reduced to half the quantity, give it to the patient to drink. It will cure the fever. If the patient feels restless because of high fever, give him the juice of basil leaves mixed with sugar.

(4) Boil 20 basil leaves, 20 corns of black pepper, a little bit ginger and cinnamon in a glass of water. Mix sugar and give it hot to the patient to drink. It will be beneficial in fever.

(5) Taking the juice of 12 gms. of basil leaves regularly cures the fever.

Cumin seeds : Raw ground cumin seeds (1 gm.) with equal quantity of jaggery taken thrice daily cures chronic fever.

Ice : In case of high fever, sponge the body with iced water. Dip a piece of cloth in iced water and sponge the entire body from head to foot repeatedly. Put a wet piece of cloth on the head and belly.

***Neem* :** Tie 21 gms. of *neem* leaves and 21 corns of black pepper in a piece of muslin cloth and boil in ½ litre of water. When the water is reduced to one-fourth quantity, allow it to cool down and give it to the patient in the morning and evening.

Clay : Wrap a wet clay pad around the belly. Change it every hour. It will provide relief from the burning sensation caused by the fever.

Sugarcane juice : It is beneficial in low fever.

***Peepal* :** Munch a twig of *peepal* tree twice a day. Swallow the juice and spit out the rest.

CHILDREN'S FEVER

Bacteria and virus thrive in the cold climate. When they somehow enter the human body, the immunization system of the body tends to raise the temperature. The bacteria and virus cannot remain alive in the high temperature, therefore, these agents causing the fever die down automatically even if no other treatment is taken for the fever. According to the researchers, the concept that fever could hit and damage the mind of a child causing his death is wrong. In reality, our body tends to build and develop a self-protecting lifelong shield, because of the infectious diseases contracted during the childhood. In the name of health and cleanliness, there is abundance of inoculation and vaccination, on the other side, a child is given over protection against any possible infection. We have a tendency to rush to a doctor on noticing even a minor common cold, cough or fever. A child is burdened with the heavy woolens during winter and very thin and light clothes are given to the child during summer. Both these practices are detrimental to the health of the child.

These over-concerned people and their children could be seen rushing to the doctor every now and then. The children are deprived of their natural experience to fight diseases. The more care you take of the child, the more incapable he becomes to withstand any disease. In case of minor fever, not only the children, but also the adults should avoid taking any medicines at least for three days. If the fever or its accompanying pain prolongs after three days, then only, one should resort to medical treatment. But today neither we have any rest nor any patience. It is advisable that a child should be allowed to learn living in fever and we ourselves should have the patience to watch it.

You will be surprised to see the results of this patience. Small and petty infections and seasonal fever do not take much time to cure. We need to understand that the nature provides us an inbuilt armour to sustain our life in the universe.

DENGUE FEVER

Symptoms : Sudden sharp fever without cough or cold, acute pain in the body. The dengue fever is generally accompanied by pain in the bones, therefore, this fever is also known as the bone-breaking fever. Severe pain in the forehead, pain in the inner-side of the eyes, muscles and joint pains. Loss of appetite and taste, appearance of small raised spots on the chest, nausea and vomiting, etc.

Hemorrhage also takes place in the dengue fever. The patient gets irritated in the light. Vomiting and feeling of restlessness is possible. Sometimes, there are repeated attacks of this fever which generally happens after rains. These all are the general symptoms of dengue fever. Mostly it spreads like an epidemic taking a heavy toll of life.

Symptoms of Hemorrhage : Continuous acute stomach-ache, cold, yellowish and sticky skin, red raised spots on the face, hands and feet. Hemorrhagic dengu could cause internal bleeding. A patient bleeds through mouth, nose and anus, which could make him unconscious. Repeated vomiting with or without blood, restless sleep, continuous crying, dryness of the mouth and feeling of thirst—these all are the symptoms of dengue fever. The hemorrhagic dengu is much dangerous. Most of the deaths are caused by it. It generally resembles the normal fever, hence, sometimes, doctors also fail to reach the correct diagnosis.

How it spreads : It is transmitted by the viral infected female mosquitoes.

Where these mosquitoes grow : These mosquitoes thrive on the stagnant water in coolers, drums, jars, buckets, tanks, water reservoirs, bottles, etc., where stagnant water is found. It is, therefore, necessary that the water collected around the houses after rains should not be allowed to stagnate.

Where it is not possible to let the water out, insecticides or burnt mobil oil should be sprinkled in the water. Kerosene oil or mobil oil creates a thin layer on the surface of the water which kills larvae. The other anti-mosquito measures could also be taken, viz., the use of mosquito nets, anti-mosquito creams, repellants and burning of *agarbattis*, etc. In the villages, the mosquitoes grow in the pens, wet, dark and humid places. In addition, full sleeve shirts and full length trousers should be used so that minimum bare part of the body is exposed.

Treatment : Normal dengue fever is not that dangerous. The symptom-based treatment should be resorted to i.e., wet pads could be used if the temperature is high. Antidotes could be administered as per the necessity. Pain-killers should not be given to the patient of hemorrhagic dengue. Pain-killers tend to increase hemorrhage. Maintaining the water balance of the body and controlling the blood pressure of the patient is also necessary. The treatment given for the patients of normal fever and malaria is applicable for the dengue fever also.

TYPHOID

There is a rapid reduction in the accumulated glycogen during typhoid and the balance of water in the body is disturbed. The patient also suffers from colitis and as a result, loose motions begin. Patients of typhoid should not be given protein-rich food. Eggs and meat are totally prohibited.

During this period, the patient should be given only liquids or easily digestible carbohydrate-rich diet. Vegetable soup and fruit juice is useful for the patient.

After the patient has recovered from the fever and weakness, he should be given plenty of protein-rich diet so that the loss of tissues can be compensated.

Large raisins : Dr. Tartlit, a Western Scientist found out on the basis of experiments that the germs of typhoid can be destroyed by burning raisins or large raisins and other dry fruits.

Mausambi **:** It is beneficial during typhoid.

Cloves : Give clove water to the patient suffering from typhoid. Boil five cloves in 2 litre of water, when the water is reduced to half the quantity, strain it. The patient should take it frequently every day for some time. Plain water should also be boiled and given to the patient when it cools down.

Salt : Heat a tsp. of salt and mix it in a glass of water. Drink this solution once every day for three days. If you feel thirsty, do not take water for an hour. After that take water only in little sips. Do not take too much water. It will cure the fever. Typhoid gets cured before time through this treatment.

Orange : It has a cooling effect and provides relief from restlessness caused by typhoid. The patient can take milk mixed with orange juice or can eat an orange after taking milk. Oranges can be eaten several times in a day. It is beneficial in typhoid.

Apple : Apple juice is beneficial in typhoid.

Banana : It is an ideal food for the patients of typhoid. It satisfies hunger and thirst.

Honey : During Enteric fever and pneumonia the digestive system is affected and it does not function properly. If hot water with some honey is given to the patient frequently, it has a soothing effect on the intestines and the patient does not become weak. The patient should not be given solid food. Honey gives energy to the patient and also provides treatment.

MALARIA

The rise of temperature in malaria fever is accompanied by cold and shivering and it subsides with sweating. It is caused by mosquito bite. The patient of malaria should not consume rice for some days.

Lemon : (1) Fill a lemon with salt and black pepper and heat it. Suck it. It will reduce the heat of the fever.

(2) Squeeze two lemons in ½ litre of water, put the rind also in the water and boil it in a clay pot and keep it overnight after the water has been reduced to half the quantity. Drinking it in the morning provides relief from malaria.

(3) Drinking lemon water with sugar provides relief from malaria. If there is a rustling sound in the ears as a result of taking quinine, lemon water will provide relief from that also. Plenty of milk and lemon should be taken with quinine.

Orange : Boil the rind of two oranges in two cups of water. When it is reduced to half strain and drink it hot.

Apple : Eating apples helps in a speedy recovery from the fever. The paroxysm of malarial fever can be checked by eating an apple before it begins.

Guava : It is useful for patients of malaria. Therefore, it should be eaten by patients of malaria.

Cumin seeds : Grind 1 tsp. of cumin seeds. Mix it with three parts of jaggery and make three pills. In periodic malaria to check the paroxysm of fever, take a pill every hour before the fever begins.

Coriander : Grind coriander seeds and dried ginger in equal quantity and take the powder thrice daily with water. It will provide relief from the fever.

Long pepper : Grind three pieces of long pepper, mix with honey and lick it. It provides relief from asthma, cough and malaria fever.

Butter milk : It provides relief from malaria with paroxysm on every fourth day.

Garlic : If the malarial fever occurs at regular intervals, apply garlic juice on the nails of fingers and toes before the occurrence of the fever and also mix a tsp. of garlic juice with a tsp. of sesame oil and put 10 drops of it on the tongue of the patient every hour before the fever. Repeating it for four days will provide relief from malaria.

Alum salt : Mix 1 gm. of alum salt with two gms. of sugar and give it to the patient twice at an interval of two hours before the occurrence of the fever. It will check the malarial fever or reduce its severity. Repeat the treatment in case of anticipated recurrence of the fever. The patient should remain free from constipation. If he suffers from it, it should first be treated.

Green chilli : A green chilli should be de-seeded and the hollow chilli should be worn around the right thumb and tied with a piece of cloth two hours before the fever comes. Repeating it twice or thrice will check the recurrence of the malarial fever. The green chilli may cause a burning sensation. Therefore let it remain on the thumb as long as you can tolerate it, otherwise remove it.

Salt : (1) Grind finely one part of rock salt and four parts of *boora.* Taking half tsp. of it thrice daily with hot water will prevent the reoccurrence of the malarial fever.

(2) Heat five tsp. of common salt on a hot plate till it turns brown. Mix a tsp. of it in a glass of hot water and drink it daily before the fever comes. **Do not take it during the malarial fever.**

Basil : The use of basil is beneficial in all types of fever. Eating basil leaves regularly prevents the occurrence of malaria. If one develops malarial fever, boil 22 basil leaves and 20 ground corns of black pepper in two cups of water. When the water is reduced to one fourth, mix sugar candy and drink it when it is cool. If it is not possible to do so, basil leaves and black pepper can be chewed.

***Neem* :** Grind 60 gms. of *neem* leaves alongwith 4 corns of black pepper, mix it with 125 ml. of water, strain and drink it. It will cure malarial fever. It is a dependable recipe.

DIABETES

Diabetes is a disease characterized by excessive flow of urine containing sugar. This disease develops gradually and the patient usually does not know for a long time that he is suffering from it. It is more common in men than women. Fat persons usually suffer from diabetes. In the past, mostly people between 40-50 years of age or after it were liable to get diabetes but now even small children become diabetic. Hereditary factors are also responsible for this disease.

In the human body, insulin is secreted by pancreas gland which is connected with the digestive system. Insulin helps the blood to convert sugar into energy. The pancreas gland retains as much sugar as is required by the body and burns the rest of it. But if the pancreas gland stops secreting insulin or its quantity is reduced or there is some obstruction due to some reason, it leads to diabetes. In these circumstances, sugar gets into the blood and does not get converted into energy and is also expelled out of the body through urine. There are two types of this disease : (1) Diabetes Mullites, and (2) Diabetes Insipidus (polyuria).

Symptoms : Diabetes is caused when pancreas does not secrete an appropriate amount of insulin. Sugar in blood and urine is a sure sign of diabetes. Excessive thirst, hunger, frequent passing of urine, frequent appearance of boils, wounds not healing, pain in the feet, poor eyesight, constipation, T.B., weakness due to increase in sugar levels, restlessness, higher blood pressure, unconsciousness, headache, dry skin, itching, etc. are the symptoms of diabetes.

Excess TV watching—A cause for Diabetes : Occasional TV watching as a part of hobby is not harmful for the health, but excessive TV watching is giving an invitation to diabetes. Researchers in USA state, men watching TV for 20 hours or more in a week are more prone to become diabetic at some later stage. Men at 40 or above, spending excessive time on watching TV are more susceptible to the dangers of this disease. The obese adults of this age group generally become its victims. The researchers are of the view that the lifestyle of watching TV for unexpectedly long hours has direct connection with this disease. Regular exercises can spare the scourge of diabetes.

Treatment : Diabetics should not eat sweet food items such as sugar, jaggery, sugarcandy, sweet fruits, rice and products made of fine flour (*maida*). Physical exercise, walking and light diet are beneficial. If diabetes is not under control, do not eat wheat flour *rotis* alone, mix it with barley and gram (3 kg. barley, 1 kg. wheat and ½ kg. gram and grind it). The patient should consume more of green vegetables, daal and curd. Bitter gourd (raw or cooked as a vegetable) and rose apple are beneficial. Taking *triphala churan* is beneficial. It also relieves constipation. Diabetes can be cured by proper diet and physical exercise. It cannot be cured with medicines alone if the required type of food is not taken. The foods mentioned below, if taken in sufficient quantity, can cure diabetes :

Diabetes causes weakness in the body. Eat raw or tender coconut to gain energy. Also take cashews, groundnuts and walnuts soaked in water. Taking curd, butter milk and soyabean is also beneficial.

Diabetic patients should observe fast on every seventh day. On the day of fast they should take only fruits, vegetables and lemon water without sugar. They should not eat anything else.

Lemon : In case of excessive thirst taking lemon water is quite beneficial in diabetes.

Orange : An orange a day is okay. for a diabetic patient. Orange peel should be dried in the shade and ground into powder form. Boil 4 tsp. of it in a glass of water, strain and drink it daily.

Mango : Mixed juice of mango and rose apple in equal quantity taken regularly for a few days will cure diabetes.

***Amla* :** Fresh *amla* juice mixed with honey cures diabetes.

Rose apple : (1) A diabetic patient should take rose apples daily. In homeopathy, the juice of rose apple known as *Cegium Jambolinum* mother tincture is used for the cure of diabetes. ½ tsp. of the *churan* of rose apple kernel taken daily in the evening with water cures the problem of sugar in the urine.

(2) Grind dried rose apple kernel and bitter gourd in equal quantity. Take a tsp. of it with water twice a day.

Tomato : Tomatoes are very beneficial for patients of diabetes. It gradually reduces the sugar in the urine. They are also useful in other urinary diseases. For homeopathic treatment, read the book '*Homeopathic Vyavaharik Chikitsa Saar*'.

Carrots : Take mixed juice of carrots (310 gms.) and spinach (185 gms.)

Radish : It is beneficial for diabetics. Its juice is also useful.

Bitter gourd : (1) Take 15 ml. of the juice of bitter gourd mixed with 100 litre of water thrice daily for three months. Also eat bitter gourd as a cooked vegetable. Taking 6 gms. powder of bitter gourd dried in the shade once every day will provide relief from sugar in the urine.

(2) Boil 250 gms. of bitter gourd in ½ litre of water. When it is reduced to half the quantity, strain and drink it.

Lady finger : Cut the stems of ladies fingers and dry it in the shade. Grind it into a fine powder and sieve it. Mix sugar candy in equal quantity and take ½ tsp. of it with cool water daily in the morning on empty stomach. It will cure diabetes. This has been corroborated by the experience of patients who have benefited from it.

Turnip : Diabetics should regularly eat the vegetable of turnip.

Wheat : The juice of wheat grass is beneficial in diabetes.

Fenugreek : (1) The use of fenugreek seeds cures diabetes. Its seeds reduce the amount of sugar in the blood. They also reduce the sugar in the urine by 65 per cent. Its effect can be noticed within ten days. Taking fenugreek seeds with water 15 minutes before the meals is quite beneficial. Its dose varies from 25 to 100 gms. It can be taken in any form—cooked as a vegetable, with water, in powdered form mixed with wheat flour and baked as *chapatis*, with rice, pulses, *chutney* or its powder mixed in milk or water.

If calories are restricted to 1200-1400 per day, its effect is noticeable within a short period. Continue its use as long as urine contains sugar. It not only reduces the sugar but also lowers the cholesterol. When you are using fenugreek seeds, gradually reduce the intake of medicines for diabetes and finally stop them altogether.

(2) Soak 60 gms. of finely ground fenugreek seeds in a glass of water. Strain and drink it after twelve hours. Take it twice daily in the morning and evening for 6 weeks to cure diabetes. Also eat fenugreek leaves cooked as a vegetable alongwith it.

Gram : (1) Soak overnight 28 gms. of black gram in milk and eat it the following morning. Also mix black gram and barley in equal quantity and grind it. Use this flour to prepare *chapatis* and eat them in the morning and evening.

(2) Eating *chapatis* made of *besan* for ten days stops the passage of sugar with urine.

Turmeric : If there is frequent and excessive flow of urine and you feel thirsty, take 8 gms. of turmeric powder twice daily with water. It will prove beneficial.

Honey : When you have an urge to eat something sweet, take a little honey instead of sugar. It will check diabetes and save you from chronic diseases of the kidney. Take honey only to satisfy your urge to eat something sweet. Otherwise, it should not be taken.

Dates : In diabetes and other diseases where eating sugar is harmful but you have a strong urge to eat it, you may eat dates in a small quantity.

DISEASES OF THE KIDNEY

Orange : Taking one or two oranges before breakfast in the morning followed by a glass of hot water or taking orange juice cures kidney problems or protects one from kidney ailments. Oranges keep the kidneys clean. Apples and grapes are also equally beneficial. Fruit juices keep the kidneys healthy if taken in the morning before breakfast.

The use of honey is beneficial in kidney problems.

Carrots : Boil 2 tsp. of carrot seeds in a glass of water and drink it. It will increase the flow of urine.

Radish : Taking half a glass of radish juice provides relief from burning sensation and pain at the time of urination.

Bathua **:** It is beneficial in kidney problems. It relieves hesitancy and strangury micturition and restores the flow.

Arbi **:** Eating the vegetable of *arbi* is beneficial in kidney diseases. It makes the kidneys strong.

Water-melon : Eating water-melon is beneficial in Nephrites.

—Ben Charles Harris : Kitchen Medicines

Long cucumber : Taking mixed juice of carrots and long cucumber or carrots and turnips cures kidney diseases.

Potato : A patient suffering from kidney problem should eat potatoes. It contains lots of sodium and very little of potassium. Too much of potassium causes excessive secretion of salt from the kidneys.

Mango : Mango is shaped like a kidney. Eating mangoes regularly strengthens kidneys.

RENAL COLIC

Stones cause acute pain in the stomach, kidneys and back. The patient feels restless because of pain. There is a hesitancy and burning sensation during urination and sometimes the patient passes blood with urine. This pain is also known as renal colic.

Grapes : Grind 30 gms of the leaves of a grape vine, mix water, strain, add salt and drink. It will provide relief to the patient squirming with kidney pain.

Bottle gourd : Cut a bottle gourd into pieces, heat them and apply the juice of these pieces on the painful part or grind some pieces and apply on the affected part. It will immediately reduce the pain.

STONES

The presence of oxalate, calcium, phosphate and purine in

excess in the food causes stones. The flour of grains without fibre is the main source of phosphate. Oxalate is found in plenty in green vegetables. Milk is the main source of calcium and phosphate. Therefore, the above mentioned things and milk should not be taken by those having a stone problem. The patient should take food which contains very little of oxalic acid and purin.

Coconut : Taking coconut water removes stones.

Spinach : Some people think that spinach causes stones, but you can take it for certain that the juice of raw spinach does not cause stones. Take spinach juice and get totally transformed.

—***Kanti Bhatt, Manhar D.Shah***

Bitter gourd : It breaks the stones into pieces in the kidney or bladder and flushes them out with the urine. The patient should take the juice of two bitter gourds daily and also eat them as a vegetable. It will check the passage of blood with the urine.

Rice : Patients suffering from stones in the kidneys or urinary bladder should not eat rice at all.

***Lajwanti* or *Chhuimui* :** The juice of the root or *panchang* (the five parts) of *lajwanti* removes the urinary obstruction and flushes out the stones and also removes the swelling on the urinary organ.

Maize : Burn maize corns and barley to ash. Grind both of them separately and store in glass bottles and mark them with labels. Dissolve 2 tsp. of maize ash in a cup of water, strain and drink it in the morning. It dissolves the stones and increases the flow of urine. Similarly, take barley ash in the evening.

Cumin seeds : Grind cumin seeds and sugar in equal quantity. Take a tsp. of it thrice daily with cool water. It will be beneficial.

Barley : Barley water flushes out the stones. The patients suffering from stones should take barley or barley products as *roti* made of barley flour, roasted barley or *sattu*. It helps in dissolving the stones and also prevents the formation of stones.

Sugar candy : Grind 15 cardamom, 1 tsp. of the kernel of melon seeds and 2 tsp. of sugar candy. Mix it in a cup of water and take it twice daily in the morning and evening. It dissolves the stones in the kidney.

Green grass : Take out the green grass with roots and remove the tender leaves. Wash the tender stems and roots with water, grind, strain and mix sugar to taste with it and drink it. Take it twice daily. It dissolves the stones and increases the flow of urine. Grind half kg. of stems and roots of grass at a time.

***Sahjan* :** Eaten as a vegetable, it breaks the stone into pieces and flushes it out with the urine.

Taking vegetables and fruits grown in summer flushes out the stones.

Melon : Melon is very useful for patients suffering from stones.

Apple : Stones are generally formed in the kidneys and the gall bladder. Even if they are removed by an operation, they are generally formed again. Taking apple juice regularly checks the formation of stones and the ones already formed get eroded gradually and are flushed out with the urine. It also checks frequent micturition at night. It cleanses the kidneys and relieves kidney pain.

Mango : Grind mango leaves dried in the shade and take 8 gms. of it in the morning with water kept overnight. It flushes out sand and stones from the body.

***Amla* :** Taking *amla churan* with radish is beneficial for patients suffering from stones in gall bladder.

Coriander : Soak 50 gms. each of sugar candy, aniseed and coriander seeds in 1½ litre of water in the morning. Strain it in the evening, grind the soaked seeds and again mix with the same water and strain and drink it. If you cannot take the entire quantity at a time, take it in two installments. Similarly, soak these things in the evening and repeat the process the following morning. It will increase the flow of urine and the stones will be flushed out.

Rose apple : Eating ripe rose apples provides relief from stones. The powder of rose apple stone taken with curd is also beneficial.

Dried dates : The use of dried dates is beneficial for patients suffering from the problem of stones.

Carrots : (1) For stones, swelling of the kidneys or for cleansing the kidneys, 150 gms. juice each of carrots, beetroot, cucumber or gourd is very beneficial. Carrot juice flushes out stones from the kidney and the gall bladder. Taking only carrot juice 3 times a day, is also beneficial. When mixed with 250 gms. juice of salad leaves, it helps in flushing out gall bladder stones.

(2) Fill a thick hollow radish with equal quantity of the seeds of carrots and turnips and close the opening. Roast it in fire. When it cools down, take out the seeds. Take half tsp. of the seeds with water twice daily in the morning and evening.

Cucumber : Cucumber juice is beneficial in stones. 250 gms. of it should be taken thrice a day. It is also beneficial in burning micturition, hesitancy and diabetes. To make the juice tasty, add a tsp. of honey and squeeze half a lemon in it.

***Bathua* :** *Bathua* taken as a vegetable prevents the formation of stones.

***Chaulai* :** This vegetable dissolves the stones.

Cabbage : Its use is beneficial in stones and urinary obstructions. The vegetable should be prepared in purified butter.

Potato : If there are stones in one or both the kidneys, it will be beneficial for the patient to eat only potatoes. Eating only potatoes and taking water frequently will flush out the sand and stones from the kidneys.

Onion : Onion juice mixed with sugar and taken as a syrup will dissolve the stone and flush it out.

Radish : (1) Boil 35 gms. of seeds of radish in ½ litre of water. When the water is reduced to half, strain and drink it. If it is taken regularly for a few days, it will dissolve the stone in the gall bladder and flush it out.

(2) Drink 20 ml. of radish juice daily and chew and eat its leaves as well. The stone will get dissolved and come out with urine. Continue this treatment for 2-3 months.

Wheat : Wheat and gram should be boiled in water and the patient should be given this water to drink. It will dissolve the stone in the gall bladder. The juice of wheat grass is also beneficial in gall bladder stones.

Gram : Soak overnight gram *daal* in water. The following morning eat it with honey. It will be beneficial in kidney and gall bladder stones.

Butter milk : It is useful for gall bladder stones.

Walnut : Grind walnuts alongwith the shell, sieve it and take a tsp. of it twice daily in the morning and evening. It will flush out the stones.

Henna : Boil 6 gms. of henna leaves in ½ litre of water. When it is reduced to 150 gms., strain and drink it hot. Take it for five days. It will flush out the stone. Kidney problems will also be solved.

Sugarcane : Chewing and sucking sugar cane is helpful in breaking the stones into pieces which are ultimately flushed out with urine.

Caraway seeds : Taking 6 gms. of Caraway seeds with water daily helps in flushing out the stones from the kidneys and the gall bladder.

***Neem* :** Take 6 gms. of the ash of *neem* leaves thrice daily with cool water. The stones in the kidney and the gall bladder get dissolved and flushed out in a few days. **Method :** Dry *neem* leaves in the shade and burn them in a pot. When they are burnt, cover the mouth of the pot with a lid. Take out the burnt leaves after four hours and grind them. You will get the ash of *neem* leaves.

Cardamom : It is beneficial in stones. It provides relief from burning sensation during urination.

***Kulthi* :** Soak overnight 250 gms. of *kulthi* in 3 litre of water and boil it the following morning. When the water is reduced to 1.5 kg., strain it and saute it with salt, black pepper powder, cumin seeds, and turmeric in clarified butter. Drink it daily. It flushes out the stones from the kidney and the gall bladder without a surgical operation. Continue with the treatment as long as the stones are not expelled. It is not harmful even if it is taken for a long time. After straining, use the *kulthi* left back as a *daal* by adding some more water.

Harmful Things to be Avoided : Those suffering from stones in the kidney and gall bladder, should avoid rice and spinach as these are quite harmful.

Beet root : Taking the juice or soup of beet root dissolves the stones and flushes them out. Take 30 gms. of it four times a day, for few weeks.

BURNING IN URINE

Cauliflower : Cauliflower is useful in this disease.

***Petha* :** Two pieces of *Agra ka petha* taken daily for a few days or drinking *petha* juice is very useful in burning micturition.

Lady finger : It provides relief from burning micturition. It increases the flow of urine.

Ridged gourd : It relieves burning sensation and clears the flow of urine.

Rice : Add sugar to half a glass of cooked rice water (*maand*) and drink it. It will relieve burning in micturition.

Wheat : Soak overnight 12 gms. of wheat in ¼ litre of water. Strain it the following morning, add 25 gms. of sugar candy to it and drink it. It will relieve burning in micturition.

Maize : To relieve burning in micturition, boil fresh maize corn in water, add sugar candy to the water and drink it.

Milk : Drink unboiled milk with water added to it.

Almonds : Grind five soaked and peeled almonds with seven cardamom and mix in a glass of water, add sugar to taste and drink it twice daily in the morning and evening.

Barley : Boil a cup of barley in 1 litre of water and drink it. It is highly beneficial in relieving burning in urine.

Kateera **:** It relieves burning in urine. Soak it overnight, mix sugar and eat it the following morning.

Water : Soak a piece of cloth in cold or iced water and place it under the navel, it will clear the flow of urine.

Amla **:** Mix 60 ml. of fresh *amla* juice with 30 gms. of honey and take it thrice a day. It makes one dose. Take three such doses. It will increase the flow of urine and provide relief from constipation and burning in urine.

Pomegranate : Pomegranate syrup relieves burning in urine.

Phalsa **:** *Phalsa* provides relief from burning in urine.

Coriander : (1) Soak overnight 15 gms. of coriander in water. Grind it like *Thandai* the following morning, strain, add sugar candy and drink it. It will relieve burning in urine. It will help control the sexual urge.

(2) Soak overnight coriander and *amla*, mash it the following morning and drink it. It will relieve burning in urine.

(3) Pound dry coriander and sieve it. Mix an equal quantity of sugar with it. Take a tsp. of it in the morning with water kept overnight on empty stomach and do not eat or drink anything else for an hour. In the same way, take another dose at 5 in the evening with water kept since morning. If you suffer from constipation, take 2 tsp. of *isabgol* husk with hot milk. It will relieve burning in the bladder.

Cardamom : Taking ground cardamom with milk increases the flow of urine and relieves pain or burning in urine.

Onion : Boil 50 gms of finely cut pieces of onions in ½ litre of water. When the water is reduced to half, strain it and drink it when it is cool. It will relieve burning in urine.

Water-melon : The juice of a water-melon exposed to dew drops during the night with sugar added to it is beneficial in burning micturition.

Isabgol **:** Soak *isabgol* in water, add powdered *boora* to it and drink it. It will relieve burning in urine.

Basil : Chewing basil leaves helps in relieving burning in urine.

POLYURIA

Excessive secretion of urine is called polyuria. It is caused by nervous disorders. Some serious problem like diabetes, swelling in the kidneys can also cause polyuria. After fever also there is excessive urination for sometime. There is frequent urination in excessive quantity. This disease can be treated by regular use of the following food items :

Turmeric : Taking a tsp. of turmeric powder twice daily in the morning and evening with cool water can cure polyuria.

Grapes : Polyuria is not good for urinary bladder. Eating grapes cures the problem of polyuria.

Amla **:** Mix the juice of three *amlas* with water and take it twice daily in the morning and evening for four days. It will provide relief from polyuria.

Banana : Eat a banana followed by *amla* juice mixed with sugar. It will check polyuria. Eating bananas alone also reduces the frequency of urination.

Pomegranate : Taking five gms. powder of pomegranate rind with water reduces the frequency of urination. Take it twice daily for three weeks. Do not eat rice while taking this treatment.

Apple : Eating apples checks nocturnal frequency of urination.

Tea : Tea is diuretic. It should be avoided.

Dried dates : In case of old people suffering from polyuria, give them dried dates to eat regularly for some time. If the problem of polyuria is severe, they should eat dried dates twice a day. They should drink milk after eating dried dates at night.

Spinach : Nocturnal frequency of urination is checked by eating the vegetable of spinach in the evening.

Gram : To check polyuria, eat 50 gms. of roasted grams followed by a little jaggery. Taking it for ten days will cure polyuria. Older people should eat roasted grams for a longer period.

***Masoor daal* :** It is beneficial in polyuria.

Sesame seeds : They are wonderfully effective in checking frequency of urination. Eating *laddoos* made of sesame seeds and jaggery in equal quantity cures polyuria.

Caraway seeds : Eating caraway seeds mixed with sesame seeds cures polyuria.

Secretion of white substance with urine : Take 250 ml. of carrot juice thrice daily. If the colour of the urine is pale, take mulberry juice mixed with sugar. It will clear the colour of the urine.

ISCHURIA

Coriander : Take 20 ml. of the juice of green coriander leaves mixed with 10 gms. of sugar. Repeat it if one dose does not work.

Onion : Boil 45 gms. of onion pieces in 1 litre of water. Strain it, mix honey and take it thrice a day. It will clear the flow of urine without any pain. The frequency of urine is checked. If urine has stopped, its secretion will restart.

Milk : Taking hot milk with jaggery is helpful in tackling urinary problems. It clears the flow of urine. There is no hesitancy. Take a glass of milk with jaggery twice every day.

Radish : If the secretion of urine stops due to kidney problems, take a dose of two ounces of radish juice. It will facilitate the secretion of urine. Taking 2 ounce of radish juice will check burning micturition and pain.

Lemon : Grind lemon seeds and put the paste on the navel and pour cold water over it. It will remove the obstruction and clear the flow of urine.

Cumin seeds : Grind cumin seeds and sugar in equal quantity and take 2 tsp. of it thrice daily with water. It will increase the flow of urine.

Turnip : If the flow of urine is obstructed, eat raw turnip and radish.

Cabbage : It is beneficial in ischuria. This vegetable should be prepared in clarified butter.

Coconut : It clears the flow of urine.

Long cucumber : It is diuretic and increases the flow of urine. Melon is also diuretic.

Banana : Four tsp. of banana juice mixed with 2 tsp. of clarified butter removes the obstruction in urine and increases the flow. It is a very good recipe for curing ischuria. The clarified butter in the banana juice cannot be retained in the stomach and the flow of urine is increased.

Rice : Take half a glass of boiled rice water (*maand*) mixed with sugar. It will clear the obstruction in micturition.

DYSURIA

Dysuria is characterized by pain and difficulty in urination. It is either frequent and slow or is obstructed altogether. Its major symptom is an acute pain at the time of urination. It is caused by gonorrhoea, stones, worms, inflammation of the urinary gland, disorders of the placenta or kidney, amoebiasis, etc. In order to get relief, these problems should first be treated. This way, dysuria will get automatically cured. Amoebiasis was suppressed by a patient by taking opium. When he got amoebiasis again, he also developed dysuria once again.

Water : Drinking hot water is beneficial in all types of dysuria. Hot water has a purifying property. Lukewarm water should be taken. It is useful in painful micturition.

Carrots : Drinking a glass of carrot juice daily clears the flow of urine. It provides relief from painful, burning and difficult micturition.

Ginger : If urine is characterized by pain and blood, mix fine and sieved powder of dried ginger in milk, add sugar and drink it.

Coriander : Put half a kg. of boiling water in a new earthen pot and mix 30 gms. of semi-pounded coriander seeds. The following morning, mash the coriander seeds, strain and add 30 gms. of *batasha*. Divide it into five doses and take it five times a day. It will be beneficial in micturition which is characterized by blood, obstruction, pain, burning and restlessness.

Cardamom : Cardamom powder with milk clears the flow of urine and provides relief from dysuria.

Urinary diseases can be cured by homeopathic treatment without a surgical operation. For the treatment of urinary diseases, please read the present author's book *Homeopathic Vyavaharik Chikitsa Saar.*

STOMATITIS

Banana : In case of the stomatitis of the tongue take a banana with curd made from cow milk in the morning.

Mulberry : Mix a tsp. of mulberry syrup in a cup of water and gargle. It will be beneficial in stomatitis of the mouth and tonsillitis.

Coriander : In case of stomatitis of the mouth, application of the fine powder of coriander seeds mixed with borax or baking powder is quite beneficial. Application of coriander powder alone is also useful. Salivation is also beneficial. Also apply the juice of green coriander. Boil Coriander seeds in water and gargle with this water.

Glycerine : In case of stomatitis of the mouth, application of glycerine is beneficial.

Basil : Chewing basil and jasmine leaves cures stomatitis.

Tomato : Those who suffer from stomatitis frequently, should eat plenty of tomatoes. They act as a medicine for stomatitis.

Bitter gourd : In case of stomatitis of the mouth, rinse the mouth with the juice of bitter gourd. You may heat the juice of bitter gourd a bit, add a little alum salt and gargle. It will cure stomatitis.

Jasmine : Chew few jasmine leaves and keep them pressed in the mouth at the affected part and spit out after two minutes. Then rinse the mouth with water. It will be beneficial in stomatitis.

***Harad* :** Take a tsp. of *harad* powder with hot milk or hot water before bed time. Apply honey mixed with fine *harad* powder at the affected part in the mouth. It will prove beneficial.

***Tumru* Seeds :** *Tumru* seeds are available with grocers. When placed on the tongue, they have a cooling effect and cause a burning sensation in the skin. For sometime, there is salivation and the pain stops. Grind the seeds into a fine powder and use it for stomatitis. Spit out after a while. Do it three times every day.

Lemon : Squeeze a lemon in hot water and gargle. Use lemon in plenty. It will provide relief from stomatitis.

Alum salt : Gargling with alum salt dissolved in water cures stomatitis.

Aniseed : Those who suffer from stomatitis frequently, should eat a little aniseed after meals. It will provide relief from stomatitis.

Camphor : Mix camphor with clarified butter and apply in the mouth four times daily and allow to salivate for some time. Then rinse the mouth.

Betel leaf : Chew a piece of camphor of the size of gram *daal* with a betel leaf and spit out the saliva. Do not swallow it.

***Arhar* :** Soak *arhar daal* in water. Use this water for gargling and rinsing the mouth. It will provide relief from stomatitis. It will also reduce the effect of heat.

Henna : Soak henna in water. Rinsing the mouth with this water will provide relief from stomatitis or you could chew henna leaves. It will also cure stomatitis.

Turmeric : Boil 15 gms. of turmeric in 1 litre of water, let it cool down. Use it for gargling twice daily in the morning and evening.

Clarified butter : Application of clarified butter before bed time is beneficial.

Black pepper : Chewing 15 gms. of black pepper together with 30 gms. of raisins provides a cure for stomatitis.

Cumin seeds : In case of swollen and painful gums, rub on them fine sieved powder of roasted cumin seeds mixed with rock salt. Spit out the saliva; it will be beneficial.

TONSILLITIS

There are two small glands situated on each side of the throat. Sometimes one or at times both of them get swollen which makes eating and drinking difficult. Swallowing becomes very painful, one also gets fever. The Hindi word for Tonsillitis is *Tundika-shoth*. The patient suffering from Tonsillitis should not be given chilled or cold things to eat or drink. Tonsils are a vital part of the body. As far as possible avoid surgical operation. They can be cured by taking homeopathic treatment or through Food Therapy. Baryta Carb is the best medicine in homeopathy for the treatment of tonsillitis. Its potency can be from 30 to lakh. The food items mentioned below are helpful in treating this disease. Whichever treatment you may take, taking the food items recommended for patients of tonsillitis will be beneficial in providing relief from the problem.

Basil : Wearing a neck band made of basil beads prevents tonsillitis and other throat problems.

Pineapple : Pine Apple is beneficial in tonsillitis.

Carrots : Carrot juice cures tonsillitis, pain in the throat and strengthens the teeth.

Water chestnut : It contains plenty of iodine. Patients suffering from throat problems and tonsillitis should specially eat them.

Salt : Gargling with hot saline water cures tonsillitis, swelling and pain in the throat. Gargle regularly till you get relief from pain.

Alum salt : Gargle with saline water with a little alum salt added to it. It cures tonsillitis.

Glycerine : Gargling with hot water mixed with the glycerine is beneficial in tonsillitis.

Tea : Boil tea leaves in water, strain and gargle. It will be beneficial.

CANCER

Cancer means the growth of a useless and shapeless tumor in the body which cannot be contained. If a lump or tumor is formed any where in the body and grows rapidly and if operated upon, recurs at another place, it is nothing but cancer. This causes decay in the body, the tumor keeps on growing and can burst at times. Early detection is not easy because the patient does not feel any inconvenience in the beginning and ultimately when it is detected it is at such an advanced stage that it becomes incurable and it is difficult to save the patient. It is such a fatal disease that when the patient comes to know that he has developed cancer he is scared to death. But if it is detected at an early stage it is possible to save the patient. The following symptoms can lead to an early detection of cancer :

(1) Any ulcers that do not heal quickly, especially those in the mouth. Any wound on the skin that does not heal even in six months, rather it keeps growing.

(2) Continuous unnatural excessive bleeding, especially in the case of women after climatic period. Bleeding while passing stool, especially when the patient does not suffer from piles.

(3) Excessive growth or tumors and lumps in any part of the body, especially in women.

(4) Difficulty in swallowing food and continuous indigestion.

(5) Continuous cough, hoarse voice or bad throat.
(6) Malfunctioning of intestines, continuous constipation and loose motions.
(7) Pain or change of colour in any speck, wart or keloid.
(8) Unexpected loss of weight and strength and aversion to food.

In case there is any of the above symptoms and you have a doubt about cancer, consult a doctor.

Saccharin

Saccharin is an artificial granular substance. Which is three hundred times sweeter than sugar. It has no food value or calories. It is derived from petroleum and coltar and has been used since 1950 as a substitute for sugar for diabetics. Since it is very sweet and its use in place of sugar is highly economical from business point of view, it is freely used in canned food and drinks.

To say that saccharin is useful for obese and diabetic persons because it will reduce the fat content in their blood is nothing but a commercial gimmick to sell things by promoting the culture of consumerism. In reality, it does not provide any such benefits.

According to studies conducted in America and Canada, the use of saccharin is harmful for human body and it increases the possibility of cancer of the bladder. Several institutes like Wisconsin Alumini Institute, American Food and Drink Organization and Health Care Department of Canada conducted experiments in 1971, 1974 and 1977 respectively in which they fed saccharin to mice and assessed its effects. It was found that most of the mice that were fed saccharin developed tumors in the bladder.

On the basis of these experiments the National Academy of Sciences in America drew a conclusion in 1978 that saccharin contains cancer causing elements in excess. As saccharin is used literally in all cold drinks and canned foods, therefore, Canada, New Zealand and several European countries have banned the use of saccharin in these things. America has also banned its use in food items. But India is usually indifferent to such matters.

Cosmetics : Women often use soaps, creams, powders shampoos, lotions, etc., as beauty aids but as these things contain harmful chemicals, they fall a prey to skin diseases and cancer.

Cancer is caused by accumulation of pollutants in the blood. Instead of getting scared, you should change your life-style to get rid of the disease. According to Heeri Research Centre in England, women who conceive before the age of 33, do not suffer from breast cancer, tumor, etc. This disease can be checked by turning to nature, living a natural life and consuming food in its natural form. Whereas allelopathic system of medicine has caused panic among the patients by telling them that it is incurable, food therapy infuses a new ray of hope in the life of cancer patients and takes them on the road to recovery. Take the following food items regularly and live a healthy life :

Cauliflower : Take ¾ cup of cauliflower juice daily in the morning on empty stomach. It will be beneficial.

Cabbage : Take atleast ½ cup of cabbage juice daily the first thing in the morning on empty stomach. It can cure cancer in its early stages.

Food : It has been proved by the on-going research that the chemical beta-carotene present in food can destroy cancer cells. It is found in plenty in whole pulses, cabbage, cauliflower, carrot, lemon and fruits of the species of *mausambi*. These fruits and vegetables should be consumed in plenty by cancer patients. Fried food causes cancer. Fried food contains cancer-causing carcinogens which get into the stomach with the food. Therefore, fried food should not be consumed.

Grapes : The cancer patient should observe fast for the first three days. Then he should be given grapes to eat. He should also be given enema sometimes. He should not be given more than 2 kg. of grapes in a day. After a few days give him butter milk to drink. Do not give anything else to eat. It is a slow process and takes several months to provide relief. The grape poultice can be applied on the wounds. Sometimes grape juice causes stomach ache or a burning sensation in the anus. But there is no cause for fear. The pain will subside after a few days. Fomentation will be beneficial at the time of pain.

—The Grape Cure : Johanna Brandit

Bel **:** The use of *bel* has been considered beneficial in bone cancer, blood cancer and other types of cancer. *Bel* can be taken in the form of juice or in any other form.

Carrots : Carrot juice is a good anti-toxicant. It can cure even the most incurable diseases such as cancer. Two glasses of carrot juice should be taken daily—one before breakfast in the morning and another in the evening. 12 oz. of carrot juice mixed with 4 oz. of spinach juice is especially beneficial in cancer.

Wheat : How is wheatgrass helpful in treating cancer? According to Dr. Vigmore, cancer is only a state of the body which indicates that there is something wrong with this wonderful machine. Nature always tries to maintain a balance in the human body. Since people have different life-styles, they suffer from different diseases—some suffer from cancer. There was a woman suffering from breast cancer. She had tried all types of treatment but of no avail. But when she was put on the diet of different types of fruit juices, she was cured in a few months. Wheat grass is an effective anti-toxicant. Its use can cure cancer and many other diseases. Its juice is known as green-blood. It is said that upto 40% of its properties are similar to those of human blood.

How to Prepare Wheat Grass Juice

Fill 10 or 12 earthen pots with clean soil without manure. Sow half a handful of wheat in each earthen pot one by one everyday and water them occasionally. Put the earthen pots in shade. When the wheatgrass is 6 inches high in one of them, uproot it and cut off the roots, wash it well and grind into a paste, put it into a piece of cloth and squeeze out the juice. Drink it immediately. Take it twice daily in the morning and evening. In this way, keep sowing wheat and taking wheatgrass juice regularly. In addition, soak ½ cup of clean and washed wheat in a pot in two cups of water.

Drink the water after twelve hours. Take it twice daily, in the morning and evening. In this way, you will see that even the deadliest of diseases get cured within 8-10 or 15-20 days and within two or three months even a patient on the deathbed would be fully cured and his normal health would be restored. Do not add lemon or salt to the juice. Also do not eat anything for some time after taking the juice. Take this treatment and inform the writer about the outcome so that the experience of one patient could inspire other patients to benefit from it. While taking the juice of wheat grass, eat as much of raw food such as fruits, vegetables, sprouted grains, etc., as possible to derive the maximum benefit. (For details refer, '*Gehun ke Jawarey*' by *Dr. Surendra Kapil*).

Curd : Karnal, 24th July, 1977. The Scientists of National Dairy Institute have opined after conducting an arduous research that curd can check the possible occurrence of several types of cancer. Curd is highly beneficial for health. Curd is a milk product but when milk is turned into curd, it acquires properties which make it much more useful than milk.

Cancer of the Stomach : Garlic prevents stomach cancer. When suffering from cancer, a few cloves of garlic should be ground and mixed in water and taken for a few weeks. It will cure the cancer. Taking garlic thrice daily after meals cleans the bowels. It causes contractions in the muscles of the stomach and thus reduces the pressure on the intestines. It stimulates the liver as a result of which the capillaries in the walls of the stomach get a supply of oxygen and blood.

Bread : New Delhi, 10th June, 1979. If one wants to avoid the cancer of the stomach, one should increase the intake of bread. This new discovery was made by the nutrition scientist Prof. Groye of Lieden University (Germany). Bread prevents cancer because according to nutrition scientist, it is more easily digestible than other food products and thus alleviates the risk of intestinal cancer.

For effective treatment of cancer it is essential that complete changes should be made in food habits. It is also necessary to avoid carbonated foods, water and smoking, carcinogen and chemicals.

REVOLUTIONARY CHANGES IN DIET

First of all, the patient should try to cleanse his skin, lungs, kidneys and intestines. Enema should be taken to cleanse the kidneys. The patient should take only the juice of oranges, grapes, pears, tomatoes with lemon, etc., for four days. The juice of carrots and other raw vegetables is also beneficial.

After a few days, the patient should be given natural foods, such as garlic, tomatoes, carrots, green leafy vegetables, cabbage, etc. Besides, sprouted grains and almonds can also be given.

In ancient times, garlic was used as a medicine for cancer. Egyptians used it as an external medicine. Hippocrates was the first to use it as food therapy. Those who consume garlic in sufficient quantity are less likely to suffer from cancer.

The Japanese scientist, Dr. Fukunir Morishale and his team who have been studying the properties of Vitamin-C in the cure of cancer are of the opinion that it can increase the life span of cancer patients. According to them, Vitamin-C and Copper are useful for patients of cancer.

Dr. Leonada Santamaria of Peevia University, Italy and his colleagues have discovered that beta-carotene found in vitamins is effective in preventing cancer.

The research being conducted all over the world shows that the use of green and yellow vegetables and fruits is beneficial in the treatment of cancer. The research going on in Japan for the last 23 years reveals that people who regularly eat green and yellow vegetables are less likely to suffer from stomach cancer.

A study conducted by Hebert University on 1200 patients shows that the families that consume carrots, tomatoes, salad, green leafy vegetables, dry fruits, water-melon in large quantities are less likely to suffer from cancer. Alongwith the above, it is also necessary that mind gets full rest and the patient is kept away from tension and depression.

AIDS

Bel **:** The use of *bel* is beneficial in AIDS. It can be used in any form.

EPISTAXIS

Lemon : In case of epistaxis, put two drops of lemon juice frequently into the nostrils. It will check bleeding from the nose.

Sugar candy : Grind 50 gms. each of dried white lotus flowers and sugar candy and mix them. Take a tsp. of it with hot milk twice daily in the morning and evening for one week. It will cure epistaxis. Do not take hot things, pickles and fried food. It is based on experience.

Grapes : Draw in the juice of sweet grapes through the nostrils. It will provide instant relief from epistaxis.

Amla **:** People suffering from frequent nose bleeding should soak dried *amla* overnight and wash the head with it in the morning daily. *Amla* preserve is also beneficial. If all the treatments are of no avail, put *amla* juice in the nostrils and apply ground *amla* paste on the head. It will surely be beneficial. If fresh *amla* is not available, soak *amla* powder in water and prepare the paste. It will remove dryness and heat from the head.

Banana : Mix sugar with milk and take it with a banana daily for ten days.

Pomegranate : (1) Putting a few drops of pomegranate juice in the nostrils will provide relief from expistaxis.

(2) Taking ½ juice of sweet and sour pomegranates mixed with 2 tsp. of sugar candy daily in the afternoon provides relief from nosebleed during the summer season.

Onion : Put a few drops of onion juice in the nostrils in case of bleeding from the nose. Onion juice cures the infection of the nose and throat. Putting a few drops of onion juice mixed with the juice of mint leaves in the nostrils is also beneficial. The extract of pomegranate flowers can also be mixed with the juice of mint leaves.

Clarified butter : Let the patient lie down with the neck bent backward. Put 5 drops of clarified butter in each of the nostrils and ask him to draw it in with the breath. In this way, inhaling of clarified butter will provide relief from epistaxis. Take this treatment for one week. Also take milk mixed with *ghee* daily.

Alum salt : Dissolve alum salt in unboiled cow milk and inhale it. If it does not provide relief from nose bleeding, dissolve alum salt in water, dip a piece of cloth in it and put it on the forehead for 5-10 minutes. It will check bleeding from the nose.

Coriander : Inhaling the juice of green coriander leaves and applying its paste on the head will check bleeding from the nose because of heat.

Basil : Putting a few drops of basil juice in the nostrils will stop bleeding from the nose.

Green grass : When suffering from nose bleeding inhale the juice of green grass and then put a few drops of the juice in the nostrils. It will be beneficial.

***Multani mitti* :** Soak overnight 10 gms. of *multani mitti* in ½ litre of water in an earthen pot, drain and drink it the following morning. It cures even chronic epistaxis in a few days.

Water : Pouring cold water on the head will stop bleeding from the nose.

Ice : Rub ice on the head and also pour cold water on it. It will stop bleeding from the nose.

Coconut : Eating coconut daily in the morning on empty stomach provides relief from epistaxis.

***Petha* :** Soak overnight two pieces of '*Agra ka petha*' in a glass of water. Eat the *petha* pieces the following morning and also drink the water. It will provide relief from nose bleeding in a few days.

Black gram : Soak black gram and grind it. Apply the paste on the forehead. It will provide relief from nose bleeding.

HEMORRHOIDS

Varicosity of the veins around the anus is called hemorrhoids. These swollen veins are of the size of a pea corn or even bigger. They are commonly known as piles. Hemorrhoids are either inside or outside the anus. External hemorrhoids keep dangling near the opening of the anus. So long as they do not get chaffed or infected they do not cause pain. When they get chaffed there is unbearable pain in them. Inner hemorrhoids start bleeding. There can be one or several hemorrhoids. When the inner hemorrhoids come out of the anus, they strangulate the opening. Until they are pushed inside, they keep causing pain. In this way, internal hemorrhoids cause bleeding while the external ones do not bleed.

Symptoms : Bleeding while passing the stool, acute or shooting pain, itching and burning in the anus are some of the symptoms of hemorrhoids. They are caused by exerting pressure while passing the stool because of constipation.

Causes : Hard stool, frequent use of laxatives, eating hot and spicy foods, drinking, damaged liver, sedentary life-style, keeping late hours, long sittings or taking such medicines that cause heat in the stomach are the causes which lead to hemorrhoids.

Medicines can provide relief from hemorrhoids but they can't be fully cured. Some persons become frustrated and get them removed through surgical operation but it has been noticed that they recur even after operation. The disease runs in the family and is passed on from one generation to another. My opinion as a doctor is that unless there is an acute disorder or pain, one should not opt for surgery. Homeopathic treatment easily provides relief in this disease. But the best results can be obtained through food therapy. The patient suffering from hemorrhoids should take care that he has no constipation and the stool is soft and not hard. For this purpose, he should eat the food recommended in the section on constipation. After passing the stool, clean the anus well with the middle finger. The detailed description of the food suggested for hemorrhoids in the present author's book, *Bhojan ke Dwara Chikitsa* is being reproduced here in brief. You can lead a healthy and happy life by using these things regularly.

NON-BLEEDING PILES

Lemon : Strain some lemon juice through a piece of clean, fine muslin cloth and mix an equal quantity of olive oil with it and inject five gms. of it inside the anus with a syringe daily at night. It will check the pain, burning and reduce the size of the hemorrhoids. It will enable the patient to pass the stool without any pain. If the patient experiences acute pain, burning or excessive bleeding, he should observe fast and drink only water with fresh lemon juice. Fill four cups with fresh milk straight from the udders. Squeeze half a lemon into one of them at a time and drink it. Take it for a week. It will provide relief from all types of hemorrhoids.

Massage : Regular massage of the body is beneficial in hemorrhoids.

Millet : Eating millet bread is beneficial in hemorrhoids .

Brinjal : Application of ground brinjal paste on the hemorrhoids is beneficial and provides relief from pain and burning. Dry the pulp and the skin of the brinjal and powder it. Put the powder on live coals and expose the hemorrhoids to the fumes. Burn a brinjal to ashes, mix it with honey and apply it on the hemorrhoids. They will dry up and fall off.

Ridged gourd : It relieves constipation. Its regular use cures hemorrhoids.

Chaulai **:** Regular use of *chaulai* as a vegetable can cure hemorrhoids.

Bathua **:** So long as *bathua* is available, eat it daily as a vegetable. Take *bathua* juice. Boil *bathua*, strain and drink the water. It will cure hemorrhoids.

Beet root : Hemorrhoids wither away by the regular intake of beet-root.

Carrots (1) **:** Eating raw carrots or taking carrot juice cures hemorrhoids. So long as carrots are available during the season, use them regularly.

(2) Mixed juice of carrots (3 parts) and spinach (one part) is beneficial in hemorrhoids.

Mango : Mix ½ cup of sweet mango juice with 25 gms. of curd and 1 tsp. of ginger juice and drink it. Take it thrice daily. It will cure hemorrhoids.

Guava : Taking guava fruit for a few days will provide relief from piles.

Onion : Acharya Baagbhatt says that onion can cure both the bleeding and non-bleeding piles.

A raw onion should be eaten every day. He says that he advises his patients to eat onions.

—*Vaidya Naveen Bhai Ojha, Shuchi Arsh Rog Visheshank*

Radish : (1) Eating raw radish stops hemorrhoidal bleeding. Take a cup of radish juice, mix a tsp. of clarified butter in it, stir well and drink it twice daily in the morning and evening. It will be beneficial both in bleeding and non-bleeding hemorrhoids.

(2) Cut a white radish into pieces, add salt to them and put them overnight in the open in the dew. Eat them the following morning on empty stomach. After passing the stool, wash the anus with radish juice.

(3) Soak 100 gms. *Jalebis* prepared in clarified butter in 125 ml. of radish juice. Taking it for a week will provide a lifelong cure of hemorrhoids.

—*Swami Jagdishwaranand Saraswati* : *Gharelu Aushadhiyan*

(4) Fry radish pieces in clarified butter and eat with sugar.

Gwar **:** Grind 11 green leaves of the *gawar* plant and 11 corns of black pepper and mix in 62 litre of water. Drink it once a day for some days. It will cure windy hemorrhoids.

Taking the juice of wheat grass is beneficial in all types of hemorrhoids.

Bottle gourd : Grind gourd leaves into a paste and apply it on hemorrhoids. They will be cured in a few days.

Sesame seeds : Eat 60 gms. of black sesame seeds followed by a glass of cool water. It will cure non-bleeding piles. Application of sesame oil on hemorrhoids regularly is beneficial.

Nutmeg : Saute 10 pieces of nutmeg in clarified butter till they turn red. Grind them, sieve and mix in two cups of wheat flour and again saute it in clarified butter. Then mix *boora* to taste. Take a tsp. of it daily in the morning on empty stomach. It will be beneficial in hemorrhoids.

Dried ginger powder : Mix equal quantity of dried ginger powder and jaggery and take ½ tsp. of it twice daily in the morning and evening.

Swallow-wort : 3 drops of swallow-wort milk in a *batasha* taken in the morning before sunrise is beneficial in hemorrhoids.

Tea : Grind tea leaves in water, heat it and apply it warm on the hemorrhoids. It will provide relief from hemorrhoidal pain.

***Harad*:** Taking ½ tsp. of *harad* powder twice daily with hot water in the morning and evening is beneficial.

Cauliflower : Cauliflower and yam taken as a cooked vegetable with a little quantity of spices is beneficial.

Milk : Take the husk of *isabgol* with hot milk before bed time. It will relieve constipation and will be beneficial in hemorrhoids.

Butter milk : Taking butter milk mixed with salt and ground caraway seeds is useful in hemorrhoids. The hemorrhoids treated with the use of butter milk do not reappear. Rock salt is more useful than common salt. Take butter milk at the end of the meal.

Castor oil : Regular application of castor oil on external hemorrhoids is beneficial. It relieves pain and the hemorrhoids dry up.

Cumin seeds : Taking the powder of cumin seeds mixed with sugar candy with water relieves hemorrhoidal pain.

Aniseed : Grind aniseed and sugar candy and take ½ tsp. with milk.

Mustard oil : If the hemorrhoids are very painful, take a little bit of mustard oil on your palm, mix with a little water, rub it and apply it on the hemorrhoids daily after passing the stool. It is very beneficial.

Basil : Grind basil leaves into a paste or extract juice from the leaves and apply it on the anus. It will be beneficial. Eating basil leaves will also be useful.

***Neem* :** Grind 10 kernels of *neem* fruit alongwith rock salt or sugar candy and take it with cool water daily in the morning and evening.

It will start giving relief after four days.

BLEEDING PILES

Lemon : (1) Squeeze the juice of half a lemon in hot milk and drink it immediately. Repeat it every three hours.

(2) Cut a lemon into two and fill both the halves with catechu. Put them overnight in the open in the dew. Suck both the pieces the following morning. It will check hemorrhoidal bleeding.

***Amla* :** Grind dried *amlas* into a fine powder and take a tsp. of it with cow milk or butter milk twice daily in the morning and evening. It is beneficial in bleeding piles.

Pomegranate : Grind the peal of pomegranate and sieve through a piece of fine muslin cloth and take 8 gms. of it with fresh water in the morning and evening.

Papaya : Taking papaya daily in the afternoon is beneficial in bleeding piles. The papaya should be fully ripe. Raw papaya should be eaten as a cooked vegetable.

Coconut : Burn coconut coir to ashes and mix it with equal quantity of *boora* and take 10 gms. with water daily.

Bottle gourd : Grind the peal of bottle gourd dried in the shade. Take a tsp. of it twice daily with cool water in the morning and evening. It checks hemorrhoidal bleeding. Take this treatment for seven days.

Onion : The use of onions is beneficial in both bleeding and non-bleeding hemorrhoids.

Radish : Eating raw radish checks hemorrhoidal bleeding. Take a cup of radish juice mixed with a tsp. of clarified butter in the morning and evening. It will be beneficial.

Bitter gourd : Taking a tsp. of the juice of bitter gourd mixed with sugar is beneficial.

Gram : Eating hot roasted gram is beneficial in bleeding piles.

***Masoor daal* :** Eating *masoor ki daal* with morning meals followed by a glass of sour butter milk is beneficial in bleeding piles.

Sesame seeds : Chew well and eat 60 gms. of black sesame seeds. It will check hemorrhoidal bleeding. Apply sesame oil on the hemorrhoids.

Tamarind : The juice of tamarind leaves is beneficial in bleeding piles.

Yam : Eating rice and yam with tamarind leaves is beneficial in hemorrhoids.

Cauliflower : Eat raw cauliflower as salad.

Curd : Eat only curd so long as you suffer from bleeding piles. Do not eat anything else. It will check the bleeding.

Clarified butter : Mix a tsp. each of clarified butter, sesame seeds and ground sugar candy and take it thrice daily. It will check the bleeding.

Fenugreek : Prepare a concoction of fenugreek seeds or boil them in milk and take it. It will check hemorrhoidal bleeding.

Alum salt : After passing the stool, wash the anus with alum salt water, also wash the inside of the anus with the help of a syringe. It is beneficial in bleeding piles.

Isabgol **:** Take a tsp. of the husk of *isabgol* with hot water or hot milk before bed time.

Raal **:** Grind 60 gms. of yellow *raal* into a fine powder. Take 7 gms. of the powder daily in the morning mixed with 125 gms. of curd. It is an effective medicine for bleeding piles. Take it for a week. Whenever you pass urine, take some urine in your hand and wash the hemorrhoids with it. If this practice is followed for two months, it will provide a permanent cure for piles. Yellow *raal* can be had from a grocer's shop. Besides bleeding hemorrhoids it is also useful in other types of hemorrhoids.

Butter milk : Mix white rock salt and one spoonful grounded and roasted cumin seeds in a glass of butter milk. Take one glass four times a day. Before going to bed rub cream skimmed from milk on the anus.

Cumin seeds : Boil 1 tsp. each of cumin seeds, aniseed and coriander seeds in a glass of water. When the water is reduced to half, strain and drink it after mixing a tsp. of clarified butter. It will check hemorrhoidal bleeding. It is more useful for pregnant women in treating the problem of piles.

Coriander : Taking coriander juice mixed with sugar candy gives prompt relief.

LEUCODERMA

'Leuco' means 'white' and 'derma' means 'skin', thus leucoderma means abnormal whiteness of the skin. This disease is usually very difficult to treat. If the patient and the physician treat this disease for a long time with patience, it is possible to cure it. During the treatment very small blackish spots appear in the white patches. These spots keep spreading and the skin gradually becomes normal. The abnormal whiteness disappears. In this way, the disease is cured. It is not an infectious disease. Only the skin becomes white.

Causes : Why do white patches appear? So far it has not been possible to find out what causes this problem. However, there are certain things which affect the human body and can cause white patches in the skin, which spread rapidly.

(1) When the quantity of melanin in the blood is reduced, the skin becomes white, (2) chronic constipation, (3) malfunctioning of the liver, jaundice, (4) ailments of the stomach, (5) worms, (6) diseases like typhoid which affect the stomach and intestines, (7) chronic diarrhoea, (8) irregular food habits, indigestion, (9) insufficient sweating, (10) heredity, (11) excessive mental tension or worries, (12) syphilis, (13) tubercular constitution, (14) hurt, burn, (15) wearing clothes tight at the waist, (16) problems of the ear, teeth and throat, (17) meat-eating.

Symptoms : White spots can appear any where in the body. Initially they appear on hands, elbows, face, ankles, feet and other parts which come under pressure such as waist, where you tie the belt, etc. Gradually, they spread and merge and cover the whole body. These white spots do not cause any type of pain. That is why the patient does not care to go for treatment when it is at the initial stage and ignores it considering it to be a small spot. But when finger tips, palms, soles, lips, etc. become white it becomes difficult to cure the disease and it takes a very long time. When the whole body becomes leucodermic, there is very little possibility of its cure. When the spots have just started appearing and they have not spread beyond two or three inches, they can be cured. While treating leucodermic patients I have noticed that some of the white patches disappear but new ones appear.

It usually takes a year or two to treat leucoderma. In the world of medicine, leucoderma can be treated by homeopathic system of medicine.

Treatment Through Food

Internal Use : Put pomegranate leaves to dry in the shade,

SINCE

आजीवन स्वास्थ्य प्राप्ति के साधनों की सही जानकारी

grind them into a fine powder, sieve it and take 8 gms. of it each in the morning and evening with fresh water.

Gram : (1) Soak a handful of gram and 10 gms. of *triphala churan* in 125 litre of water. After 12 hours tie the soaked gram in a piece of coarse cloth and pour the remaining water on the bundle. Open the bundle after twenty four hours. This way, you will get gram sprouts. If they do not sprout due to weather conditions, you may eat them without sprouting. Chew the sprouted gram well. Eating them regularly for six months will cure leucoderma.

(2) During treatment of leucoderma, if you stop taking salt, you will derive greater benefit. Eat *rotis* made of gram flour without salt for a long period. You can apply clarified butter on the *rotis*. Eat gram *daal* also. Eating gram flour *rotis* without salt regularly for a considerably long period will cure leucoderma without any medicines. If you find it difficult to eat gram flour *roti* for a long time, mix wheat and gram flour in equal quantity, add rock salt and eat the *rotis* daily. Similarly, in place of gram *daal*, you may some time take *moong daal*. Among other vegetables, you may take spinach, carrots, *parwal* and potatoes in a small quantity.

The use of calcium-rich food with Vitamin-D is highly beneficial. You get Vitamin-D from the Sun. Sun-bath is beneficial for leucodermic patients.

Abstinence : Do not take sour things, meat, especially fish, rice, salt, oil, jaggery, chillies.

Besides the above eatables, also use one of the things for external application on the white spots for a long time.

Bathua : Boil *bathua*, squeeze out the juice and drink it. Also eat *bathua* as a vegetable. Wash the affected skin with boiled *bathua* water. Grind raw *bathua* leaves and squeeze out the juice and mix ½ cup of sesame oil with two cups of *bathua* juice and heat it slowly. When the juice evaporates and only the oil is left, strain it and store it in a bottle. Apply it regularly on white spots. It will be beneficial.

Ginger : Mix 15 gms. of *bapchi* with 30 ml. of ginger juice. When both of them get dry, mix 45 gms. of sugar and grind. Take a tsp. of it daily with cool water once in the morning an hour after meals. Apply *bapchi* oil on white spots. Sometimes a patient develops blisters or latches because of the application of *bapchi* oil. Therefore, great precaution should be taken in its application. Even, if there is a slight problem do not use it. Initially, apply bapchi oil only on patch of half an inch at one place for four days. If there is no reaction, you may use it on all the white spots. If the disease is in its early stages, it gets cured in five months.

Walnut : Walnut tree has such a toxic effect that the soil around the roots of the tree gets blackened. There are several accounts in books saying that eating walnuts regularly cures leucoderma.

***Neem* :** Grind dry *neem* leaves, flowers and fruits in equal quantity and take a tsp. of it daily with water.

Alfa-alfa : Mix 100 gms. each of alfalfa and cucumber juice and drink it daily. It will cure leucoderma. Drink it daily twice in the morning and evening for a few months.

Garlic : Grind *harad* in garlic juice and apply on white spots. Eating garlic will also help.

Butter milk : Taking butter milk is beneficial in leucoderma.

Black gram : Grind black gram in water and apply on the white spots for four months. It will cure leucoderma.

Turmeric : Mix 125 gms. of turmeric powder in 500 gms. of spirit in a glass bottle and cork it and put it in the Sun. Stir it well three time everyday. After three days, strain and again store in a glass bottle. This will be turmeric tincture. It will be beneficial to apply it thrice daily on the white spots. Take a tsp. of turmeric powder twice daily in the morning and evening with hot milk for six months. It is beneficial in leucoderma.

Basil : Take a basil plant with its roots. Wash it and clean it well. Pound it and cook it slowly in ½ litre water mixed with ½ litre oil. When the water evaporates and only the oil is left, mash and strain it to get the basil oil. Apply it on white spots.

Spomia Fistulosa (Swallow-wort) : It is a wild plant and can be found easily everywhere. Application of its milk on the white spots cures them in a month or two. Do not apply it near the eyes and on the lips.

Leucoderma can be cured by taking homeopathic medicines, prescribed food items and by applying one of the above mentioned local medicines. Leucoderma should be treated not only by medicines but also by food. Those who want to know more about it, should correspond with the present writer.

ABSCESS

Guava : If you have got an abscess, whelks, blood disorder and itching, eating 250 gms. of guava daily in the afternoon for four weeks will be helpful. It will cleanse the bowels, remove the heat from the blood, also cleanse the blood and solve the problem of abscesses, whelks and itching.

***Harad*:** In case of suppuration of the abscess, burn a *harad* and grind it into a fine powder, mix it with vaseline and prepare an ointment. Boil a tsp. of ground *harad* in a glass of water, strain and foment the abscess with the water when it is lukewarm and wash it. Also wash the spot where there is itching with that water. It will be beneficial.

***Bathua* :** Mix dried ginger powder and salt with pounded *bathua.* Put it in a piece of wet cloth, make a little bundle, wrap it with wet clay and roast it on live coal. When roasted, dress the wound with it when it is hot. The abscess will subside and burst.

***Masoor daal*:** Prepare poultice by using *masoor ki daal* and apply it on the abscess. It will soon burst and the pus will get dried up.

Cumin seeds : If a suckling mother develops a lump or

abscess, grind cumin seeds in water and apply on the affected part. It will be beneficial.

***Dhatoora* :** Apply clarified butter to a *dhatoora* leaf, heat it and put it on the abscess. It will relieve pain and the abscess will subside.

Red chilli : Apply red chilli powder on abscesses and whelks.

Water : First foment the abscess with hot water for three minutes, then with cold water for a minute. In this way, fomenting for ten minutes twice daily in the morning and evening will be beneficial.

Carrots : Application of hot carrot poultice on an abscess or a whelk is beneficial. It helps the congealed blood to thaw.

Tamarind : Mash and mix tamarind pulp in water and drink it. It is beneficial in abscesses, whelks and ulcers.

Onion : If the abscess is suppurating and has become intolerably painful, pound and grind an onion, mix turmeric powder, wheat flour, water and clarified butter with it and heat it for some time and prepare poultice. Apply it hot on the abscess. It will allow the abscess to burst and there will be no need for an operation.

Garlic : The use of garlic accelerates the healing process of abscesses and wounds. Application of garlic paste on abscesses and whelks in the initial stage is quite beneficial. It is not useful after suppuration. The abscesses which have worms can be cured with garlic.

Rice : Prepare ground rice poultice in mustard oil and apply it on the abscess. It will burst and the pus will come out.

Black gram : If the pus in the abscess is thick and excessive, use black gram poultice.

Curd : If there is swelling, pain and burning because of the abscess, apply curd after straining out the water content. For it put the curd in a piece of cloth and hand it on a peg. The water will drip away. Apply the curd on the abscess and bandage it. Change the bandage thrice in a day.

Caraway seeds : In case of swelling because of an abscess or whelk, grind caraway seeds in lemon juice and apply.

Henna : Boil henna in water and wash the abscess with the boiled henna water.

***Neem* :** Grind *neem* leaves in water and apply the paste on the abscess. It is beneficial in the initial stages. If you find the abscess is not likely to subside or if it has not reached the stage of suppuration, grind *neem* leaves with honey and apply on the abscess. It will suppurate and burst. After it has burst, grind *neem* leaves, heat it with clarified butter and apply on the wound. It will facilitate its healing. Grind *neem* bark in water and apply on the whelks. Boil *neem* leaves in water and wash the wound with it. It is beneficial to heat *neem* leaves and swathe them on the wounds.

Ointment for Abscesses and Whelks : Abscesses and whelks are caused by disorders of the blood. The wounds do not heal easily. Application of *neem* ointment on them is beneficial. **Method :** Grind 175 gms. of *neem* leaves without adding water and make a paste. Pour similar quantity of mustard oil in a copper utensil and heat it. When the oil is quite hot, put the paste in it. When it gets blackened. Remove it from stove and let it cool down. Then grind it in the same oil. The ointment will be ready. Apply this on the abscesses and whelks.

Green grass : Regular application of the paste made of green grass on an abscess allows it to suppurate and burst.

Clay : If the abscess is big and hard and it does not burst, apply wet soil on it. The abscess will burst and the pus will come out. Keep using wet soil pads on the abscess for sometime.

Basil : Boil basil leaves in water and wash the abscesses with it. Grind fresh basil leaves and apply on the abscesses. Mix 250 gms. each of the juice of basil leaves and coconut oil, heat it on slow fire. When the water gets evaporated, add 12 gms. of wax in it and stir. The application of this ointment will be beneficial.

ITCH

The use of salt is harmful in itching. Fruits and vegetables are beneficial. Fruits and vegetables increase the alkali content in the blood which is good for health. Patients suffering from itching should stop taking salt and increase the intake of fruits and vegetables in their raw and natural form without adding anything like spices, etc. It will be highly beneficial.

Banana : Grind banana pulp in lemon juice and apply on parts affected with itch and ringworm or bald patches. It will be beneficial.

Lemon : Suck a lemon and mix lemon juice with coconut oil and massage the skin with it. It will be very beneficial in itch.

***Harad*:** Boil 2 tsp. of *harad* powder in two glasses of water and strain it. Use this water to wash the parts affected with itch or soak a piece of cloth in the water and wipe the affected part with it. It checks the itching.

Jasmine oil : (1) Mix lemon juice and jasmine oil in equal quantity and massage the body with it. It will be useful in dry itch.

(2) Mix camphor with jasmine oil and massage the body with it. It will provide relief from itching.

Garlic : Boil garlic in oil and massage the body with it. It is beneficial in itching. It also cleanses the blood.

Wheat : Application of kneaded wheat flour provides relief from skin diseases, inflammation, itch, painful abscesses and whelks and burn wounds.

***Arhar*:** Grind *arhar daal* with curd and apply on the affected part. It will be beneficial in itching.

Gram : Eating gram flour *roti* for 64 days without salt will provide relief from shingles and itch.

Milk : Mix water with milk and apply it on the body with a swab of cotton. It will provide relief from itching.

Coconut : Mix coconut oil with lemon juice and massage the body with it. It will reduce the severity of itching.

Cumin seeds : Boil cumin seeds in water and use it for washing yourself. It will provide relief from itching and nettle-rash. It is based on experience.

Black pepper : Taking black pepper powder with clarified cow butter provides relief from all types of itch and toxins.

Green grass : Mix the juice of green grass with sesame oil and use it for massaging the body. It will provide relief from itching.

Mix 63 ml. of the juice of green grass in 250 ml. of sesame oil, boil it, let it cool down, strain and use it for massaging the body for a week. It will provide relief from all types of skin diseases.

Red chilli : Boil red chilli powder in oil and apply the oil on the affected parts. It is usually beneficial in swelling, itching and other skin-diseases. It is especially useful in whelks that occur during the winter season.

Basil : Mix the juice of basil leaves with equal quantity of lemon juice and apply it on the affected parts. It is usually effective in providing relief from itching. Mix 250 gms. each of the juice of basil leaves and coconut oil and heat it on slow fire. When the water content has evaporated, mix 12 gms. of wax in hot oil and stir well. The ointment will be ready for use. It is highly beneficial in whelks and itching.

Aniseed : Grind aniseed and coriander seeds in equal quantity. Mix one and half times clarified butter and double sugar with it. Take 30 gms. each in the morning and evening. It will be beneficial in itching.

Alum salt : In case of itching in the procreative organs, mix alum salt with hot water and wash the affected parts.

Tomato : Massage the body with a tsp. of tomato juice mixed with 2 tsp. of coconut oil. Take a hot bath afterwards. It will provide relief from itching.

Yam : Eating yam as a vegetable provides relief from itching. You may take it for a long period.

Bathua **:** Boil *bathua* and squeeze out the juice and drink it regularly. Also eat *bathua* as a vegetable. Wash the skin with boiled *bathua* water. Mix four parts of the juice of raw *bathua* with one part of sesame oil, heat it till the water content has evaporated. Massage the skin with this oil.

Parwal **:** Eating *parwal* as a vegetable is beneficial in itching.

Green gram whole : Soak green gram whole in only as much water as can be absorbed by it. After two hours, grind it and apply it on the affected part. It will be beneficial.

Jaggery : A patient suffering from blood disorders should take jaggery instead of sugar in tea, milk, lassi, etc. It will purify the blood and provide relief from itching.

Caraway seeds : Grind caraway seeds in water and apply on the parts affected with itching. Boil caraway seeds in water and wash the affected parts with it.

Sugar : Those suffering from itch should not eat sugar or things made of sugar like toffees, sweets, etc. They can instead eat sweet fruits. In this way, they will get relief from itching.

Camphor : Mix 10 gms. of camphor with 100 ml. of coconut oil and apply it on the affected parts. It is quite beneficial. Mix the camphor in slightly warm water. Camphor makes the skin numb and thus provides quick relief from itching.

Neem **:** It cleanses the blood. Apply *neem* oil or grind *neem* fruit in water and apply on the affected parts. Taking 25 ml. of the juice of *neem* leaves, in the morning, is beneficial in itching. Take it regularly for a few days.

ACNES, PIMPLES, BEAUTY OF THE FACE

During the youth, acne or pimples usually appear on the face. They spoil the beauty of the face or rather make it ugly.

Pimples are caused by hormonal disorders, stomach problems and lack of cleanliness of the skin. They appear on oily skin. Therefore, it is advisable not to apply cream or oil on the face. If you scratch a pimple with your fingers, it will leave a mark on the skin. It is beneficial to keep the bowels clean and not to have constipation during treatment for quick relief.

Pimples are the result of wrong food habits like irregular and inadequate meals, too much of starch, sugar and oil in food. If the digestive system does not function properly, the waste matter is not expelled from the body regularly in time which leads to formation of toxins in the blood. The skin makes an additional effort to expel the waste matter from the body but when this process is blocked, the consequence is acne or pimples.

Other Causes : Taking too much of tea, coffee, alcohol, tobacco and mental tension or menstrual irregularities.

To solve the problem of acne, take at first fruits for a week. Take fruits thrice a day. You may take grapes, pineapple, pomegranate, etc. and other fruits of the season. Bananas, fruits with citric acid, tinned fruits, etc. must not be taken. Take water with lemon juice without sugar or plain cold or hot water.

After eating fruit for a week, the patient should take a balanced diet. Every month, only fruit should be taken for three days.

The food which is rich in starch, protein or fat should be avoided. Also do not take meat, sugar, strong tea or coffee, pickles, refined or processed foods, soft drinks, ice-cream, white sugar and fine wheat flour or things made of them.

Treatment for Acne/Pimples : Two vitamins, niacin and Vitamin-A have been successfully used for its treatment.

Vitamin-E should be used so that acne or pimples do not leave any marks on the face or it should be used to erase them.

As far as local treatment is concerned, first of all wipe the skin with a piece of cloth dipped in hot water and then do it with cold water. Sun- bathing and open air are especially beneficial. Cleansing the affected parts with lemon juice has been noticed to have produced good results.

Mint : If the beauty of the face has been spoilt by pimples and marks, apply mint *chutney* on the face daily. It will restore the beauty of the face in a mouth.

Butter milk : Knead gram flour in butter milk and apply it as a face pack. It will cure pimples.

Black pepper : Grind 20 corns of black pepper in rose water and apply on the face before bed time and wash the following morning with hot water. It removes acne, pimples and wrinkles from the face and it begins to shine.

Tomato : Knead fuller's earth powder in tomato juice and make a paste. Use it on the face as a face pack for thirty minutes. Wash the face with hot water afterwards. Drink a glass of tomato juice daily. It will provide relief from pimples.

***Neem* :** *Neem* draws out oil from the skin. Wash the face with *neem* oil. Boil *neem* leaves in water and wash the face with it. If the skin is not oily, there are little chances of your getting pimples.

Almonds : (1) Rub almond oil on the face, especially around the eyes. You will not get wrinkles on the face.

(2) Grind two almonds, mix ½ tsp. of honey and 2 tsp. of lukewarm milk. Apply and rub it on the face and hands. Wash after twenty minutes. It will keep the skin soft.

Orange : Grind dry peel of oranges in water and rub the paste on the face, it will provide relief from acne.

Lemon : (1) Mix the juice of a lemon with a tsp. of fresh cream from hot milk and rub it on the face to get relief from pimples.

(2) Mix one part of lemon juice with four part of glycerine and rub it on the face. It will provide relief from acne and pimples and beautify the face. If you massage the entire body with it, the skin will become soft and smooth.

Mustard : Soak overnight 3 tsp. of mustard seeds. Use only as much water as can be absorbed by the seeds. Grind it the following morning and apply on the face. It will provide relief from pimples and acne.

Masoor daal **:** Soak *masoor daal* using only as much water as can be absorbed by the daal. Grind it and mix with a little milk. Use it as a face pack twice daily in the morning and evening. Grind nutmeg and black pepper in unboiled milk and apply on the face before bed time.

Caraway seeds : Grind 30 gms. of caraway seeds into a fine powder, mix with 25 gms. of curd, grind once again and apply on the acne and pimples before bed time. Wash the face with hot water the following morning. It will provide relief from acne and pimples.

Basil : Mix the juice of basil leaves with lemon juice in equal quantity and apply on the face. It will remove black spots, freckles, discolouration and pimples from the face. Three hours after this, apply the juice of basil leaves mixed with butter on the face.

Nutmeg : If you have black spots or pimples on the face, grind nutmeg in milk and apply the paste on the face. It will enhance the beauty of the face.

Water : Apply dew drops on the face in the morning. You will find dew drops on grass blades in the morning. It will provide relief from pimples.

Cumin seeds : Boil cumin seeds in water and wash the face with it. It will enhance the beauty of the face.

MEASLES

It is an eruptive, infectious disease of childhood. It spreads rapidly from one child to another. It is caused by a kind of virus which spreads from one person to another through breathing. Its major symptoms are sneezing by a child, running nose, red eyes and continuous dry cough with a grating sound. The child continues to cough for a long time. The temperature in fever rises to 103-104 degrees. Within three days of the development of fever there appear red eruptions on the face and chest. After the eruptions subside, the fever and cough also begin to subside.

Sometimes measles lead to pneumonia. Other children should not be allowed to come in contact with the child suffering from measles.

Cloves : Grind cloves and give it to the patient with honey. It will provide relief. It is based on experience.

***Amla* :** If there is burning and itching in measles boil dry *amlas* in water and wash the body with it when it is cold. It will provide relief from burning and itching.

Butter : If heat has been generated in the body because of measles, mix butter and sugar candy in equal quantity and lick 2 tsp. of it in the morning.

STAMMERING

An involuntary interruption or inability to utter a letter or syllable is called stammering. Because of defective control of muscles of the speech organs there is an obstruction in pronunciation of certain sounds or one utters them with repetition. There is a difficulty in the necessary movement of the tongue and lips and there is also a sound in the voice organs which leads to stammering. This difficulty is usually limited to words beginning with sounds produced by letters like p, b, t, d, g, k. Because of stammering one pronounces words like *kabooter* as *tabooter*. When these sounds occur in the middle of a word, there is no difficulty in pronouncing them. The person who stammers should be given regular practice in pronouncing them correctly and in controlling the breath. He should be taught to speak slowly and patiently.

***Amla* :** Chewing fresh *amla* is helpful in curing stammering of children. The tongue becomes thinner and the speech becomes clear. Mix a tsp. of *amla* powder with clarified butter and lick it daily. It will help overcome stammering.

Almonds : (1) Soak 12 almonds, peel them and grind them, mix with 31 gms. of butter and eat it regularly for a few months. It will provide relief from the problem of stammering.

(2) Grind finely an almond alongwith 10 corns of black peeper and sugar candy to taste and lick it.

Cinnamon : Chewing and sucking cinnamon provides relief from stammering. You may consult the writer of the present book for the treatment of stammering.

Dried dates : Clear Voice—Boil dried dates in milk and take it before bed time. Do not take water after it for two hours. It will clear the sharp and bad voice.

INSOMNIA

It is said that Henry IV about whom Shakespeare has written a play suffered from insomnia. He used to say, "Uneasy lies the head that wears a crown." The patients of insomnia can be divided into seven categories. The first and the largest category is of those who are victims of excessive insomnia—people who keep awake during the night because they do not get any sleep or if their sleep is disturbed because of some reason, they can't go back to sleep.

The second category belongs to those who drink; they take sleeping pills or use some other sedatives. Another category of people are those who have been suffering from sleep disorders from the very beginning. People in the fourth category suffer from acute depression or worries. The fifth category belongs to those who are somnolent—such people are sleepy most of the time. Whatever vocation they may be engaged in and whatever the time may be, they feel drowsy and want to go to sleep. The sleep of the people in the sixth category is continuously disturbed because of breathing problem. People in the seventh category indulge in sleep-walking, gritting teeth or moving the muscles during sleep.

Patients should not be encouraged to use sleeping pills. There are other ways to overcome sleep related problems, for example, the patient should be asked not to take coffee in the afternoon. He should be told to do exercise and go to sleep regularly. Besides, he should not go to sleep in the afternoon. He should learn to relax his muscles and do exercises which induce sleep and relaxation. —*Nyaya, Ajmer, 2.11.78*

It has been noticed during treatment that patients of insomnia do a lot of thinking while going to sleep, as a result, they do not get sleep. Homeopathic medicine Calcaria Carb-200 is effective in insomnia.

Remembering God : While going to sleep it is good to remember God. It will help you in getting good and refreshing sleep.

Massage : Massage the neck, backbone and shoulders well for ten minutes before going to sleep. Massage the backbone with both upward and downward movement of the hands. Take a little stroll before bed time. Go to bed after passing the urine. It induces good sleep. If you do not get sleep soon after you get into the bed, do not worry. It is a good time for rest. You will get good sleep after this rest.

Keep regular sleeping hours. If you do not go to sleep in time, it is difficult to get sleep later. When you feel sleepy, go to bed alone. While trying to sleep, concentrate on breathing and to reverse counting from 100 downwards.

Eating the following food items is sleep-inducing :

(1) Eating apple preserve, and

(2) Taking carrot juice.

Onion : If you do not get sleep, eat raw or cooked onions or roast onions in hot ashes and take four tsp. of its juice. It will induce good sleep.

Mustard oil : According to *Bhavprakash*, massaging the soles of the feet with mustard oil provides calmness and good sleep.

Aniseed : Boil 10 gms. of aniseed in ½ litre of water, when the water is reduced to one-fourth quantity, strain and mix with 250 ml. of milk and 15 gms. of clarified butter. Add sugar to taste and drink before bedtime.

Mango : Eat a mango at night followed by a glass of milk. It will induce good sleep.

Carrots : Carrots contain nutrients of a balanced diet. It cures insomnia. Take a glass of carrot juice daily.

Cabbage : It is good for patients of insomnia. Cabbage should be taken as a vegetable cooked in clarified butter.

Milk : (1) Eating 50 gms. of *mawa* or *khoya* made of milk before bedtime induces good sleep.

(2) Take a glass of milk mixed with sugar and a tsp. of clarified butter before bed time. It will quickly induce sleep.

Nutmeg : Grind it in water or clarified butter and apply on the eyelids. You will quickly go to sleep.

Tea : It is harmful for a patient of insomnia. Taking tea in the evening causes sleeplessness.

Coriander : Grind fresh coriander leaves and mix with sugar and water and drink. It induces good sleep and provides relief from headache.

Curd : Curd mixed with black pepper powder, aniseed and sugar is sleep-inducing.

Honey : Mix a tsp. each of lemon juice and honey and take it at bed-time. It facilitates sleep. If sleep is disturbed, again take the above mixture and it will induce sleep. If lemon is not available drink a glass of water with 2 tsp. honey mixed in it. It is helpful.

Water : If you are not getting sleep, put your feet and legs in warm water for ten minutes before going to bed. It is known as washing the feet with warm water. If you feel giddy, put a wet handkerchief on your head. In summer it is better to wash your feet with cold water before going to bed. You will get good sleep.

TOO MUCH OF SLEEP

Aniseed : A person who sleeps too much, feels drowsy and lethargic all the time, should boil 10 gms. of aniseed in ½ litre of water and when it is reduced to one-fourth, should mix a little salt and take it twice daily in the morning and evening for five days. It will check drowsiness.

Red chilli : Capsicum Anum is a homeopathic medicine made of red chillies. Take 5 drops of its mother tincture in a tsp. of water twice daily in the morning and evening. It will check sleepiness.

INSANITY

Pomegranate : Boil 15 gms. of fresh green pomegranate leaves alongwith 15 gms. of fresh roses in ½ litre of water. When it is reduced to one fourth, strain it and mix 20 gms. of clarified butter and drink everyday. It helps in relieving bouts of insanity.

Guava : Eat 250 gms. sweet Allahabadi guavas twice daily in the morning and at 5.00 p.m. in the afternoon for 6 weeks. For taste, you can add lemon juice, black pepper powder and salt to the guava. It will provide energy to muscles, remove heat from the body and cure insanity. Eating guava relieves tension and worries.

Caraway seeds : Half a tsp. of ground caraway seeds mixed with 4 ground large raisins and dissolved in half cup of water taken twice a day for a considerable period cures insanity.

Gram : If the insanity is due to *pitta*, soak 60 gms. of gram in water overnight. Grind it well the following morning with loaf sugar and mix in a glass of water and drink. It is beneficial. Soak gram *daal* in water. Drinking this water can also cure insanity.

Red chilli : A few drops of the homeopathic medicine *Capsicum Anum* mother tincture made of red chilli, given during the bout of insanity can bring the patient back to consciousness.

Black pepper : Grind 12 corns of black pepper with 3 gms. *brahmi* leaves, mix with half a glass of water, strain it and drink it twice daily.

Water-melon : If the insanity is due to the excess of

whimsical notions or apprehensions, mix a cup of water-melon juice with a cup of milk and 30 gms. of sugar candy, fill it in a plain bottle and hang it on a peg in the open in the moonlight overnight. The following morning give it to the patient to drink. Give it to him for 21 days. It will provide relief from whimsical or apprehensive behaviour.

SEXUAL DISEASES

In the absence of proper knowledge about sex, sexual diseases are increasing day by day. Sexual diseases start at the young age of 12 years and if untreated, at the peak of youth, that is, between 25-30 years of age, they cause extreme despair and a feeling of helplessness in the youth. This is the story of thousands of young men I have known personally. The basic cause of sexual diseases which I have discovered, while working in my hospital, is masturbation or onanism.

In adolescence they masturbate so much that the sexual organ becomes weak and as a result their married life is unhappy. They acquire the habit of masturbation from bad companions. They fantasize and fall a prey to nightfall or emission and wet their clothes with their semen. The semen gradually becomes thin and after marriage they find it difficult to retain and there is early ejaculation and finally they become impotent. The disease is usually kept secret and the patient does not discuss it with the physician but he takes medicines given by quacks and jugglers and is often trapped by sex advertisements and thus spoils his health and life becomes hell.

All medicines for providing sexual vigour or semen support contain intoxicants like marijuana, opium, etc. which lead to an increase in sexual indulgence, destroy the health and causes various diseases. Every young man should remember that artificial treatment will not bring results. Only the use of natural things can lead to good health and enable one to get rid of sexual diseases.

Having sexual relations outside marriage also causes sexual

diseases. It is a despicable disease. One who looks at the patient can judge that he is suffering from a sexual disease and he begins to hate him. The patient gradually falls into the pit of despair and his death is certain. To protect yourself and others from sexual diseases is a noble work and basic to the construction of a beautiful and healthy society. Acquaint yourself with the various sexual diseases described here, take proper treatment and get a new lease of life. Never commit a sexual indiscretion in future.

Syphilis : It is a contagious venereal disease which is caused by promiscuous sex. The germs of the disease enter the body through sexual intercourse. Consequently, the sinning man takes the disease to his wife also.

Its germs affect a person in two-three weeks. Wounds appear on the private parts of the man. These wounds are painless and there is no itching. Painless wounds are the first sign of syphilis. On the first appearance of such a wound, immediate treatment is essential. If treatment is not taken even then the wounds will disappear and the patient thinks he has recovered, but it is a wrong notion and the disease keeps developing inside the body and affects the whole body.

After two or three weeks the germs strike again. Swelling as is caused by the sting of an insect appears over the entire body. Even this swelling is painless and free from itching. It is the second stage of the disease. If treatment is taken even at this stage, the patient recovers. Gradually this swelling disappears. But after a month wounds appear on the chest and the patient remains constantly sick. It is the third and final stage of the disease. If treatment is taken even at this stage, the patient will recover.

But if treatment is not taken, the disease becomes permanent and then its treatment is not possible. In such a situation any important part of the patient's body may be damaged. The patient may suffer from heart problem, blindness, deafness, insanity, impotence or he may even die.

Women suffering from this disease develop black spots on

palms and soles. If an affected woman gives birth to a child, the germs do not spare even the young one. The blisters on the private parts of an infant give a clue to this disease.

Gonorrhoea : Pain on micturition and the secretion of pus from the private parts is an indication of gonorrhoea. The external sign of this disease in an infant delivered by an affected woman is redness of eyes.

Rativran : It is characterized by ulceration in the private parts and painful swelling in the thighs.

AIDS : AIDS (Acquired Immuno Deficiency Syndrome) has turned into a huge problem and is a terrible disease. In 99% cases the chief reason for AIDS is multiple sexual relationship.

AIDS spreads through the virus named H.I.V. The virus connects itself with lymphocyte alongwith T. lymphocyte and fits in as a socket and affects the activities of the cells and gradually destroys the immune system. The immune system does not get destroyed immediately but comes to nought gradually and finally the patient dies.

Sexual relationship with other than the life partner should be avoided. We should enlighten the people in this regard.

Genovenosis : It is characterized by constantly increasing pinkish growth in the private parts. If not treated properly, it can turn into cancer. In case there is painful swelling in the thighs, it can be lyphogranuloma venereal.

Venereal warts : The disease is characterized by slow but constant growth of pinkish warts in the private parts, which are painless. These are venereal warts.

Candidacies : If the skin in the private parts becomes scaly and cracks with a burning pain and there is a butter-like thick and white secretion from the private parts, the disease is known as candidacies. Diabetic patients can acquire it quickly through sexual intercourse. It can be treated by applying one per cent Jensen Violet.

Trichomoniasis : If there is a foul-swelling yellowish liquid secretion from the private parts and is accompanied by burning pain, the disease is known as Trichomoniasis.

Riviserp which is an itch of the generative organs causes very painful wounds in the private parts. Women are usually not aware of this disease. The wounds occur in the Vagina and the germs travel through intercourse to the body of the man. It is also known as Herpes Genitalis. The application of one per cent Gention Violet is useful in this disease also. It is available at Chemist shops.

To avoid sexual diseases it is advisable that the man should not have sexual relations with women other than his wife and should take pure and *satvik* food.

EMISSION

Semen is secreted in testicles. Two small bags of testicles are contained in the scrotum under the penis. Semen is constantly produced in them. Consequently, after a stage, there is no room to store extra semen. The testes, therefore, frequently emit the semen in order to make room for further fresh secretion. This process is known as Emission. In this way, emission is a natural activity. Even frequent emission does not cause any physical or mental loss. Mentioned below are the ways to check excessive emission :

Rose apple : Four gms. of the *churan* of the rose apple kernel taken with water morning and evening effectively checks excessive emission.

***Amla* :** (1) Taking one piece of the preserve of *amla* daily is beneficial in emission.

(2) Put 200 gms. of *amla* powder in a glass tumbler. Add 60 ml. of water to it and soak for 12 hours. Then strain it and add 1 gm. of turmeric powder and drink it. It is a good medicine for emission among youths. *Amla* revitalizes the semen.

Pomegranate : 5 gms. of the powder of pomegranate rind taken with water, in morning and evening, checks emission.

Banana : It is beneficial in emission and the related disease in which sperm and other vital hormones of the body emanate through urine. Take two bananas daily followed by a glass of hot milk for three months.

Garlic : Crush a clove of garlic with teeth and swallow. It will provide relief from emission. Take the clove of garlic after washing your hands and feet before bed-time.

Onion : Mix 10 ml. of the juice of white onions, 8 ml. of the juice of ginger, 5 gms. of honey and 3 gms. of clarified butter and take the mixture at bed-time. It checks emission.

Coriander : (1) Taking coriander powder and sugar candy with cool water provides relief from emission, burning micturition, gonorrhoea and syphilis. Those who want to be relieved of sexual urge should take 12 gms. of coriander powder mixed in water for a few days.

(2) Grind dry coriander seeds and sieve. Mix equal quantity of ground sugar. Take a spoonful of this powder on empty stomach in the morning with a glass of water kept overnight and do not eat or drink anything thereafter for an hour. Similarly take another dose in the evening at 5.00 with a glass of water kept since morning. If the patient suffers from constipation he should take 2 tsp. of *isabgol* husk with warm milk. It provides quick relief from emission.

Basil : Cut the roots of basil plant into small pieces and grind into powder. Take it mixed in water. It will be beneficial. Do not take hot milk at bedtime. Do not sleep on your back. Lie on one side. Wash your hands and face before going to bed. Get up early in the morning. Avoid bad company and bad habits. While taking your bath wash and clean the urinary organ well. The loss of semen leads to the weakening of body's resistance power. People suffering from emission should take lukewarm milk three hours before going to bed. Do not go to bed immediately after taking milk.

VIRILITY, EJACULATIO PRAECOX

Kateera **:** Soak half tsp. of pounded *kateera* in a glass of water overnight. Next morning mix sugar and eat it. It will rectify the consistency of semen.

Large raisins : Blood and Virility—Wash 60 gms. of large raisins and soak them in water. Eat them after twelve hours. Soaked raisins cure the ailments of the stomach and increase virility. The quantity can be gradually increased upto 200 gms. Eating 3-4 kg. of large raisins in this way in a year is very beneficial.

Rose apple : If the semen is thin and emission takes place at the slightest excitement, the patient should take 5 gms. of the *churan* of rose apple kernel every day in the evening with hot milk. It also increases virility.

Pear : It strengthens the semen.

Dried dates : Patients of Ejaculatio Praecox and those who have thin semen should eat 5 dried dates with their caps everyday in the morning.

Gram : (1) Eating roasted gram or soaked gram with equal quantity of almonds followed by milk thickens the semen.

(2) Eat soaked gram *daal* mixed with sugar at bed-time. Do not drink water after it. It strengthens the semen.

Almonds : Those who suffer from premature ejaculation at the beginning of intercourse should take 6 almonds, 6 black pepper corns, 2 gms. of dried ginger powder, sugar candy to taste followed by hot milk.

Ber **:** It strengthens the semen.

Cinnamon : Grind it fine. Take 4 gms. each in the morning and at bed-time with hot milk. It strengthens the semen and helps in the digestion of milk.

Isabgol **:** Mix 5 gms. each of *isabgol*, *khus-khus* syrup and sugar candy in water and drink it. It will check premature emission.

Basil : (1) A piece of the root of basil plant or its seeds taken with a betel leaf check premature ejaculation, enhance retentive power and strengthen the semen.

(2) Grind well 60 gms. of basil seeds and 75 gms. of sugar candy. Take 3 gms. of the powder daily with milk. It is beneficial in cases of enfeeblement.

(3) Taking 3 gms. of basil seeds or the *churan* of basil root with equal quantity of old jaggery followed by milk enhances virility. It strengthens and increases the semen.

IMPOTENCE—WAYS TO INCREASE VIRILITY

There are two main reasons of impotence—physical and mental. We will discuss physical impotence later. First we will take up mental reasons. In modern age, man leads stressful life. Sometimes even during sexual intercourse he is not free from useless anxieties. Under such circumstances, during sexual intercourse either full erection does not take place, or if it does take place it is only momentary and the man falls a prey to premature emission. For full strength in the penis it is essential that nerves, blood containing arteries and veins, hormones, muscles and the mind should all function in coordination.

Even with the malfunctioning of one part, the pleasure of intercourse goes away. It is also necessary that your partner is willing and ready for the intercourse. If you are ready and the partner is not prepared, you will not be able to enjoy it because the very word 'intercourse' implies full participation of both the partners. Besides mental preparedness of both the partners, proper atmosphere is also required. If there is no privacy or there is noise in the vicinity, the enjoyment of intercourse will not be complete.

Sometimes one indulges in sexual intercourse while in a state of stress or tension but he does not derive full satisfaction and this leads to another anxiety. He apprehends that he may have gone impotent. This unknown fear overtakes him and whenever he tries to indulge in sex he is afraid that he may not succeed. He is obsessed with these thoughts and consequently he suffers from premature emission or impotence. Because of these mental apprehensions, erectile dysfunctioning occurs. The constitution of body is the greatest wonder of nature. The penis contains two sponge like tubes. When we are prepared for intercourse, blood flows towards these tubes and they are filled with blood. As a result, the enlargement and erection of the penis takes place. But, for proper erection, it is necessary that the various related parts of the body function in coordination.

Mentioned above was the mental factor for impotence. Let us now discuss the physical factors. It has been generally observed that in 50% cases of impotence, there is a physical disablement such as illness, operation, accident, masturbation, the imbalance of hormones or the ill-effects of some medicines.

Diabetes : It is also one of the causes of impotence. Just as diabetes does not allow wounds in the feet to heal, affects kidneys and eyes, similarly, it causes impotence by affecting arteries and veins.

Diseases of the Heart and Arteries : When the walls of arteries harden and thicken, the flow of blood to the penis is reduced and it leads to impotence. The main causes for Athro Sclerosis are excess fat intake (clarified butter and oil) and lack of exercise. If the flow of blood has been reduced by any other reason (such as clogging of the arteries or defect in the arteries by birth), it can also lead to impotence.

If there is a defect in the veins, they cannot retain blood at the time of intercourse and erectile dysfunction takes place.

High blood pressure and the medicines taken for its treatment can also cause impotence.

Alcohol : It causes imbalance in the hormones. It can also affect the nerves but if it is checked at the right time, one can regain his potency.

Smoking and Tobacco : The use of tobacco in any form,

such as cigarette, *bidi, hukka* or *gutka* can cause obstruction in the flow of blood and lead to impotence.

Malfunctioning of Lever or Kidneys : Surgical operations on the parts below the abdomen (such as Cancer Operations) or in the prostate, rectum or bladder can sometimes cause a problem or obstruction in veins or arteries leading to impotence.

Damage to Spinal Cord : Impotence can also occur because of damage to the spinal cord.

Sometimes impotence occurs because of a reaction to some medicines. But such problems can be solved through proper treatment. Modern medical science has made great strides in this direction and impotence can be effectively treated.

It depends on the individual case as to which tests are needed but impotence can be diagnosed by proper investigations of the flow of blood, obstructions in the flow of blood, the clogging in the arteries, the shape and structure of the penis and mental impotence. The following things are important :

- ❖ Medical History
- ❖ The History of Sexual Activity
- ❖ General Physical Check-up
- ❖ Information about mental factors.
- ❖ Information about changes in the penis during sleep at night.
- ❖ Information about the flow of Blood.

Blood Investigations

- ❖ Blood sugar (For Diabetics)
- ❖ Investigations of the liver and kidneys
- ❖ Hormones

Treatment of Impotence : The treatment depends on what is the cause of impotence. After ascertaining the cause, the treatment can be given accordingly.

Smoking : Smoking by middle aged persons, eating fatty food can cause impotence.

Mango : Taking mango juice for two to three months

enhances virility and imparts strength to the body. The body gains weight. It strengthens the nervous system and sexual powers.

Coconut : It arouses sexual urge and thickening of the semen.

Carrots : It is an energy giving tonic for everybody. It thickens the semen. It is very effective in curing impotency. It is advisable to take carrot juice.

Onion : It arouses sexual urge and produces semen. It imparts energy to perform sexual act for a longer duration. A citizen of Iran, Yayah Ali Akbar Beg Noori married 168th time at the age of 88. The secret of his youth even at that age was that he ate 1 kg. of raw onions daily.

To gain virility and improve potency take onion juice mixed with honey. Mix the juice of white onions with honey, juice of ginger and clarified butter (6 gms. each) and lick it. Its use for a month makes an impotent man sexually virile and potent.

Pomegranate : Eating it daily keeps the stomach soft and strengthens the sexual organs.

Dried dates : In the case of premature emission and thinness of semen, the patient should eat dried dates every morning. Dried dates soaked in milk become more nutrient and energizing.

Cigarette : It adversely affects the sexual powers. Dr. Virendra Singh of Jaipur, Skin Specialist and Sexologist has proved that regular smoking of ten or more cigarettes for 6-12 months reduces sexual powers.

Smoking : According to world famous physician and sexologist Dr. Eishfield, excessive smoking adversely affects the sexual activity of men. He writes in his book *Sexual Pathology* that too much smoking can lead to impotency. It disturbs the hormonal functions in the human body.

Chilgoze **:** It is highly energizing. Eat 15 pieces every day.

Honey : Honey mixed with milk is beneficial in the case of premature emission or loss of semen. It is energizing and increases the semen. It is highly useful in imparting manly vigour and removing defects of semen.

Basil : Eating a piece of the basil root or ¼ tsp. of basil seeds with a betel leaf checks premature emission and increases the durability of the sexual act. It strengthens the semen.

Black gram : Eating a *laddoo* prepared from black gram followed by a glass of milk increases the potency and strengthens the semen and sexual power.

Milk : (1) Eat a banana with 10 gms. of clarified butter in the morning followed by a glass of milk. In the afternoon take two bananas, 30 gms. of dates and a spoonful of clarified butter followed by milk. It will strengthen the semen. Banana increases the virility.

(2) Mix the paste of 5 almonds in hot milk, put a tsp. of clarified butter in it. Drinking it after the sexual act provides energy. To cure impotence, add a pinch of saffron to milk during the winter season.

Garlic : (1) To cure impotence and gain virility take 50 gms. of garlic fried in clarified butter daily.

(2) Grind 200 gms. of garlic and mix in 600 gms. of honey. Store it in a bottle in a sack of wheat for a month. After a month take it out and take a dose of 15 gms. each in the morning and evening followed by hot milk. Follow this routine for a month. It will be highly beneficial. It will give energy and increase virility.

(3) Munch five cloves of garlic in the morning and drink a glass of milk afterwards. Follow this routine throughout the winter.

Wheat : (1) Soak wheat in water for twelve hours. Then tie up the soaked wheat in a thick piece of cloth and after thirty six hours wheat sprouts will be ready. Eat the sprouts without cooking. For taste, you can add jaggery or raisins. These sprouts are full of Vitamin E. It is beneficial in impotence and infertility. It is full of health and energy. For fertility eat wheat sprouts for three days and then black gram sprouts for the next three days. Follow this routine alternately for a few months.

(2) Soak 100 gms. of wheat in water overnight. In the morning grind it on a stone slab and liquefy by adding water. For taste add some sugar. A week's treatment will cure the problem of secretion of semen with urine.

Pistachio **:** It is full of Vitamin E which is helpful in the increased production of semen.

HEART DISEASES

Women live longer than men. Usually they don't have the problem of clogged arteries before the age of 50. Even after 50, the incidence of heart disease is lower in women than in men. The tender and compassionate nature of women does not let their coronary arteries harden up. Men should also cultivate the virtue of compassion and their face should reflect love and tenderness instead of demonic anger.

Men are destroying themselves with over-ambition, tension and a lifestyle which is full of challenges. Even at an early age of 30-40 a man's coronary arteries are clogged. The lack of exercise and physical labour results in his becoming idle and obese. The misleading slogan of "eat, drink and be merry" has led him to smoking and drinking and the path of self-destruction. He likes good taste and rich food only. The lack of fiber in his diet affects his health. Fried food items and sweets harden up our coronary arteries. We should not allow our tongue and teeth to become agents of death.

For keeping the heart healthy reduce the intake of clarified butter, sugar and salt after the age of 40. Games, exercise and walking should be a part of the daily routine. When tired and exhausted men reach home, women can make them feel relaxed with a welcoming smile and fresh nutritious food. It is the way to spare the heart from diseases.

Do you know ?

(1) A man's heart constantly works for him without rest from the time he is unborn till the moment of his death. The

muscles of heart are stronger than the muscles of a wrestler.

(2) The average weight of heart is 250-300 gms. In size it is not larger than two fists.

(3) It beats for one lac four thousand times every day and pumps 7200 litres of blood daily. If it stops beating for three minutes, a man dies. The total length of arteries and veins in the human body is 60,000 miles.

(4) Heart diseases are more common in people who suffer from mental tension and stress—people like leaders, wealthy men, officers, advocates, doctors and city dwellers. The possibility of heart disease among the uneducated is higher by 40 to 50 per cent than in the educated people. With the spread of education the incidence of heart disease gets reduced.

(5) Heart disease is not so common in women, postmen, those who do regular exercise and villagers.

(6) Heart disease is closely related to obesity, diabetes, smoking, drinking, fatty food and strain and stress of modern lifestyle. Smoking increases the heart palpitation. 51% men and 54% women who smoke possibly develop heart problem.

The Possible Symptoms of Heart Disease

(1) The use of more than two pillows for better sleep.

(2) To have cramps in the feet thrice or more than three times in a week.

(3) To have a wheezing breath in the cold, especially after exercise and physical labour.

(4) Coughing again and again while in the room.

(5) Increased palpitation on walking.

(6) Finding the routine exercises difficult to perform suddenly. If a person sweats profusely while sitting (usually during heart attack or immediately before it one sweats profusely), it is a symptom of heart disease. When these symptoms appear consult a heart specialist.

(7) The following are the symptoms of the acute stage of heart disease :
   (a) Terrible pain on the left side of the chest.
   (b) Difficulty in breathing
   (c) Unconsciousness
   (d) Restlessness
   (e) During heart attack there is a sudden pain in the chest and the man feels exhausted, sits down and becomes unconscious. All this happens in a few minutes.

(8) Symptoms of the Chronic stage of heart disease :
   (a) Shortness of breath after even a little exertion.
   (b) To feel compelled to go to sleep while sitting at night.
   (c) Swelling in the feet.
   (d) Physical weakness.
   (e) Enlargement of the liver and dropsy.

(9) Can the heart disease be prevented? The answer is "yes."
   (a) If the food taken is regular, limited and balanced. Never over- eat.
   (b) If you do not eat the yellow portion of the egg and limit the intake of *halwa*, butter and salt. Eat vegetarian food.
   (c) If you can check your obesity by regular exercise.
   (d) If you stop smoking.
   (e) If you can keep away from anxieties and stress and strain of today's life.
   (f) If you can regularise your ways and coordinate between your work, rest and exercise.

People who are compassionate towards the poor and the sorrow-stricken are free from heart ailments.

One can save oneself from heart-attack by hard work. One who walks for 16 kms. does not develop heart problem. Hard work between 35 and 40 years of age also reduces the possibility of heart disease.

Heart patients should stop taking solid food, items hard to

digest, strong spices, fried things, tea, coffee, tobacco, alcohol, clarified butter and butter.

In heart diseases, proper diet acts like a medicine. Such patients should take low calorie food. The diet should be free from saturated fat and cholesterol. The cooking medium should be sunflower oil or saffola. The patient should be given only fat-free milk. Cheese, vegetables, fruits, etc. can be included in the diet.

A heart patient should take complete rest. He should not move about and pass the stool and urine in bed. The patient should not climb stairs and should not run.

PALPITATION

Onion : Those who have quickened action of the heart in which it beats too rapidly, to safeguard against heart disease, should eat a raw onion daily with their meals. It will normalize the heart beat. The research conducted by the Neurological Department of George Medical College, Lucknow shows that the right quantity of onion juice is helpful in the flow of blood and protects one from several heart-related problems.

Grapes : If the patient lives only on grapes, he can quickly recover from heart-disease. The palpitation can be normalised with the help of grape-juice. The patient gets quick relief and the emergency situation is averted.

***Pistachio*:** It normalizes the palpitation. Soak five pistachios overnight. In the morning discard the water and eat the pistachios followed by two draughts of water.

Milk : Drink a glass of fresh milk with sugar candy or honey added according to taste and 10 soaked and ground raisins every-day for 40 days. It will normalize the palpitation and provide strength to the body.

Carrots : Carrots are beneficial for patients who have rapid palpitation and thick blood.

Coriander : If it seems the palpitation is rapid, the patient should take a tsp. of coriander powder mixed with equal quantity of sugar candy with cool water.

Pomegranate : Grind 50 fresh leaves of pomegranate, dissolve the paste in water and strain and drink it. Take it twice daily in the morning and evening. It will be beneficial.

ENERGIZERS FOR HEART

Lemon : It has special qualities which are beneficial for the heart. Its regular use makes the arteries flexible and soft and removes their hardness. Lemon is, therefore, very useful in treating high blood pressure. It keeps the heart strong till old age and there is no fear of heart failure. When there is restlessness and burning in the chest squeeze a lemon in cool water and drink. It will be very beneficial.

Pineapple : It contains several juices which act as digestive enzymes. Its use helps one to get rid of common heart ailments. Its sour elements expel the unnecessary substances from the body and give extra energy to the body.

Apple : Eating fresh apples or apple preserve for 15-20 days is a good treatment for debility and sinking of heart.

***Phalsa* :** (1) For heart patients *phalsa* juice mixed with water, ginger powder and sugar is beneficial.

(2) Grind 10 gms. of ripe *phalse*, 5 corns of black pepper and a pinch of rock salt. Mix a cup of water and a little lemon juice. Take this treatment regularly for a few days. It is good for a weak heart and palpitation. It increases the semen and give strength. It also has a cooling effect.

Asafoetida : It gives strength to a weak heart. It also prevents blood from clogging and facilitates blood circulation.

Jaggery : It is beneficial because it strengthens the heart and the body.

Ginger : For a weak heart, palpitation and heart-sinking it is beneficial to take daily a cup of the concoction prepared by boiling ginger powder with a pinch of salt.

Brinjals, black gram and *lychee* are energizers for the heart.

Black gram : Soak overnight 50 gms. of black gram. Next morning grind it, mix half glass of milk and sugar to taste and drink. It gives strength to the heart.

Honey : Honey is the best tonic for heart. The heart gains as much strength from it as a horse gets from eating green millet. The use of honey alleviates the swelling in the muscles of the heart. It not only provides energy to a diseased heart but also makes a healthy heart stronger and averts heart-failure.

When it is feared that the patient will fall unconscious because of the lack of glycogen in the blood, the patient can be saved by giving him honey at this crucial time. Honey provides instant energy and stimulation. When the heart begins to beat faster because of cold or weakness and there is a feeling of suffocation, 2 tsp. of honey at that time would give new energy. If the heart is weak, there is a feeling of sinking of heart or some such trouble a tsp. of honey in hot water will be beneficial. A tsp. of honey daily strengthens the heart. A tsp. of honey contains 100 calories.

Basil : During winter, grind together 7 basil leaves, 4 corns of black pepper and four almonds and mix in water. Take it daily. It strengthens the heart and cures various ailments of the heart.

***Mausambi*:** Its juice strengthens and stimulates the digestive system, brain and the liver. Its regular use makes the arteries soft and flexible. The cholesterol which accumulates in the arteries and which obstructs the blood-flow and causes heart-failure, is expelled from the body and the body gains fresh blood, vitamins and the necessary minerals. Mausambi is the best fruit which strengthens the cardiac system, arteries and capillaries.

Mustard oil : The food cooked in mustard oil may cause heart disease. This information was given by renowned heart specialist Dr. A. Olson in an interview. Dr. Olson says that the acid present in mustard oil turns into cholesterol when food is cooked in this oil and thus it leads to heart problem.

Amla **:** (1) Taking *amla* powder with cow milk cures heart problems.

(2) Mix *amla* powder with equal quantity of sugar candy powder. A tsp. of this powder taken with water daily cures heart diseases.

(3) When you are half through your meal, take 35 ml. of *amla* juice in half a glass of water followed by the remaining meal. Follow this routine for 21 days. It will strengthen the heart and the brain and improve the health.

Chaulai **:** Its juice is beneficial for heart patients. It can also be eaten in the form of cooked vegetable.

Arbi **:** 25 gms. of *arbi* taken as a cooked vegetable daily is beneficial to heart patients.

Gram : It is beneficial to heart patients.

Lychee **:** It gives energy to the heart.

Curd : It is said to be very useful in high blood pressure, kidney problems and obesity. According to Prof. George Shemon of America curd is good for the prevention of heart disease. It curbs that fatal substance called Cholesterol in the blood which clogs the arteries and obstructs the flow of blood. Curd is, therefore highly beneficial.

PAIN IN THE HEART

Banana : Eating two bananas with 15 gms. of honey is beneficial to patients who develop pain in the heart.

Caraway seeds : Caraway seeds relieve pain and stimulate the heart.

Grapes : Grape juice provides quick relief from pain in the heart.

HEART BURN

Tamarind : The juice of ripe tamarind mixed with sugar candy provides relief from heart-burn.

Potato : Potato juice is beneficial in heart-burn. If it is difficult to extract its juice, crush a piece of raw potato with your teeth and gulp the juice and spit out the pulp. It provides relief from heart-burn. It has a cooling effect in heart-burn.

Garlic : When it seems that the heart is going to fail, immediately chew 4-5 cloves of garlic. It will prevent heart failure. Subsequently the patient should be given garlic boiled in milk. Garlic expels gas from the stomach and thus relieves the heart from pressure and provides strength to the heart. Garlic is very effective in reducing cholesterol level and thus preventing heart disease. It does not allow the arteries to harden. It even expels the clogged cholesterol from hardened arteries and makes them normal again. Garlic is a preventive medicine.

Cloves : Grind three cloves in cool water and mix in a cup of water, add sugar candy to taste. Take this prescription twice, daily. It will provide relief from heart-burn.

ANGINA

Severe pain in the chest arising from an inadequate blood supply to the heart is called angina.

Any obstruction in the artery obstructs the blood-supply to the heart and it calls for the open heart surgery, in which the veins from the hands and feet are taken out and transplanted in the heart. However, even after this kind of major operation, some patients re-develop the same problem, resulting in another operation. The second operation becomes more risky and complicated as compared to the first. In this context, Dr. Manubhai Kothari of Mumbai has come up with a new experiment.

The Experiment and its method : Take one medium size **bottle gourd** and grate it after washing and without peeling it off. Add 8 basil leaves and 6 mint leaves. Grind the mixture and strain through muslin cloth. Prepare the juice of approximately 150 gms. Add equal quantity of plain water, powder of 4 grains of black pepper and 1 gram rock salt. This becomes one dose for an adult. This diluted juice should be taken 45 minutes after each meal, i.e. after breakfast, lunch and dinner, thrice a day. Everytime fresh juice should be prepared. To begin with, the quantity of the juice could be less, but it should be increased gradually as one becomes used to it.

The bottle gourd juice cures all the digestive problems, cleanses the stomach and extracts the mucous out. In the first 4 days, one might experience rumbling sounds in the stomach. It could cause loose motions also. This is a natural phenomena and one should not get scared. It automatically stops, once the stomach is cleansed.

While experimenting with the above prescription, it is necessary to walk a bit, even if it is for 10-12 steps to begin with, however the distance should be gradually increased to 10 km. The patients afflicted with angina could experiment with this recipe.

The patients experimenting with this recipe are requested to share their experiences with the author, to help encourage the treatment through food.

HEADACHE

Headache can be felt in the forehead, temples, the back or the upper part of the head or anywhere in the head. Headache may just be a symptom in a few diseases as fever, flue, small-pox, etc. Sometimes headache is not the result of any other disease. Such a headache in itself is a disease.

Causes of Headache : (1) When blood accumulates in the veins of the brain, it causes headache. (2) Constant headache can be a symptom of increased blood pressure. When the blood pressure is low it also leads to headache, because the brain does not get enough blood-oxygen. (3) During fever headache is caused by the expansion of brain arteries. (4) Headache can be caused by the dilatation of arteries in the head because of extreme anger or severe mental tension. Anxiety causes tension in the muscles of the face and head leading to occipital headache. (5) Lack of sleep or sleeplessness causes headache. (6) Toxins in the blood because of urine problems, constipation, dyspepsia, etc. also cause headache. (7) Ulcer, swelling, etc. in the brain causes pain. (8) Weak eyesight, diseases of the eyes, ears, nose, throat, teeth cause headache. (9) Some medicines or introduction of some adverse external protein can cause headache. (10) Constant chronic headache is caused by acidity and diseases of the eyes.

Treatment : Headache can be cured by treating the patient taking into account the cause, nature, condition and the humour of the body. First of all try to remove the cause.

The headache caused by catarrh, over-exertion, mental tension, keeping awake at night and accumulation of blood does not require any treatment. Reduction in the use of oily food leads to whiteness in the eyes and dryness in the brain. It causes headache. In this type of headache the use of milk, butter, clarified butter, *halwa* and such other oily foods is beneficial. The headache caused by physical and mental exertion requires rest. Sleep provides relief in all types of headache. If sleeplessness, constipation, acidity, gas, etc., are responsible for headache, take the treatment prescribed in the present book. Given below are the details of food items which can treat headache :

Water : If headache is due to catarrh, immersing the feet in hot water provides relief. If the cause is high blood pressure put wet pads on the head.

Eucalyptus oil : It is available at Chemists shops. If the cause of the headache is catarrh apply the oil on the forehead and smell it. It provides quick relief.

Lemon : Lemon tea is useful in headache. Crush lemon tree leaves and smell them. The patients who have chronic headache should take this treatment. It provides a lasting cure. Smelling dry lemon tree leaves and drinking tea prepared from those leaves has a miraculous effect.

—Vaidya Sushil Kumar, Jaipur

Apple : Taking a salted apple every day for 20-25 days is beneficial in headache. Take one or two salted apples in the morning on empty stomach. Chew the apples well. Follow it with hot water or hot milk.

Coconut : Eating dry coconut with sugar candy before sunrise provides relief from headache.

Carrots : Mixed juice of carrots (185 gms), beetroot (150 gms.), cucumber (125 gms) cures headache.

Tamarind : The headache caused by heat can be cured by taking tamarind water twice a day. Soak the tamarind in water, mash it and mix sugar before taking it.

***Phalsa* :** *Phalsa* syrup is beneficial in the headache caused by the disorders of bile.

Onion : If the headache is because of hot wind and heat-stroke, apply onion paste to soles of the feet, which is in fact beneficial in all types of headache. Smelling at cut onions also relieves headache.

Garlic : In all types of headache including the migraine, application of onion paste on the temples, provides relief. The application of garlic paste may cause blisters on the skin. It is therefore, advisable to be cautious while applying it. After a little while the spot should be cleaned and washed. If it is migraine, put two drops of garlic juice in the nostril of the side affected by migraine. Eat two cloves of garlic every two hours followed by a glass of water.

Black gram : Prepare a paste from soaked black gram and apply it on the forehead. It will provide relief from the headache caused by heat.

Clarified butter : Massaging the soles with clarified butter at bed-time provides relief from the headache which develops all of a sudden.

Mustard oil : If the headache is due to cold, taking bath with cold water or walking in cold winds, apply mustard oil in the nose, ears, navel and soles. It will provide relief.

Tea : When the headache is due to cold and is marked with sneezing and a running nose, taking tea is beneficial.

Aniseed : Chew a tsp. of aniseed followed by milk. It is beneficial in headache. Chronic patients should use it daily.

Wheat : Sprinkle wheat flour on live coal and smell at it and take the fumes in. It cures the headache caused by cold, catarrh, chronic coryza, sinusitis and the one which grows severe with the rising sun. Smell and inhale the fumes of wheat flour for three minutes everyday in the morning and evening. Old headache considered to be incurable will get cured.

***Gwar-patha* :** Take some pulp out of *gwar-patha*, knead it with wheat flour and prepare two *batis*. After baking them, press them with your hand and immerse in clarified butter. Eat them early in the morning before sunrise and go to sleep. This treatment if taken for 5-7 days will cure any type of chronic headache.

Gram : Eating *motichur laddoos* with clarified butter and black pepper will cure the headache caused by weakness.

Cloves : (1) Application of the paste of cloves on the forehead provides immediate relief from headache. Clove-oil is also effective.

(2) Boil five cloves in a cup of water. When the water is reduced to half, mix sugar and drink it. Take it twice for few days in the evening and before bed-time to get relief from headache.

Asafoetida : If the headache is due to cold, dissolve some asafoetida in water and apply it on the forehead.

Black pepper : Burn a corn of black pepper attached to a needle and inhale its fumes. It also cures the headache caused by wind.

Mint leaves : Application of the paste of mint leaves on the forehead and temples is beneficial in headache.

Coriander—Headache caused by heat : (1) Soak overnight coriander seeds (10 gms.), dry *amla* (5 gms.) in a glass of water in an earthen pot. In the morning mash the ingredients well and strain and drink after adding sugar candy to it. It is beneficial in headache.

(2) Application of coriander paste to the forehead is especially beneficial in headache caused by the excess of bile.

Salt : (1) Put a pinch of salt on the tongue, follow it with a glass of water after ten minutes; it will provide unexpectedly great relief.

(2) Mix 3 gms. of salt in 62 ml. of water and smell it. It provides relief from headache.

Ginger : If the headache or migraine has been caused by an upset stomach, prepare ginger paste, mix a little water and apply it to the painful spot.

Initially, it will cause a little burning. But the pain will subside soon. The above experience was narrated by Dr. B.L. Jain of the Botany Department, University of Rajasthan, Jaipur. If the headache is due to catarrh, grind the ginger in a little water and then apply to the forehead.

Cardamom : Application of cardamom paste on the forehead relieves headache.

Cassia leaves : Application of slightly warm paste of cassia leaves on the forehead will provide relief from all types of headache caused by cold or heat.

Nutmeg : If the headache is due to cold, apply nutmeg paste on the forehead. It will be beneficial.

Cinnamon : Application of cinnamon paste on the forehead and temples will be beneficial.

Basil Leaves : Take powder of basil leaves dried in the shade. Smell it for sometime. It will provide relief from pain and pacify the excitement of madness. The juice of basil leaves mixed with lemon juice in equal quantity relieves headache.

Water-melon : Take a glass of water-melon juice mixed with sugar candy in the morning. It is beneficial if the headache has been caused by heat.

Clay : Putting wet clay pads on the forehead provides relief from headache.

MIGRAINE, HEMICRANIA

This is a severe type of pain and is usually on one side of the head. The youth between the age of 14-22, especially young women, suffer from it and in several cases it goes upto middle age. It starts from one part of the head and spreads to one side or occasionally to the whole of the head and neck. It is a disease inherited from paternal side.

Causes : Emotionally charged mental state, physical exhaustion, anger, anxiety, tired eyes, food-related disorders, dyspepsia, allergic condition, etc. are the main reason for migraine.

Symptoms : As you rise from bed in the morning you feel giddy. There is darkness before the eyes or flashes seem to appear in the dark. Besides, the patient feels sickness of stomach and nausea. After it, there is a piercing pain in the temples. The pain starts in the opposite side of the eye which is overtaken by darkness. The pain spreads gradually and gains severity. Movement, light and noise make it worse. Vomiting provides some relief. After 2-4 hours the pain begins to subside. The pupil of the eye on the painful side often gets dilated. At last, the patient falls asleep and when he wakes up the pain has disappeared. In this way, it takes a day for the patient to recover. The patient's face appears to be dull. The bouts of pain last for years. After middle age, their frequency is reduced and gradually it stops. Migraine gains or loses severity with the cycle of the sun.

Treatment : Often wrapping the head, using cold pads, retiring to a quiet place and sleep provide relief. Giving a massage to the head quickly reduces the pain. The patient should avoid over-exertion, constipation and dyspepsia. Items fried in oil or clarified butter, meat, tea and coffee should not be consumed. Do not over-strain the eyes. Regular use of the following food items is beneficial for patients of migraine :

Grapes : A cup of grape juice taken in the morning before sunrise provides relief from migraine.

Milk : If the severity of the pain in migraine increases or lessens with the cycle of the sun, take *jalebis* with hot milk or *rabri* before sunrise.

Curd : (1) If the pain increases with the ascendancy of the Sun, eat rice and curd in the morning before sunrise.

(2) You could take curd, rice and sugar candy—all mixed together. It provides relief from migraine.

Clarified butter : If the pain increases or decreases with sunrise, smell clarified butter in the morning and evening. If the headache is because of heat then massage the head with normal clarified butter, otherwise use hot clarified butter.

Asafoetida : Dissolve asafoetida in water and smell it. It relieves pain. Also apply the solution on the forehead.

Salt : Mix half tsp. of salt with half tsp. of honey and lick it. It will provide great relief.

Dried ginger powder : Grind dry ginger in a little water and heat it. Apply it on the forehead. Also smell it. It will provide relief from migraine and other types of headache.

Mustard oil : It is beneficial in migraine. Put 8 drops of mustard oil in the nostril on the painful side and inhale the smell. It relieves migraine. Do it for five days.

Jaggery : If the pain increases or decreases with sunrise, eat 12 gms. of jaggery with 6 gms. of clarified butter.

Black pepper : Chew 12 gms. of black pepper and follow it with 30 gms. of clarified butter. It will provide relief from migraine.

Honey : (1) If the pain begins with sunrise and subsides with sunset, put a drop of honey in the nostril other than the one on the painful side. It will relieve pain.

(2) In case there is a sudden spurt in the migraine pain, the patient vomits, feels relieved after vomiting and it happens frequently, take 2 tsp. of honey with meals regularly. It will check the pain. If the pain develops suddenly, taking 2 tsp. of honey on that occasion will provide relief.

Basil Leaves : Licking powder of basil leaves with honey in the morning and evening is beneficial.

Sugar : If the pain increases with sunrise and decreases with sunset, stand infront of the sun at sunrise and drink 150 ml. of water slowly with 60 gms. of sugar dissolved in it. It will provide relief from migraine.

HYPERTENSION

The heart circulates the blood in the body through arteries. When the blood gets into the arteries, their walls also help in blood circulation by exerting pressure. Sometimes the walls of the arteries thicken up and lose their flexibility. Under such circumstances, the heart has to work harder and use greater force for proper circulation of blood. This extra force or pressure is known as blood pressure.

Hazards : High Blood Pressure can lead to heart attack, arresting of heart, paralysis of the brain, failure of kidneys, problems of eyesight and even death.

Symptoms of High Blood Pressure : Headache, nausea, giddiness, exhaustion, general body-aches and pain, increase in palpitation of the heart and pulse rate. Often blood pressure in itself does not show any symptoms. If one develops blood pressure after the age of 35, he should go in for regular periodical check-up of heart, eyes and kidneys, especially if there is a family history of the disease or if you are living in stressful conditions.

Causes of Hypertension : Disorders of kidneys, emotional stress, hectic lifestyle, loss of peace, hereditary factors, obesity, excessive smoking and drinking.

Patients of Hypertension should take proper treatment as suggested by the Physician and should take regular diet and exercise. The diet should not only be regular, but also controlled and with limited salt intake. Yogic exercises, e.g., *shavasan* is beneficial. Avoid stress, anger and anxiety and lead a peaceful life. After the age of 35 one should have periodical check-up of blood pressure. Sleep for full nine hours during the night. Have a nap during the day after lunch. To lower high blood pressure limit the intake of salt from ½ gm. to 1 gm. in a day. Take liquid diet every seventh day. Take plenty of water. Do not take intoxicants. Dr. Evans in his book *Cardiology* says that medical treatment in common blood pressure cases has proved to be unsuccessful. Dr. James C. Thomson in his book *High and Low Blood Pressure* has written that the gains of medicines in high blood pressure are not verifiable. At best, they are tentative. According to homeopathic system, it is not the disease but the patient who needs to be treated.

Treatment

The patients of high blood pressure should keep the bowels clear. For this, they should regularly take lemon water, *isabgol*, *amla* juice, *moong* sprouts, *moth*, gram and salad.

Fasting : It is good for patients of high blood pressure. They should observe fast once a week. During the fast, they should take fruit and vegetable juices.

Tobacco, coffee, tea, non-vegetarian food are harmful to patients of high blood pressure.

***Shavasana*:** Lie down straight on your back. Keep the arms and legs straight and the heels joined. Close the eyes and let the body relax completely. Stop thinking. Concentrate on breathing and breathe slowly. It will give peace and relaxation within five minutes.

Bottle gourd : Half cup of the juice of bottle gourd mixed with a little water should be taken thrice a day regularly. It will be beneficial.

Banana : The juice of the stem of banana plant (½ cup) taken twice a day cures high blood pressure.

Lemon : It has special virtues which can strengthen the heart. Its regular use makes the blood arteries flexible and soft and they lose their stiffness. Therefore, lemon is beneficial for patients of hypertension. The heart remains strong till old age and there is no risk for heart failure. Whatever the type of blood pressure, taking lemon in water several times a day is useful. In the morning, it is beneficial to take lemon juice in warm water.

Apple : It is beneficial to eat apples in hypertension.

Papaya : It is highly effective in hypertension. The patient should eat a papaya everyday in the morning. It will soon check hypertension.

Mint leaves : (1) It regulates both high and low blood pressures. Therefore, it should be used every day in the form of *chutney* or juice. The patients should use mint leaves without adding salt or sugar.

(2) The patients of hypotension can take mint leaves *chutney* with rock salt, black pepper and raisins.

Tomato : It lowers high blood pressure.

***Amla* :** Taking *amla* preserve every day in the morning is useful in hypertension and heat of the blood. It is a blood purifier.

Long cucumber : It has a great deal of potassium. Its juice is useful both in low and high blood pressures.

Potato : It normalises the blood pressure. Boil potatoes in water with salt added to it. Because of the peel the potatoes do not absorb much salt. But it becomes a tasty food item. It is useful in high blood pressure. Potatoes contain magnesium which lowers the blood pressure.

***Petha* :** It prevents hypertension.

***Arbi* :** It lowers high blood pressure.

***Tinda* :** It lowers high blood pressure. It is diuretic.

Rice : Prolonged use of rice reduces cholesterol levels. It also cures hypertension.

Massage : Regular massage of the body improves the condition of a hypertensive patient.

Water-melon : The juice of the seeds of water-melon contains an element known as *Kurkur bosytrine* which broadens the capillaries. It acts on the kidneys and thereby lowers the blood pressure. Grind water-melon seeds and put them in a cup of boiling water and let them soak for an hour. Then stir, strain and drink. Take four doses daily. Water-melon juice is also beneficial.

Carrots : 310 ml. of carrot juice mixed with 125 ml. of spinach juice daily cures the problem of blood pressure.

Garlic : 6 drops of garlic juice mixed in 3 tsp. of water taken four times every day is useful. Eating raw garlic after meals cures hypertension. The juice of garlic leaves mixed in water is more useful. As you get better, reduce the dose.

***Chaulai* :** Its juice is beneficial for hypertensive patients. It can also be eaten as a cooked vegetable.

Butter milk : It is beneficial in both high and low blood pressures.

Henna : Hypertensive patients get relief by the periodic application of henna paste on hands and feet.

Honey : It has a favourable effect on the human body, reduces the hyper activity of arteries and lowers blood pressure.

***Neem* :** 25 ml. of *neem* juice every morning is beneficial for patients of hypertension.

***Triphala* :** Soak overnight 2 tsp. of *triphala* powder and 30 gms. of sugar candy in a clay pot. Strain it the following morning and drink. It is beneficial in hypertension.

***Rudraksha* :** Wearing five-faced *rudraksha* is beneficial.

The use of butter milk with asafoetida is beneficial in *Hypotension.* Mix a small quantity of salt also.

INFLUENZA

In short, influenza is known as flu. It causes sudden fever and pain in the muscles of the body. Usually it occurs in winter or spring season. The cause of its spread is infection. There is often some or the other change in its symptoms. It starts with a sudden feeling of cold and shivering and then fever develops which goes upto 102-103°C.

Alongwith fever, the other symptoms are sneezing, bodyache, headache, dry cough, indigestion, and debility. The fever begins to subside after two days. It spreads rapidly from one person to another.

Safety Measures : Avoid going to crowded places. Do not over tire yourself. Gargling daily with saline warm water helps. Give massage to your body with mustard oil and also smell at it every morning.

Treatment : Taking lemon juice in warm water protects the various limbs of the body; it helps in fractured bones, pain, coryza, catarrh and flue. Lemon water should be taken frequently in the above problems.

Orange : It is believed in some parts of the world that during the spread or epidemic of influenza eating oranges protects you from the disease. Even if you are suffering from flue, oranges are beneficial.

Caraway seeds : (1) Boil 3 gms. each of caraway seeds and cinnamon in water and drink.

(2) Boil 12 gms. of caraway seeds in two cups of water, when it is reduced to half, let it cool, then strain and drink. Taking it this way four times a day cures influenza.

Ginger : Boil together 3 gms. of ginger or dried ginger powder, 7 basil leaves, 7 corns of black pepper, a bit of cinnamon in ¼ litre of water. Add sugar and take it hot. It cures influenza, coryza, cough and headache. It also provides preventive treatment during the spread of influenza.

Cinnamon : Boil 5 gms. of cinnamon, two cloves and ¼ tsp. of dried ginger powder in 1 litre of water. When it is reduced to one-fourth strain it and make three doses. Take them thrice during the day.

Long pepper : Boil two long pepper or ¼ tsp. of dried ginger powder in milk and drink.

Honey : Mix 2 tsp. of honey and ½ tsp. of baking powder in 250 ml. of hot milk. Take it twice in the morning and evening. It will cause a lot of sweating. Do not expose yourself to wind while you are sweating. It will cure catarrh and influenza. Honey kills the germs of cough and reduces the severity of fever and headache.

Basil : Boil 12 gms. of basil leaves in $\frac{1}{4}$ litre of water. When it is reduced to one-fourth, strain it, and add rock salt and drink it hot.

Do not eat cereals till the fever lasts. Tea, milk, *mausambi* juice and large raisins can be taken.

DIAGNOSIS OF DISEASES THROUGH NAILS

Nails are a good mirror of your health and beauty. Nails in themselves are colourless. They are transparent. In a healthy condition the pink colour of the nails is because of the healthy blood underneath. If you press hard a nail, it appears milky because the blood underneath is displaced.

Those who suffer from anemia or are living under stress or are suffering from some disease do not have pink nails. Their nails appear white or yellow. Smooth, spotless nails without lines are an indication of good health and beauty.

Heart Disease : Twisted or bent nails at the edges are an indication of heart or lung disease.

Ligamentary Weakness : Twisted and *tawa*-shaped nails are caused by anemia. Crooked protuberance on the nails impedes the growth of nails. Its main cause is general debility and ligamentary weakness. Sometimes a child is born with fingers without nails. Such a child is usually bald by birth.

Brittle Nails : In case the nails are broken, torn, or detached from the skin, immerse your fingers in warm mustard oil for ten minutes. Then rub them gently so that blood circulation is restored in them. If the nails are very brittle, take calcium-rich food and milk in plenty. Milk is beneficial in all types of the problems of the nails.

To make the nails bright and strong, massage them with olive oil. If olive oil mixed with alum salt is applied on the nails regularly, the nails will not be brittle.

Coconut or turpentine oil also helps in maintaining the natural brightness and strength of the nails. Similarly, glycerine removes the dryness of the nails and they look beautiful.

Lack of Calcium : Roughness, lack of smoothness and nails-biting by children are an indication of lack of calcium. The nails do not grow to full size because of the lack of calcium and they lose their brightness. If the nail grows, it remains very thin and soft. —*Nyaya, 16-12-1979*

Lemon : (1) If the nails do not grow in the normal way, immerse your fingers in hot lemon water for five minutes, then immediately put them in cold water. It will facilitate the growth of the nails.

(2) Application of lemon juice on the nails makes them very strong and beautiful. Wash the fingers and rub the nails with lemon and let them dry up.

(3) After squeezing the juice out of lemons, rub the nails with the rind. It will brighten them.

ENURESIS

***Amla* :** Mix 1 gm. of *amla* powder, 1 gm. of the powder of black cumin seeds and two gms. sugar candy powder. Take this dose with cool water. It will cure the problem of wetting of the bed during sleep.

Rose apple : Grind the kernel of the rose apple and take a tsp. of the powder with water. It will provide relief from the problem of bed-wetting.

Dried dates : If the child wets the bed during sleep, give him dried dates to eat at night daily for a few days. If old men suffer from incontinence and pass urine too frequently, they should also be given dried dates to eat. Eat dried dates twice during the day and at night follow them with milk.

Walnut : Children who are in the habit of bed-wetting should be given 2 walnuts and 20 raisins daily for two weeks. It will give relief from the problem of bed-wetting.

Sesame seeds : Take 50 gms. black sesame seeds, 25 gms. caraway seeds and 100 gms. jaggery and mix. Take 8 gms. each in the morning and evening regularly. It will cure incontinence and bed-wetting during sleep.

Honey : The use of honey before bed-time by children checks the involuntary discharge of urine during sleep.

Large raisins : Taking 5 large raisins before bed-time provides relief from the problem of bed-wetting.

CHECKING OF ABORTION

The premature expulsion from the womb of a foetus less than three months old is known as miscarriage. During miscarriage there is a great deal of blood-loss. If it is only bleeding, it is called threatened abortion. If bleeding is accompanied by pain the possibility of miscarriage increases.

Causes : New diseases, e.g., pneumonia, infections; old diseases, e.g.; syphilis, T.B., Uterus-related problem, a blow in the stomach, fear, mental shock, impeded growth of the foetus in the womb, tendency towards miscarriage, lack of Vitamin E, and some problem of internal glands can lead to abortion. If a woman has had two abortions, there is a possibility of the third abortion also. After three abortions, the fourth abortion is almost a certainty. Women suffering from T.B. and who are delicate and soft by nature, usually fall a victim to miscarriage.

Auxiliary Methods to check Abortion : Women who are prone to abortion should not lift heavy things. They should take rest. During miscarriage and stomachache one should take complete rest. During miscarriage, the bed on the side of the feet should be raised a little. Any problem which can be solved be taken care of. The husband should not sleep with the wife at this time. The mother should take care of her health. Only a healthy mother can deliver a healthy child.

Treatment : Frequent abortions require precautionary treatment from the very first month of conception. If a women has a tendency towards abortion, she should be cautious even before conception and should take food items which are preventive.

Vitamin E : It is found in wheat and other sprouts, in tender leaves and milk. It is essential for conceiving and healthy pregnancy. The lack of Vitamin E destroys the duct which produces sperms in men, consequently men lose the vital power to produce a child. Men who do not have sperm in their semen, should take Vitamin E regularly. The following items contain Vitamin E in plenty :

Wheat : Soak wheat for 12 hours in water, then tie it up in a wet coarse cloth for 24 hours. You will get wheat sprouts. These sprouts are full of Vitamin E. For detailed information on this topic please consult the book *Bhojan ke Dwara Chikitsa.*

Pistachio **:** It also contains Vitamin E. Vitamin E checks abortion.

Pomegranate : Grind 100 gms. of fresh pomegranate leaves, mix water, strain and drink. Also apply it on the belly. It will check abortion.

Water chestnut : In case the uterus does not sustain pregnancy because of weakness and miscarriage takes place, eating fresh chestnuts for a few weeks will be beneficial.

Gram : If it is feared that miscarriage will take place, drink the concoction of gram.

Alum salt : ¼ tsp. of alum salt in a cup of milk and diluted with water checks the possibility of abortion. In case of pain and bleeding during abortion take the above dose every two hours.

Aniseed : In case miscarriage takes place again and again, (1) take 62 gms. of aniseed, 31 gms. of *gulkund* made from roses, grind them together, mix water and drink it once every day to check the possibility of miscarriage.

(2) Take aniseed water during the entire period of pregnancy.

Barley : Take 12 gms. of barley flour, sieve it, and mix it with 12 gms. each of ground black sesame seeds and sugar and add honey to it and lick on it. It will be beneficial.

LEUCORRHOEA

Leucorrhoea is a discharge of white yellowish or greenish mucus from the vagina. It is not a disease in itself but is the result of several other diseases.

To cure leucorrhoea it is necessary to keep good health and complete hygiene, take light exercise, avoid constipation, give up tea, fine flour and fried food and take instead, fruits and vegetables. Also avoid sexual activity, anger, sorrow, anxiety and other emotional perturbations.

Treatment through food

Amla **:** (1) 3 gms. of *amla* powder mixed with 6 gms. of honey taken once daily for 30 days is beneficial. Do not take sour things.

(2) 20 ml. of *amla* juice mixed with honey taken for a months is also beneficial.

Banana : (1) Eating a banana followed by milk and honey is beneficial for the patients of leucorrhoea.

(2) Take a banana with 8 gms. of clarified butter for eight days. *Kheer* prepared with banana and milk is also useful.

(3) Eat raw bananas cooked as a vegetable.

(4) Eat two bananas with 3 tsp. of honey.

Phalsa **:** It is beneficial for patients of leucorrhoea.

Tomato : Tomatoes are useful in leucorrhoea.

Water chestnut : *Halwa* prepared with the flour of water chestnuts cures leucorrhoea and its *rotis* cure bleeding.

Pomegranate : Grind 30 fresh green pomegranate leaves with ten corns of black pepper, mix in half a glass of water, strain and drink it twice daily in the morning and evening.

Gram : Grind roasted gram and mix with sugar. Eat it daily followed by milk with clarified butter. It will cure leucorrhoea.

Rice : Soak half cup of rice in one cup of water. Roast 100 gms. of *moong* on a hot plate, grind and store in a bottle. Dissolve a tsp. of this powder in a cup of soaked rice water and drink it once daily. It is beneficial in leucorrhoea.

Masoor daal **:** Grind *masoor daal* and prepare *churma.* It is beneficial for the patients of leucorrhoea.

Alum salt : ¼ tsp. of alum salt powder taken with water thrice daily cures both leucorrhoea and bleeding. Dissolve alum salt in water and wash the vagina deep inside with a syringe daily in the morning and evening.

Cumin seeds : Roast cumin seeds and eat them with sugar to get relief from leucorrhoea.

Dried ginger powder : Boil 10 gms. of dried ginger powder in ¼ litre of water. When it is reduced to one fourth strain it and drink. Take this treatment for three weeks.

Basil : (1) Taking the juice of basil leaves mixed with equal quantity of honey, mornings and evenings, is beneficial.

(2) Take the juice of basil leaves mixed with cow milk. The juice of basil leaves mixed with sugar candy cures leucorrhoea.

HYSTERIA

Symptoms : There are no definite symptoms to diagnose hysteria. Its main symptom, however, is an attack of unconsciousness or fainting. It can last from 24 to 48 hours. Some people have frequent and repeated attacks. During the attack, the patient becomes senseless. Greater attention should be paid during an attack to the mental and nervous symptoms shown by the patient. Women are more prone to this disease.

Causes : Usually such young women who know that there are sympathetic people around who will take care of them are prone to this disease. If the feeling that 'they will get sympathy' is not there, the disease will also go. The chief reasons behind hysteria are hatred between husband and wife, sexual dissatisfaction, anxiety, fear, grief, family troubles, sudden mental shock, pregnancy, problems pertaining to menstrual cycle, dyspepsia, etc.

Treatment : The treatment should be for the root-cause of the problem. The attack of unconsciousness should not be a cause for worry. The patient should go for a walk every day in the open air. Fruits should form a major part of the meals. The patient should read good literature. It is more beneficial to take honey than sugar in milk. From the point of view of treatment, as soon as the patient experiences an attack, make him lie down in a comfortable position and sprinkle cool water on his face. At this time, make him smell things with a sharp smell and rub such things around his nose.

The above mentioned treatment is instantaneous but the lasting cure can be provided only by tackling the mental problems which have caused the disease. For this, it is necessary to establish a close rapport with the patient at the mental level and tackle him affectionately looking into his problems and solving them. This is the only effective treatment. If the root-cause of anxiety is removed, the disease will automatically disappear. Often the severity of the disease diminishes with age. Sometimes, sexual satisfaction one gets after marriage relieves the problem.

The patients of hysteria should take nutritious food, milk, clarified butter, rice, grape juice, apples, pomegranate, oranges, etc.

Hysteria is a mental disease, it should, therefore, be treated at the psychological level. Neglect in proper treatment can be fatal at a later stage.

Lemon : Take lemon, salt, cumin seeds, roasted asafoetida and mint leaves in warm water at least for a month.

Pomegranate : Boil 15 gms. each of pomegranate leaves and fresh rose petals in ½ litre of water. When it is reduced to one-fourth quantity, strain it and add 20 gms. clarified butter. Taking it regularly is beneficial for patients of hysteria.

Milk : Take fresh unboiled milk with sugar candy or honey and 10 raisins soaked in water daily in the morning for 40 days. It will be beneficial.

Onion : Making women patients of hysteria smell onion juice on fainting brings them back to consciousness.

Garlic : A few drops of garlic juice put in the nostrils brings the patient back to consciousness.

Asafoetida : Making the patient smell asafoetida brings him back to consciousness.

Red chilli : There is a homeopathic medicine made from red chillies known as Capsicum Annum. A few drops in the nostrils of the patient bring him back to consciousness.

LACTATION

Mother's milk is the best diet for infants. Infants should be fed milk in a cheerful mood. If they are fed in an angry mood, it causes stomach-ache and spasms. Mother's milk should not be fed to infants for the first three days after birth. If the mother's milk is not sufficient and the infant is not fully fed, the following lactogenic food items will be helpful :

Grapes : Grapes are lactogenic. They stimulate milk production. Mothers with insufficient milk should eat grapes.

Papaya : Raw papaya eaten as a cooked vegetable increases lactation. Ripe papaya is also lactogenic.

Carrots : Lactating mothers should take carrot-juice to stimulate milk production.

Onion : Raw onions eaten in sufficient quantity with meals stimulate better milk production.

Peas : Peas are also lactogenic.

Black gram : Eating black gram *daal* with clarified butter stimulates milk production.

Gram : Soak overnight 62 gms. of *Kabuli* gram in milk. Strain the milk next morning. Eat the gram by chewing them thoroughly followed by hot milk in which the gram had been soaked. It is lactogenic.

Castor oil : Massaging the breasts with castor oil for a month or two stimulates better milk production.

Cumin seeds : Roast cumin seeds and eat them with sugar. It increases milk production.

CRACKED LIPS

Groundnut oil : Take ¼ tsp. of groundnut oil in your palm and using this oil massage your lips with your index finger before taking your bath. It is beneficial for lips.

Mustard oil : Applying mustard oil on the navel before bedtime prevents the cracking of lips.

***Mausambi* :** Apply *mausambi* juice on the lips thrice daily. The lips will lose their blackishness and they will regain their natural pink colour. —*Care 31-10-1998*

Clarified butter : Add a little salt to clarified butter and apply it on the lips and navel. It will prevent the cracking of lips.

Almonds : Taking 5 almonds daily prevents the chapping of lips.

Glycerine : It is beneficial to apply glycerine on the lips.

FRACTURING OF BONES

Tomato : The use of tomatoes makes the bones strong. Tomatoes contain more calcium than other fruits and vegetables.

Garlic : Garlic is useful if the bone has been fractured and displaced. In fact, it is useful in any disease of the bones.

Wheat : Licking 12 gms. of the ash of burnt wheat with honey is helpful in joining broken bones.

Turmeric : Regular use of turmeric powder is beneficial in the case of fractured bones.

Honey : Regular use of honey helps in joining the broken bones. For further details please read the present writer's book *Shaktivardhak Bhojan.*

PAIN IN THE JOINTS OF BONES

***Kateera* :** It is a kind of gum and is available at grocer's shop. Pound it to make smaller pieces. When soaked, it absorbs a lot of water and swells a great deal. It should, therefore, be soaked in a bigger vessel. Soak half tsp. in a glass of water overnight. It will get swelled up by the morning. Mix sugar with it and eat it. It cures pain in the joints of bones.

Black gram : Boil 5 tsp. of black gram *daal* in a glass of water. When it is reduced to half, strain and drink. Take it twice daily. It relieves pain in the joints of bones.

NEUROPATHY

Symptoms of neuropathy : Lack of patience, insomnia, exhaustion, lack of concentration on work, despair, negative thoughts and lack of confidence are the main symptoms of neuropathy.

Causes : The disease is caused by economic loss, anxiety, grief, tensions in the family, over-exertion, masturbation, over-indulgence in sexuality and unbalanced diet.

Treatment : Neuropathy makes the digestive system weak. It is, therefore, advisable not to take meat. Go for a walk daily, take exercise and nutritious diet, especially protein, B-Complex and Phosphorus rich food. For details of diet please read the present author's book *Shaktivardhak Bhojan*.

RHEUMATISM

Rheumatism is an acute disease with painful inflammation and swelling of one or more joints and often with endocarditis. In the initial stages pain is accompanied by fever. When it gets chronic, fever disappears. But the patient is unable to walk or move about. There is greater pain in the feet. It is marked by foul smelling sweat, thirst and headache. There are several types of Rheumatism. It includes stiffness of the chin, losing the sense of taste, stiffness of the neck, the lumber region and hands and feet and paralysis. When the joints become deformed and twisted, it is called Rheumatoid Arthritis. When you get up in the morning, you feel stiffness in the fingers and hands.

Causes : It is caused by dirty teeth, anxiety, lack of peace, fear, grief, working or doing business against your wishes, getting drenched with water, feeling cold, syphilis, gonorrhoea, over-indulgence in sex, eating stale and fried food, keeping awake during nights, restraining the natural pressures, getting hurt, excessive bleeding, over-exertion, obesity, etc.

It is also caused by the deposition of uric acid in the joints, accumulation of toxins, T.B., germs of various diseases and the lack of minerals and vitamins in the diet.

Treatment : Fomentation, massage, sweating and steam-bath are beneficial in Rheumatism. It is sometimes accompanied by pneumonia. In such a case, treatment should be taken for pneumonia first. The diet should include blood-purifying food items. If the cause of rheumatism is gonorrhoea, it should be treated first.

Do not take food items like rice which cause the morbid affection of the windy humour. The use of sprouts is beneficial in rheumatism.

Relief through Spiritualism : Instead of considering the disease a result of one's bad deeds, if one thinks positively and finds solace in religion or spiritualism, the patient could get a great relief. American scientists have found in their study that the patients afflicted with the incurable disease of rheumatoid arthritis get a great relief from pain and get better if they take shelter in religion and spiritualism. Faith is the great healer.

The patients having positive thinking and faith in religion or spiritualism have been seen having effective control over their pain. The negative thinking to consider the disease a divine wrath aggravates the pain. Besides, the patients who have faith in the God and who love their life get social support also.

Points to Remember : Usually a patient of rheumatism suffers from constipation. He should solve the problem of constipation. The use of castor oil is beneficial.

The patient should avoid oil, butter, clarified butter, fried food, etc. Similarly, lady's finger, jack fruit and rice should not be taken. The use of wheat, millet and barley is beneficial.

The use of very hot spices and chillies is not advisable. The medium hot spices like dried ginger, black pepper, cumin seeds, cloves and cinnamon are useful.

The patient should keep away from curd, pickles, tamarind, vinegar and other sour items. If the patient likes, he can take a little quantity of butter-milk but it should not be sour.

Lemon : Take a lemon in cool or warm water as per the weather daily. You can add honey to it for taste, that is, you can take lemon water with honey.

The juice of green leafy vegetables like spinach, *bathua* and *chaulai* is harmful.

Walnuts, *petha*, bottle gourd, cucumber and melons are beneficial.

Wheat : The juice of wheat grass is very beneficial in this disease. To get more information on this topic please go through the present author's book *Bhojan ke Dwara Chikitsa*.

Patients of rheumatism can get relief by taking only juice of sour fruits and vegetables like bottle gourd and tomatoes.

Curd : It is harmful for patients of rheumatism. Only a little quantity of fresh sweet curd can be taken.

Meat and *masoor daal* is also harmful in rheumatism.

Calcium, Phosphorous : If the bones have been affected by rheumatism, calcium and phosphorous-rich food should be taken. For details, please go through the present writer's book *Shaktivardhak Bhojan*.

The use of sprouts is also beneficial in rheumatism.

Tomato : Tomatoes are good for the patients of gout.

Mint leaves : Boil 50 fresh mint leaves or ½ tsp. of the powder of dry mint leaves in a glass of water. When it is reduced to half of its quantity, strain it and drink it twice daily in the morning and evening. It is beneficial in gout pains.

Carrots : Its juice cures rheumatism and gout. The juice of carrots, cucumber and beetroot taken together in equal quantity are much more beneficial. If all the three vegetables are not available at the same time, take the juice of whatever is available.

Potato : Keep a little potato in each of the two pockets of your *pyjama* or pants. It will protect from rheumatism. Eating potatoes is beneficial. Application of the paste of raw potatoes on the toe reduces gout pain. Also apply the paste on the painful spot.

Onion : (1) Onions are beneficial in neuropathy and rheumatism. In Greece, homeopathic doctors used to permit patients to eat cooked onions (*Refer Unan's Therapeutic Hints by Dr. K. D. Goswami*).

(2) Mix onion juice and mustard oil in equal quantity. Massaging the painful parts with it proves to be beneficial.

Garlic : Daily massage with garlic oil is helpful. Clean and peel a big pod of garlic, cut it in two piece and boil in milk. If the *Kheer* prepared in the above manner is taken for six weeks, it can cure gout. Take it at bed-time. You can prepare this *kheer* by grinding the garlic and boiling it in milk. The quantity should be increased gradually. Sour food, sweets should be avoided. Ground garlic mixed with sesame oil is also beneficial for the patients of rheumatism. It is a tried formula.

—*Vaidyaraj Pt. Ram Narain Sharma*

Half tsp. of garlic juice mixed with a tsp. of hot clarified butter taken twice a day in the morning and evening is also beneficial in rheumatism.

Salt : (1) The patients of gout have increased levels of acid in the blood. Salt further increases these levels. It is, therefore, not advisable for patients of gout to take salt.

(2) Foment the swollen parts with heated salt or sand tied in a piece of cloth.

Fenugreek : (1) It is a useful vegetable for patients of rheumatism and gout. Roast fenugreek seeds in clarified butter, grind and make small *laddoos*. Eat them twice a day in the morning and evening for ten days. It is beneficial in rheumatism. Candy prepared with jaggery and fenugreek seeds cures gout.

(2) Soak overnight four tsp. of fenugreek seeds in a glass of water. Strain in the morning and heat the water slightly and drink. It is quite beneficial. Eat the soaked, fenugreek seeds after sprouting them.

Ginger : Its juice mixed with clarified butter or honey is useful in rheumatism, backache and pain in the thighs.

Boil 10 gms. of dried ginger powder in 100 ml. of water. Let it cool down, mix sugar or honey and drink it. It is a tried formula. Grind dried ginger and *harad* in equal quantity and take this powder twice daily with hot water. It helps in joint pains.

Honey : Patients of rheumatism should take sufficient honey over a prolonged period. It is highly beneficial. It reduces pain in the joints.

Basil : Boil basil leaves in water and steam the painful parts of the body and also wash them with the hot water. Eat basil leaves with black pepper and cow's clarified butter. It is beneficial in rheumatism.

Asgandh : Grind *asgandh* and loaf sugar in equal quantity and mix them. Take 3 tsp. of it every morning and evening with hot milk.

Sand : Heat some sand on a hot plate, put it in a piece of cloth and foment the painful parts.

Beet root : Its use provides relief from pain in the joints.

Long cucumber : If rheumatism is because of the presence of excess uric acid in the body, taking half glass each of mixed carrot and cucumber juice is beneficial. Its juice is also useful.

Kulthi : Boil 60 gms. of *kulthi* in 1 litre water. When it is reduced to one-fourth, mix a little rock salt and half tsp. of dried ginger powder and drink it. It is beneficial.

Sesame seeds : Massaging the body with sesame oil provides relief from rheumatism.

If body-ache has been caused by gout or windy humour, pound and grind 20 gms. dried ginger, 40 gms. walnut kernel and 160 gms. black sesame seeds and mix with 100 gms. of jaggery. Take 20 gms., twice a day, with hot water.

Caraway seeds : (1) Applying the extract or oil of caraway seeds on the joints provides relief from pain. Boil caraway seeds in sesame oil to prepare the oil.

(2) Mix salt to taste with a tsp. of ground caraway seeds and take it with hot water in the morning on empty stomach.

Tea : It increases the level of uric acid in the urine. It leads to pain in the joints and weight gain. Therefore, rheumatic patients should not take tea.

PAIN IN THE KNEES

Cucumber : Take plenty of cucumber with meals and also garlic to get relief from pain in the knees.

Potato : In case of synovitis of the knee, swelling and pain in the joint, grind raw potatoes and apply the paste on the knee. It is highly beneficial.

***Moth* :** Any type of pain in the knees whether new or old can be cured by eating *laddoos* prepared with kidney beans.

The above treatment has been tried by my mother Smt. Bhauri Devi. To prepare *laddoos* you need kidney beans, sugar and clarified butter in equal quantity. Roast the kidney beans in hot sand. Grind and sieve them. Roast the flour in clarified butter. Add sugar syrup to it and prepare *laddoos*. Eat two *laddoos* at a time in the morning on empty stomach. While taking this treatment, do not consume oil, pungent spices and sour food. It will provide relief from pain.

PAIN IN THE THIGHS

Ginger : To get relief from pain in the thighs take a tsp. of ginger juice with half tsp. of clarified butter in the morning on empty stomach.

BACKACHE

Lemon : Mix a tsp. each of lemon and garlic juice and 2 tsp. of water and drink it. Take it twice, daily in the morning and evening. It will provide relief from backache.

—*Dr. Poddar Jalendra Maharathi*

Fenugreek : Taken as a vegetable is beneficial in backache.

***Sahjan* :** Eaten as a vegetable, flowers or pods of *sahjan* are beneficial in backache.

Dried dates : It is beneficial in backache.

Potato : Prepare a poultice from raw potatoes and apply it on the back to get relief from pain.

Wheat : Licking 12 gms. of the ash of burnt wheat and an equal quantity of honey provides relief from backache and pain in the joints. Bake a *roti* of wheat flour on one side. On the other side apply sesame oil and tie the *roti* on the painful part. It will provide relief from pain.

Castor oil : Grind 5 kernels of the seeds of castor plant in milk and drink it. It is beneficial in backache.

Nutmeg : Grind nutmeg in water and heat it well in sesame oil. Let it cool down for sometime. Massage the back with it. It is beneficial and relieves pain.

Ginger : Take ginger juice mixed with clarified butter. It will provide relief from backache.

DENTAL DISEASES

People these days develop problems of the teeth at an early age. The main reason is that man in the initial stages used to eat hard substances which gave ample exercise to the teeth and gums. But today's man eats easy to chew, cooked and soft food which does not require much dental exercise. These days the use of sugar, biscuits, toffees, chocolate, ice-cream and ice has increased a great deal. These items are responsible to some extent, for the decay of the teeth.

The teeth of some children are very weak and yellowish from childhood. The chief reason is that during pregnancy the mother did not get full nutrition. Pregnant women should take milk and calcium regularly. The child will have healthy teeth.

For the protection of the teeth it is essential to clean them well after eating something so that the food particles trapped between the teeth can be cleaned out. Meals should be taken with patience and after thorough chewing.

The health of the body depends upon the health of the teeth. Bad teeth are due to a bad stomach. Anyone suffering from constipation, dyspepsia and lack of appetite affects the teeth. It is, therefore, advisable to take treatment for the stomach while taking treatment for the teeth. Sugar and sweet food are harmful for the teeth. Sugar sticks to the teeth and leads to decay. Therefore, whenever you eat something rub the gums and teeth with your finger properly and rinse your mouth. A little precaution will keep the teeth healthy for life.

Milk : Milk (except for mother's milk) spoils the teeth of children at an early stage. The diseases of the teeth begin at an early age. Children who are not fed on mother's milk during infancy develop more dental problems than those who have been suckled by their mother.

Children subsisting on milk diet get used to sugar because of its presence in milk. Therefore, they prefer taking only sweet things till the age of three-four years but this habit, later, spoils their teeth. If proper care is taken in this direction from the very beginning, the child will have strong teeth and they will not get spoilt easily. Actually, the sugar mixed in milk is responsible for the infection in teeth in children. Therefore, they should be given milk without sugar.

Lemon : Squeeze a lemon in fresh water and rinse your mouth. It will provide relief to the teeth. Rub the skin of the lemon on the teeth. It will make them clean, beautiful and bright.

CLEANLINESS OF THE TEETH

Given below are the recipes for homemade tooth powders which not only clean the teeth but also cure some general ailments of the teeth.

Cassia leaves : Grind dry cassia leaves into a fine powder. Use this powder to massage your teeth with, every third day. It will make the teeth bright.

Turmeric : Mix 5 gms. of roasted alum salt with 50 gms. of turmeric powder. Massage your gums and teeth with it daily. It will prevent bleeding and toothache. It will cleanse the teeth and make them strong.

Lemon : Grind dry lemon rind into a fine powder and use it as a tooth-powder. It will cleanse the teeth and check foul breath. Massage the teeth with lemon juice mixed with salt and mustard oil daily. It will make them strong and cure almost all dental ailments. Cleaning the teeth with small pieces of lemon rind will make them bright. If the teeth have become yellowish and the gums have become weak and blackish, apply on the gums and teeth half tsp. of salt mixed with 5 drops of lemon juice in the morning before cleaning the teeth. Rinse after five minutes. Then clean the teeth with tooth paste or tooth-powder. Do not brush the gums because brushing makes them loose. To make the teeth bright apply glycerine and then rinse with warm water.

***Neem* :** Burn a dry branch of *neem* with leaves and turn it into ash. Grind it and use it as a tooth powder. For taste and fragrance, add cloves, mint and salt. It cures pyorrhoea and makes the teeth strong. It is beneficial to brush the teeth with a neem stick.

—Shri Bhojraj Bapna

***Harad* :** Massaging the teeth with *harad* powder cleanses them.

Almonds : (1) Burn almond shells and keep them under cover for a day. Grind them the following day and mix one-fifth part of alum salt with it and again grind. Used as a tooth powder, it will cleanse the teeth and cure almost all dental ailments.

(2) Prepare a tooth powder with the ash of burnt almond shells and add rock salt to it. It will make the teeth strong. You can add rock salt and alum salt to the ash of almond shells.

STRONG TEETH

The fact that the teeth should remain strong throughout life comes next to cleanliness of teeth. They should not get loose, there should be no cavities and no decay. Eating pungent, hot and cold things like ice-cream or taking only soft things weakens the roots of the teeth. It is, therefore, necessary to be careful about diet. If the teeth are loose and painful, do not get them extracted unless there is no alternative. If there is a cavity, get it filled. Munching on roasted gram gives an exercise to the teeth which makes them strong. Given below are the recipes for making the teeth strong :

Mango : Chew fresh mango leaves and spit them out. After a few days, the teeth will become strong. The gums will stop bleeding. Burn dry mango leaves and turn them into ash. Use it as a tooth powder. It will strengthen the teeth and brighten them. It will also check bleeding.

Sesame seeds : Eat 32 gms. of black sesame seeds by chewing them well in the morning on empty stomach after brushing your teeth. Do not mix jaggery, sugar or any thing else with it. Follow it with a glass of cool water. If you wish you can repeat it in the evening also. It makes the teeth strong.

Turmeric : Mix turmeric powder, salt and mustard oil and massage the gums and teeth.

Clay : If the teeth are loose and it appears that they will fall out, application of wet clay (black or red) on the gums in the morning and evening daily will strengthen the teeth.

Tomato : Eating tomatoes strengthens the teeth.

Carrots : Carrot juice if taken daily prevents the diseases of the teeth and gums. The roots of the teeth get strengthened.

Salt : Massaging the teeth with fine rock salt brightens them.

TEETHING

Butter milk : If a child is given butter milk to drink daily he will have no teething problems and it will protect him from dental diseases.

Honey : Massaging the gums with honey will facilitate teething without any trouble.

Basil : The application of the juice of basil leaves mixed with honey on the gums of the child and making him lick a little of it makes dentition easy. The powder of basil leaves given with pomegranate syrup also makes teething easy.

Grapes : During teething period, give the child 2 tsp. of grape juice daily. It helps in early teething. The child also gets healthy. For the sake of taste, honey can be added to grape juice.

Aniseed : If teething is painful and the child cries, boil 2 tsp. of aniseed in a cup of water and give him a tsp. of it four times a day. It will facilitate teething.

SENSITIVITY TO WATER

Gallnut : It is available at a grocer's shop. Grind it into a fine powder. Using it as a tooth powder and massaging the gums with it daily solves the problem of the sensitivity of the teeth to water. The teeth become strong and the bleeding stops. It also checks general dental diseases.

BLEEDING TEETH

Tomato : Tomato juice taken thrice a day is beneficial and checks bleeding.

TARTISH TEETH

Almonds : In case the teeth become tartish, eat almonds. It will remove tartishness of the teeth.

Salt : If the teeth have become sour because of eating sour things, rub a little salt on the teeth.

TOOTHACHE

Onion : In case of toothache or pain in the gums, place a piece of onion at the exact spot. It will bring relief.

Bottle gourd : Grind 24 gms. of bottle gourd and 20 gms. of garlic and boil in 1 litre of water. When it is reduced to half kg. strain it and rinse the mouth with it. It will provide relief from pain.

Mustard oil : Inhaling the smell of mustard oil from one nostril once or twice relieves pain. Mix mustard oil, lemon juice and rock salt and massage the gums. It will clean the teeth, relieve the pain and tighten the gums. Mix very finely ground and sieved salt with mustard oil. Massaging the gums and teeth with it will provide relief from toothache and swelling of gums.

Asafoetida : If the teeth are rotten and painful, place a little asafoetida beneath the painful ones. It will relieve pain. There is a homeopathic medicine made from asafoetida. Paint the rotten teeth with its mother tincture. It will provide relief from pain. Soak a cotton swab in warm asafoetida water and put it between the painful teeth. It relieves pain.

Salt : Gargling with warm saline water is beneficial in toothache. Massaging the teeth and gums with finely ground rock salt is quite helpful. If tooth is loose, mix black salt in sesame oil and massage the gums.

Caraway seeds : Every type of toothache can be relieved by the use of caraway seeds. Put some seeds on live coal and smoke the painful teeth. Put a tsp. each of salt and ground caraway seeds in boiling water and keep it covered for some time. When the water is warm, take a draught and retain it in the mouth for some time, then spit out. Repeat it several times. There should be a gap of two hours between the smoking of the teeth and rinsing of the mouth. Repeat both the activities thrice a day to get relief from toothache.

Basil Leaves : Grind black pepper in the juice of basil leaves and make small globules. Putting it between the painful teeth provides relief from pain.

Mint leaves : Massaging the gums with the paste of mint leaves provides relief from toothache.

Water : First retain for two minutes hot water in the mouth. Follow it with very cold water for two minutes. Repeat it four times. Start with hot water and finish with cold water. Continue with it at least three days even after the pain is over. For swollen gums rinsing with hot water is beneficial. It provides relief from toothache.

Lemon : Cut a lemon into four pieces. Pour salt on them and heat them one by one and put them on the aching molar one at a time and compress. It will be helpful in relieving pain.

***Amla* :** If the teeth have become rotten and painful, mix a little camphor in *amla* juice and apply it to the aching teeth. It will bring relief.

Clay : Using clean clay as a toothpaste and massaging the gums with it daily provides relief from pain.

Cloves : (1) Grind five cloves and add lemon juice to it. Massage the teeth with it to get relief from toothache.

(2) Boil 5 cloves in a glass of water and rinse the mouth with it. Do it thrice daily for relief from toothache.

(3) In case of rotten teeth, put a clove between the teeth or apply clove oil.

***Neem* :** Boil *neem* leaves in water and rinse the mouth. It relieves toothache.

Camphor : To get relief from toothache, put camphor between the aching teeth. In case of cavity, fill it with camphor. It will bring relief from pain and kill the germs.

Turmeric : Roast it and then grind it. Massage the aching teeth with it to get relief from pain. It destroys the germs. Massaging the teeth with only turmeric powder is quite effective. If you compress a piece of turmeric between the aching teeth, it will reduce the pain.

Guava : Chewing guava leaves relieves toothache. Boil guava leaves in water and rinse the mouth. It relieves toothache and pain and swelling of gums.

Alum salt : In case of a cavity and toothache, put a cotton swab between the teeth with a little alum salt in it. It will provide relief from pain.

Ginger : To get relief from toothache put a piece of ginger between the teeth with a little salt on it.

Rock salt : It is beneficial to rinse the mouth with hot water mixed with rock salt. Gargling with hot saline water daily before bed-time prevents dental diseases.

DISEASES OF THE GUMS

Lemon : Squeeze a lemon in fresh water and rinse the mouth with it and drink some of it. It checks the swelling of gums and foul breath.

Alum salt : Grind finely one part salt and two parts alum salt. Massage the gums with it thrice daily. Then mix 5 gms. of alum salt in a glass of hot water and rinse the mouth. It will strengthen the gums and teeth and check bleeding and pus.

Water : Rinse the mouth with hot saline water. The gums will remain healthy.

Apple : In case of decay of teeth, cavities and swelling of gums eat an apple daily after meals. It will restore the health of the teeth and gums and prevent their going worse in future.

Carrots : Taking 70 ml. of carrot juice daily prevents dental diseases and gum problems.

Onion : Put a piece of onion between the teeth to get relief from toothache and pain in the gums.

Turnip : Chewing a raw turnip with the teeth helps solve dental and gum problems and cleanses the teeth.

Henna : Boil henna leaves in water and rinse the mouth with it. It cures incurable diseases of the teeth and gums.

Cumin seeds : Grind roasted cumin seeds and rock salt in equal quantity and massage the gums with it and spit out the saliva.

Ginger : In case of swollen gums, take 3 gms. of dried ginger powder with warm water once daily. It will also relieve toothache.

Caraway seeds : Roast caraway seeds on a hot plate to the extent that they become black. Grind and massage the gums with it. It will cure gum diseases and cleanse the teeth.

PYORRHOEA

Salt : Grind finely rock salt and sieve it through a muslin cloth. Mix one part salt and four parts mustard oil and massage the gums daily to cure pyorrhoea. Continue with this treatment for a prolonged period. Besides curing pyorrhoea, it will also provide relief from general dental problems like toothache and hyper sensitivity of the teeth. Also eat carrots or drink carrot juice. Avoid sugar, tea and coffee. It will keep your teeth healthy.

Oranges : Eating oranges is beneficial for the patients of pyorrhoea. Grind dry rind of oranges and massage the teeth and gums with it daily.

Mango : Grind finely mango kernel and massage the teeth and gums with it. It will cure pyorrhoea and other diseases of the teeth.

Cabbage : Eating raw cabbage provides relief from pyorrhoea and other diseases of the teeth.

Camphor : In case of pyorrhoea, apply camphor mixed in clarified butter four times daily and let the saliva drip out. Then rinse the mouth.

Castor oil : Mix castor oil and camphor and massage the gums with it twice daily in the morning and evening. It is beneficial for patients of pyorrhoea.

Spinach : It is preventive in nature and protects the teeth from diseases like pyorrhoea. Its juice makes the teeth strong. Chew and eat raw spinach. Taking spinach juice in the morning on empty stomach cures pyorrhoea. If carrot juice is added to it, it checks bleeding.

Alum salt : In case of pyorrhoea, bleeding gums, pain and swelling in the gums, grind finely one part of salt and two parts of alum salt and massage the gums thrice daily. Follow it with rinsing of the mouth with a glass of hot water with 5 gms. of alum salt in it. It will strengthen the gums and teeth and check bleeding and pus.

Kerosene oil : Rinsing the mouth with it cures pyorrhoea.

Betel leaf : Chew a betel leaf with a very small quantity of camphor and spit out the saliva. Be careful and do not swallow the saliva. It will be beneficial.

Garlic : In case of pyorrhoea, pain and swelling of gums and foul smell, add twenty drops of garlic juice to a tsp. of honey and lick it. Grind some garlic cloves and add to 60 ml. of mustard oil and then heat it.

When the garlic gets burnt up, strain the oil and add 30 gms. of burnt and ground caraway seeds and 15 gms. of rock salt. Massage the gums with it. It will cure the common ailments of the teeth. Its regular use for two-three months will also cure pyorrhoea.

Soap nut : Burn 250 gms. of the shells of soap nut on a hot plate, grind finely and sieve. Massage the gums daily with ¼ tsp. of this powder with 5 drops of mustard oil added to it. Continue with the treatment for two months.

Amla **:** Burn dry *amla* and grind and mix rock salt. Massaging the gums with it and mustard oil cures pyorrhoea.

Lemon : Use plenty of lemon. Rinse the mouth with water with a lemon squeezed in it. Applying lemon juice and honey on the gums checks bleeding and pus. The teeth become strong.

Clay : Soak clean clay in water and put in the mouth for sometime. Then spit it out and rinse the mouth. Do not eat sweets. It will cure pyorrohea.

GRINDING OF THE TEETH

Caraway seeds : Eating ¼ tsp. of ground caraway seeds with a little rock salt or taking it with water provides relief from the problem of grinding of the teeth.

WOUNDING OF TONGUE

Coconut : If the tongue has been cut and wounded by betel chewing, eating dry coconut alongwith sugar candy will be beneficial.

Cloves : In case of wounding of tongue by betel chewing, sucking on a clove will heal the tongue.

UNCLEAN TONGUE

Tomato : Eating red tomatoes with rock salt cleanses the tongue.

FOUL SMELL/BAD BREATH

Pomegranate : If foul smell emanates from your mouth and there is too much of salivation, take ½ tsp. of ground pomegranate rind with water twice daily in the morning and evening. Boil the rind in water and rinse the mouth.

Cumin seeds : Eating roasted cumin seeds removes smell.

Basil : Basil leaves provide relief from all types of foul smell. Chewing basil leaves after meals checks bad breath.

Lemon : Gargling with fresh lemon water is beneficial. Also drink a glass of it. It will remove bad breath.

Mint Leaves : If you suffer from bad breath, dissolve ground mint leaves in water and rinse the mouth with it twice or thrice daily. It will freshen up the breath.

Coriander : Eating coriander leaves freshens up the breath.

Ginger : For freshness of breath mix a tsp. of ginger juice in a glass of hot water and rinse the mouth.

Cardamom : Chewing cardamom or **liquorice** removes bad breath.

Water : Whenever you drink water, wash hands if water is available and rinse the mouth repeatedly.

Large raisins : Eat 10 large raisins daily for 15 days. It will remove bad breath.

Bad breath is caused by constipation and lack of cleanliness of the teeth. Therefore, it is advisable to take care of these problems as per recommendations made in the present book.

HOARSENESS, APHONIA

Hoarseness is caused by swelling in the vocal cords, too much of shouting, catarrh, coryza, excessive coughing, wounds in the throat, etc. Cancer of the throat, hysteria and paralysis also make the throat hoarse. If the throat remains hoarse for a prolonged period, great care should be taken in treatment. Specialists should be consulted.

The following recipes remove disorders of the throat and make voice clear. Even if the patient is taking some other treatment, e.g., homeopathic or allelopathic, the use of above recipes will expedite relief and will not have any harmful effect. Also use the recipes mentioned in Catarrh and Coryza.

Clarified butter : Mix 1 tsp. each of clarified butter and sugar candy with 15 ground black pepper corns and lick in the morning and evening. It will provide relief from hoarseness. Do not take water for a few hours after licking it.

Amla **:** A tsp. of *amla* powder taken with hot water clears the throat. The voice also becomes clear.

Salt : Gargling with hot saline water in the morning and evening brings relief.

Liquorice : Suck on a piece of liquorice or a little bit of the essence of liquorice at a time. Repeat it several times a day. It is quite beneficial.

Lemon : If the throat becomes hoarse, redness or swelling appears, squeeze a lemon in fresh or hot water and gargle thrice or four times a day.

Ginger : (1) Make a hole in a piece of ginger, fill it with asafoetida, wrap it in a piece of cloth and roast it. Then grind it and make pea-sized globules. Suck on a globule eight times a day. It is useful in aphonia. Licking ginger juice with honey opens up the vocal cord.

(2) Half tsp. of ginger juice taken every half an hour cures hoarseness due to cold or eating sour things. Let the ginger juice remain in the throat for a few seconds. It clears the throat.

Rose apple : Grind rose apple stones, mix with honey and make tablets. Suck on two tablets, for four times, daily. It clears the hoarseness and removes the heaviness of the voice. Taking it over a prolonged period rectifies the defects of voice. It is wonderfully beneficial for singers and those who have to speak a lot.

Garlic : Gargle with hot water with garlic juice added to it.

Asafoetida : If hoarseness occurs because of coryza or change of weather, gargle with hot water with ½ gm. asafoetida added to it. It will improve the voice.

Black pepper : (1) Black pepper powder mixed with clarified butter taken with meals is beneficial in hoarseness.

(2) Chew 12 black pepper corns with 12 *batashas* at bedtime. Do not follow it with water. It will cure hoarseness caused by cold and catarrh.

Honey : Gargling with a cup of water with honey in it clears the hoarseness.

Radish : Taking the powder of radish seeds with hot water clears the throat.

Turnip : Boil a turnip in water, strain the water, add sugar to it and drink it. It is beneficial.

Water : Boil water in a pan. When steam rises, draw it through your mouth into the throat. Also gargle with hot saline water. Foment the throat.

Caraway seeds : Boil caraway seeds and sugar and drink it. It clears the throat.

Betel leaf : Take a betel leaf with liquorice powder before bed-time and go to sleep. When you get up in the morning you will find that the throat has been cleared.

Barley : Chew and swallow 25 grains of barley in the morning. It will clear the voice.

DRYNESS OF THROAT

Dried dates : In case of a dry throat sucking a stone of a dried date is beneficial.

Plum : Eating plums relieves dryness of the throat.

THROAT PAIN

Pain in the throat is caused by eating hot and spicy food, the use of medicines, cold, flu and swelling in the throat. Do not take cold drinks if you have pain in the throat.

Coriander seeds : Chew 2 tsp. of coriander seeds every three hours. It is beneficial in all types of throat pain.

Salt : Gargling with hot saline water is beneficial.

Tamarind : Rinsing the mouth with tamarind relieves throat pain.

Lemon : Squeeze a lemon in a glass of water and rinse the mouth and gargle. Drink hot water with lemon juice.

Spinach : Boil 250 gms. of spinach leaves in two glassful water and strain. Gargle with hot spinach water. It will relieve pain.

Mulberry : Taking mulberry syrup removes dryness of throat and relieves pain.

THROAT WOUNDS

Radish : Mix radish juice and water in equal quantity, add some salt and gargle. It will heal wounds in the throat.

TONSILLITIS

Cinnamon : Grind cinnamon finely and apply some powder on the tonsils with your thumb. It will check the enlargement of tonsils.

EYE DISEASES

Clear bowels are necessary for healthy eyes. While bathing in the morning immerse your face in a bucketful of water and repeatedly open your eyes. Keep the mouth full of water. Wash your hands, feet and eyes and rinse your mouth before going to sleep. Massage the soles of the feet with mustard oil. It keeps the eyes healthy and cures several disorders of the eyes. Massaging the head with mustard oil and walking barefoot on green grass gives the eyes stamina. When the eyes are tired and stressed, cover the eyes with your palms and feel the darkness. The use of nutritious food makes the eyesight sharp. Never look at the sun during an eclipse; it damages the eyes.

Water : Cold fomentation is required in eye diseases. It is essential for conjunctivitis. If the eyes have become red, hot and swollen, repeated splashes with cold water, rose water or fomentation with a piece of ice in a piece of cloth are helpful. With this treatment the smaller veins get contracted and the eyes get relief from burning sensation and inflammation. If eyes have got swollen, do not continue with cold fomentation after the initial stage. *The Method of Fomentation* : Fold a piece of cloth five times and prepare a pad, soak it in ice-cold water and foment the eyes with one side first and then with the other side. If there is no ice, use only the cold water.

Fomentation with Cold Water : In case of pain, redness, swelling and dazzling effect of a light on the eyes, fomentation with cold pads is required. When the cold pad becomes warm, soak it again in cold water. If the above eye problems have been caused by cold, fomentation with hot water is advisable. Put a handkerchief on your mouth, make it warm with your breath and then foment the eyes with it.

Exercises for the Eye : (1) Move the eyeballs in a circular manner. First begin from the left side, then from the right side. Then cover the eyes with your palms. It will provide relief.

(2) Look straight in front of the eyes, then look up and down towards the feet. Repeat it ten times.

(3) Move the eyeballs left up, right down, then right up and left down. Then look straight. Repeat it for ten times.

Effect of Darkness : Cover your closed eyes with both palms making a rounded cavity creating the effect of darkness inside. Open the eyes for a minute and observe the darkness. It refreshes tired eyes, relieves pain and redness.

Palming : Reading for a long time or working under bright light tires the eyes. Looking at some thing by straining the eyes or looking into the distance creates tension in the eyes. In this case creating the effect of darkness with your palms is helpful. Rub the eyes slowly with the ball of the thumb. It is known as palming exercise. After it, again create the effect of darkness. It refreshes tired eyes and relieves tension promptly.

Red lines in the eyes appear because of excessive smoking or drinking. The dark circles under the eyes appear because of anemia or tension. Place two pieces of cucumber on the eyes. It will reduce tension.

SQUINT

Squint is the uncoordinated action of the eyeball, so that the visual axes of the two eyes fail to meet at the objective point. Squint can be corrected by practising looking straight and in a coordinated way. For this, use spectacles without power. Paint the glasses black leaving a circular spot at the centre unpainted. Put the spectacles on and try to see with the squinted eye through unpainted portion in the glass. It will rectify the squint.

Watching the Finger : It is an easy way of curing squint. Place the index finger of the right hand on the fore part of the nose and try to look at it with both eyes. Turn the finger towards the right temple and again look at its tip with both eyes. Bring it back between the eyebrows and try to look at it. Then move it towards the left temple and look at it. Repeat the exercise several times. It helps in straightening the nerves and veins of the eyes. While looking at the tip of the finger repeatedly blink the eyes.

The patients who have eye ailments should not take salt, red chillies, sour things and oil.

Common causes of Eye Diseases : Gazing at things minutely or gazing at glaring things or dazzling light for a long time, awakening late nights, sorrow, anger, too much of sex, overuse of intoxicants and lack of energy-giving nutritious food are the factors that cause eye diseases. Treatment through the food, mentioned below, will cure eye diseases and will be beneficial in keeping the eyes naturally healthy.

HEALTHY EYES

***Triphala* :** Soak overnight 2 tsp. of *triphala* in a glass of water in a clay pot. The following morning strain it and splash the water on the eyes. It cures almost all the diseases of the eyes.

Rose water : Putting a cotton swab soaked in rose water on the eyes provides relief from the eye ailments caused by heat.

Almonds : Soak 8 almonds in water overnight. The following morning grind them, add water and drink it. Follow it with a glass of milk. It will provide relief from eye diseases such as oozing of fluid from the eyes, sore eyes, weakness and tiredness of the eyes, etc.

Milk : If the eyes have got hurt or burnt, chilli powder or spices have been put into them, some insect has got into them or bitten them or if the eyes have become red, sore, muddy and are not able to tolerate light, put a cotton swab soaked in milk on them. It is beneficial. Keep the swab on the eyes for the entire night for better results. Put two drops of milk into the eyes also.

Coconut : Eating dry coconut and 60 gms. of sugar everyday for a week is beneficial in general diseases of the eyes. Eat a *roti* with clarified butter, sugar and black pepper.

Banana and Sugarcane : Both of them are beneficial for the eyes.

Lemon : A lemon a day in a glass of water will keep the eyesight intact for life.

Water : A lot of eye problems come up during the summer season—sore eyes, itching, redness, etc. In such cases wet pads are quite beneficial. Lie down on your back and put a wet pad soaked in cold water on one eye first and then on the other. The wet cloth should touch the eye-lids. Put a slight pressure on the pad with your fingers. It will provide relief and freshen up the eyes.

EYES HEALTH REVITALIZER

***Amla* :** The use of *amla* sharpens the eyesight. Soak overnight 6 gms. of dry *amla* powder in ¼ litre of water. Next morning strain it and wash your eyes with it. It cures all types of eye ailments and improves the eyesight. Take a tsp. of *amla* powder with water every day at bed-time.

Carrots : Vitamin A in carrots strengthens the eyes. Even in old age it is possible to read without spectacles. A glass of juice at 4.00 p.m. daily for forty days will keep the eyes healthy.

***Masoor daal* :** Fried in clarified butter *masoor daal* strengthens the eyes.

Onion : Onion juice used as eye drops sharpens the eye sight. Use it daily.

Cloves : Cloves are beneficial for the eyes.

Rose water : Cleaning the Eyes—Mix 12 ml. of rose water with 5 drops each of lemon juice and honey. Put a drop in each eye four times a day. It will keep the eyes clean.

Lemon : Mix a drop of lemon juice in a tsp. of water. Put two drops in each eye. It will keep the eyes healthy and cure common eye diseases.

CLEAR EYESIGHT

Eyesight becomes weak because of watching horror movies, anxiety, headache, dandruff and excessive sexual activity. Anxiety and mental tension are especially responsible for weak eyesight. Do not go for spectacles as soon as you find that your eyesight has become weak. Relax. Try to improve your eyesight.

To improve the eyesight softly massage the area around the eyes with your fingers. Do not use any oil. Before going to bed massage the forehead with clarified butter.

Sun Rays : At sunrise, stand before the sun and cover your eyes with your fingers in such a way that sun rays filter through them and touch your eyes. Do this for ten minutes. Then wash your eyes with cold water and massage your face. Similarly, when the sun is not very bright in the evening, sit down facing the sun and close your eyes and move the upper part of your body from left to right and right to left. Do it for twenty minutes daily. Then wash the eyes with cold water. It provides relief to the eyes and protection from several diseases.

The Moon : On the full-moon night look at the moon for fifteen minutes.

Close the eyes and splash cold water on them several times during the day. Fold a piece of clean cotton cloth four times, soak in cold water and put it on the eyes. Remove it when it gets warm. Repeat it several times in a day. It will keep the eyes healthy. It is beneficial in all types of eye ailments.

Cauliflower : Its juice strengthens the eyes.

***Parwal*:** This vegetable is beneficial for the eyes in several diseases.

***Amla* :** If the vision gets blurred taking *amla* juice mixed with water in the morning and evening for four days will be beneficial.

Onion : (1) The whiteness on the pupil of the eye is known as cataract. Soak a cotton wick in onion juice and let it dry. Burn it in sesame oil and prepare *kajal*. Apply it in the eyes daily. It will cure cataract. Regular use of onions improves the eyesight. It can also be used as eye drops to improve the eyesight. It is a proven formula.

(2) Its regular use improves the eyesight. Put a few drops of onion juice in the eyes. It cures dimness of sight, pteryglum and cataract. It is a proven medicine.

Milk : Fresh unboiled strained milk with sugar candy or honey and mixed with water in which 20 raisins have been soaked overnight taken for forty days improves the eyesight.

***Ber*:** It has in essence a cooling effect on the eyes, purifies blood and improves the eyesight.

Tomato : Tomatoes are beneficial for patients of short-sightedness.

Carrots : Take mixed juice of carrots and spinach (125 gms. each). It improves the eyesight.

Wheat : Taking the juice of wheat shoots improves the eyesight.

Clarified butter : (1) Take clarified butter prepared from cow milk alongwith sugar candy to improve the eyesight. Clarified butter is beneficial for the eyes.

(2) Grind 10 corns of black pepper, mix with a tsp. of hot clarified butter and take it in the morning. It improves the eyesight. If this treatment is taken over a prolonged period, it restores the eyesight and there is no need to use spectacles.

Mustard oil : Massaging the soles of the feet with mustard oil improves the eyesight.

Almonds : Soak 10 almonds overnight. Remove the skin in the morning and take the almonds with 12 gms. of butter and sugar candy. To improve the eyesight it should be taken for a month or two. Grind 7 almonds alongwith 10 gms. each of sugar candy and aniseed and take it with hot milk before going to bed for forty days. It improves the eyesight. Do not take water after it throughout the night. It will obviate the need of spectacles.

Aniseed : (1) Taking aniseed after meals improves the eyesight.

(2) Mix half tsp. of ground aniseed with a tsp. of sugar and take it with milk. It will improve the eyesight.

Black pepper : (1) Mix clarified butter with black pepper powder and sugar candy and lick. It improves the eyesight.

(2) Mix black pepper powder with clarified butter and put it in the open in the moonlit night. Take half tsp. of it daily.

Coriander : Grind coriander leaves alone or with *amla* and eat it. It strengthens the eyes and improves the eyesight.

Green grass : Walking barefoot on the green grass in the morning improves the eyesight.

Lemon : Mix 9 parts of honey of smaller bees, one part each of the juice of ginger, lemon and onions, strain and put one drop into each eye mornings and evenings daily. Prolonged treatment will cure cataract. If you mix 12 ml. of rose water with it, it will improve the eyesight and obviate the need for spectacles. This recipe was given by Naturopath Dr. Hiralal to Dr. S.R. Chawla and was tried by himself and found reliable.

Spinach : Its juice improves the eyesight.

CONJUNCTIVITIS

Symptoms : During conjunctivitis the white portion of the eyes becomes red. There is a secretion of water and mud like substance from the eyes. The eyelids become sticky; there is swelling in the eyes marked with friction and pricking pain. It is difficult to stand light. Some patients like hot food, others cold food.

Causes : It is caused by exposure to bright sun, cold wind, bright light, smoke, plague and gonorrhoea. Sometimes, the eyes are infected severely.

Treatment : Keep the eyes clean. Mix boric acid in warm water and wash the eyes in the morning and evening. Keep the bowels clear.

Salt : Do not take salt in conjunctivitis or reduce its intake to the minimum. Mix a minute quantity of salt in a cup of water, soak a cotton swab in it and put it on the eyes repeatedly. It is beneficial in conjunctivitis.

Bathua **:** *Bathua* taken as a cooked vegetable daily relieves swelling and redness of the eyes.

Cumin seeds : Roast cumin seeds and grind them. Take a tsp. of this powder with a tsp. of honey every day after meals. It is beneficial in conjunctivitis.

Sugar : Eating *roti* with loaf sugar or *batasha* is beneficial in conjunctivitis.

Alum salt : Mix 1 gm. of alum salt in 40 ml. of rose water and store in a small bottle. Put two drops of it in each eye several times a day. It will relieve pain, redness and prevent the secretion of mud from eyes. It refreshes the eyes if used at bed-time. It can be used daily.

Turmeric : In case of redness and throbbing pain in the eyes and secretion of pus, boil a tsp. of turmeric powder in ½ litre of water. When it is reduced to one-fourth, strain it through a fine piece of cloth.

Put a few drops in the eyes in the morning and evening. It will be beneficial. Prepare it afresh every third day. Grind a piece of turmeric in water, warm it a little and apply it on the eyelids. It is beneficial.

Pomegranate : Grind pomegranate into a fine paste. Its application with a bandage on the eyes is useful in relieving pain.

Red chilli : Grind red chillies into a paste. Apply this paste on the big toe of the foot on the side of the eye affected with conjunctivitis. If both eyes are affected, apply the chilli paste on both the toes.

Coriander : (1) In the case of a child suffering from conjunctivitis tie some coriander seeds in a piece of clean cloth and soak in water for ten minutes. Then put it lightly on the affected eyes of the child.

(2) Soak green coriander leaves in water for some time, then mash it and strain. Washing the eyes with this coriander water is highly beneficial. It cures conjuctivitis.

STYE

Stye is an inflammatory condition of the eyelash. A little whelk appears on the eyelash. Relief comes when it matures and bursts. Sometimes, it appears again and again.

Tamarind : Grind tamarind seeds on a stone slab as we rub sandal-wood. Apply it on the stye. It will have a cooling effect. It is a very good treatment for styes.

Water : Foment the affected eyelash with a piece of cloth soaked in hot water for three minutes. Then foment with cold water immediately thereafter. The stye will disappear in two days.

Dried dates : Grind the stone (kernel) of a dried date in water and apply on the affected eye. It will provide relief.

Cloves : Grind a clove in water and apply on the eye affected with styes. It provides relief from styes and swelling.

The homeopathic medicine—Pulsatia-30 is useful for styes. Take 8 pills at a time. Take it five times in a day. If the styes recur again and again take Staphysagria-200 twice, daily. Take 1 dram pills from a homeopath.

NIGHT BLINDNESS

Mango : Night blindness is caused by the lack of Vitamin A. Mangoes contain maximum Vitamin A which is beneficial in night blindness. The mangoes which you can suck are more useful.

Honey : Apply honey into the eyes like *kajal.* It cures night blindness. It also improves the eyesight.

Tomato : Tomatoes are useful in night blindness and short-sightedness.

***Gwar* :** It is beneficial in night blindness. *Gwar* leaves eaten as cooked vegetable also cure night blindness.

Coriander leaves : Consuming green coriander leaves in good quantity daily with meals cures night blindness. It can be combined and used with *daal*, *chutney*, *kadhi*, vegetables, *raita*, etc.

Carrots : It is beneficial to take carrot juice and milk in night blindness.

Water : Taking a plunge in cold water and opening the eyes while in water cures day blindness and enables one to see during the day.

TRACHOMA

Do not use *kajal.* Fasting will be beneficial. But do take water during the fast. In the morning, eat large raisins and drink water.

SAND PARTICLE IN THE EYES

Milk : If a sand particle, a bit of dry grass or straw or anything foreign gets into the eye, put three drops of milk into the eye. The foreign particles will be expelled because of the lubricity provided by milk.

Castor oil : If a sand particle or a piece of stone gets into the eye or if the eyes are painful because of smoke or pungent smell, wash and clean the eyes with water and put a drop of castor oil in them. After putting the drop of oil in them, foment the eyes after every twenty five minutes.

CATARACT AND OPACITY

Cataract is clouding of the Crystalline lens in the eye obscuring vision.

Potato : Grind a raw potato on a stone and apply into the eyes like *kajal* in the morning and evening. It will cure 5-6 year old cataract and 4 year old phula in three months.

Onion : (1) Soak a cotton wick in onion juice and allow it dry. Burn it in sesame oil and make *kajal.* Apply it into the eyes. It cures cataract.

(2) Putting drops of onion juice into the eyes cures cataract.

With the formation of cataract the vision gradually becomes obscure. In allelopathic system it is removed by a surgical operation. Take plenty of vegetables and vegetable juices to prevent the growth of cataract. Their regular use is required. Application of sandal-wood paste on forehead checks the growth of cataract.

Treatment Through Food

Honey : Jaipur, 25th June, 1977 (S). The use of honey has proved to be very beneficial for the treatment of black cataract and other terrible diseases of the eye. Dr. R.G. Sharma, Eye Specialist, Sawai Man Singh Hospital, Jaipur states that a drop of honey into each eye daily can save you from cataract. Even those who have developed cataract can get sure relief by the use of honey simply for four weeks at the initial stage of the disease. Swami Sadhananand in his book *Motiabind Ke Prakritik Upchar* says that the application of the honey of neem or lotus flower in the eyes at bed-time cures cataract.

Lemon : Mix 9 parts of the honey of small bees and 1 part each of the juice of ginger, lemon and white onions, strain and put a drop in the eyes mornings and evenings for a prolonged period. You can mix 12 parts of rose water to it and use it regularly. It improves the eyesight and obviates the necessity of spectacles. This prescription is based on the practical experience of Dr. Hiralal who passed it on to Dr. S.R. Chawla.

Carrots : Take 310 ml. of carrot juice mixed with 125 ml. of spinach juice daily. It can cure cataract.

Coriander : Boil a tsp. of coriander powder in a cup of water. Strain it and when it is cool, put a few drops into the eyes. It will certainly be beneficial.

GLAUCOMA

Glaucoma usually occurs after the age of 40, but it can occur earlier also. It is also known as glaucosis. It is marked by a hardening of the eyeball due to interference with normal circulation of the eye-fluids. The initial stage of glaucoma is marked by occasional headache. Then there is a deterioration in the vision and tension in the eyes.

Glaucoma is not a disease in itself but it is caused by other diseases of the body. If it is treated at the initial stage, the patient recovers easily. The eyes of the patients of high blood pressure are usually tense. When glaucoma is caused by other ailments of the body, treatment through operation does not help because it does not cure other ailments which are the root-cause of glaucoma. Dr. Michal M. Krenov of Soviet Medical Institute is also of the opinion that it is better to get rid of glaucoma without undergoing an operation.

INTOXICANTS

Once you take to intoxicants, there is a habit formation and then, it is very difficult to get rid of the habit. Initially, it appears that intoxicants bring relief from exhaustion and activate the body and make you feel cheerful. But the positive effect does not last long. As you get used to it, the effect of relief diminishes and the quantity of intoxicants has to be increased. It is characteristic of all intoxicants. It is, therefore, advisable not to smoke, not to take to hemp, alcohol or any other intoxicating substance. Cannabis causes madness for which there is no treatment.

A good way of giving up intoxicants like alcohol and narcotics is to announce your decision in the presence of friends. Say with determination that you will not take for example, alcohol or narcotics.

Such an announcement will reinforce your determination. If the promise has been made quietly and only to yourself without making it known to anyone else, the onus of keeping the promise solely rests with you. Whether you keep the promise or break it only you will know and only your self-respect will be involved. But a promise made in the presence of others is difficult to break because you will feel that your image could go down in the eyes of others.

If your decision has been made publicly, you are morally

bound to honour it and you take it as a challenge. You feel if you fail, you will be betraying not only yourself but also others.

First, know your habit, then announce your decision to give it up and do not allow excuses or laxity to undermine your determination and to deviate from the path you have chosen.

SMOKING

Health check-ups of chronic smokers and those who chew tobacco have revealed that their lungs are damaged upto 40 to 60 per cent. Smoking gradually leads to mental imbalance.

—*Rajasthan Patrika, Jaipur 1-5-1995*

Cigarette smoke could become a cause for the sudden death of infants, therefore, they should not be exposed to it.

SMOKING AND IMPOTENCE

Smoking is injurious to health from every point of view and its each puff takes the smoker nearer to death. Some people, however, consider smoking to be a symbol of manliness and they are unable to get rid of this addiction. Ringing bells of danger, American scientists have warned in a study, that a patient of blood pressure used to smoking, runs 27% higher risk of impotence. Even those smokers who stop smoking, run 11% more possibility of impotency than the pure non-smokers.

All tobacco products contain nicotine which is more dangerous than alcohol, marijuana, heroin and cocaine.

Lemon : Discontinue the habit of smoking and tobacco-chewing and whenever the urge to smoke or chew tobacco is too strong suck a lemon. Put a few drops of lemon on the tongue to create a sour taste in the mouth. It will put a check on the urge. Use lemon as often as required.

Aniseed : If you want to give up smoking, use aniseed. Fry aniseed in clarified butter and store in a bottle. Whenever the urge to smoke overtakes you, chew half a tsp. of the aniseed. It kills the urge to smoke. Also try to keep control over your desire.

Caraway seeds : Take 50 gms. each of caraway seeds and aniseed, mix black salt to taste, soak in lemon juice and stir well with a spoon. Let them dry in the shade. Then roast on a hot plate. Whenever you feel like smoking or chewing tobacco, chew half a tsp. of the above mixture. You will be able to give up the habit of smoking. It will also cure flatulence, strengthen the digestive system and improve appetite. It is an effective recipe for flatulence and wind related problems.

***Hari Om* :** Get up early in the morning. Sit down on the bed and say to yourself with firm determination that you will smoke two cigarettes or *bidis* less today. Repeat the words *Hari Om - Om - Om.* Feel that you have got enough determination to quit smoking. *Hari Om - Om- Om.* Try this experiment for 12 days. You will be able to quit smoking.

INTOXICATION

Onion : A cup of onion juice will considerably reduce any type of intoxication.

Salt : Make the patient drink 60 gms. of salt dissolved in water. It will provide relief from any type of intoxication. It will cause vomiting and expel the intoxicating or poisonous substance from the stomach.

Water : Drinking a lot of water diminishes the evil effects of intoxicants.

Grapes : Living only on grapes enables one to get rid of smoking, tea, coffee, tobacco and alcoholism.

Tamarind : Soak 50 gms. of tamarind in ½ litre of water for two hours. Then mash well and mix unrefined yellow sugar or sugar candy or plain sugar, strain and drink. It will diminish the effect of intoxication from hemp and alcohol.

***Chaulai* :** Taken as a vegetable it reduces the effect of intoxicants.

Coffee : Strong coffee can diminish the poisonous effect of alcohol and opium.

—Medicine for the Million by Family Physician, London

Tea : It is harmful for those taking intoxicants because it aggravates the problem.

ALCOHOLISM

Orange : Taking an orange before breakfast checks the urge for alcohol.

Apple : Taking apple juice several times a day or eating apples alongwith the meals helps one in giving up the habit of taking opium or alcohol.

Long cucumber : It diminishes the effect of alcohol. Drunk person who has lost his sense, can become normal and come back to his senses if he is made to drink long cucumber juice.

Clarified butter : Licking sugar candy mixed with clarified butter prevents intoxication.

Alum salt : (1) Drinking a glass of water with 6 gms. of alum salt dissolved in it brings you back to normalcy from a state of drunkenness.

(2) A tsp. of alum salt powder mixed in 250 ml. of milk brings you to normalcy.

INTOXICATION BY HEMP

Guava : Eating guava fruit or taking the juice of its leaves enables one to recover one's senses.

Tamarind : Soak ripe tamarind in water, wash well and drink. It will enable you to come back to your senses.

Rice : Drinking rice water helps you in coming back to your senses.

***Arhar* :** Boil 31 gms. of *arhar daal* in water or soak it in water. Drinking it will bring you back to your senses.

Curd : Fresh curd enables you to recover from intoxication by hemp.

Butter milk : Sour butter milk accelerates recovery from intoxication by hemp.

White Paper : Rub a white paper in water, strain it and

make the patient drink this water. It quickly brings an inebriate back to senses.

Basil Leaves : Grind 12 basil leaves and 6 black pepper corns and mix in a cup of water. Give it to the patient to drink. It will enable him to recover from the intoxication by hemp.

Take milk several times to get relief from intoxication by hemp. Put two drops of mustard oil in each ear. A tsp. of ginger juice and the juice of a lemon mixed in a glass of water quickly relieves intoxication by hemp.

DISEASES OF THE EAR

Diseases of the ear are caused when water, sand or an insect gets into it or by hurt, loud noise, accumulation of wax in it, scratching it or by cold or a whelk, etc. Keeping in mind the above factors, proper care should be taken of the ears.

EARACHE

Sometimes an ear develops a terribly sharp pain. It is caused by cold, injury or a whelk. It should be treated after ascertaining the cause.

Mustard oil : (1) Putting warm mustard oil in the ear provides relief from pain.

(2) Burn a few cloves in mustard oil. Putting drops of this oil in the ears will be beneficial. Mustard oil is useful if an insect has got into the ear, there are ear-noises or there is deafness.

(3) Boil garlic in mustard oil and strain. Putting these oil drops in the ears relieves pain, heals wounds and controls pus-formation.

***Neem* :** Boil *neem* leaves in water. Steam the ears with it. It will clear wax and relieve pain.

Brandy : A drop of brandy will bring relief from intense pain.

Ginger : Put three or four drops of strained lukewarm ginger juice in the ear. It will bring relief from pain caused by cold, accumulation of wax, or injury. If the pain persists, put the drops in the ear again.

Basil Leaves : The juice of basil leaves used as ear drops relieves pain. If there is pus in the ear, continue the treatment for some days.

OTORRHOEA

Lemon : Squeeze a lemon in water and drink it daily in the morning. It is beneficial in otorrhoea.

Garlic : Heat a clove of garlic and 12 gms. of *sindoor* in 60 ml. of sesame oil. When the clove of garlic gets burnt up, strain the oil and store it in a bottle. Put two drops of this oil in the ear daily. It will bring relief from otorrhoea, itching, tinnitus etc. Boil garlic in mustard oil and use this oil as ear drops to get relief from ear-ache, injury, otorrhoea, etc.

Onion : Put 5-7 drops of warm onion juice in the ear. It will bring relief from ear-ache, otorrhoea, rustling noises in the ears and deafness.

INSECT IN THE EAR

Mustard oil : Put a few drops of warm mustard oil into the ear and the insect will be expelled.

Alum salt : If an ant has got into the ear and you have a strange sensation, dissolve alum salt in water and put a few drops into the ear to expel the ant.

Water : If an insect has got into the ear, dissolve a little salt in warm water and put it into the ear. Then tilt down the ear. The insect will die and get out.

WATER IN THE EAR

While bathing, swimming or getting drenched water sometimes gets into the ear and does not get out fully. In such a case :

(1) Put warm sesame oil into the ear.

(2) Stand on one foot on the side of the affected ear and tilt the head on the same side and jump a few times. The water will get out.

DEAFNESS

Garlic : Fry 8 cloves of garlic in 60 ml. of sesame oil, strain the oil and put two drops in the ear daily for some days. It will cure deafness.

Basil Leaves : Putting drops of warm juice of basil leaves is beneficial in problems related to loss of hearing.

Mustard oil : Putting drops of warm mustard oil into the ear is beneficial in deafness.

TINNITUS

Sometimes there is a whistling sound or ringing in the ears. Mostly it happens at night. If it is not cured, gradually it leads to deafness. Actually, ringing in the ear or other ear noises are considered to be an incurable disease but there is no need to despair. Take the following treatment :

Do not pay any attention to the ear noises. Eat nutritious food which provides energy to the brain.

Garlic : The use of garlic as prescribed for pus in the ear is also beneficial in tinnitus.

Mustard oil : Putting drops of warm mustard oil in the ears cures ringing in the ears caused by cold.

Dried ginger powder : Mix jaggery and clarified butter with dried ginger powder, heat it and then eat it. It cures rustling noises in the ears.

VERTIGO

Lemon : If giddiness of the head has been caused by the disorders of the liver or flatulence, taking warm lemon water will be beneficial. Mix one and a half (1½) tsp. of lemon juice in a cup of warm water.

Large raisins : Fry 25 gms. of large raisins in clarified butter, add a little rock salt and eat them. It will bring relief from vertigo.

***Amla* :** (1) If giddiness occurs during the summer and you feel restless, drink *amla* syrup.

(2) If you are a teacher, advocate or student or if you do a lot of mental work, your head gets heated and you feel giddy, *amla* preserve is a panacea. Its daily use in the morning will enhance your intellectual and mental powers. Drink a glass of hot milk after eating *amla* preserve.

Black pepper : Grind black pepper and fry in clarified butter. Strain the clarified butter and mix it with wheat flower and prepare *halwa* by adding jaggery or sugar, also add the fried black pepper powder to it. Eat it daily in the morning and evening before meals. It will provide relief from vertigo.

Coriander : Boil 4 tsp. of coriander powder in a glass of water, strain it, add sugar candy and drink it. It is beneficial in vertigo.

Basil : Taking the juice of basil leaves mixed with sugar relieves vertigo.

Sugar : Chew 2 tsp. of coriander powder mixed with 2 tsp. of sugar. It will be beneficial.

ENERGIZING THE MEMORY

Memory-power does not increase with medicines—In the universe of commerce, medicines to enhance the memory-power, are sold on the basis of advertisements. In fact, these medicines do little good. Most of such medicines contain more than 50% sugar syrup and the contents are also not pure. Repeated advertisements and publicity create a psychological effect on the minds of the people. The people are advised to beware of such medicines and avoid their use. If these medicines could improve the memory-power, all the rich people would become vigorous and would have a dominating memory.

Memory-power can be improved only through

concentration, revision of the matter stored in the mind and by remaining healthy and following laws of nature.

From health point of view the reasons for a weak memory are physical and mental debility, indulgence in unnatural sexual activity, fickleness and lewdness. The following items for treatment through food are beneficial :

Apple : Apples energize the memory. Persons with a weaken brain and sinews and students who do not have a retentive memory should eat one or two un-peeled apples by chewing them thoroughly daily 15 minutes before meals.

***Amla* :** (1) Eating preserved *amla* daily in the morning, energizes the memory.

(2) Take green *amla* juice mixed in 30 ml. of water when you are half way through your meals. Take the remaining food then. It should be taken for 21 days. It will provide strength to the heart and mind and improve physical health.

Eating coconut, *lychee* and pistachio also improves mental powers.

Carrots : Eat seven almonds daily in the morning followed by 125 ml. of carrot juice mixed with 500 ml. of milk. It will be beneficial.

Wheat : The juice of wheat grass energizes the memory. Please consult the present author's book *Bhojan ke Dwara Chikitsa* for information regarding preparation of the juice of wheat grass.

Clarified butter : Massaging the head with clarified butter invigorates the memory.

Almonds : Soak ten almonds overnight. Peel them in the morning and eat them with 12 gms. of butter and sugar candy. It will strengthen the brain. If it is not possible to do so, grind 7 almonds and 10 gms. each of sugar candy and aniseed and take it with hot milk at night. Take it for 40 days. It invigorates the brain and memory. If it is not possible to do that also, grind finely 10 almonds and mix in 500 ml. of milk and heat it to three boils, allow it to cool down, mix sugar and drink it or grind almonds and aniseed in equal quantity. Take a tsp. with cool water before bedtime. It will invigorate the memory and provide strength.

Aniseed : Pound aniseed lightly, remove its husk and sieve. Take a tsp. of it each in the morning and evening with cool water or hot milk. It invigorates the memory and keeps the mind cool.

Black pepper : Take 8 corns of black pepper with 30 gms. of butter and sugar daily. It energizes the memory and keeps the mind cool. It also provides physical strength.

Basil : Prepare *thandai* with the following ingredients : 10 basil leaves, five corns of black pepper, five almonds, a little honey and water. Drinking it invigorates the memory.

Gulkand : Take it thrice daily. It will energize the memory.

Mango : Mix a cup of mango juice, ¼ cup of milk, a tsp. of ginger juice, add sugar to taste and drink it daily. It provides strength to the brain and cures chronic headache due to debilitated brain. It keeps the body healthy.

Black gram : Soak overnight 30 gms. of black gram *daal.* Grind it in the morning into a paste, mix it with milk and sugar and drink it. It is beneficial for the brain.

Sesame seeds : It contains protein. The brain is made of lasithene and it is found in sesame in plenty. Prepare *laddoos* with sesame and jaggery in equal quantity. Take a *laddoo* each in the morning and evening followed by milk. It provides energy and removes mental debility and tension.

Walnut : Walnut is shaped like the brain. Eating walnuts invigorates the brain.

Coriander : Grind 125 gms. coriander seeds and boil in ½ litre of water. When the water is reduced to one-fourth, strain it and add 125 gms. of sugar candy and heat it. When it becomes thick remove it from the stove. Lick 10 gms. of it daily. It is beneficial in mental debility.

BRAIN HEAT

Henna : Application of henna paste removes heat from the body and gives coolness to mind and body. The brain gets cool and peaceful.

Basil Leaves : Grind 5 basil leaves and 5 corns of black pepper. Mix it in a glass of water and take it every morning for 21 days. It enables the mind to lose heat and become cool.

MARASMUS

Milk : Soak three almonds, grind them and mix with milk. Drinking it is beneficial in marasmus.

Mango : Soak the powder of dried raw mangoes, mix with honey. It is good for children. Give a little quantity of it to the child twice daily. It cures marasmus.

Tomato : Its use is beneficial in marasmus in children. Juice of red tomatoes given to a child four times a day makes him quite healthy.

Grapes : Give as much grape juice to the sick child as he can take. It should be given twice daily. It will be more beneficial if it is given alternately with tomato juice.

—Dr. Poddar Jalendra Maharathi

OEDEMA

Symptoms : Oedemo is caused by accumulation of serum in cellular tissue. It is marked by serious swelling. It is demonstrable by the 'pitting' produced by pressure of the finger. It is also a form of waterlogging under the swollen part. The symptoms of oedema are dyspepsia, thirst, light or high fever, debility and dry skin. Oedema in itself is not a disease. It is a symptom of some other disease. Oedema related to cardiac disease, first affects thighs and hands. Hepatic oedema is marked by swelling on the stomach first. Renal oedema is marked by swelling on the face first. Women usually have swelling on hands, feet and face due to menstrual disturbance.

Treatment Through Food

To cure oedema it is essential to treat the root-cause of oedema. It is, therefore, necessary to first identify its root-cause and then start the treatment. Given below are some common prescriptions :

Clearing the bowels by taking a laxative is beneficial in all types of oedema. If the patient gives up cereals and salt and lives solely on milk, he gets well without losing much time. With any type of treatment it will be beneficial to take milk, fruit, green vegetables, *parwal*, brinjals, green gram *daal* and bathing with hot water. Homeopathic medicine has proved to be much more successful than other medicines in the treatment of oedema.

Ash : Burn dried cow-dung cakes and turn into ash. Apply some ash on the swollen part and tie it with a bandage. It will absorb water and reduce swelling.

Banana : It is beneficial in all types of oedema.

Pineapple : In case of oedema accompanied by micturition and albumin passes through urine, the liver is enlarged, the patient suffers from dyspepsia and there is swelling near the eyes and on the face, eat ripe pineapple daily and subsist only on milk. Take this treatment for three weeks. It will bring relief.

Turmeric : (1) Take a tsp. of turmeric powder in hot milk with sugar added to it to taste once daily. It is beneficial in oedema. Take this treatment for a few weeks. (2) Taking ¼ tsp. of turmeric powder with water regularly brings relief from oedema.

Potato : Cut 250 gms. of potatoes and boil in ½ litre of water. Foment the swollen parts with it and apply potato paste on them. It brings relief from swelling caused by injury.

Cumin seeds : Grind cumin seeds and sugar in equal quantity and take a tsp. of it thrice regularly. It will bring relief from oedema.

Water : Fomenting the affected parts with cold and hot water alternately brings relief from oedema. Foment first for three minutes with hot water and then with cold water for one minute.

Dates : It cures oedema.

Carrots : Boil 2 tsp. of carrot seeds in a glass of water and drink it. It is diuretic and beneficial in oedema and diseases of the kidney.

Wheat : Boil wheat and foment the swollen part with the boiled hot water. It reduces the swelling.

Black pepper : Grind black pepper, mix it with a little quantity of milk. It is useful for oedema in children.

Red chilli : Heat 125 gms. red chilli powder in 375 gms. mustard oil. Remove it from the stove when it boils, strain it and apply the oil on the swollen part.

Salt : Fomentation with salted hot water is beneficial in swelling caused by injury.

Dried ginger powder : Taking 12 gms. of dried ginger powder with jaggery reduces swelling.

Barley : Boil a cup of barley in 1 litre of water, allow it to cool down and drink it. It is highly beneficial in oedema.

Water-melon : It is beneficial in oedema to take the juice of water-melon seeds. It is good for the kidneys. It reduces the swelling around ankles. ***How to prepare it*** **:** Water-melon seeds should be first dried in the shade and then ground. Put 3 tsp. of the ground seeds in boiling water and allow them to soak for an hour. Strain it and drink it. Take four doses daily.

WEIGHT GAIN

Sometimes persons having thin body want to put on weight. The use of the following food items over a prolonged period increases weight.

Barley : Soak barley in water for 12 hours. Spread them on a sheet on a cot to dry. When they are partially dry, pound them and separate the husk from the grain. You can get barley grain without the husk from the market also. Prepare *kheer* with a cup of barley grain in milk and eat it daily in the morning. Within a few weeks thin and skinny people gain weight.

Banana : Eat two bananas daily followed by 250 ml. of hot milk for three months. You will gain weight.

Pomegranate : It raises blood level and makes the body strong.

Coconut : It enables a person to put on weight.

Dried dates : It makes blood, provides strength and enables one to put on weight. Eat dried dates boiled in milk.

Peas : They increase blood and muscle and strengthen the body.

Peanuts : Eating a few peanuts daily helps in gaining weight.

Black gram : Eating black gram *daal* with husk increases the muscle of the body.

Clarified butter : Eating clarified butter with sugar enables one to gain weight.

Carrots : Regular use of carrot juice enables one to gain weight.

Massage : Regular massaging of the body with oil makes a weak body strong.

Almonds : Soak seven almonds in water overnight. Peel them in the morning and grind into a paste. Mix 30 gms. of butter with it and add sugar to taste. Spread it on bread and eat it. Follow it with 250 ml. of milk. Continue with this treatment for six months. It will not only enable you to gain weight but will also sharpen your intellect.

Honey : To gain weight take honey in milk regularly.

Water : Slimmer persons should take plenty of water and water based drinks. Put fresh water in the sun for four hours. Use this water to bathe children daily at a fixed time. It will strengthen their body.

WEIGHT REDUCTION

It is very difficult for overweight persons to lose weight. It is, therefore, advisable not to be overweight. For men 70 kg. and for women 60 kg. is the upper limit., Obesity is a curse and root cause of problems. It is an early invitation to death. Obesity means serious ailments which call for costly check-ups and investigations and high fees to the doctor. If you want a sweet smile on your face and want to have fun in life get rid of extra weight. Do not over-eat. It makes you sick. Abstemious meals mean a long life. Take a spare diet, go for a walk regularly and you will be able to shed weight. Without changing dietary habits, it is very difficult for an overweight person to lose weight. Just taste, do not fill yourself up with food. Increased weight is a call for by-pass surgery. If you want a basic change in your body-weight, take as little of *bati*, *burfi*, almonds, *vade* and biscuits as possible, take regular exercise and go for a walk daily.

People who do not do much physical exertion need 1500 to 2000 calories a day through food to compensate for the daily loss of calories but it has been noticed most people take 3000 to 4000 Calories a day which leads to accumulation of fat in the body and obesity.

Obesity is caused by the accumulation of fat in the body. If you want to lose weight, do not take fats and carbohydrates. Obesity leads to high blood pressure, diabetes, arthritis and makes walking difficult.

Causes : The use of fatty substances like meat, clarified butter, rice, potatoes, fried foods, sweets, granular sugar, bananas, grapes and oily foods leads to obesity. Oversleeping during the day, lack of proper physical exercise, frequent eating and indigestion also cause obesity. Lack of proper menstruation among women also leads to obesity.

To tackle obesity, take frugal meals. Instead of big meals take fruit and vegetables, take water an hour after meals and take cold baths. Do adequate physical work and occasionally observe a fast. To reduce weight it is advisable not to eat to your fill, rather leave the dining table before the feeling of satiety occurs. Doctors often advise that one should listen to music or read a book while eating to divert your attention from food.

It would be better not to take meals of any type except fruit for a few days. Do not partake of clarified butter, sugar, rice and sweets.

For a shapely and beautiful body and shedding obesity related ugliness :

(1) Take balanced and healthful food that will bring about internal purification and expel toxins from the body.

(2) Expel the toxins in the body through stool, urine and sweating. For this, tackle constipation and take more of diuretic substances and liquids for increased flow of urine. Allow the body to sweat out the toxins.

(3) Take long and deep breaths to inhale more of oxygen and destroy toxins in the body.

(4) Take exercise regularly. It makes the body shapely and beautiful and then depletes the accumulation of fat from certain parts of the body.

(5) Massage the body well with oil. Take special care of the particular parts of body where fat has accumulated.

(6) ***Relaxation*** **:** Allow the body and mind to relax completely. It removes tension and improves blood circulation and expels toxins from the body.

(7) Both overweight men and women should do skipping on empty stomach or five hours after meals.

(8) Scientists lay stress on the intake of calcium instead of exercises or dieting to become slim and thin. Calcium releases a kind of hormone which maintains balance between the metabolism and blood-circulation. It burns the calories and the excess weight automatically reduces. Calcium intake in the food should be increased.

Know the correct weight : The ideal weight of an adult should be according to his height, that is a kilogram to an inch. The weight of an adult of five feet should be 60 kg.

Obesity makes one look unshapely and ugly. The buttocks and hips of women generally become large and heavy. The buttocks become heavy because of the lack of proper movement. The muscles also lose their flexibility for want of movement. They lose their shape and begin to expand outwardly. The buttocks not only become heavy but also become extra large. They can get enlarged even without the consumption of fat.

You can keep the body fit and shapely by remaining active and taking proper nutritious diet. For a fit and shapely body, exercise is necessary. Go for a brisk walk daily for half an hour and take some exercise. Skipping is also a good exercise. Take exercise regularly for 15 minutes daily.

Walking : One should not lose weight in one go, it should be done gradually. Walking 3 miles in an hour every day is a good way to reduce 1 kg. of weight in a month.

Bitter gourd : Take the juice of bitter gourd with lemon every morning to shed weight.

Vegetables and Fruits : Vegetables and fruits are low calory foods, therefore, eat more of them. Banana and *cheeku* increase the weight, hence do not eat them. Do not add salt to fruits and vegetables for taste. Reduce the salt intake to the minimum. Also do not consume sugar, oily and fatty substances like clarified butter, butter and sweet potato.

Tea : To reduce weight take tea with mint leaves added to it.

Salt : Take salt-free food to lose weight. It is quite helpful.

Massage : If you have a bulging belly, give a massage to your body and do sit-ups every day. Skipping also reduces the bulge in the belly.

Lemon : (1) Squeeze a lemon into a glass of warm water, add rock salt to taste and drink it in the morning every day for two months. It will be beneficial in reducing weight. It is much more helpful in the summer.

(2) Squeeze a lemon into a glass of warm water and add 2 tsp. of honey to it. Take it daily for four months to shed obesity.

(3) Spinach juice with lemon also helps in reducing fatness.

Gram : Eating soaked gram *daal* with honey daily in the morning helps in shedding obesity.

Tomato : For persons who are overweight and take regular exercise and practise yoga, tomatoes are beneficial because they are a great help in expelling foreign matter or substances and food trapped in the intestines from the body. If you take raw red tomatoes with salt and onions daily, it will certainly reduce fatness gradually.

Curd : It is beneficial for those who want to shed obesity.

Butter milk : Drinking butter milk with black salt and the powder of caraway seeds helps in reducing fatness.

Basil Leaves : Mix the juice of basil leaves and honey in a cup of water and drink it daily. It will help in reducing fatness.

Potato : Potatoes in themselves do not increase weight. But when they are fried and spices are added to them, they certainly increase fatness. It is therefore recommended that potatoes should be taken either boiled or roasted. They are beneficial and safe.

***Kulthi* :** Eat 100 gms. *kulthi daal* daily to reduce fatness.

Juice : To shed obesity, take only juice or fruit once in a week and no other food like *roti* and milk.

Long pepper : Grind four pieces of long pepper and mix with ½ tsp. of honey and lick it daily. It is beneficial in reducing obesity.

Salad

Take as per requirement two or three seasonal fruit, salad leaves, radish, carrots, tomatoes, cabbage, ginger, green chillies, coriander leaves, lemon, soaked Bengal gram, black pepper and rock salt.

Method : Wash the salad leaves and cabbage leaves and spread them in the salad tray. Cut the fruit and place on the leaves. Slice the tomatoes and shred radish, carrots and ginger and put them on the fruit and also add soaked Bengal gram and coriander leaves and green chillies cut finely into small pieces. Squeeze a lemon and sprinkle black pepper powder and rock salt. You will have a very tasty and nutritious-rich salad. Take it with meals or with the afternoon tea or eat it without meals in the evening. It should be chewed properly.

Those who want to shed the bulge in the belly or fatness of the back and thighs, should eat only salad in the evening for meals. They may also take tomato and spinach soup with it. Watch your weight and see the difference after 40 days. It is a very good device to reduce as much fat as you wish. Though you will reduce fatness gradually but it is a sure and proven remedy.

Mixed Juice : Take lemon juice in hot water in the morning. Follow it with mixed juice of carrots (12 oz.) and spinach (4 oz). It is beneficial in reducing obesity.

Water : (1) Fat people should always take lukewarm water in plenty. If you take a glass of lukewarm water before meals. You will not be able to consume much food. If you take this treatment for two months, it will help in reducing fatness. Dr. Lencus suggests that you should boil three glasses of water daily and add a pinch of salt to it. Take a glass of it in the morning on empty stomach, another in the afternoon and the third one before bed-time.

(2) Take a glass of as much hot water as you can tolerate after meals.

EXERCISE FOR A THIN WAIST

To reduce waist-line, lie down straight on your back. Keep the hands on the thighs. Lift the legs 6-7 inches above the ground. Then lift the shoulders also to the same height and keep the legs and shoulders in that position as long as you can conveniently tolerate. The hands should not touch the ground.

Stand straight and keep the feet close together. Put your hands on the back and lift the right leg as much as you can. Do not allow yourself to bend and keep the leg straight. Keep it in that position for 4-5 seconds, then bring it down. Do it for ten times. Repeat the exercise with the left leg. Walking makes the hips shapely.

Tummy—Using both palms, the distended flesh of the tummy should be pressed sliding the palms from down to upward position. This should be repeatedly done atleast for 10 minutes daily. This method of massage will not allow the accumulation of excess fat in the flesh. Similarly, the excess fat accumulation in the back and legs can also be reduced.

EPILEPSY

It is a disease of the brain characterized by unconsciousness, convulsive fits etc. Hands and feet begin to tremble and there is frothing at the mouth.

The patient regains consciousness after some time. During the attack of epilepsy there is an excessive flow of current from nerve cells and there are contractions in the body resulting in the imbalance of the brain.

Epilepsy is related to the brain. Countless cells of the brain release innumerable directive waves. Another part of the brain contracts these directive waves and ensures the compliance of only the right directions. When an imbalance occurs in this function, epilepsy takes place. Other factors causing epilepsy include brain injury, high fever, meningitis, brain cancer, etc. This disease can strike any one at any age.

Symptoms : Epilepsy can be categorised in several ways according to its symptoms. The two main categories are the serious one, i.e., grand-mal epilepsy and the ordinary one i.e., petit-mal.

The patient usually suffers from a convulsive fit when he is physically or mentally stressed. Any situation which can create excitement—great height, depth or very rapid flow of water—can start an epileptic fit. Usually, the patient can feel that it is coming. It may start with headache, giddiness and restlessness and the patient seeks support. Then soon he collapses. There is a sharp contraction in his hands and feet and he begins to froth at the mouth. Sometimes, the tongue is cut and injured as it comes between the contracting teeth and jaw. The colour of the face and the size of the pupils can also undergo a change. Sometimes the patient passes stool and urine in his clothes.

The grand-mal epileptic fit can last from a few minutes to an hour. Afterwards the patient is overcome by weakness and exhaustion. The ordinary or petit-mal epileptic fit lasts only for a few seconds. It is characterized by momentary impairment of consciousness and amnesia. The patient suddenly becomes quiet, stares and comes back to what he was doing as if nothing had happened.

Things to Remember : Epilepsy is not caused by ghosts and evil spirits or bad wind but is a disease and is curable.

If the disease lasts for a long time, it affects the behaviour of the patient and he can become short-tempered, intolerant and peevish. Do not quarrel or argue with him.

Do not allow the patient to go to great height or depths, sights of fire or water and fighting.

Such a patient should not be allowed to drive in public places.

The patient should carry an identification card with details of his ailment. It will help in his treatment and contact with his relatives.

Primary Treatment : As soon as the patient has an attack of epileptic fit, insert some clean object between his jaws. It will protect the tongue from getting cut and injured. If the teeth are tightly contracted do not insert any thing forcibly because it can hurt the teeth or gums.

Make the patient lie down on one side. Loosen his clothes. Remove his belt, tie, shoes, etc.

If the patient finds it difficult to breathe, give him artificial respiration. Do not give him anything to eat until he becomes normal.

If the patient is a child, rush him to a hospital because such a fit can be the fit of meningitis also. It is also a serious disease.

If a person who is prone to epileptic fits is marriageable, make it sure before marriage that the fiance does not suffer from the same disease. After marriage, giving birth to a child should be with the advice of the physician and the treatment should not be discontinued without his permission.

Symptoms showing that the disease is incurable : If there is excessive convulsion of the muscles, the body has become very weak, there is a movement of eye brows, according to Ayurvedic system of medicines the disease is incurable.

Food : The patient should be given vitamin and protein-rich food. Lesser the quantity of salt, the better it would be. It increases the possibility of recovery of the patient. Vegetarian food and milk will make the best diet for the patient. Do not give him stimulants like coffee, peppermint and meat. For some days it is better to give him only fruit, vegetables and milk. The patient should avoid situations of fear, grief and anxiety. The patient should not be left alone because the epileptic convulsions start all of a sudden without any warning signals.

Lemon : Sucking a lemon with a pinch of asafoetida is beneficial.

Onion : Drinking 3 Oz. onion juice mixed with a little water in the morning prevents epileptic attacks. Take the treatment at least for 40 days. During an epileptic attack making the patient smell onion juice brings quick relief.

Garlic : (1) Pound garlic cloves and make the patient smell it. It will bring him back to consciousness. Boil ten cloves of garlic in milk and let the patient take it. It cures epilepsy. It should be continued over a prolonged period.

(2) Eat garlic cloves fried in oil daily.

(3) Grind three parts sesame seeds and one part garlic. Take a dose of 30 gms. daily. It is beneficial in epilepsy caused by the humour of wind.

Orris root : Mix 10 gms. of orris root powder with a tsp. of honey and lick it or take it with a cup of milk regularly. It is beneficial.

***Karaunda* :** Grind about 50 *karaunda* leaves and mix the paste in butter milk. It prevents the occurrence of epilepsy. This treatment has proved to be particularly effective in bile generated epilepsy. The attack of this kind of epilepsy takes place in about 15 days. —*Vaidya Sushil Kumar Jain*

Henna : Giving 60 ml. of the juice of henna leaves mixed with 250 ml. of milk brings relief beyond expectation.

Mustard : Grind mustard seeds and make the patient smell it during an attack of epilepsy. It will bring him back to consciousness.

Red chilli : Put a few drops of homeopathic medicine mother tincture *Capsicum Anum* into the nostrils of the patient. It will bring him back to consciousness.

Black pepper : Putting a few drops of ground black pepper in water into the nostrils brings the patient back to consciousness.

Basil Leaves : Grind basil leaves into a fine paste and massage the body of the patient of epilepsy with it daily. It is beneficial.

Nutmeg : Putting a 21-nutmeg string around the neck is beneficial for an epileptic patient.

Pomegranate : Boil 100 gms. pomegranate leaves in ½ litre of water. When the water is reduced to one-fourth, strain it and add 60 gms. each of clarified butter and sugar. The patient should take it twice daily in the morning and evening. He will soon recover from epilepsy.

MENSTRUAL DISCHARGE

Climatically India is a hot country and girls here attain puberty after the age of 13. Menstruation begins at this age. Menstrual discharge is the periodical or monthly flow from the uterus of women. The blood stain of menstrual discharge on the clothes can be washed off. If the blood stain is not washed off, it is the symptom of a disease. The flow usually lasts three days. During these three days women should take rest. They should not have a head-wash. They should not wash clothes, floors, etc. She should eat hot fresh food.

Coconut : Eating coconut facilitates menstrual discharge.

Peas : Eating peas removes obstruction in menstrual discharge.

Mustard : In menstrual disorders it is beneficial to take 2 gms. of ground mustard with the first bite of the meals.

Basil : Allow basil root to dry in the shade, grind it into powder and take ¼ tsp. of it with a betel leaf. It will check unnecessary bleeding.

DYSMENORRHOEA

Menstrual discharge is a natural activity of the female body. But in some cases menstruation is painful. It is called dysmenorrhoea. It usually happens to women who have a sedentary life-style and are physically inactive between the ages of 18-25 years. It is of two types : (1) Congestive dysmenorrhoea, and (2) Spasmodic dysmenorrhoea.

Congestive Dysmenorrhoea : Married women suffer from it and the pain is located in the parts around the uterus. The pain starts three-four days before menstruation and is relieved after menstruation starts. Women who do not do much physical work usually suffer from it. One gets relief by eating more of sugar and taking exercise.

Spasmodic Dysmenorrhoea : Out of the women with menstrual problems visiting hospitals, a large number of them suffer from spasmodic dysmenorrhoea. Usually unmarried women suffer from it. It usually begins with menstruation and lasts till the first child is born. The pain is located in the uterus. Acute pain lasts for an hour. It may be accompanied by shivering, vomiting sensation and vomiting.

Causes : It has not been possible to completely identify the causes of dysmenorrhoea. However, some of the known causes are : small uterus, insufficient blood in the uterus and lack of coordination in the functioning of reproductive organs. Hormonal imbalance is the chief reason. The food taken by us usually does not have sufficient sodium and potassium, which are necessary for maintaining a balance between the nerves and mental impulses. As a consequence, women suffer from mental tension. After marriage and first delivery, the disease automatically disappears. For details, refer present author's book *Stree Rogon ki Chikitsa.*

Treatment Through Food

Take balanced diet. Take as little of pungent food, sweets, polished rice and meat as possible. During menstruation period unmarried women should take lemon water or orange juice. It supplements potassium in the body. Foment the painful parts.

Radish : Grind radish seeds into powder and take 4 gms. thrice a day each in the morning, afternoon and evening with warm water. It facilitates free flow of menstrual discharge and relieves pain.

Asafoetida : The use of asafoetida is beneficial in relieving pain during menstruation period.

Caraway seeds : Eating *halwa* prepared with jaggery and caraway seeds in clarified butter relieves menstrual pain and clears the flow of menstrual discharge.

Dried ginger powder : Prepare a concoction with dried ginger powder and old jaggery. It will relieve menstrual pain. Avoid cold drinks and sour food. It will be beneficial. It is a proven formula.

***Neem* :** If the pain is in the thighs during menstruation take the juice of *neem* leaves (6 gms.) mixed with ginger juice (12 gms.) in equal quantity of water. It will bring prompt relief.

Carrots : If menstruation does not take place, boil 2 tsp. of carrot seeds and a tsp. of jaggery in a glass of water and take it hot twice a day in the morning and evening. It will facilitate the menstrual activity and relieve menstrual pain.

MENORRHAGIA

Sometimes excessive menstrual bleeding takes place and lasts for several days and in some cases excessive bleeding takes place during climacteric period. When there is excessive bleeding, raise the bed of the patient by a few inches on the side of the feet. Do not give oily, spicy and hot food to the patient to eat. Cold drinks will be better. Do not let her work in a hot place like the kitchen.

Pomegranate : Grind dried pomegranate rind finely and sieve it. Take a tsp. of the powder with cool water. It checks bleeding.

Coriander : (1) Boil 20 gms. coriander seeds in 200 ml. water. When it is reduced to 50 gms., strain it and add sugar candy and give it to the patient to drink. It checks excessive bleeding during menstruation.

(2) Mix ground coriander seeds with loaf sugar and clarified butter in equal quantity. Take 2 tsp. thrice daily. It will check bleeding.

DEFICIENT MENSTRUAL DISCHARGE

Asafoetida : Its use is beneficial for women who suffer from deficient menstrual discharge.

AMENORRHOEA

Lack or stoppage of menses is called amenorrhoea. There are several reasons for stoppage of menses—diseases of the local reproductive parts, absence of uterus, lack of proper development of generative and other internal parts and lack of hormonal coordination. Menses stop after child-birth also. Other factors include anemia, mental shock, stress and strain, catching cold before and after menstruation, getting drenched with water, etc. The natural reasons of amenorrhoea are pregnancy, menopause, breast feeding the infant, etc. While taking treatment for amenorrhoea, it causes should be looked into.

Radish : Grind radish seeds, carrot seeds and fenugreek seeds in equal quantity, sieve and take 2 tsp. with hot water. It will cure amenorrhoea.

Sesame seeds : Boil 15 gms. each of black sesame and jaggery in two cups of water and strain. Take it regularly for some days. It will facilitate menstrual discharge.

Salt : If the menstruation has stopped because of exposure to cold wind or working in water, take 2 gms. of salt in hot water thrice in a day. It will be helpful.

Caraway Seeds : Take 6 gms. of ground caraway seeds twice daily with hot milk. It will ensure free flow of menstrual discharge.

Basil : Boil a tsp. of basil seeds in a glass of water; when it is reduced to half a glass, drink it when it is cool. It will be beneficial in amenorrhoea.

***Neem* :** Boil 50 tender *neem* leaves in a glass of water. When it is reduced to half a glass, strain it and drink it. It will cure menorrhoea.

UTERUS PROPASE, VAGINAL CONTRACTION

Sometimes a women's uterus is displaced. It is known as uterus propase. The vagina appears to be loose. In such a case, mix 3 parts of alum salt and 1 part finely ground gallnut. Tie a tsp. of the powder in a clean piece of cloth or gauze and insert it in the vagina before going to bed. It will tighten the vagina and remove looseness. Allelopathic doctors recommend surgery for uterus propase. But homeopathic treatment is also beneficial in this respect. For the successful treatment of all types of diseases please read the present author's *Homeopathic Vyavaharik Chikitsa Saar* which is also available with the writer.

STEAM BATH

Steam-bath enhances the beauty of face and it also proves useful in the treatment of boils, pimples, spots etc. Heat some water to the boiling point, in a wide-mouthed pan. Add a spoon of glycerine in the boiling water. Wash your face with lukewarm water followed by a wash with normal cold water. Wipe your face gently with a clean towel. Now massage the face with plain unsalted butter. The fingers should move from downwards to upwards direction. The cheeks and chin should be massaged using the tips of fingers making circular motions.

When the butter applied on the face melts, bend your face towards pan and start using the steam of the boiling water. Cover your head, face and the pan with a large towel so that the steam does not escape. Keep yourself in this position for 5-10 minutes. When your face becomes sweaty, remove the towel and wipe it with a dry towel. After 5 minutes, sprinkle ice-cold water on your face, apply cold cream on face and lightly massage with the palm. Again wash your face after half an hour and wipe.

Do not use soap. Facing the mirror, you will notice the freshness and splendour on your face. The steam cleanses the face, opens up the mouth of the boils and pimples and extracts the filth out.

This method leaves no spots or marks on the face. To get rid off the pimples, take steam bath at nights. Apply the mixture of lime and coconut oil lightly on the face with the lukewarm water. The pimples will disappear in few days.

Extracting the pimples by pressing with fingers leaves scars/ spots on the face. The pimples are caused by constipation or other stomach disorders, therefore, one must be careful about one's eating habits.

Salt : Mix salt in the ginger juice and anoint your face with it, before going to bed. Wash your face in the morning with lukewarm water. Take a glass of carrot/cucumber juice etc. according to the season. It will keep your face free from pimples.

To remove the scars and black spots left by the pimples, apply juice of fresh lime on the face. Mix few drops of lime juice in a little bit of fresh milk cream. Massage the face for 5-6 minutes. Wash your face and wipe, it increases the blood circulation on the face. Face becomes radiant and the spots become lighter. The spots can also become lighter by applying the paste of *chiraunji* and cucumber juice.

Taking a glass of fresh lime juice daily, also cleanses the stomach, which in turn cures pimples. Paste of the bark of the *neem* tree, (prepared by rubbing the bark like a piece of sandal-wood), if applied on the boils and pimples, dries them. Soak some *amla* powder in a glass of water, at night. In the morning, wash your face by rubbing it over your face.

BEAUTY OF THE FACE

It's not necessary to use expensive cosmetics products available in the market, to enhance your beauty. Facial beauty can be achieved by using fresh fruits and vegetables, which are easily available. One should take nutritious diet with sufficient intake of pure water. According to beauty specialist, Mrs. Vandna Luthra, fast and junk food should be avoided.

Tomato : Apply the juice of red tomatoes on the face. Slice a red tomato and rub on the face. After it dries up, wash the face. It removes the wrinkles of the face and the skin acquires a glow.

Potato : Apply the juice of raw potatoes on the black rings under the eyes or slice a raw potato and rub it on the face, especially the black circles. It removes darkness from under the eyes.

Orange : Apply orange juice on the face. It will enhance the beauty of your face.

Cucumber : Cucumber juice can also be used to beautify your face.

Gram : Mix a little salt in gram flour, knead it and rub the face with it. It will make the face beautiful.

Lemon : After squeezing a lemon, use the rind to rub the darkish parts of the elbows. It will remove blackishness.

Milk : Rub cream or milk on the dark parts of the face, it will enhance its beauty.

Steaming : While water or milk is boiling do not miss the opportunity to steam the face. It cleanses the face.

Almonds : If a blackish layer has appeared on the lips, take an almond. Grind it in a little water. While grinding it, mix with it a saffron leaf. Apply this to your lips. After ten minutes rub it off with the help of a finger. A few day's treatment will make your lips rosy.

FAIR COMPLEXION

- Massage the face with unboiled milk and after it has dried a little, rub a little salt on the facial skin. It will remove the dirt and cleanse the skin and you will get rid of the extra and dead skin.
- After that apply a mixture of lemon juice and honey on the entire face. When it gets dry, wash the face with lukewarm water. It improves the complexion of the skin.
- Make a paste with ½ tsp. *chiraunji* and 2 tsp. milk and apply it on the face. Wash after 15 minutes. Its application regularly for one and a half month clears the complexion and makes the face beautiful.
- Prepare a paste with gram *daal* flour, turmeric powder, lemon juice, curd and rose-water and apply on the face once a week. It can also be used as a face-pack. It can be used for the entire body also. It makes the skin smooth and the complexion of the face and body fair. It is particularly useful for oily skin.
- To make the dark complexion of the feet and arms fair, massage them with lemon juice mixed with cream. This mixture can be used regularly.
- Take a handful of sieved barley flour, tie it in a handkerchief, soak it in milk and rub your body with it while bathing. Do it at least thrice a week. If you use it regularly, it will gradually make the dark skin fair. It is quite convenient to use while bathing.

- Mash a raw tomato and mix butter milk and apply on the face or hands and feet or wherever the skin has become dark. Wash off after half an hour. It can be used regularly.
- Mix 4 tsp. of lemon juice with 2 tsp. of honey, 2 tsp. of curd and 1 tsp. of lemon juice and apply on the skin. After half an hour wash off with lukewarm water. Then take a piece of ice and rub the skin of the face with it. It makes the complexion fair.
- Cucumber juice is very helpful in making the dark skin fair. Its juice alone can be used or you can mix honey or other substances that can make the skin fair.
- To remove the dark circles under the eyes, take two slices of a potato and put them under the eyes and lie down for fifteen minutes with closed eyes or rub the slices on the dark skin for some time. If you use it before the make up, the dark circles will not be visible after make-up.

In addition to the above remedies, we should protect our skin from the ultraviolet rays of the Sun. Sun rays blacken the skin rapidly.

Also eat tomatoes, carrots, spinach, cucumber, coriander leaves and green vegetables in plenty. The most important point is to keep cheerful.

FRECKLES, SPOTS AND SCARS ON THE FACE

Tomato : (1) Take a glass of tomato juice daily in the morning with salt, cumin seeds and black pepper powder. Apply coconut water on the face.

(2) Remove the black spots on the face by rubbing cotton dipped in tomato juice.

Nutmeg : (1) Make a paste by rubbing nutmeg in raw milk, mix powder of 10 grains of black pepper and apply on face. Wash it after two hours.

(2) Grind nutmeg into a fine powder and strain through a muslin cloth. Mix it with a little quantity of cow-milk. Apply

this face-pack four times a day for few days. It clears freckles and flecks.

Lemon : (1) Wherever freckles appear on the skin, rub a piece of lemon on them. Fill the piece of lemon with alum salt and then rub the skin with it. It will make the freckles light and the skin fair.

(2) Mix ground *samudri jhag* in lemon juice. Apply on the spots on the face at bed-time. It will clear the spots in a few days. If *samudri jhag* is not available rub only lemon juice. Apply lemon juice with cream on dark circles under the eyes.

(3) Rubbing the rind of lemons on the neck removes dark spots from around the neck.

(4) Lemon juice mixed with honey in equal quantity is very useful in cleansing the skin and making it fair.

(5) Mix cream and a little bit of gram *daal* flour in lemon juice. Its application makes the skin glowing and removes dryness.

(6) Grind dried orange rind, mix coconut and a little rose water. Its application makes the skin soft.

(7) Grind dried orange and lemon rind finely, mix in a little milk. Its application will make the skin of the face beautiful.

Cleansing mask : Mix 1 tsp. of *multani mitti*, 3 tsp. of curd and 1 tsp. of honey and prepare a paste. Apply it on the face. It is a deep pore cleanser of the skin. It opens up the closed pores, removes dead cells and dirt and this completely cleanses the skin.

Mask for Oily Skin : Mix 1 tsp. of *multani mitti* with 3 tsp. of orange juice and apply it on the face. It is an excellent mask for removing spots and marks from the face. It removes the extra oil from the skin.

Deep Cleansing Mask : Mix a little milk with a tsp. of gram flour and massage the face well with it. It will help in deep cleansing the skin and removing well-entrenched dirt.

Peel off the mask after 20 minutes. Any kind of make-up should not be done at least for two hours after the mask has been peeled off. Masking should be done twice a week. Masks prepared with natural things are not harmful. After the application of the mask rub the face in a circular manner, it improves the blood circulation and the skin begins to glow and becomes healthy.

To remove black spots and freckles, apply the paste prepared by grinding *masoor daal* and tender leaves of the banyan tree. Or you can apply ground cinnamon mixed with cream. To remove the dark shades from the face, grind sandal-wood powder and almonds and apply on the face. Wash off after an hour.

Turmeric : (1) Grind together turmeric and black sesame seeds. Prepare a paste daily with 1 tsp. of the above powder and apply on the face and go to sleep. Wash the face in the morning. It will remove freckles and black shadows from the face and make the complexion fair.

(2) Mix turmeric with the *malai* of milk and apply it on the spots. Black spots will be removed leaving the face beautiful.

***Neem* :** Application of the paste prepared out of the kernel of the small fruits of *Neem* on the face clears spots and patches on the face within a few weeks.

Curd : (1) Persons afflicted with boils, pimples, dry skin, black spots or patches, etc., should use curd like a paste and massage it on the body five minutes before taking bath.

(2) Mix and blend *Besan* and curd, apply it on the face, and when it gets dried, wash off your face. It brings lustre on the face. Sunburns also get cured. The mixture of curd and orange juice works like cleansing milk. Curd is a skin freshner. Application of the mixture of rice flour and curd on the face could also cure pimples.

***Siras* :** Paste made from the flowers of the siras tree if used daily for a month, cures pimples, sports and flecks.

Basil : Grind basil leaves in the lime juice and apply on the face. It cures black spots.

Orange : Grind dry peels of orange, make a paste by mixing water and apply on the face, it improves the lustre.

Orange Pack for Flecks and Spots : Take one large spoon of *Besan*, half a spoon of turmeric powder, two spoons of dried orange feel powder, one spoon each of curd, milk, rose-water, lime juice, coconut oil, and beat it and mix it well.

Apply this blend on the face, and wash off your face when it gets dried. 3 to 4 applications a week for two months could cure all types of blemishes on the face. Take 100 gms. dried orange peel powder, equal quantity of millet flour; 10 gms. turmeric powder, a bit of line juice, add some water to knead the mixture, and blend it into a dough. Apply this pack on the face.

***Amla* :** Grind dry *Amla* and mix in the water. Use it like a paste on the face, it brings splendour.

Bottle gourd : Grind peels of fresh bottle gourd and apply on the face, it also brings splendour.

Fenugreek : Application of the paste prepared from the fresh fenugreek leaves cures flecks, black sports, dryness of the skin, and wrinkles on the face. Its seeds can also be used in place of the leaves, it brings freshness on the face.

Mustard : Soak mustard in water just sufficient for the soaking, overnight. Mix equal quantity of *chiraunji* and grind in the milk. Use this paste on the body, it brings splendour.

Coconut : Application of the coconut milk on the boils, pimples, smallpox marks, and patches cures them. If coconut milk is not available, grind Batasa (a light, hollow sugar-cake) in the milk, apply on the face and wash after one hour.

Lime and Milk : Mix one spoon each of milk and fresh lime juice, and apply it on the face and all around the neck before going to bed. After fifteen minutes was off the face with lukewarm or cold water according to the season. It not only cleanses the skin but also makes it soft. The paste prepared by mixing two spoons of lime juice, milk-fat and besan (gram flour), if applied on the face, cures dryness and brings lustre on the face.

Cucumber and Lime : For the treatment of the oily skin, cut a cucumber into pieces, grind it, and extract its juice by squeezing it in muslin cloth. Add half a spoon each of lime juice and rose-water and apply the mixture on the face. Wash your face after 15 minutes. It is a good toner for the oily skin.

Gram, Milk and Turmeric : Soak two spoons of *chana daal* in half a cup of milk, overnight. Make a paste of this mixture in the morning. Add a pinch of turmeric powder and 6 drops of lime juice, mix well, and apply on the face. When it dries, wash your face with lukewarm water. Use this pack thrice a week.

***Multani mitti* :** Take a lump of *multani mitti* and grind it into a fine powder. Add water, just sufficient to make a paste. Apply this paste on the face, let it dry for 15 minutes, and wash off your face with lukewarm water. Use of this face-pack twice a week freshens the face.

***Masoor daal* :** Soak some *Masoor daal* in water overnight. In the morning, grind it into a fine paste, and one spoon curd, and blend it by beating. Apply it on the face and when it gets dried, wash off your face with lukewarm water.

Soak overnight three spoons each of soyabean and *Masoor Daal.* In the morning, grind it with raw milk and make a fine paste. Application of this face-pack brings splendour on the face. Roast some quantity of *Masoor daal* in the clarified butter, and grind it into a fine powder. Every morning and evening, take one spoon of the powder and two spoons of raw milk, blend it and apply on the face. Your countenance will bristle with splendour and softness.

Polished *Masoor daal* has the quality to extract the filth and muck out of the skin-pores. Soak overnight some polished *Masoor Daal,* some dry rose-petals and sandal dust in raw milk. In the morning, grind and blend this mixture. Apply this blend lightly on the face and remove it by rubbing your face with your hands. After that, expose your face to the Sun for an hour and wash it with lukewarm water. It provides coolness to skin during summer.

Radish : Cut fresh radish into small pieces, grind it and extract juice by pressing it through muslin cloth. Mix equal quantity of butter. Keep it in a bottle. Apply on the face daily before taking bath. Your face would brighten up with luster.

Banana : Take out the pulp of one banana and mash it finely. Add two spoons rose-water, two drops of *khus* scent, and four drops of glycerine. Blend it and put it in a bottle. If you have a dry skin, use it as a cream and massage your face with it just before make-up, let it dry and wash your face with lukewarm water. This face-pack can be prepared for 7 days. If there is any possibility of its getting spoiled, add some more rose-water.

Potato : (1) Rubbing peel of the boiled potatoes on the face cures pimples.

(2) For the face having pockmarks, spots of pimples, or shadow marks, pound a raw potato, add three drops glycerine, vinegar, and rose essence. Blend them well and rub this pack on the face for three minutes. Using this pack regularly for few days can perform magic to improve your countenance.

Rice : Make a paste of rice flour, add a pinch of sandal-wood sawdust, a pinch of turmeric powder, 2 tsp. rose-water. Beat the mixture well and keep it in the sun for half an hour. Half an hour before make-up, apply it on the face, massage a bit and wash your face with lukewarm water. Your face is ready for doing make-up. Your countenance will glow with splendour.

Papaya : The chemical substance obtained from the papaya is quite effective to tone down the oily layer on the face. Mash well the pulp of papaya and apply the paste on the face. Let it remain for 15 minutes and thereafter, rub it off the face, then wash off your face with lukewarm water. For dry skin, add rose-water, sandal-wood sawdust, turmeric powder, blend them, and apply the past on the face. After some time, wash your face with cold water.

Carrots : Make a paste of sandal-wood sawdust, rose-water, *besan* and carrot juice. Rub your face with this paste.

Apple : Peel off the apple and take out its seeds. Add *besan*, sandal-wood sawdust, turmeric powder, and grind it. Apply the paste lightly on the face and massage. It is quite effective for treating the wrinkles, pimples, and other spots.

WRINKLES ON THE FACE

Some people develop wrinkles on the face at an early age. Such wrinkles can be reduced with a little bit of efforts. One needs to exercise. Some of the simple exercises are given below.

The wrinkles generally appear on the cheeks. Pronouncing 'E-O' loudly is helpful in making the cheeks strong. First of all, wide open your mouth, pronounce E and stretch your lips as good as possible, thereafter pronouncing O let the cheeks squeeze inward. Repeat this process many a times.

Spread small bits of shredded paper on the table, and try to blow up these bits with your mouth as far as possible. Blowing exercise will bring tension to your cheeks, which is helpful to cure wrinkles.

Fill your mouth with water, do not drink it, retain in the mouth, try swelling your cheeks one by one. Repeat this process every morning while cleaning your mouth and face.

Like swelling with water, try to do this exercise with air in take. Try swelling your cheeks turn by turn. This exercise is quite effective.

ROUGHNESS OF HANDS

Wash you hands with water mixed with vinegar, regularly. Squeeze on lime in the lukewarm water, and dip your hands in it for some time. It will cleanse all the filth of your hands. Later, apply cream on the hands. Regular practice can bring softness on the hands.

To remove roughness and wrinkles on the hands, add one tsp. of sugar in the lime juice in the cup of your palm and rub both the palms together till the sugar dissolves. It cures roughness and wrinkles on the hands. Before going to bed in the night, take some *malai*, add juice of one fourth of a lemon, a little bit of glycerine, one tsp. rose-water, and almond oil. Blend them well and massage your hands thoroughly with it. Wash it off with a glycerine soap and lukewarm water. This will enhance the beauty of the hands.

Mix some barley flour in water and rub it on the hands. Take out the juice of fresh potato and massage your hands with it. It cures wrinkles.

Add pure wax and camphor in the sesame oil, stimulate it by heating, and keep the mixture in a bottle. Apply on the hands daily before going to bed. It saves from cracking in the hands.

PHYSICAL BEAUTY

Beauty is godliness. Efforts to maintain the physical splendour of your body is worship, and living in the society by keeping yourself splendid and handsome is the awareness of the supreme spirit. Handsomeness is attractive and is liked by everyone. The following are some of the useful tips for maintaining your physical beauty.

***Harad* :** *Harad* is an important beauty aid. 2 tsp. of the *Harad* powder taken with warm water in the night every fourth day extracts toxic matter out of the body. The *Harad* is an alchemic elixir which keeps body active.

Salad : Use salad of raw vegetables like cabbage, tomatoes, carrots, cucumber, radish, etc.

Turmeric : *Chutney* made from the raw turmeric, or raw

turmeric added in the vegetable, if taken regularly, purifies the blood and brings luster to the skin.

Black Spots : Mix cucumber and tomato juice and apply on the face, it cures the black spots.

Potato : Grind a raw potato and rub it one the body, the body will gain splendour. Boil potatoes in water and use this water to wash your body. It gives luster to the skin.

Honey : Apply a coat of honey on the face and let it remain for two hours. Wash it off with lukewarm water. It will brighten up the glow of the face.

Masoor daal **:** Soak *Masoor daal* in the lime juice day-long grind it and apply the paste on the face during the night before going to bed. Wash off your face in the morning, it will enhance the luster of the face.

Breast (of women) : (1) To give shape to the breast gone slack, lie down straight, take a deep breath and stretch your head backward by slowly lifting the breast part of your body. This exercise is helpful in giving shape to the slack breast. Do this exercise every morning for ten minutes, month-long on empty stomach.

(2) Make a paste by rubbing coarsely the **Gallnut**, add a little bit of honey, apply on the breasts, and wash it off after two hours. Massage the breasts with almond oil in the night.

Mustard : Soak equal quantity of mustard and *chiraunji* in cow milk for two hours. Grind it, heat it, and apply the paste on the face in the night. Wash off your face the next morning, the splendour will glow.

Triphala churan **:** Mix *triphala churan* with the lime juice, apply on the face, wash off your face after half an hour. The face will glow.

Besan **:** Mix 2 tsp. turmeric powder, 5 tsp. *besan*, 2 tsp. mustard oil. Add a little water and knead it. Application of this paste on the face adds luster.

Orange : Take equal quantity of dried peel of orange and lime, grind together, add rose-water in the powder, mix them, and apply the paste on the face. The face will become soft and cold.

Lime : Rub a lime all around the neck, thereafter, massage with raw milk and wash with water. Neck will look clean.

Rose-petals : Make a paste of fresh rose-petals, 5 grains of *Chiraunji*, and *malai*. Apply it on the lips. Wash it off after it dries. It will make lips red and shaped. Lips will also get cured.

Sandal-wood : Mix sandal-wood, sawdust and milk, add paste obtained by rubbing nutmeg. Blend it and apply on the face while going to bed. Wash off your face the next morning. It will remove black spots on the face.

Coconut oil : Squeeze lemon in the coconut oil and massage your body with it. This supplements the natural oil deficiency of the skin and the body gets toned up.

Coconut milk : Blend *besan*, turmeric powder, and coconut milk, and rub it on and off the skin. Take a hot bath followed by a cold bath. For making coconut milk, grate a fresh and raw coconut and add water. Strain it after one hour to obtain the coconut milk.

Skin diseases are caused by the stomach heat. We should eat lime and onion to maintain the balance of stomach heat. To bring splendour on the skin, soak *moong daal* in water, grind it when it becomes tender, add dry orange peel powder and a little bit of *malai*. It is a fine paste. Use it on the face and other parts of the body before taking bath.

PRETTINESS OF SKIN

Dry Skin—It your skin is dry, mix *Besan* in mustard oil, a pinch of turmeric powder rose-water, blend it into a fine paste, and apply it on your face. After some time, rub it off your face, and wash your face with lukewarm water.

Oily Skin—Make a paste of the mixture of *Besan* turmeric powder, rose-water, lime juice, and sandal-wood sawdust, Apply it on the face and let it dry. Wash off with lukewarm water after half an hour. Mix two spoons of *multani* clay powder, half a spoon of glycerine, 2 spoons raw milk, and 2 spoons curd. Blend the mixture and apply on the skin. This is useful for the normal type of skin.

Amla murabba **:** Taking one jammed *Amla* a day brightens up the texture of the skin.

Multani mitti **:** Mix *multani mitti* in water and make a paste. Apply it on the face, once a week. Wash it off after half an hour with water. It will brighten up the glow of the countenance.

Tamarind : Soak 60 gms. tamarind in ¼ litre water. When it fully swells, mash it and make its chutney-like paste. Application of this paste on the body makes the colour fair, and cures flecks and spots. Experiment this for two weeks in the summer.

Aniseed : Chewing 6 gms. regularly after dinner, purifies the blood and gives fairness to the texture of the skin.

Carrots : Half a glass of carrot juice taken empty stomach twice a day, regularly for twenty days, purifies the blood and the H.B. count also goes up. The carrot juice, if taken regularly for two months, makes the skin smooth, cheeks pink, and the countenance glows with luster.

Rub your body with dry palms slowly before taking bath. Do this from head down to the toes. The friction causes the filth gathered in the skin pores to come out and it stimulates the blood circulation, which makes the skin fresh and live.

HAIR

The hair become dry on a account of the filth collected in the skin of the skull, and they fall. The dirty skin creates dandruff, which is a dead enemy of the hair. One must, therefore, take due care of the cleanliness of the head and hair. Insufficient sleep, indiscriminate use of medicines, and worry are harmful for the health of the hair. It cause the hair to fall, break, and gray. Application of oil on the hair is necessary for healthy hair. The present day fashion to avoid the use of oil on the hair is harmful for the health of the hair.

Wash the hair with *reetha* or with *shikakai* with the water added with the lime juice by rubbing on the hair and its roots. It cures the dryness of the hair and brings splendour to the hair.

Domestic shampoo : Pods of ***shikakai***, dry *amla*, and *reetha* 250 gms. each, camphor *kanchali*, dry leaves of *mehendi*, and ***nagarmotha***—grind all these ingredients into a powder, domestic shampoo is ready. Boil a spoon of this powder in water and wash your hair with it. It cleans hair and the hair regain blackness and shine.

HEELS

Just before daily bath, dip your heels in water for some time, then rub the heels with a sandstone, scrubber, or nylon brush, and apply vasline. It cures cracks.

Heels often crack during extreme summer or extreme winter. It happens because of the collection of dust and filth in the pores of the heels. Wash your feet with lukewarm water added with few drops of lime juice, daily before going to bed, and apply vasline or glycerine.

It the cracks are deep and bleeding, wash feet with hot water before going to bed and apply hot was in the cracks, it is curative.

Application of **henna** on the heels keeps the skin soft and the heels remain pink.

The following crude form of the locally made ointment could also help cure the cracked heels :

Ingredients : White vasline 100 gms., wax 50 gms., glycerine 20 gms., juice of two fresh limes (strained), any essence of your choice.

Method : Put vaseline and wax in a small empty container. Take a large container, fill it half with the water and heat it, when it starts boiling, put the small container in the large container in such a way that water should not enter the small container. When the vaseline and wax melt, stir it with a small rod of wood or twig, add the glycerine and mix it well, take the small container out, and mix any essence of your choice, rose, jasmine, *mogra*, etc. and also add the lime juice, blend it when it is still hot, and fill it in a small bottle or phial. This ointment is very useful for the feet.

Use this ointment on your feet before going to bed. Apply it on the sole, heel, and toes of your feet and massage lightly. It will soften the skin and cracks will get cured. Do not use this ointment during the day, otherwise dirt and dust will stick to the feet and will spoil the skin.

CHEEKS : TIGHT and RED-GLOWING

The sunken and hollow cheeks give the impression of age, older than the real one, whereas the puffy cheeks make you a laughing stock. The shape of the cheeks could be improved with the exercise suggested below:

- Breathe in, and exhale slowly sounding 'O'. Repeat it for five times.
- Like you wrinkle up your nose and brows on seeing something unpleasant, make your face–wrinkle your nose, brows, and face. Keep it like that for two seconds. Repeat it for five times.
- Swell your cheeks by inhaling and draw in your lips like you do for inflating a balloon. Keeping in this condition, press your cheeks with three fingers of each hand, slowly, continuously for 10 minutes, and exhale. This exercise is most useful for the sunken lips.
- Sit down facing the mirror, draw in your lips. Now, inhale and fill your mouth by inhaling and emulate laughing. Repeat it. It brings tightness to the cheeks.

- ❖ Press your cheeks using your both palms, and act like laughing, keeping the cheeks pressed. Keep repeating it till you feel any sensation in the cheeks. It improves the blood circulation in the cheeks, which imparts red glow to the cheeks.
- ❖ Take banana shake daily to treat the sunken and hollow cheeks.

SOFT and LOVELY LIPS

- Take one spoon milk, one spoon milk-fat, and add a bit of saffron. Blend it by beating and keep it in the fridge. Apply a thin layer on the lips, and wipe it out with wet cotton wool. It keeps lips clean and gives them a pinkish shade.
- Take a little quantity of milk, dip few rose-petals. After some time, mash the rose-petals in the milk, and take out the residue. The milk will become pinkish. Add to it, ground almonds.

  Beat and blend, and store in the fridge. Apply it on the lips and after some time, wipe it off with the wet cotton wool. Its regular use will keep the lips soft glowing with natural pink.
- Apply pure clarified butter on the lips before going to bed. It will keep the lips soft and tender.
- Apply clarified butter on the hot *chapatti*. Wipe a little bit of this application with the finger and apply on the lips. It is very useful for the lips.

MASSAGE

Take two or three tsp. of salt, mix it with one and a half tsp. of coconut oil and ½ tsp. of lemon juice and massage the body with it daily before taking your bath. It will make your skin healthy and smooth.

Hirsute Body : (1) If there are excessive hair on the face and body, it mars the beauty. To remove unwanted hair mix 1 tsp. of gram *daal* flour with a tsp. of turmeric powder and a little bit of mustard oil and prepare a paste for smearing the body with. Use it on the hairy parts over a prolonged period.

(2) Get *guggal* from the grocer's shop. Grind it finely. Prepare a paste with 1 tsp. of this powder by adding a little milk and apply it on your face rubbing well. It will remove the unwanted hair.

Conditioning and Nourishing Mask : Mix a few lemon drops with a tablespoon of cream and apply it on the face. It will enliven the skin and make it smooth and soft.

The New Beauty Mask : Prepare a paste with two tablespoon of carrot juice, a little carrot pulp and a tablespoon of gram flour and apply it on the face. It is especially beneficial for elderly women. It makes the face beautiful by removing ugly scabs, wrinkles and dead cells and restores the beauty of the skin.

SOFT SKIN MASK

Mix cucumber juice (1 cup), hot water (1 cup), ¼ tsp. of boric acid powder, ¼ cup of glycerine and 1 tsp. of benzine tincture (available at allelopathic medicine store). Apply on the skin, rub and sponge. It will make the skin soft.

Barley : Mix ½ cup barley flour, 1 tsp. cream and the juice of half a lemon. Add a little water and prepare a paste. Smear the face and neck with it and wash off after 15 minutes. Do it regularly. The face will become beautiful and the skin will begin to glow.

Long cucumber : Its juice cleanses the skin. It removes spots and copper coloured marks from the face. If you have pimples, drink long cucumber juice daily. Rub the face with it and wash with water. It will cleanse the oily skin.

Spots and Marks on the Face : (1) Take a cup of cucumber juice daily. Apply the juice on the face and wash when it is dry. It will remove all types of spots, marks, freckles and marks of pimples except those of small-pox and beautify the face.

(2) To enhance the glow of the face, mix a tsp. of cucumber juice with 5 drops of lemon and a pinch of turmeric powder. Apply this mixture on the face and neck and rub well. Wash off after half an hour and wipe with a towel. This treatment brings elegance to the face.

BEAUTY PASTE

Mix well the following ingredients : ½ cup of gram *daal* flour, 1 tsp. of rose water, 2 tsp. of glycerine, 1 tsp. fine powder of sandal-wood, 1 tsp. of turmeric powder, ½ tsp. of milk and 6 drops of lemon. If you want to thicken it, add a little more of gram *daal* flour and if you want to make it thinner, add some glycerine. During winter, you can add a few drops of *kewra* or *henna* scent for fragrance. During summer or rains, add rose or *khus* scent. Massage the entire body with this paste. It will make the body beautiful.

Application on the Face : Mix ½ tsp. each of the juice of tomatoes, radish, cucumber and rosewater. Add 6 lemon drops to it. Also add 1 tsp. butter and a pinch of turmeric powder and prepare a paste. Apply this on the face in the evening. Let it dry for half an hour. After that wash with warm water and wipe with a clean coarse cloth in the upward direction. Now take a little glycerine and rosewater in your palm and rub on the skin of the face. It will make the skin smooth, soft and clean.

***Amla* :** Massage the face twice daily in the morning and evening with any oil of your choice. Soak overnight a tsp. of *amla* powder in a glass of water. In the morning strain it and use the water to wash your face with it. Do it daily. It will remove freckles and wrinkles.

Coconut : Application of coconut water on the skin of the face twice daily removes spots, pimples and small-pox marks.

Almonds : Soak overnight five almonds. Peel them in the morning and grind finely. Store in a bottle. Add 60 ml. of rose-water and 5 drops of sandal-wood scent and stir well. Apply it on the face wherever there are spots thrice daily. Where the spot is dark, apply a little extra quantity.

Turmeric : Mix 1/4 tsp. each of turmeric powder and black sesame seeds and grind in hot milk. Apply it on the face. It will remove freckles.

***Neem* :** Grind green *neem* leaves and apply the paste on the face before bed-time. Wash the face with cold water in the morning. Do it continuously for 50 days. It will clear the small-pox marks.

Rice : Soak white rice in water. Use this water to wash the face. It will clear freckles.

Milk : Apply hot milk on the face and wash it before bed-time and then give a thorough massage to the face. Again wash the face with clean water after half an hour. It will enhance the beauty of the face. Massaging the face with the froth of the freshly produced milk clears the spots. Application of milk cream on the face before bed-time also clears pimples and freckles.

Clarified butter : Application of clarified butter on the face before bed-time clears black spots and marks of injury.

Castor oil : Mix gramflour with castor oil and rub on the face. It will clear freckles and beautify the face.

Nutmeg : Grind nutmeg and black pepper in milk and apply a thick coating on the face. It clears spots and improves complexion.

Water : For a beautiful skin you should drink plenty of water daily. At least eight glasses of water are required for internal cleaning.

Meat-eating : Women who do not eat meat or take very little of it have soft skin and it is a pleasure to touch it. For spotless beauty meat-eating is harmful.

Basil Leaves : (1) Mix the juice of basil leaves and lemon juice in equal quantity. Its application on the face will clear dark shadows, freckles, pimples, black spots, etc.

(2) If there are dark freckles on the face, grind mint leaves

in the morning and apply the juice on the face and let it remain for half an hour. In the evening, grind basil leaves and apply the juice on the face and let it remain for half an hour. Wash off afterwards. If this treatment is taken for three months, it will clear the freckles.

BURNING SENSATION IN THE SOLES OF THE FEET

Mustard oil : Mix a tsp. of mustard oil in two glasses of hot water. Immerse both the feet in the water for five minutes. Then rub the feet with a pumice stone or something like that. Wash the feet with cold water. It will cleanse the feet and expel the heat.

Bottle gourd : Mash bottle gourd and rub the pulp on the soles. It will provide relief from heat and burning sensation.

Bitter gourd : Massaging the feet with the juice of bitter gourd leaves is beneficial and relieves burning sensation of the soles.

Henna : People who feel constant burning in their feet during the summer should apply henna paste on the soles. It will bring relief.

Mango : The burning of the feet and hands is relieved by rubbing the blossom or small flowers that grow on mango trees.

Clarified butter : Rubbing clarified butter on the soles, feet and hands relieves burning sensation.

***Kateera*:** It is a form of edible gum and is available with the grocer. Pound it and make very small pieces. It soaks water and swells a great deal. It should, therefore, be soaked in a bigger vessel. Soak overnight 2 tsp. of it in water. It will swell by the next morning. Eat it after adding sugar to it. It relieves burning sensation in hands and feet. It can be used in all the seasons. However, it is especially beneficial in the summer.

Butter : Eat 2 tsp. of butter with sugar candy added to it every morning. It is beneficial in burning sensation in hands and feet.

Coriander : Grind dry coriander seeds and sugar candy in equal quantity. Take 2 tsp. of it four times daily with water. It will be beneficial in relieving the burning sensation.

DEVITALIZING OF TOES

Henna : If the toes have been devitalized or are prone to cuts, apply mustard oil and then sprinkle henna powder on them. If the toes have been devitalized because of exposure to water, apply henna mixed with half the quantity of turmeric powder twice daily. It is quite beneficial.

DISEASES OF THE LUNGS

Grapes : They are beneficial for all types of diseases related to lungs—T.B., Cough, Coryza, Asthma, etc.

Fig : Boil 5 figs in a glass of water, strain it and drink it. It should be taken twice daily in the morning and evening.

Garlic : The use of garlic reduces the severity of phlegm. Take garlic after meals.

Honey : It is beneficial in diseases related to lungs. Honey is much used for the treatment of asthmatic patients.

Spinach : In case of cough, sore throat and burning gargling with spinach juice is beneficial.

Milk : Boil 5 pieces of long pepper in milk. Add sugar and drink it every morning and evening. It will bring relief from cough and strengthen the lungs. Take the treatment for some months.

Basil : If phlegm has accumulated in the lungs, grind dry basil leaves, catechu, camphor and cardamom in equal quantity. Add nine times sugar; take a pinch of it in the morning and evening. It will act as an expectorant. It is nothing but homeopathic medicine called Trituration. Please also go through the details on T.B. in the present book.

PIERCING OF A THORN

Sesame seeds : Try to get the thorn out with the help of a needle. In case it does not get out, soak a swab of cotton in sesame oil mixed with salt, put it on the spot where the thorn has pierced and put a bandage on it. The thorn will come out.

Jaggery : If thorn has pierced deep and does not come out easily, scrapple a little with a needle and apply hot jaggery with caraway seeds. The thorn will come out.

Asafoetida : Application of asafoetida solution where the thorn has pierced is quite helpful. The thorn comes out after some time.

NAVEL

Navel is the centre of gravity of the human body. It must, therefore, remain at its natural location. The navel, sometimes, gets displaced, when one gets up with a jerk, lifts something very heavy, or for any other reason also. It gets displaced to the upside, down, right or left side, and the displacement causes constipation, gastric problems, loss of appetite, or stomachache, etc.

To find out whether the navel is displaced or not

(1) Make the patient lie down flat. Put a little pressure on the navel of the patient with your thumb and two fingers. You will come to know whether the navel is in the centre or it has displaced upside, down, right or left side.

(2) Make the patient lie down flat. If the patient is a male, take a thread and put one end on the navel and measure the distance of both the nipples, one by one, with the thread. If the navel is at its original place, the distance will be equal, otherwise it has displaced. If the patient is a female, keep her arms straight on the sides alongside the boy, both the heels together and toes should remain loose. Take a long thread, put one end on the navel and measure the distance of both the big toes, one by one, by taking the other end of the thread to the

big toe-nail turn by turn. The equidistant shows no displacement, otherwise the navel is displaced.

Method to bring the navel back to its right place

(1) Make the patient lie down straight. The patient should press his rump with both the hands keeping the arms straight, and his back to the bed, he should lift his head and both the legs together slowly, making a curb like a boat. Remain in that position for some time, and slowly return to the original position. Repeat the process. The improvement can be seen by measuring with a thread as explained above.

(2) Take a medium sized *Lota* (a round pot of brass, copper, or steel), keep it on and in the centre of the bed upside down. Put a folded towel on the bottom of the *Lota* which is facing up. The patient should lie upside down in such a way that his navel rests on and in the centre of the bottom of the *Lota*. Keep the legs straight and the hands folded behind the neck. Let him in this position for sometime. Now let the patient lie down straight and measure the distance as explained above, and notice the improvement.

(3) Let the patient lie down straight keeping the arms straight along the body line. If the patient is a female, fold the leg of the side which measures less distance, bring that knee closer to the stomach and try touching the bed with this folded knee. Do not put more force. Do it several times as long as it is convenient, and thereafter, measure the distance as explained above. If the patient is a male, fold the leg of the side which show less distance and let the patient try touching the bed with the folded knee as explained.

NAVEL DISPLACEMENT

When the navel is displaced or it does not function properly, it usually causes stomachache, flatulence, diarrhoea and lack of appetite. In order to get relief from these problems the navel should be readjusted. Eat something after the readjustment.

Navel is also known as umbilicus. When you press the stomach, under navel you feel a throbbing sensation. Sometimes this throbbing or sensation appears to be on the right of the navel, at other times it appears to be on the left. It is known as navel displacement. It occurs when you lift something heavy or if there is a jerk.

If it has gone to the right side, press on the left side of lower limb in the middle, otherwise press the right side. It will bring it back to the right place.

Mustard oil : Application of oil, especially mustard oil is beneficial. If the problem is severe, soak a cotton swab in oil and put it on the navel. You may bandage it.

Aniseed : Grind 2 tsp. of aniseed, mix with jaggery and take it daily for five days. It checks navel displacement.

Curd : Take 500 gms. of curd mixed with 1 tsp. of turmeric powder. Do not eat anything else during the entire day. Before taking the curd readjust the navel. Navel displacement will not occur repeatedly.

Jaggery : Eat a little jaggery with some salt after the readjustment of the navel. Displacement will not recur.

SUPPURATION OF THE NAVEL

Betel nut : Sometimes, after suppuration blood and pus begin to secrete from the navel. After severing umbilical cord of infants, the navel begins to suppurate. For this, grind polished betel nut in hot water and apply on the navel twice daily in the morning and evening. It will heal the navel.

DISEASES OF THE DIGESTIVE SYSTEM

Lemon : If your digestive system does not function well, the food does not get digested, you feel heaviness and a pressure on the heart because of flatulence, the stomach distends and you don't get sleep at night, squeeze a lemon in a glass of warm water and drink it. Repeat it several times in a day. It will cleanse the digestive system. All the poisonous substances in the blood and the body are excreted through the urine. You will begin to feel that you have gained a fresh energy and agility. In case of indigestion smear a piece of lemon with salt, heat it and suck it. It will improve digestion. Lemon is useful in all the diseases of the liver.

Orange : Those who have a bad digestive system should mix one part orange juice with three parts water and take it daily.

Mint leaves : Mint leaves are beneficial in many diseases of the stomach. Therefore, mint leaves should be used daily in one form or the other.

Spinach : The juice of raw spinach relieves constipation in a few days. It is useful as a vegetable in the diseases of the intestines. Spinach mixed with *bathua* is also beneficial in constipation. Take spinach in sufficient quantity for some days. It will be beneficial in several diseases of the stomach.

Ginger : (1) Cut 6 gms. of ginger into small pieces, add a little salt and eat it before meals. If it is taken for ten days, it will improve the digestive system, sharpen the appetite, will relieve flatulence and constipation, improve the taste and you will begin to like your food. It will also cleanse the mucous in the throat.

(2) Grind dry ginger and caraway seeds and soak in lemon juice. Then dry it in shade and mix a little salt. Take a gram each in the morning and evening with water. It provides relief from digestive disorders, stomachache due to gas and sour belching.

(3) Grind dry ginger, asafoetida and black salt and prepare a powder. Its use expels gas from the stomach.

(4) Fry ginger piece in clarified butter, add salt to taste and take it twice daily. It is beneficial in flatulence and indigestion. It cures common ailments of the stomach.

(5) Take a tsp. of ginger juice in ¼ cup of water. It is beneficial in every type of disease of the digestive system. Whenever the stomach is upset, take ginger.

(6) Cut ginger into small pieces, wrap them in a betel leaf as

you do with betel nut pieces. Also pierce a clove in a way that the ginger pieces do not fall out. Immerse the betel leaf in lemon juice for twenty days. Add salt to lemon juice to taste. Take a *paan* daily after meals. It will help in the digestion of food and improve the digestive system in general.

STOMACH AILMENTS

Rose apple : It is beneficial in the ailments of stomach. It has the potency to regulate the motion. Take rose apple juice with rock salt to get relief from stomach-ache, diarrhoea and loss of appetite.

Banana : For different kinds of stomach related ailments, eating bananas as a part of the meals helps in recovery. It is a nutrient for the weak person and children. In the case of diarrhoea, gastritis, colitis and gastric ulcer, banana is healthful food. It removes the swelling of the intestines.

Pomegranate : It helps in recovery from debility of stomach, spleen and liver, sprue, diarrhoea, vomiting and stomach-ache. It is constipative. It being sour and sweet, it improves the digestive system and is diuretic. It helps in producing digestive juices in sufficient quantity.

Carrots : Carrots contain Vitamin B-Complex which strengthens the digestive system. It helps in recovery from dyspepsia and flatulence. It also provides relief from intestinal gas, spasms, swelling, ulcers, dropsy, appendicitis, colitis, stench, scratching, etc. and the stool is free from disagreeable smell. As soon as you take carrot juice, you feel a sense of relief. It is also effective in mucus related ailments. It clears the bowels, improves appetite and removes foul smell. Please consult the present author's book on treatment through medicines *Pet ke Rogon ki Homeo Chikitsa* for further details.

Onion : It enhances the taste of the food and improves the appetite. It helps in the digestion of the food. It stimulates the liver, spleen and bile and improves their functioning. It expels wind from the stomach and relieves stomach-ache and flatulence. It also nullifies the ill-effects on health because of the change of place and climate. It provides relief from acidity. Roast an onion in fire, crush it and extract juice from it. Mix 1 gm. of salt and drink it. It will provide relief from stomach-ache.

Radish : Eat a radish daily for two months with salt and black pepper powder with meals. It is beneficial in loss of appetite, sickness of stomach, chronic constipation and flatulence. For diseases of the stomach radish can be used in the form of *chutney*, pickles and vegetable.

***Gwar-patha* :** Mix fresh juice of *gwar-patha* (25 gms.) with 12 gms. honey and the juice of half lemon. Take twice daily in the morning and evening. It is beneficial in all types of stomach ailments.

***Chaulai* :** It is beneficial in diseases of the stomach.

Apple : It is beneficial in diseases of the stomach especially for children. Take one to three apples at a time daily according to your need and capacity.

***Bathua* :** Take it as a vegetable regularly till it is available in the season. It provides relief from the diseases of the stomach like those of the liver, spleen, flatulence, dyspepsia, worms and piles.

***Masoor daal* :** It is beneficial in the diseases of digestive system.

Bread : Its excessive use leads to several diseases of the stomach. Food items made of fine flour cause constipation. Gradually it causes peptic ulcer.

Ginger : (1) Mix 1 gm. dried ginger powder with a little asafoetida and rock salt and take it with hot water. It relieves stomach-ache.

(2) A tsp. of dried ginger powder and a little rock salt in a glass of hot water relieves stomach-ache.

(3) Fry small pieces of ginger in clarified butter and add salt to taste. Take it twice daily. It provides relief usually from all types of common stomach ailments.

HEAVINESS OF STOMACH

Aniseed : Eating aniseed soaked in lemon juice after meals relieves heaviness of the stomach, improves appetite and clears the bowels.

ERUCTATION

Asafoetida : If belching persists take a minute quantity of asafoetida with jaggery or a banana.

Cumin seeds : Grind roasted cumin seeds and take 1 tsp. of the powder with a tsp. of honey. It is beneficial in belching.

EXCESSIVE THIRST

Banana : Thirst can be controlled by eating two bananas at a time thrice a day. The dryness of the throat disappears.

Millet : Eat millet flour *rotis* with butter milk daily. It reduces thirst. People with weak body and those who are rheumatic should not take millet flour *rotis*.

Salt : It evaporates glandular juices, therefore, one feels thirsty after taking salt. Those who feel too much thirsty, should take very little of salt.

Barley : Pound one cup of barley and let it soak in water for eight hours. Then boil it. Gargle with hot barley water. It will reduce the feeling of thirst.

Water-melon : It reduces thirst. Mix sugar candy in water-melon juice and drink it. It is very beneficial.

Orange : It reduces thirst.

***Gulkand* :** Take three tsp. of *gulkand* made of roses twice daily in the morning and evening followed by a glass of water. It will quench the thirst.

Coriander : Prepare *chutney* using green coriander leaves and dry *amla* powder. Eating it daily will bring relief from excessive thirst and dryness of the throat.

Apple : Drinking apple juice mixed with water reduces thirst. Persons suffering from flatulence should not take it.

Plum : Sucking a plum reduces thirst.

Guava : Guava, *Lychee*, Mulberry and Cucumber—all help in quenching thirst.

Cloves : When the thirst is very powerful, boil cloves in water and drink. It reduces thirst. It is a proven formula.

Nutmeg : Sucking a piece of nutmeg will relieve thirst in any ailment.

Basil : Grind basil leaves, mix in water, add lemon drops and sugar candy and drink it. It will reduce thirst.

Water : If the thirst is due to dryness, taking hot water brings relief.

Lemon : Taking lemon water quenches thirst.

Cardamom : Boil the skin of 12 cardamoms in a glass of water. When the water is reduced to half, divide in into four doses and take a dose every two hours. It will control thirst in any ailment.

FLATULENCE COLIC

Lemon : When the stomach distends like a ball it is known as flatulence. 2 tsp. of lemon juice in hot water provides relief from flatulence.

Castor oil : 2 tsp. of castor oil in a glass of hot water is beneficial.

Salt : Mix one part rock salt and four parts *desi* sugar (unrefined sugar powder) and take it thrice daily. It provides relief from gas.

Caraway seeds : Grind 1 tsp. of caraway seeds, ¼ tsp. of black salt, mix in a glass of butter milk and drink it. It is beneficial in flatulence.

SPLEEN

Lemon : Cut a lemon into two pieces, heat a piece, add a little salt and suck it before meals for some days. It will bring the enlarged spleen back to its normal size.

Mango : Mix 70 gms. mango juice with 15 gms. honey. Take it daily in the morning for three weeks. It is beneficial in the swelling and wounds of the spleen. Do not take sour food during the treatment.

Papaya : Regular use of papaya is beneficial in the ailments related to spleen.

Carrots : Eating carrot pickles reduces the enlarged spleen.

Bitter gourd : 25 ml. of the juice of bitter gourd mixed in a cup of water taken thrice a day cures the problem of spleen.

Brinjal : Eat fresh long brinjals cooked as a vegetable as long as the season lasts. It provides relief from enlarged spleen.

Caraway seeds : Soak 15 gms. caraway seeds in the morning in a clay pot. Keep it inside a room during the day but on the open terrace under the sky, during the night. Next day, strain and drink it. Do it for 15 days continuously. It will cure the enlarged spleen. If it is not possible to take the above treatment, take caraway seeds in sufficient quantity in any form you like. Caraway seeds are highly beneficial in this ailment.

Clay : Application of wet clay on the stomach for a month is beneficial.

***Bathua*:** Take the juice of *bathua* leaves or boil *bathua* leaves and take the water. It cures the problem of spleen. For taste salt can be added to it.

WOUNDS IN THE INTESTINES

Apple : Taking apple juice helps in the healing of wounds in the intestines.

***Ber*:** It heals intestinal wounds.

INTESTINAL DISEASES

Butter milk : It clears and purifies the channels and pathways in the body and allows the circulation of digestive juice effectively. It prevents the diseases of the intestines.

Honey : To cure intestinal ailments, soak overnight three tsp. of ground *amla* in a glass of water. In the morning, strain, mix 4 tsp. of honey and drink it.

Radish : Its juice acts as an antiseptic for the intestines.

Curd : According to Gastro-enterologist, Prof. Tashev Tasho of Bulgaria the ill-effects of antibiotics on the intestinal bacterial flora can be set off by taking curd.

Juice : Ulcer patients as well as patients with intestinal disorders can take fruit juices. Some people think that taking fruit juices or fruit causes hydrochloric acid in the stomach which is harmful for the ailments of the stomach and ulcers. But their belief does not hold good.

Ulcer and intestinal patients should give up pulses and eggs.

SWELLING IN INTESTINES

Carrots : Mix 185 gms. carrot juice with 150 gms. juice of beet-root and 160 gms. juice of cucumber and drink it. It is beneficial in the swelling of intestines.

Curd : Use of plenty of curd daily to get relief from the swelling of intestines. Eat it frequently. Whenever you feel hungry, eat curd instead of *roti*.

INTESTINAL CONSUMPTION

Garlic : Mix garlic juice (5 drops) with 3 tsp. of water and drink. It is beneficial in intestinal consumption.

MUCOUS

Ginger : (1) Grind dried ginger and mix with jaggery in equal quantity. Take two tablets of the size of peas daily in the morning and evening. It will check the secretion of mucous from the intestines.

(2) Mucous gets formed in the stomach because of indigestion. To get relief, boil ½ tsp. of dried ginger powder in 250 ml. of milk, then let it simmer for some time. Allow it to cool down. It should be taken before bed-time for 4-5 days. It will check the secretion of mucous.

Neem **:** If mucous passes with the stool, clean green *neem* leaves with water and dry them in the shade. Grind the dry leaves into a powder. Take ½ tsp. of it twice a day, with cool water. After a few days the secretion of mucous will stop.

Garlic : (1) Take a clove of garlic with a minute quantity of opium. It will provide relief from mucous.

(2) Mix 5 cloves of garlic with ½ tsp. of clarified butter and eat them by chewing properly. It brings relief from the problem of mucous.

Aniseed : (1) 5 drops of aniseed oil with ½ tsp. of sugar taken four times daily will provide relief from mucous.

(2) Roast 100 gms. of aniseed and grind with 100 gms. of sugar candy. Take 2 tsp. of it after meals in the morning and evening with cool water.

Coriander : Grind 50 gms. coriander leaves alongwith 25 gms. aniseed, dissolve in a glass of water, strain and drink it. It cures the problem of mucous. If a child suffers from mucous, give him the concoction of coriander and dried ginger powder.

Isabgol **:** (1) Take a tsp. of *isabgol* husk in hot milk before bed-time. In the morning take another tsp. in curd mixed with dried ginger powder and cumin seeds. If you take it for four days continuously it will provide relief from the problem of mucous.

(2) Mix one part each of *harad* and the dry pulp of *bel* and three parts of *isabgol.* Take 2 tsp. of it in the morning and evening with hot milk. It will bring relief from mucous.

GASTRIC ULCER

Garlic : Take four cloves of raw garlic after meals daily. It will help in the healing of gastric ulcer.

Bathua **:** It strengthens the stomach.

Banana : Cook green raw bananas as a vegetable and eat without adding salt or chilli powder or take 3 tsp. of the powder of dried raw bananas twice daily in the morning and evening with cool water. It facilitates the healing of gastric ulcer.

COLITIS

Ulcerative Colitis is an inflammatory and ulcerative condition of the colon. It leads to loose motions and passing of mucous and blood with the stool.

Carrots : Carrots contain Vitamin B-complex which strengthens the digestive system and cures colitis. For details about the use of carrots in this disease please read the present writer's book *Bhojan Ke Dwara Chikitsa.*

Banyan tree : Take 1 kg. of the hanging roots of the banyan tree of the thickness of a human finger and cut into small pieces of the size of an inch. Boil them in 5 litre of water. When the water is reduced to 1 litre, allow it to cool down, strain and store in a glass bottle. Take 2 tsp. of it twice daily in the morning and evening. It provides relief from both ulcerative and amebic colitis.

Water : Taking hot water, as hot as you can tolerate, after meals provides relief from colitis.

AVERSION

Extreme or intense dislike for food is called aversion.

Pomegranate : Grind ½ tsp. of black pepper, 1 tsp. of roasted cumin seeds, very little quantity (equal to the weight of 1 piece of gram pulse) of roasted asafoetida, rock salt to taste and 70 gms. of dried pomegranate seeds. It will make a tasty *churan.* Take it daily. It will provide relief from aversion and keep you cheerful.

***Phalsa* :** Take *phalsa* with black pepper powder and rock salt to get relief from aversion.

Radish : Eat a radish daily with black pepper and salt with meals for two months. It will be beneficial.

Mint leaves : Mix 3 gms. paste of mint leaves, cumin seeds powder, asafoetida, black pepper powder and salt in a glass of hot water and drink it. It is quite beneficial.

Moth **:** Eating fried and salted *moth* available with *namkeen* vendors provides relief from aversion.

Coriander : Grind coriander seeds, cardamom and black pepper in equal quantity and eat after adding ¼ tsp. of clarified butter and sugar. It brings relief from aversion.

Sugar : Mix tamarind pulp, ¼ tsp. of black pepper powder and sugar to taste in a cup of water and strain it. Take it four times daily. It will provide relief from aversion and improve the appetite.

Caraway seeds : Grind caraway seeds, add salt to it and take it with hot water. It will solve the problem of aversion.

CANCER OF THE STOMACH

Garlic : The use of garlic prevents cancer of the stomach. Cancer patients should be given ground garlic dissolved in water. It can cure cancer of the stomach. Eating garlic after meals thrice a day keeps the bowels clean. It causes contraction in the stomach muscles. As a consequence, the intestines do not have to over-work. It also stimulates the liver which facilitates the flow of oxygen and blood to the capillaries of the stomach walls.

Bread : If you want to protect yourself from cancer of the stomach, increase the intake of bread with your meals. This finding has been made by the nutrition expert, Prof. Groen of Lieden University, Germany. Bread plays a preventive role because according to nutrition experts bread is more easily digestible than other edibles. As a result, it eliminates the chances of cancer of the stomach. (See—'Cancer' at *pg.129*).

BAD SMELL

Curd : If bad smell emanates from your body, mix curd with black gram flour and rub on the body.

Basil : Smelling the juice of basil leaves or the powder of dried leaves removes bad smell from the nose and kills germs.

Onion : After eating onions, eat jaggery or a betel leaf to curb onion smell. Or you may chew coriander seeds or cardamom. It will also serve the purpose. To curb the onion smell from the vegetable cooked with onions, add a little sugar dissolved in water when the cooking begins. To remove onion smell from utensils, clean them with salted lukewarm water.

Garlic : Chew coriander seeds after eating garlic to curb its smell.

Radish : Eat jaggery after eating a radish. It will check the smell expelled with burps.

Carrots : Carrot juice improves the digestive system. It checks the strong smell in the stool and kills the germs. 'Take Juice and Transform Yourself.' — *Kanti Bhatt* and *Manhar D. Shah*

PROLAPSE RECTI

Guava : While passing the stool in some cases the anus emerges out. Press it in and apply the paste made by grinding guava leaves. It will provide relief from the problem.

Alum salt : Dissolve alum salt in water and insert the solution into the anus with the help of a syringe. It is beneficial. Also dissolve ½ tsp. of alum salt in a glass of water and cleanse the anus with it. Soak a piece of cloth in alum salt water and place it on the anus.

Gallnut : Grind two gallnuts and mix in a glass of water and boil for some time. Allow it to cool down. Clean the anus with it. It will check the emerging out of the anus.

CORN

Lemon : Application of lemon juice on the corns makes them soft. You can put a piece of lemon on the corn and bandage it with gauze. Or soak a swab of cotton in lemon juice and put it on the corn and bandage it.

Castor oil : Application of castor oil on the corns for two months provides relief from them.

Onion : Apply onion juice on the corn thrice daily. When it becomes soft, cut it off.

EXPECTORATION

Grapes : Grapes make the lungs strong and cure coryza and cough. Mucus is expectorated. Do not drink water after eating grapes.

Mint leaves : ¼ cup of the juice of mint leaves mixed with equal quantity of hot water taken thrice daily provides relief from cough.

Banana and Mulberry : They both provide relief from cough.

Mustard oil : In case of cough and accumulation of mucus in the chest, massage the chest with mustard oil mixed with rock salt. It will bring relief. It checks asthma and expectorates mucus.

Turmeric : (1) In case of discharge of mucus, take ½ tsp. of turmeric powder with hot milk.

(2) If it is hard to get sleep due to cough, take turmeric powder and salt mixed in hot water.

(3) If the discharge of mucus takes place in coryza and asthma, take 2 gms. of turmeric powder thrice daily with hot water.

Black pepper : Boil 30 *neem* leaves and 5 ground corns of black pepper in two cups of water. When the water is reduced to one-fourth, strain and add a tsp. of honey. Take it twice daily in the morning and evening. It brings relief from cough, mucus and congestion in the throat.

Basil : Mix 5 tsp. of sugar in 50 gms. juice of basil leaves and prepare a syrup. Take a tsp. of it daily. It will provide relief from cough. The juice of basil leaves can facilitate expectoration by thinning the mucus.

PAIN IN RIBS

Asafoetida : Dissolve asafoetida in hot water and apply the solution on the painful ribs.

Ginger : Grind 30 gms. dried ginger and boil in ½ litre water, strain and make four doses. Take it four times in a day. It will relieve pain in ribs.

Honey : Mix a little *sindoor* in honey, put it on a clean piece of cloth and place the cloth on the painful ribs. Foment the ribs. It will relieve pain in the ribs.

Water : Take a glass of hot water, as hot as possible, after meals regularly. It will relieve pain in ribs.

CRAMPS

Onion : Massaging the sole of the feet with warm onion juice relieves cramps and twitching.

Honey : If the eyelids of the patient close down repeatedly and there is twitching in some part, he should use honey regularly. It will bring relief from cramps.

MUMPS

Salt : Gargling with hot saline water helps. Foment the swollen glands with hot saline water.

Clay : Application of wet black clay on the swollen glands is beneficial.

PAIN RELIEVERS

Pain Relieving Medicines are Harmful : The chief pain relieving medicines are : Anacin, Crocin, Ibuprofen and commonly used Aspirin.

The use of 300 mg. or a higher dose of aspirin does not do any good to heart patients, rather it is harmful.

Pain relievers, it is true, provide prompt relief from pain but they also damage extensively several parts of the body. Pain killers can cause ulcers in the stomach and sometimes the patient can die of bleeding. Pain killers are harmful in the long run.

Elderly persons, women, smokers and drinkers have a greater possibility of having stomach ulcers. Therefore, such persons should be specially careful about the use of pain-killers.

—*Rajasthan Patrika, Jaipur, 13-4-1995*

Garlic : Grind two bulbs of garlic and mix in 100 gms. sesame oil. Apply on the painful parts. It will relieve pain.

Mustard oil : Mix 5 gms. of camphor in 50 ml. of mustard oil and massage the painful parts. It is beneficial and relieves pain.

Water : Whatever type of pain in any part of the body, first foment with hot water for 3 minutes, then foment with ice-cold water for one minute. It will be beneficial.

Wheat : Bake a wheat flour *roti* only on one side. The other side should be unbaked. Smear the unbaked side with sesame oil and place it on the painful part and bandage it. It will provide relief from pain.

Gram : If the pain is located in the back, hands and feet, massage with gram *daal* flour. The massage will bring relief from pain.

Cardamom (large) : Grind large cardamom into fine powder and apply it on the painful part. It will be beneficial.

Cardamom : "Eat Cardamoms and Remove Pain"— A survey conducted by Cardamom Board says that cardamom has the power to remove headache, stomachache, vomiting sensation and the chronic disease of pain in the joints. To know about how cardamom should be used in different types of pain, please go through the present author's book *Bhojan Ke Dwara Chikitsa.*

Coffee : Whatever type of pain, it is reduced by taking coffee. It contains the element known as Caffeine which affects the experience centre of the brain called sensor cortex by stimulating it. Thus it reduces pain.

Fenugreek : Roast 100 gms. fenugreek seeds on a hot plate in such a way that they remain half-roasted. Then pound them to a little extent. Mix 25 gms. of black salt. Take 2 tsp. of it twice daily in the morning and evening with hot water. It will provide relief from joint pain, back-ache, knee-pain, rheumatic pain and all types of pain. It will also check flatulence.

Turmeric : Taking a tsp. of turmeric powder in a glass of hot milk relieves body-ache.

Cumin seeds : Boil 2 tsp. of cumin seeds in a glass of water and foment the painful parts. Grind the boiled cumin seeds and apply the paste on the painful parts.

INJURY

Gwar **:** Boil sesame seeds and *gwar* in equal quantity, grind and apply on the sprained or injured part. It will relieve pain.

Green grass : If the bleeding is because of a cut or injury, grind green grass and soak a piece of cloth in its juice and bandage it on the injured part to stop bleeding.

Kerosene oil : Application of kerosene oil twice a day after bathing provides relief from injury, sprain or swelling because of injury and sprain or from chronic pain.

Ice : If there is bleeding because of injury, use an ice pack and also a piece of ice. It will stop the bleeding.

Banana : In case of injury or abrasion : (1) Place a banana peel on the injured spot and bandage it with a piece of cloth. It will check swelling.

(2) Knead a ripe mashed banana and wheat flour in water, heat it and apply on the injured spot.

Garlic : Grind garlic cloves with salt and use it as a poultice on the injured spot and bandage it with a piece of cloth. It will be beneficial in injury and spasms.

Fenugreek : Apply the poultice made of fenugreek leaves and bandage it up. It will relieve swelling caused by injury.

Castor oil : (1) In case of an injury or bleeding or wound, apply castor oil and bandage it up. It is beneficial.

(2) Smear a leaf of the castor tree with sesame oil and heat it. It provides relief from swelling and pain caused by injury.

Alum salt : If the injury is internal taking 4 gms. of ground alum salt mixed in half a glass of milk is beneficial.

Turmeric : (1) Taking a tsp. of turmeric powder in a glass of hot milk relieves pain and swelling caused by an injury. It mends the wear and tear of the body. Knead turmeric powder in water and apply the paste on the injured spot. If there is bleeding because of injury, fill the injured place with turmeric powder. It will come off only with the dry incrustation. Turmeric powder is useful even in an eye injury.

(2) Mix 2 tsp. of turmeric powder, four tsp. of wheat flour, a tsp. of clarified butter, ½ tsp. of rock salt and make *halwa* using a little water. Spread it on the injured spot and bandage it up. You can reduce or increase the quantity of the ingredients as per your need. Mix ½ tsp. rock salt in 500 ml. of boiling water. Cover the pot and keep it for some time. When it is bearably hot, soak a piece of cloth and foment the injured spot with it. It will provide relief from pain.

(3) In case of a bone fracture, the use of turmeric powder is beneficial.

(4) Grind an onion and mix a tsp. of turmeric powder and tie it in a piece of cloth. Heat it in sesame oil and foment the injured part. After fomenting for a little while spread the contents on the injured part and bandage it up.

(5) Mix two parts of turmeric powder and one part of lime and apply the paste on the injured or swollen part. It will relieve pain.

(6) Grind 10 cloves of garlic with ½ tsp. of turmeric powder and heat it in a tsp. of oil. Apply it on the swollen part, place on it a little cotton and bandage it up. It will relieve swelling.

Sesame seeds : Cook oil cake in water and spread it on the sprained part while it is bearably hot. It will provide relief from pain.

Onion : Mix a tsp. of turmeric powder with 2 tsp. of onion juice. Tie it up in a piece of cloth and soak it in hot mustard oil and foment the injured part with it. Afterwards spread the contents on the injured spot and bandage it up with the same piece of cloth. Also put some cotton and use another bandage. Mix 2 tsp. of onion juice with 1 tsp. of honey and take it twice daily. It will relieve both pain and swelling caused by injury.

Water : When you slip and fall or injure yourself and there is swelling on and around the injured spot it is painful. If there is swelling due to injury do not do hot fomentation. Cold fomentation is helpful. Foment with ice or cold water. It reduces or removes swelling. As soon as you receive an injury, foment with ice or cold water. Then bandage it and position it upwardly. Cold fomentation should be done for fifteen minutes and then repeat it every two hours for ten hours. Increase the gap in the next ten hours. Then do alternate cold fomentation with hot fomentation. For details, see the present author's book "*Bhojan Ke Dwara Chikitsa*".

Wheat : When you have a bone fracture, injury or sprain, eat *halwa* made with jaggery and wheat flour. Mix 2 tsp. of wheat ash with jaggery and clarified butter and eat twice daily in the morning and evening. It will relieve pain and help in the joining of the bone.

Rock salt : Mix rock salt and unrefined sugar powder in equal quantity and take a tsp. twice daily in the morning and evening. It will relieve pain caused by injury.

Salt : (1) Heat salt on a hot plate. Tie it up in a piece of coarse cloth and foment the bruised or sprained part while it is hot. It will relieve pain.

(2) Foment with hot saline water.

Ginger : If you have developed pain due to injury, lifting something heavy or because of some part of the body has been crushed, apply a thick layer of ginger paste and bandage it up. Remove the bandage after two hours and apply hot mustard oil on the layer of ginger paste and foment. Repeat it for a few days. It will relieve pain.

Potato : Sometimes there are blue spots because of an injury. Grind a raw potato and apply the paste on the affected part.

HEMORRHAGE

***Phalsa* :** To check bleeding from any part of the body, taking *phalsa* syrup regularly proves to be quite effective.

BLEEDING : CUTS

Amla **:** To stop bleeding caused by a cut apply fresh *amla* juice.

Green grass : Soak a piece of cloth in the juice of green grass and bandage it on the injured spot. It will help in checking bleeding.

Kerosene oil : To control bleeding caused by a cut, soak a piece of cloth in kerosene oil and bandage it tightly on the injured spot. The bleeding will stop. It will also relieve pain. Keep adding a few drops of kerosene oil to the piece of cloth tied on the injured spot every now and then.

BLEEDING : INJURY

Banana : If the bleeding has been caused by an injury apply the juice of banana stem. The bleeding will stop. There will be no pus formation in the wound. It will also accelerate the healing of the wound.

Ice : If the bleeding is because of an injury, put an ice pack on the injured spots and also place a piece of ice on it. The bleeding will stop.

WOUND

Orange : Eating oranges will accelerate the process of healing of a wound.

Grapes : Eating grapes helps in the prompt healing of wounds.

Sahjan **:** Grind *sahjan* leaves and apply the paste on the wound. It will quicken the healing process.

Carrots : Boil carrots and prepare pulp. It helps in the healing of rotten wounds. It is a common practice in England. Taking carrot juice is also beneficial. The application of carrot pulp on a cancerous wound is also beneficial.

Cabbage : Its juice is beneficial and helps in the healing of wounds. Add 5 times water to cabbage juice.

Onion : (1) Homeopathic doctors Kook, Gabriel and Minchen told that washing a wound with onion juice mixed with four times water and putting a gauze soaked in the same juice on the wound helps in the healing of a wound.

(2) Application of onion poultice made in clarified butter on a wound is beneficial.

Garlic : If you have got a wound caused by a cut, soak a piece of gauze in garlic juice mixed with two parts water and put it on the wound. It will accelerate the healing process. Also eat garlic.

Wheat : Grind wheat grass and apply its paste on boils and wounds. It will be beneficial.

Castor oil : It is beneficial to apply castor oil on the wound and bandage it.

Alum salt : If the wound is fresh, it has been caused by injury or scratch and it is bleeding, wash the wound with alum salt water and sprinkle alum salt powder on it. The bleeding will stop.

Turmeric : (1) Mix turmeric powder in clarified butter or oil, heat it and soak a piece of cotton in it and bandage it on the wound.

(2) Grind a piece of turmeric in water and apply it on the wound. It kills the germs. Sprinkle some turmeric powder on the wound.

Honey : (1) Dressing the wound with gauze soaked in honey brings relief.

(2) Dress the wound with one part yellow wax and four parts honey. Heat the wax and mix honey, you will get an ointment. It cures even the incurable wounds.

(3) Mix honey with sesame oil and soak a piece of cotton or gauze in the mixture and dress the wound. It facilitates the healing process.

Basil : Smelling at the powder of basil leaves is beneficial in the healing of wounds. Grind dry basil leaves finely, sieve through a fine muslin cloth and sprinkle the powder on the wound. Or you can grind green basil leaves and apply the paste on the wound.

Water : If the wound has been caused by an injury, soak a piece of cloth in cold water and dress the wound with it. Keep the cloth wet. It heals the wound. In case of swelling caused by an old wound, drink hot and cold water twice a day.

***Neem* :** (1) Boil 2 tsp. of the juice of *neem* leaves, 2 tsp. of mustard oil and four tsp. of water. When the water evaporates and only the oil is left, let it cool down, strain and apply it on the wounds and dress. The wounds will heal soon.

(2) If the wound has been caused by the pinching of shoes, apply *neem* oil and sprinkle the fine powder of dried *neem* leaves on the wound.

(3) Grind green *neem* leaves and squeeze out the juice. Soak a cotton swab of the size of the wound in the juice and heat it in clarified butter. Dress the wound with it when it is hot. It helps the wound to heal quickly. Even old incurable wounds get healed. It is based on my personal experience.

Clarified butter : Heat a tsp. of clarified butter in a bowl. Put in it a swab of cotton soaked in water but after squeezing out the water. When the wet cotton swab loses its moisture, dress the wound with it when it is bearably hot, place a betel leaf on it and bandage it up. Change the dressing daily. The wound will get healed.

Millet : Eating millet is beneficial in the healing of wounds.

VERMINOUS WOUNDS

Basil Leaves : Boil basil leaves and wash the wounds with the water. Sprinkle the powder of dry basil leaves on the wounds. Soak a piece of gauze in the juice of basil leaves and dress the wound with it.

Mint leaves : Grind mint leaves, prepare a poultice and dress the wound with it. It kills the worms.

SINUS

Lemon : Squeeze two lemons in one glass of water and take it daily in the morning to get relief from sinus.

Mustard oil : Soak a cotton wick in the medicinal plant swallow wort's milk and allow it to dry. Then light it like a lamp in mustard oil and prepare *kajal* in a clay pot. Apply the *kajal* on the sinus.

Cloves : Grind cloves and turmeric and apply it on the sinus. It will provide relief.

***Neem* :** Dress the sinus with the poultice of *neem* leaves.

Turmeric : Sprinkle turmeric powder on the wound. It will kill the worms in the wound and facilitate its healing.

Garlic : Grind ten cloves of garlic with ¼ tsp. of salt and fry it in clarified butter. Apply it on the verminous wound and bandage it. It will kill worms and accelerate the healing process.

FISTULA

Pomegranate : Boil a handful of fresh pomegranate leaves in two glasses of water. When the water is reduced to half, strain and use it to foment the anus when it is bearably hot and then wash. It will provide relief from the fistula.

Wheat : Taking the juice of tender wheat grass is beneficial in the healing of fistula.

HEMIPLEGIA

Paralysis of one side of the body, e.g., the paralysis of the right arm, is known as hemiplegia.

Black gram : Boil black gram and dried ginger in water as you boil tea and give the boiled water to the patient of hemiplegia to drink.

Bitter gourd : It is beneficial in hemiplegia.

Dried dates : It is beneficial in hemiplegia but one should not take more than 4 pieces at a time, otherwise they generate a great deal of heat in the body. If you eat them after soaking them in milk, they are more nutritious.

Onion : Taking onion juice in adequate quantity facilitates blood circulation and the use of onion is beneficial in hemiplegia.

—*Veer Vani, Jaipur* 3-1-1976

Garlic : (1) Grind 10 cloves at a time and eat with hot clarified butter twice daily in the morning and evening.

Dry massaging of the affected parts of the body with hands is helpful. Do it for two months.

(2) In case of hemiplegia, boil 25 gms. of peeled and ground cloves of garlic in milk. When it becomes thick like *kheer,* eat it when it cools down. Take it regularly for some time.

(3) Boil 250 gms. of ground garlic in 500 ml. of mustard oil and 2 liters of water in an iron pan. When the entire water has evaporated, allow it to cool down. Strain it and massage the body regularly with it. Its use for a month will enable the patient to recover from hemiplegia.

(4) Grind 7 cloves of garlic, mix with a tsp. of butter and eat it. It is also beneficial in hemiplegia.

(5) Take two cloves of garlic and a cup of milk. Take 3 cloves the following day. Chew a clove at a time and take a draught of milk. Increase the number by one clove every day and also the quantity of milk by one sip every day. This way continue the treatment for twenty five days, that is, take 25 cloves of garlic with milk on the 25th day. After 25 days decrease the number of cloves by one each day and the quantity of milk by one sip each day. After 50 days the patient will recover from hemiplegia. If it is not possible to take one big dose of garlic and milk, divide it into two or three doses and take them after an interval of a few hours.

Ginger : (1) Grind 500 gms. of black gram *daal* and fry in clarified butter. Add jaggery to it to taste and 200 gms. of ground ginger. Make *laddoos* and eat one *laddoo* daily.

(2) Boil 20 gms. dried ginger and 50 gms. of black gram. Take the boiled water. It cures hemiplegia.

Honey : Boil one ounce water. Add 2 tsp. of honey when it is bearably hot and give it to the patient to drink. It will provide enough calcium to him. In this way, give honey to the patient for three weeks. The parts affected by hemiplegia will begin to function again.

Walnut : Apply walnut oil into both the nostrils daily in the morning. It will provide relief from hemiplegia.

Black pepper : Grind black pepper into a very fine powder. Mix 1 tsp. of this powder with three tsp. of clarified butter and apply it on the parts affected by hemiplegia.

Basil : Boil basil leaves in water and steam the affected parts and then wash them with the boiled water. Grind basil leaves with rock salt and curd. Apply on the affected parts with this unguent.

Mixed Fruit Juice : Take mixed juice of apple, grapes and pear in equal quantity. It provides relief from hemiplegia. It has to be taken for a few months. For details refer, *'Lakwe ki Prakritik Chikitsa'* by *Dharam Chand Saravgi.*

Sugar : As a preventive measure do not let children eat sugar as a safeguard against hemiplegia.

FITS

Onion : If a woman has fainted or gone hysteric, making her smell onion juice will bring her back to consciousness and make her normal.

Red chilli : Putting a few drops of the homeopathic medicine Capsicum Annun in the nostrils brings a man back to consciousness.

Basil Leaves : Grind basil leaves with salt and put a few drops of the juice into the nostrils of the patient. It is beneficial in bringing the patient back to consciousness.

Water : Sprinkling cold water on the face of the person who has fainted helps him in regaining consciousness.

Mustard oil : Sometimes a woman faints because of

miscarriage or a man faints because of an injury or excessive bleeding. The eyes remain wide open and the person loses consciousness. There is a gurgling sound in the throat caused by cough. In such a case, first massage the head and then the body with mustard oil. Make him drink a little clarified butter. He will regain consciousness.

Ginger : (1) Mix 2 tsp. of ginger juice and 2 tsp. of ground sugar candy in a cup of cool water and make the patient drink it. He will soon come round.

(2) Mix a tsp. of ginger juice and a tsp. of honey and make the patient drink or lick it. He will regain consciousness.

Mint leaves : The smell of mint leaves is helpful in regaining consciousness.

BERIBERI

Orange : Those who usually live on polished rice, develop the disease called beriberi because of the lack of Vitamin B-1. It is characterised by pain in the sinews, paralysis, the dryness of muscles and swelling. Orange juice is beneficial in beriberi.

Potato : Beriberi means 'unable to walk'. The main symptom of the disease is the weakness in the veins of the thighs. Grind potatoes and squeeze out the juice. Give a dose of 1 tsp. of the juice to the patient at a time. Or the patient can chew a raw potato and swallow the juice. This is equally beneficial.

DIPTHERIA

It is an infectious disease of the throat and glands in which false membranes are formed. It is characterised by pain and swelling in the throat and obstruction in breathing.

Lemon : Dr. E.P. Andrews in his book, *Therapeutic Byways* writes that a German physician successfully treated 80 patients with lemon juice and only one of the patients died. He made the patients gargle with lemon water or asked them to suck a little piece of lemon.

Pineapple : Its juice destroys the false diptheric membrane and keeps the throat clear. Pineapple is the chief medicinal fruit for diptheria. Fresh pineapple contains pepsin which is the main element of bile. It is beneficial for a sore throat.

Garlic : Chewing and slowly sucking 60 gms. of garlic cloves in four hours is beneficial in diptheria. Children should be given garlic juice mixed with syrup. It should be frequently repeated.

DIABETES

Banana : It is beneficial in diabetes. It increases the weight. Eat two bananas followed by a glass of hot milk daily for three months. If you suffer from flatulence do not eat bananas.

SCROFULA

Turmeric : Take 8 gms. of turmeric powder twice every day in the morning and evening. Grind a knob of turmeric in water on a stone and apply it on the affected part. Its use for some days brings relief from scrofula.

Carrots : Taking 310 ml. of carrot juice with 125 ml. of the juice of spinach provides relief from scrofula.

PATIENTS WITH KIDNEY PROBLEMS SHOULD NOT EAT THE FOLLOWING ITEMS IN EXCESS

1. Milk, curd, cottage cheese, and other items made of milk.
2. Meat, fish, chicken, etc.
3. Items containing potassium in excess—chocolate, coffee, milk, churan, beer, wine and dry fruits.
4. Fruit, vegetables, etc.
5. Items containing sodium in excess—bread, cake, pastry, etc.
6. *Namkeen*, butter, cheese, etc.
7. Chutney, papad, pickles, etc.

ADENOIDS

Carrots : Carrot juice provides relief from Adenoids.

HYDROCELE

Mango : Grind 25 gms. mango leaves and 10 gms. rock salt, heat it a little and apply it on the testicles. It will provide relief from hydrocele.

Raisins : In case of dropsy of the scrotum or testicles, eating twenty raisins daily will be beneficial.

***Arhar* :** In case of hydrocele in a child, grind soaked *arhar daal* and apply the paste on the testicles.

Water : Fomenting with hot and cold water alternately provides relief from hydrocele.

HERNIA

When the viscera in the abdomen forms a bunch and protrudes through a rupture in the abdominal wall and passes into the blood vessels of the thighs causing protrusion of the size of an egg, it is known as hernia.

When the patient lies down, the protrusion disappears. When he stands, the protrusion reappears. While passing the stool with pressure, sneezing or coughing the protrusion of hernia is clearly visible. While sneezing, the hand automatically reaches the part where the protrusion is and presses it. There appears to be a soft swelling there. In fact, hernia is not a disease as such. It is the weakness of the muscles of stomach walls because of which intestinal protrusion occurs.

Causes : As mentioned above, hernia occurs because of the weakness of the muscles of stomach walls. The stomach wall becomes so weak that the intestines get a chance to protrude and swell like a balloon. The common factors, though not principal causes, which lead to hernia are constipation, jerk, severe coughing, falling down, injury, pressure, or exerting pressure while passing stool.

The patients of hernia should eat abstemiously and avoid constipation and should not pass the stool by exerting pressure otherwise the likelihood of your developing hernia will increase. Dyspepsia and constipation should certainly be avoided in hernia. If you have bulging belly, reduce the bulge.

Castor oil : In case you have hernia testes in which the protrusion has entered the scrotum and the testes seem to be blown up with air and are painful, take 2 tsp. of castor oil in a cup of milk daily for a month. It will be beneficial in hernia.

Coffee : Taking coffee repeatedly and washing the affected part with solution of coffee expels the air and the blown up part becomes normal. It is beneficial even in near fatal hernia.

PROTECTION FROM HEAT

Daily Routine During the Summer : (1) Take a sun-bath for 15 minutes at the time of sunrise. Then take your bath with cold water and rub your body fully well.

(2) **Eyes :** Splash cold water frequently on your eyes during the summer. It will keep your eyes refreshed and healthy.

(3) Do not go out in the sun with empty stomach. Keep the head covered when you move out.

(4) After taking your lunch lie down on your bed for a little while during summer days.

Mulberry : Eat mulberry fruit daily during summer days.

Barley : *Sattu* made of barley has a cooling effect on the body and imparts stamina to tolerate heat.

***Harad*:** Grind *harad* and mix with jaggery in equal quantity and make pea-sized pills. Take two pills with water daily after breakfast. It prevents the disorders common in summer days.

***Amla* :** Taking *amla* syrup during summer days quenches the thirst and prevents common disorders.

Pomegranate : Pomegranate has a cooling effect on the body. One should take pomegranate syrup during the summer.

Rice : It has a naturally cool effect. When the stomach is full of heat eating rice will provide a cooling effect during summer days.

Coriander : If due to hot weather you feel giddy, nausea or the palpitation of the heart goes up, soak 100 gms. coriander powder in ½ litre water in a new clay pot for an hour. Take half cup of the water at a time and mix 5 *batashas* and drink it. Repeat it after every three hours. It will provide relief from all disorders caused by excessive heat.

Water : In case of pain or burning in hands and feet or restlessness, cold water pads are highly beneficial. Soak a piece of cloth in cold water and put it on the face and the belly.

SUFFOCATION IN SUMMER

Lemon : If you have a feeling of suffocation because of heat, take lemon water. It will give you a refreshing feeling.

Cucumber : Eating cucumber is beneficial in summer.

SWEATING

Sweat mainly consists of water which contains various kinds of salt as chlorides of sodium and potassium and other chemicals. It is, therefore, saltish in taste.

Sweat is formed in sweat-glands which are situated below the skin, especially that of the palms of hands and the soles of feet and also that of the head. Usually their number ranges between 20 to 30 lakhs in a human body. Women have greater number of sweat glands than men. Yet, they do not sweat so much as men because of the testosterone hormone.

The formation of sweat depends upon the instruction received from the brain which is activated by hypothalamus. When our body is heated up due to some reason, the heat passes on to the blood and when the hot blood reaches the hypothalamus part of the brain, it gets agitated. Consequently, the process of keeping the heat under control and making the temperature normal begins through vibrating nerves and the forming of sweat in the sweat-glands starts and the various parts of the body begin to sweat. Due to atmospheric heat and dryness, the sweat begins to evaporate. In this process it uses body-heat thus reducing body temperature. During the summer season the human body excretes ½ litre sweat every hour to keep the body temperature normal. As a result the body loses 125 calories of heat every hour. This is how we feel cool.

Normal sweating is an indication of good health. Sweating keeps the pores in the skin open and the skin gets proper oxygen. Consequently, it retains its shine and smoothness.

Excessive sweating results in the loss of two much water and salts leading to headache, sleepiness, peevishness and sometimes vomiting. The patient finds himself at a loss. The body becomes cold, breathing becomes fast and the pulse rate goes up.

The patient should be given tomato juice mixed with salt and water in a small quantity, frequently. Lemon water also compensates for the loss of water and salts in the body. Do not work for long hours with empty stomach in hot weather.

Green gram : Roast kidney beans and grind them into powder. Knead it by adding water and smear the body with the paste. It will check excessive sweating.

***Harad* :** Grind *harad* finely. Smear the part which sweats excessively with the paste. Wash yourself after ten minutes. It will check excessively sweating.

***Moth* :** Roast *moth* and grind it. Mix ½ tsp. of salt in a handful of *moth* flour. Rub it dry on the body part which sweats excessively. It will check excessive sweating.

***Arhar* :** Mix a handful of a *arhar daal* with 1 tsp. of salt and ½ tsp. of dried ginger powder and fry it in mustard oil and then grind it. Massage the body with it. It will check excessive sweating. It can also be used for excessive sweating during delirium.

Salt : If your sweat is foul smelling reduce the intake of salt to the minimum.

Water : If your feet sweat profusely, immerse the feet first in hot water and then in cold water. Rub the feet together and then wipe them with a towel. Continue with the treatment for a week. It will be beneficial.

Brinjal : Application of the raw juice of brinjals on palms and soles checks profuse sweating.

Alum salt : Wash hands and feet with two glasses of cold water mixed with 1 tsp. of alum salt. It will check sweating.

PRICKLY HEAT

Henna : During the summer season prickly heat appears on the neck and the tender skin of the body. Application of henna paste is beneficial and relieves pain. It is a proven formula.

Bitter gourd : Application of the juice of bitter gourd is helpful in prickly heat during the summer season. Mix 1 tsp. of baking powder in ¼ cup of the juice of bitter gourd. Two or three applications will provide relief from prickly heat.

SUN-STROKE

You may have a sun-stroke if you move about in the hot sun during the summer season.

Symptoms of Sun-stroke : Lack of sweating, redness of face, high fever (106-108°C), increased pulse rate, difficulty in breathing and giddiness.

Precautions :

1. Do not move about in the hot sun. If you have to go out in the sun, cover your head and neck with a piece of cotton cloth. Use an umbrella and a cap.
2. Do not go out in the sun with empty stomach.
3. Keep away from crowded places and suffocating atmosphere.
4. Take cold drinks, salt, onions and raw mango juice in water.

Treatment :

1. Take the patient to a shaded and cool but open place.
2. Remove his clothes or loosen them.

3. Place cold wet pads on the forehead.
4. Give him some cold drink, salt and lemon.
5. Do not give anything hot to drink.
5. If the fever is high and the temperature does not come down, consult a doctor.

Mango : It is beneficial to take raw mango water during a heat stroke. If the patient of heat stroke complains of dryness of the mouth and tongue, sweating on the forehead and hands and feet, restlessness and excessive thirst, give him raw mango boiled and diluted with water. Boil or roast a large raw mango. Keep it in cold water for some time. Remove the skin, mash it well, add jaggery, cumin seeds, salt and black pepper powder to the pulp and then add water to it as per your requirement. Take a cup at a time thrice daily. It will be beneficial in a heat stroke.

Onion : Massaging the temples and the chest with onion juice and drinking the juice is also beneficial in a heat stroke. Eat onions twice daily during summers and also keep one with you to protect you from a sun-stroke. Whenever you take your meals, take onions also. If you take the *chutney* of mint leaves and onions regularly during the summer it will minimize the risk of your having a heat stroke.

Cardamom : If you want to protect yourself from the scorching sun, chew a cardamom before you venture out. This recipe has become quite popular in Gulf countries. Most of the Arabs chew cardamom to save themselves from the scorching sun.

Coriander : Mix sugar in coriander water and drink it to protect yourself from a heat stroke.

Basil : Mix sugar in the juice of basil leaves and drink it. It protects you from a heat stroke. If you have already suffered, even then it will be beneficial. It relieves giddiness.

Ice : Remove the clothes of the patient and let him have some air. Make him cool by sponging his body with ice cold water. Soak a sheet in iced water and wrap his body with it. Thus bring his temperature down to 102°C.

Water : Taking water frequently during the summer is a good antidote to heat-stroke. Sponge the body of a heat stroke patient with water. As a safety measure or to relieve heat the cold water pads are highly beneficial for the patient of heat stroke. Put cold water pads on the head, chest, abdomen and other parts of the body.

Lemon : Squeeze a lemon in a glass of water, add sugar to taste and drink it. It will reduce the severity of a heat stroke.

Mulberry : Eat mulberry fruit as a preventive measure.

Tamarind : Smear the palms and soles of the patient with ripe tamarind pulp. It will reduce the severity of the heat stroke. Drinking tamarind water in summer is beneficial. Soak tamarind in water, mash it, strain and drink it. It will be more beneficial if you mix jaggery in tamarind water.

***Phalsa* :** *Phalsa* syrup is a wholesome drink in a heat stroke. It releases the unnecessary heat from the body and fulfils the essential requirement of water in the body.

DISEASES OF THE RAINY SEASON

Lemon : The typical diseases of the rainy season are : stomach disorders, fever and boils and ulcers. The use of lemon is beneficial during the rains. Squeeze a lemon in a glass of lukewarm water and take it daily in the morning at least for 95 days.

CHANGE OF CLIMATE

Red chilli : Fry red chillies in clarified butter. If people travelling inland and abroad eat such fried chillies, the change of climate and water will not affect them adversely.

LIGHTENING/ELECTRIC SHOCK

Basil : If someone has fainted because of electric current or because he has been struck by lightening, massage his head and face with basil juice. He will come round.

SKIN DISEASES

There are several skin diseases which affect the skin—itching, eczema, boil, whelks, prickly heat, psoriasis, herpes, etc.

Causes : Skin diseases are caused by increased levels of acidity and decreased levels of Vitamin A and C and calcium in the body. These are caused by infection or contagion also. Skin diseases can be suppressed by the application of strong and effective ointments or taking strong medicines but are not totally cured. They appear again after some time.

Treatment : The first and basic thing to treat skin diseases is purification and cleansing of blood. To know about it, please read the chapter on blood disorders and blood purification in the present writer's book *Shaktivardhak Bhojan* and use the food items mentioned therein. Keep the bowels clean. Observe fast. During the fast take lemon water. Observe fast for three days and take only lemon water and nothing else. Thereafter take orange juice for three days and nothing else. After that take boiled vegetables, salad, raw vegetables, seasonal fruit, carrot juice and *amla* juice in sufficient quantity. Make minimum use of strong spices, sugar, salt and soap. Take sun bath.

Lemon : It cleanses the skin. Application of lemon juice on skin disorders like boils, whelks, eczema, ringworm, etc. or washing the wounds with lemon water or drinking it is beneficial. Squeeze two lemons in water and take it in the morning daily. It is beneficial in skin diseases.

Apple : Eating two apples daily is beneficial in skin diseases. If your skin is oily, grind an apple into a fine paste and apply a thin layer of it on your face. Wash after ten minutes with hot water.

Tomato : Tomatoes are sour. This sourness cleanses the blood. For blood purification take tomatoes alone, that is, without mixing them with anything else. If because of blood disorders, red blotches appear on the skin, bones of the face are swollen, gums bleed, possibility of your developing scurvy exists, diseases like eczema and beri-beri appear, taking tomato juice thrice a day will be beneficial. It will purify the blood. If you take tomato juice regularly for a few weeks, skin diseases will disappear.

Carrots : Carrot juice is antibacterial and checks infection. It also checks the irritability and stench of the blood. It purifies the blood and is beneficial in itching, boils and whelks. It checks blood disorders. It also provides relief from acne and makes the face beautiful. Thus carrot juice is highly beneficial in skin diseases.

The skin usually becomes dry because of the deficiency of Vitamin A. Dryness of the skin is more prominent during winter. Carrots are available in plenty during the winter and they contain plenty of Vitamin A. Therefore, you can get rid of dryness of the skin by eating carrots.

Cucumber : It is beneficial in skin diseases.

Onion : Eating raw or cooked onions removes yellowishness of the skin and makes it healthy. The skin becomes beautiful. If you roast it in fire and dress boils and tumours with it, the pus will come out. It provides relief from swelling, burning and pain and accelerates the healing of a wound. Even infectious wounds get healed up. Homeopathic doctors Kook, Gabriel and Minchen maintain that using one part onion juice mixed with 4 parts water to wash rotten, suppurating wounds and then dressing them with a piece of gauze soaked in the same solution will heal the wound. Onion juice purifies the blood, it is germicidal and provides relief from itching.

Cauliflower : It contains alkaline elements. The combination of sulphur and chlorine in cauliflower cleanses the mucus membrane and the intestines. It cleanses the body and blood and cures skin diseases.

***Bathua* :** Boil *bathua* leaves, squeeze and take the juice. It is beneficial in skin diseases. Wash the skin with *bathua* juice. Grind raw *bathua* leaves and squeeze out the juice. Mix ½ cup of sesame oil in two cups of *bathua* juice and heat it on slow fire. When the water content has entirely evaporated, strain the oil, store in a bottle and apply it on the skin eruptions. It will bring relief in due course of time.

Poppy seeds : Skin diseases due to summer heat can be cured by taking regularly the syrup made of poppy seeds. If can cure infectious diseases of the skin and boils and whelks among children.

—Dr. Virendra Singh, Samachar Jagat, Jaipur dt. 26-5-1984

Sugar : Those suffering from skin diseases like itching should not eat sugar and things made of sugar like toffees and sweets. They will get relief from itching.

Mint leaves : Grind green mint leaves and apply on the face for 20 minutes. It removes the heat and cools down the skin.

Wheat : Heat the wheat on a hot plate to the extent that it gets burnt up. Then grind it into a fine powder and mix it in pure mustard oil. Apply it on the affected part. It will cure old and incurable skin problems. It is especially beneficial in hard-to-heal skin diseases of private parts and dry skin ailments.

Red chilli : Rubbing the red chilli oil on the skin is beneficial in skin diseases. It is especially beneficial in case of boils which develop during the rainy season. Heat 125 gms. of red chilli powder in 375 ml. of mustard oil. Let it boil for some time. Strain it and you will get red chilli oil.

Salt : Bathing with hot saline water is beneficial in skin diseases which develop during the winter.

If the skin becomes dry and drab, cracks develop in hands and feet, wash them with hot water mixed with salt, foment them well. It will make the skin soft.

Caraway Seeds : Grind caraway seeds in hot water and rub the paste on the parts affected with shingles, eczema, itching and whelks. Boil caraway seeds in water and use the boiled water to wash the affected parts. It will be beneficial.

***Neem* :** Grind tender *neem* leaves, dissolve in water and drink it. If it is taken in the first week of April, it will provide relief from ulcers, boils, ring worm, itching and other diseases caused by disorders of the blood and will also bring relief from rheumatic problems, bile and cough. Use 30 gms. of tender *neem* leaves at a time. Drink it regularly for some days. If a boil has suppurated and there is secretion of pus from it, grind *neem* leaves, mix some honey and apply the paste on the affected part.

Boils, shingles, scales on the skin, whelks and wounds are caused by blood disorders. It is difficult to cure them. But *neem* ointment is beneficial in skin diseases.

Method : Grind 175 gms. *neem* leaves without adding water and make a fine paste. Put 87 gms. mustard oil in a copper vessel and heat it. When the oil is fully heated add the *neem* paste to it. When the paste is blackened, allow it to cool down for a while. Then add camphor and a little yellow wax and grind it. You will get *neem* ointment.

Glycerine : If the lips and skin are cracked application of glycerine is beneficial.

Gram : Make a paste of gram *daal* flour by adding a little water to it. Apply the paste on eczema, itch, boils, whelks, etc. Rub it off when it gets dry and wash with water.

Water : Soak a piece of cloth in water, squeeze and wrap it around the neck of a child and cover him with a blanket. If this treatment is taken for a few days, it will save the child from skin diseases.

Honey : (1) Soak overnight three tsp. of *amla* powder in a glass of water. Strain it in the morning and drink it after adding 4 tsp. of honey to it. It will cure skin diseases.

(2) Taking honey mixed in water cures several skin diseases like itch, light spots on the body, boils, whelks and acne.

CHILBLAIN/CRACK OR CHAP ON HEELS

Turnip : Boil turnip in water. Use the water to wash the affected part of the feet. Then rub turnip on it. After the application at night wrap the foot with a piece of cloth. It will cure chilblain.

Clarified butter : Mix salt in clarified butter and rub on cracks in the heel. It makes the skin soft. It also prevents the heels from cracking.

Mustard oil : Massaging the feet with mustard oil prevents the heels from developing cracks.

Application of warm mustard oil on the feet facilitates the healing of cracks.

Sesame oil : Native yellow wax is available at a grocer's shop. Mix one part of this wax with four parts of sesame oil, heat it and make ointment. The application of this ointment will help in the healing of cracks and chaps on the heels.

Henna : Application of henna paste on the cracks is beneficial.

Black pepper : Mix black pepper, resin, catechu in equal quantity and grind. Mix 2 tsp. of clarified butter, four tsp. of jasmine oil and heat it in an iron vessel. Then store it in a bottle. Its application on cracks and chaps helps in their early healing.

Salt : Washing and fomenting hands and feet with hot saline water is beneficial in chilblain.

Onion : Grind raw onions and apply the paste on the affected part. It will be beneficial.

Papaya : Grind dried peel of papaya into a fine powder. Mix it with glycerine. Its application on cracked heels twice a day will bring prompt relief.

Castor oil : Wash the feet with hot water and massage them with castor oil. It will prevent the heels from cracking.

Turmeric : Mix turmeric powder in unboiled milk. Massage hands and feet with it. It will make the skin soft. Hands and feet will not get cracked or chapped. If they are already cracked fill the cracks with turmeric powder. It will help in their early healing.

If the skin has become dull and drab because of cold, mix lemon juice in unboiled milk and soak a swab of cotton in it and lightly apply on the face. After a little while wash it with clean water.

If the heels are cracked and have developed fissures, massage them with mustard oil before going to bed. In the morning rub the heels lightly on the floor and wash them. It should be done regularly for fifteen days. Do not keep your feet wet for a long time. Apply oil on the heels during the day.

If your fingers have gone black because of household chores, mix lemon juice and few drops of glycerine in milk. Apply it on the hands for fifteen minutes, then wash them.

During the winter, chapped and rough hands are a common problem. Wash and clean the hands with lukewarm water. Then massage the hands with oil for ten minutes. The skin of the hands will become soft and smooth and you will get rid of roughness.

WARTS

Apple : Rubbing the juice of sour apples on the warts is beneficial. Warts disintegrate and fall off.

Onion : Application of onion juice on the warts destroys warts.

Castor oil : Soak a piece of gauze in castor oil and dress the warts and bandage them. It will provide relief from warts.

Coriander : Grind coriander leaves and apply the paste on the warts.

DRY AND OILY SKIN

Skin is of two types—oily and dry. Dry skin is hard. It does not get natural oils to keep it soft because its sebaceous glands do not function properly. Therefore, the skin is not fully hydrated. On the other hand, because of vapourization water disappears from the skin. As a result, the skin becomes dry.

The water level in the millions of skin cells is regulated by hormones and atmospheric changes. If the weather is hot, water will evaporate from the skin quickly and the skin will get dry. If it is rainy season, the skin retains moisture. There are some natural substances in the skin which also help it to retain hydrate. But with the advancing age, such natural resources dry up and the skin becomes dry.

Dry skin needs moist and oily substances. The skin around the throat and eyes especially becomes dry because the secretion of natural oils in these areas is not sufficient and fine wrinkles appear around the throat and eyes.

The use of bathing soap makes the skin drier. Therefore, the use of soap on these spots should be minimized. Also avoid the sun as far as possible because it reduces the water level of the skin still further.

After 40 years of age a woman nears the menopausal stage. As a result of hormonal changes, the sebaceous glands begin to contract and the output of natural oils is diminished. Therefore, the skin becomes dry and dehydrated and cracked. It also loses its smoothness.

Despite the dryness of the skin, the problem of acne can come up even at this late age and can be accompanied by burning sensation and redness.

In such a case, avoid hot drinks and chillies and spices. Do not use too oily a lotion or cream for treatment.

Special care should be taken of diet. If you are a vegetarian, make sure that you are getting sufficient protein. Take a balanced oily diet and plenty of green vegetables and fruits. Also ensure that you are taking sufficient fibre in your food. Reduce the intake of salt. Drink plenty of water. Reduce the intake of tea, coffee and soft drinks.

Make it a point to take exercise every day atleast for 20 minutes. Massage your body with oil.

Smoking and drinks dehydrate the skin. Avoid them.

Treatment for Dry Skin :

Orange : Grind orange peel dried in the shade. Knead the powder in milk and rub the dry skin with it. The skin will regain its softness.

Clarified butter : Mix the powder of ten corns of black

pepper in a tsp. of clarified butter. Take it daily in the morning for two months. It will tackle the problem of dryness of the skin.

Milk : Rubbing the skin with milk cream (*malai*) makes it soft. To protect your skin from sun burn rub milk cream mixed with rose water. Alternatively, milk cream can be mixed with honey.

Papaya : Grind a ripe papaya and rub the pulp on the face. It will make the facial skin smooth and soft and enhance the beauty.

Oil : Apply any suitable oil on the dry skin and give a massage to your body with oil.

OILY SKIN

Oily skin has a shine and is sticky. Till the age of twenty, the skin is usually oily. The reason behind this is the hyper-activity of sebaceous glands which become over-active because of hormones. Besides, the skin is affected by changes in the weather. During the winter, the oily glands become more hyper-active. Some people are naturally more affected by it than others. They also have to face the problem of acne.

But the oily skin has its own advantages. Oily skin is less prone to wrinkles and the signs of old age are not so loudly visible in them.

Whenever you feel that your skin is oily, take care of your emotions, diet, health and activities because the state of your skin can be an indication of imbalance in one of the above factors. Do not partake of oily food items, pastries, cream based items and fatty foods. Instead, taking fresh fruits and green vegetables will be better. Take at least eight glasses of water daily. Have your full quota of sleep. Take exercise in fresh air so that blood circulation in the body improves, thus, a few changes as indicated above will rectify the imbalance. Also try to control your emotions.

TREATMENT FOR OILY SKIN

Water : If the extra oil in the skin is removed the problem will be solved. For this, cleanse the skin with hot water.

Sandal-wood : Knead sandal-wood powder in rose-water and rub on the face. It removes spots on the facial skin as well as acne and pimples.

Lemon : Spots, stains and pimples appear on oily skin. People with oily skin should wash the face with soap and water twice daily. Rubbing lemon on the facial skin is beneficial.

Apple : Grind an apple fully well and apply the paste on the face. Wash it off after ten minutes.

Gram *daal* flour : Mix gram *daal* flour in rose-water and rub it on the face and the body. Take your bath after 10 minutes. It will remove the extra oil from your skin.

SWELLING OF FINGERS IN WINTER

Peas : During winter, an inflammatory swelling of toes, feet or fingers occurs due to the influence of cold. To get relief, boil peas in water and use the water to wash toes and fingers.

Turnip : Boil 50 gms. turnip in 1 litre of water. Immerse the hands and feet in this hot water. It will provide relief from swelling.

Alum salt : If your fingers have got swollen or developed itch on account of working in water for a considerable time in winter, boil alum salt in water. Use the water to wash your fingers. It will bring relief from chilblain.

Mustard oil : Mix four tsp. of mustard oil with 1 tsp. of finely ground rock salt. Then heat it. Apply the oil on the toes before bed-time and wear socks. It will bring relief from swelling.

URTICARIA

Mint leaves : Boil 10 gms. mint leaves and 20 gms. of jaggery in 200 ml. of water, strain it and drink it. It provides relief from oft recurring urticaria.

Gram *daal* flour : Eating *laddoos* made of gram *daal* flour with black pepper powder sprinkled on them relieves urticaria.

Clarified butter : Massage the body with clarified butter mixed with rock salt. Then lie down and cover yourself with a blanket and let your body sweat. It will relieve urticaria.

Asafoetida : Mix asafoetida with clarified butter and massage the body with it.

Cumin seeds : Boil cumin seeds in water. Use the boiled water for bathing. It provides relief from itch and urticaria.

Black pepper : Take clarified butter mixed with black pepper powder. Also massage the body with it.

Caraway seeds : (1) Take a tsp. of caraway seeds with rock salt added to taste on empty stomach in the morning with water. It will be beneficial in urticaria.

(2) Boil 1 tsp. of caraway seeds and 2 tsp. of jaggery in two cups of water. Drinking it is beneficial in urticaria.

(3) Mix 1 gram of caraway seeds with 3 gms. of jaggery and eat it. It will provide relief from urticaria.

Honey : (1) When the patient does not get any relief even after trying costly medicines and taking injections, he will certainly get relief if he takes 6 gms. of nag-kesar with 25 gms. of honey twice daily in the morning and evening. It is a proven prescription.

(2) Take a tsp. of honey with a tsp. of *triphala* twice daily in the morning and evening. It will provide relief from urticaria.

Turmeric : (1) Mix 1 tsp. of turmeric powder, 2 tsp. of wheat flour, 1 tsp. of *ghali*, 2 tsp. of sugar and prepare *halwa* by adding ½ cup of water. Allow it to cool down. Eat it daily in the morning followed by a glass of milk. It relieves urticaria.

(2) Mix ½ tsp. each of turmeric powder and sugar candy or honey and take it twice daily. It will provide relief from urticaria.

***Neem* :** Mix *neem* oil with mustard oil and heat it or burn the kernel of *neem* seeds in mustard oil. Give a massage to your body with this oil. Chew *neem* leaves unless you find them very bitter. It relieves urticaria.

Mustard oil : First, take a laxative and cleanse the bowels. Then massage the body with mustard oil and take a hot bath. It is beneficial in urticaria.

Alum salt : Dissolve ½ of alum salt in ½ cup of hot water and apply the solution on the affected parts and wash. It will be beneficial.

Onion : It is beneficial to eat onions in urticaria.

Betel leaf : Grind three betel leaves and 1 tsp. of alum salt by adding a little water. Apply the paste on the affected parts. It will provide relief from urticaria.

Basil : Eat one piece of *amla* preserve daily twice with ¼ tsp. of basil seeds. It will relieve urticaria.

***Siras* :** Grind *siras* flowers in a little water and apply the paste on the affected parts. Also mix 1 tsp. of honey with a tsp. of the paste of *siras* flowers and lick. It will be beneficial.

BOILS

Small boils and sometimes larger ones, appear on hands, face and the body with the onset of summer and rainy seasons. They are quite painful. They become red in colour and suppurate. The older ones disappear but new ones come up. Such boils can appear in other seasons also, but mostly they appear in summer. There are several reasons:

(1) *Accumulation of sweat in the skin*—The body dispels filth through sweat. If because of some reason the sweat accumulates in the skin, boils appear and the filth comes out through them. During summer when sharp hot winds blow, a lot of dirt settles on the body and blocks the sweating process.

(2) *Eating food items of hot nature*—Eating mangoes, melon, water-melon, etc., in excess, increases heat in the body which causes boils.

(3) *Synthetic clothes*—Nylon and terylene clothes, plastic shoes, etc. have an adverse effect on the skin and cause boils.

Treatment : Take bath twice daily. Take cool drinks and

food items which have a cooling effect on the body. Eat blood-purifying food so that the blood remains clean. Please read the chapter on blood disorders and blood purifiers in the author's book '*Shaktivardhak Bhojan*'.

Multani mitti **:** Soak *multani mitti* and then grind it. Mix camphor and smear the body with it. Bathe yourself after an hour.

Lemon : Lemon cleanses the skin. Application of lemon juice or washing and bathing with lemon water is beneficial in the various diseases of the skin like boils, whelks, shingles and eczema. There is a marked increase in the appearance of boils and whelks in the rainy season. The use of lemon is highly beneficial in this season. Take warm lemon water every day in the morning at least for three months.

Pineapple : Application of pineapple pulp on the boils is beneficial. Pineapple juice makes the unhealthy tissues healthy.

Cumin seeds : Grind cumin seeds in a little water and apply the paste on eczema, boils and on painful parts. It is beneficial.

Water : Foment the swollen part and boils first with hot water for three minutes followed by cold fomentation for a minute. In this way, fomentation for about ten minutes twice daily in the morning and evening will bring results beyond expectation.

Guava : Eat 250 gms. of guava daily in the afternoon for four weeks. It will bring relief from boils and itch. Guava will clear the bowels, remove excess heat from the body, cleanse the blood and heal boils and whelks.

Tamarind : Mash ripe tamarind in water, strain it and drink it. Take it regularly for some days. It will be beneficial.

Ber**:** If boils have developed in and outside the nose, smelling *ber* and application of its pulp will be beneficial.

Carrots : Dress the boils with carrot poultice. It allows the coagulated blood on the boils to melt down.

Potato : Drinking the juice of raw potatoes provides relief from boils.

Walnut : If you are prone to boils, eat four walnuts daily throughout the ear.

Henna : Boil henna in water and wash the boils with it.

Caraway seeds : Boil caraway seeds in water and wash the boils with it. Grind caraway seeds in water and apply on the boils. It will be beneficial.

Honey : Prepare a paste by mixing wheat flour and honey. Spread it on a piece of cloth and dress the boil with it. Take three tsp. of honey in a glass of hot water daily for a few months.

Basil : If a boil has developed inside the nose, smelling at ground dry basil leaves is beneficial. Heat the juice of basil leaves mixed with coconut oil in equal quantity. When the water part has evaporated mix 12 gms. of yellow wax and stir. An ointment will be ready. Its application on burns, eczema, boils and whelks is beneficial.

***Neem* :** In the months of March-April you can get tender *neem* leaves. Grind 30 gms. of reddish tender *neem* leaves alongwith rock salt and eat on empty stomach daily in the morning. It purifies the blood and the boils are healed. Apply the paste of *neem* leaves on the whelks. If the pain is too much, heat the paste and then apply. You can grind *neem* bark in water and apply on the boils. *Neem* ointment is also highly beneficial.

Method : Grind 175 gms. *neem* leaves without adding water. Heat 100 ml. of mustard oil in a copper vessel. When the oil gets heated, add the *neem* paste to it. When the paste eventually gets blackened, allow it to cool down. Add 5 gms. camphor and 20 gms. yellow wax and grind well. The ointment is ready.

Camphor : Mix 5 gms. camphor in 50 ml. of coconut oil and apply on the boils. It checks itching. If coconut oil is not available you can use an edible oil.

***Bathua* :** Grind *bathua* leaves, dried ginger and salt and tie the paste in a wet piece of cloth. Wrap wet clay around it and heat it. Untie it and apply it hot on the boils. It will reduce pain and help in the excretion of pus.

Black pepper : Grind black pepper in a little water and apply it twice daily on the small whelks as long as they do not subside.

Red chilli : Boil red chilli powder in oil, then strain the oil and apply it on the boils. It will be beneficial.

Garlic : Taking ¼ tsp. of garlic juice mixed in ¼ cup of hot water thrice a day facilitates the healing of boils.

Please read the chapters on boils, disorders of blood, purification of blood in *Bhojan ke Dwara Chikitsa* and *Shaktivardhak Bhojan*. Take anti-bacterial food items mentioned in '*Shaktivardhak Bhojan*'.

ECZEMA

Pomegranate : Grind pomegranate leaves and apply the paste on the part affected with eczema. It is beneficial.

Yam : It provides relief from eczema if eaten as a vegetable for a considerable period.

***Bathua* :** Boil *bathua*, squeeze out the juice and take it daily. Also eat it as a vegetable. Use the boiled water for washing the affected part. Grind the raw *bathua* leaves and squeeze out the juice. Mix two cups of the juice with ½ cup of sesame oil and heat it on slow fire. When the water part has evaporated, strain the oil and store it in a bottle. Apply it on the affected part for a considerably long period to derive full benefit.

Lemon : Scratch the affected part a little and apply lemon juice four times a day. It will provide relief from eczema.

Banana : Grind banana pulp and add lemon juice to it. Its application will be beneficial. If the affected part appears to be swollen, do not worry. Application of banana pulp with lemon juice will bring relief.

Papaya : Application of papaya juice on the part affected with eczema is beneficial.

Carrots : (1) Grate carrots finely. Add rock salt and heat it. Dress the affected part with it when it is hot. It will bring relief.

(2) Mix 185 ml. of carrot juice, 250 ml. of the juice of beet-root and 125 ml. of cucumber juice and drink it.

Potato : Drinking the juice of raw potato provides relief from eczema.

Garlic : Burn garlic cloves into ash, mix it with honey. Its application on the parts affected with eczema in infants is quite beneficial. For grown ups both internal and external use of garlic is beneficial.

Radish : Grind radish seeds in lemon juice into a paste, heat it and apply on the affected part. On the first day, its application may cause burning and pain but it will diminish on the second day. Gradually healing will take place. It is beneficial in both dry and wet eczema.

Water chestnut : Grind a dry water chestnut in lemon juice. Its application at first will cause burning but soon it will have a cooling effect. Its application for some days will help in the healing of eczema.

Green gram : Soak green gram in only as much of water as can be absorbed by it. After two hours grind it into a paste and apply on eczema and ring-worms. It will be beneficial.

Gram : Eating *roti* made of gram flour without salt for 64 days brings relief from eczema, itching and other blood disorders. You can consume clarified butter with it.

Turmeric : Application of turmeric paste thrice during the day and once at night helps in the healing of eczema.

Black pepper : Grind black pepper and take it mixed with clarified butter made from cow's milk. It helps in the healing of all types of itch and eczema.

Red chilli : The applications of red chilli oil in eczema is beneficial. Mix 175 gms. of red chilli powder in 375 ml. of mustard oil and then heat it. Strain it after it has been boiled properly. It is known as red chilli oil. It cures eczema.

Salt : Anoint every hour the part affected with eczema with salt water. It will help in the healing of eczema in a week.

Caraway seeds : Grind caraway seeds in hot water and apply it on the affected part or boil caraway seeds in water and use the water to wash the affected part.

Basil : (1) Take 12 ml. of the juice of basil leaves every day if you are suffering from eczema.

(2) Application of the juice of basil leaves mixed with lemon juice in equal quantity is helpful in the healing of eczema.

(3) Grind 100 basil leaves and ¼ tsp. of salt and mix with ½ tsp. of lemon juice. Its application on eczema is useful.

(4) Grind 100 basil leaves and five cloves of garlic and apply the paste on the part affected with eczema.

(5) Clean the affected part, rub a piece of lemon on it, then grind basil leaves into a paste and apply it on that part. Do it twice a day for fifteen days.

***Neem* :** (1) Drink 12 ml. of the juice of *neem* leaves daily to get relief from eczema.

Taking the juice of 30 gms. of tender *neem* leaves daily in the first week of April is very useful in the healing of eczema.

(2) Burn a piece of green *neem* wood. When you burn it, tiny water drops will be secreted by the unburned portion. Apply these drops on the affected part.

(3) For total healing of eczema, apply the paste of *neem* leaves prepared by grinding the leaves in curd.

Milk : Taking milk with *gulkand* is beneficial in eczema.

Sesame seeds : Prepare an ointment by mixing 2 tsp. each of sesame oil, *taramira* oil, ground resin and 1 tsp. of yellow wax (used in medicine). Its application on the affected part provides relief. **Method :** Heat sesame oil, mix 2 tsp. of ground resin and 1 tsp. of yellow wax. Then mix *taramira kajal.*

How to Prepare *Kajal* : Light an earthen lamp using taramira oil. Allow it to remain lit for four days and collect the soot for *kajal.* Mix this *kajal* with the above preparation.

Use : Its use provides relief from eczema, boils, cracking or chapping of the skin of the fingers, heels, etc.

Onion : Application of the paste prepared by ground onion seeds in lemon juice twice a day for a month or two brings relief from eczema.

LEPROSY

Symptoms : Leprosy is caused by *Myobacterium lepriae.* It is not hereditary or venereal. It is of two types : infectious and non-infectious. The infectious one is called lepromatus leprosy in which nodular cutaneous lesions are infiltrated and the patient's nose, throat and skin are infected with leprosy. The skin of his face, ears and at other places becomes thick. The affected parts lose the feeling of sensation. The patient is not sensitive to cold and heat. Even if a nail pierces his soles he will have no sensation of pain. The germs of leprosy and T.B. are almost similar. That is why leprotic patients also suffer from T.B. Leprosy is more common among the poor. The disease does not necessarily disfigure the body. The bodies of 20 per cent patients can be disfigured. Leprosy can now be treated and one can fully recover from it. At the social level, the patients deserve sympathy and not hatred. There are effective homeopathic medicines for the treatment of leprosy. Below are mentioned some of the general prescriptions which can be beneficial if the treatment is taken over a prolonged period. These can be used alongwith whatever treatment the patient may be taking. These will be beneficial.

Yam : Eating yam as a vegetable provides relief from leprosy. It should be taken regularly over a prolonged period.

Bathua **:** Boil *bathua* leaves, squeeze out the juice and drink it. Also eat *bathua* as a cooked vegetable. Wash the skin with the water in which *bathua* has been boiled. Grind raw *bathua* leaves and extract the juice. Mix two cups of *bathua* juice with half cup of sesame oil and heat on slow fire. When the water content has evaporated, strain in a bottle and apply on the affected part daily.

Gram : Eating gram sprouts regularly for three years is beneficial to a patient of leprosy. If the patient does not eat anything except gram for six months he will recover from leprosy. Soak gram overnight in water, next morning boil it in the same water and eat it. Whenever you are hungry, eat gram— roasted or otherwise or *roti* prepared from gram flour. Also drink the water in which gram has been boiled. Do not use any salt or chillies.

Amla **:** Take a tsp. of *amla* powder twice daily in the morning and evening with water.

Turmeric : Take a tsp. of turmeric powder twice daily in the morning and evening with water. Grind turmeric in water and apply on the affected part.

Basil : Eat 15 leaves of basil daily and also grind some leaves in water and apply on the affected parts.

Neem **:** (1) Mix *neem* and *chalmogra* oils in equal quantity and apply on the affected parts.

(2) The use of *neem* is helpful in every respect in treating leprosy. The patient should be kept under the shade of a *neem* tree. Massaging the body with *neem* oil, taking four tsp. of the juice of *neem* leaves twice daily in the morning and evening, spreading fresh *neem* leaves daily on the bed and bathing yourself with the water in which *neem* leaves have been boiled or the juice of *neem* leaves has been mixed are beneficial. The treatment should continue for a considerably long period.

Pomegranate : Application of the juice of pomegranate leaves on leprotic wounds is beneficial.

Cauliflower : It contains a lot of sulphur which is beneficial in itching, leprosy and such other skin diseases.

Parwal **:** Eating it as a cooked vegetable is beneficial for patients of leprosy.

Conch Shell : Listening to the sound of a conch (*shank*) destroys the germs of leprosy. The germs react to the sound of a conch and are destroyed. Leprosy patients should therefore listen to the sound of a conch.

POISONOUS BITES

Lemon : Dr. Herring says that lemon juice should be applied to get relief from sharp pain of a mosquito bite. The application of lemon juice mixed with salt relieves pain if you have been bitten by a scorpion, spider, wasp, bee, bed-bug or flea.

Mango : If you have been bitten by a rat, monkey, mad dog, poisonous spider, scorpion or wasp, grind mango kernel in water and apply on the affected part. It will provide relief from burning sensation and pain.

Swallow-wort : Immediate application of the milk of swallow-wort on the affected part provides relief if you have been bitten by a snake, scorpion, wasp or bee. It diminishes the effect of the poisonous bite. Swallow-wort is a wild plant. When you pluck its leaves, a kind of milk is secreted.

Pomegranate : Application of the paste of pomegranate leaves is beneficial if bitten by a scorpion, wasp, etc.

Water : If you have been bitten by a scorpion, wasp, bee, chameleon or rat, apply clarified butter on the bitten spot and then place it under a tap and release water with pressure on it continuously for some time. It will relieve pain of the bite.

Onion : If bitten by a dog or jackal, application of onion paste mixed with honey and taking onion juice dispels the poisonous effect. The application of onion paste is also beneficial if bitten by a bee, poisonous insect, wasp, scorpion, etc. In case of a scorpion bite, eat onion pieces with salt. You can also eat jaggery.

Mint leaves : If bitten by a poisonous creature you can apply the juice of mint leaves on the bitten spot. The poison will gradually begin to subside.

Garlic : Application of garlic juice will eliminate the effect of the bite of a poisonous insect.

Asafoetida : The homeopathic medicine Mother-tincture of Asafoetida should be used if bitten by a scorpion or wasp.

Salt : When stung by a poisonous flea or wasp, pour water over the sting and then rub salt. It will relieve burning and pain and check swelling. Also drink some saline water.

Honey : If bitten by a jackal, dog, scorpion, etc., application of honey on the bitten part is beneficial. Also eat some honey.

Basil : Grind basil leaves, mix some salt in it and apply on the part stung by a wasp, black bee or scorpion. It will promptly relieve burning and pain. The juice of basil leaves is quite beneficial. If it is applied on the body, mosquitoes will not bite you. Also drink some juice mixed with water.

***Neem* :** Grind *neem* leaves and apply on the part stung by a bee or scorpion. Also chew some leaves.

Clay : A wet clay bandage on the part stung by a scorpion or wasp is useful.

Match-stick : If a wasp or bee has stung you, grind the firework part of a match stick in water and apply on the sting.

SCORPION BITE

Garlic : (1) Eat three tsp. of honey mixed with the juice of one garlic bulb. Grind ½ tsp. of salt with 6 cloves of garlic and apply the paste on the affected part. It will neutralize the poison. As soon as you get relief, wash off the paste.

(2) Grind garlic and dried raw mango and apply it on the part stung by a scorpion. It will provide relief.

Radish : (1) Apply salt on a piece of radish and place it on the affected part. It will relieve pain. Those who eat radish regularly are not affected severely by the poisonous sting of a scorpion.

(2) Give to the patient radish to eat and apply radish juice on the affected part.

Mint leaves : Smear the affected part with ground mint leaves and drink mint juice. If bitten by a rat, bandaging the affected part with mint poultice is especially beneficial.

Bottle gourd : Grind bottle gourd and apply on the part

stung by a scorpion. Also drink its juice. It will neutralize the poison.

Alum salt : Grind alum salt in water and apply on the affected part.

Red chilli : Grind red chillies and apply it on the part stung by a scorpion. It will have a cooling affect.

Salt : Put four drops of salt saturated solution in the ear on the opposite side of the part bitten by a scorpion. If the scorpion bite has taken place on the right foot, put the above drops in the left ear. It will bring prompt relief. Also apply the solution on the part stung by scorpion and take a sip. It is a proven and successful experience.

How to Prepare the Solution : Keep adding salt to water and keep stirring. When the salt does not dissolve in water anymore even after stirring, you will have salt saturated solution.

(1) Add one part of salt to 5 parts of water and apply it into the eyes like *kajal.* It will quickly neutralize the poison of scorpion bite. The above saturated solution provides relief from the poisonous bite of insects also.

(2) Mix four tsp. of salt in two glasses of hot water and immerse the affected part in the solution or put a gauze soaked in it on the part stung by a scorpion. It will relieve pain and burning.

Pomegranate : Grind pomegranate leaves and apply the paste on the part stung by a scorpion or wasp. It will be beneficial.

To know about the prescriptions of mango, onion, asafoetida, honey, basil leaves, clay, etc. read the chapter on '*Poisonous Bites*'.

Water : If you have been stung or bitten by a scorpion, wasp, bee, chameleon, rat, etc., continuously spray water on the affected part with a syringe. It will relieve pain and burning caused by the poisonous bite.

Apple : Grind an apple into a fine paste and apply on the affected part. Also eat an apple.

Tamarind : Break tamarind kernel into two, soak one piece in water and put it on the affected part and press it so as to make the kernel well stuck there. It will suck the poison and fall off automatically.

Caraway Seeds : Grind caraway seeds in water and apply the paste on the part stung by a scorpion. It will relieve pain and burning.

SNAKE BITE

Identifying a snake bite : The taste of red chillies will not appear to be bitter to a victim of snake-bite. It is how you can recognise a snake-bite.

Banana : As soon as a person has been bitten by a snake, remove his clothes and let him lie down on banana leaves so that the juice of banana leaves enters his skin through the pores. Also extract 20 gms. juice from the stem of banana tree, strain it and mix 12 ground black pepper corns and give it to the patient to drink.

If the patient has become unconscious, spoon-feed the juice to him. When he comes round give him half a glass of banana juice every 20 minutes. This treatment neutralizes the effects of snake poison in the body of the patient and death can be averted. Till the patient does not get the expected relief keep feeding the juice to him every little while. After extracting the juice, use the pulp and skin to dress the bitten part and bandage it. Also you can use the juice of the stem of banana tree for massaging the body of the patient. Drinking the juice of the stem of banana tree neutralizes snake poison.

Onion : Crush onions and squeeze out 15 ml. of juice, mix 15 ml. of mustard oil and give it to the patient to drink. It will make one dose. Give three such doses at an interval of 30 minutes each. The patient will recover and the snake poison will be neutralized.

Garlic : Snakes do not appear in the house where garlic bulbs are kept. If the appearance of a snake is apprehended, place some garlic bulbs there. The snake will not come near.

Castor oil : Grind 10 gms. of tender leaves of castor oil plant and 5 gms. of black pepper corns, mix some water and give it to the patient to drink. It will cause vomiting and expectoration. After a little while repeat the dose. It will expel the poison.

Alum salt : Give alum salt dissolved in water to the patient to drink.

Basil Leaves : Grind basil leaves, mix water and give it to the patient to drink.

***Neem* :** If the person bitten by a snake chews *neem* leaves and they taste bitter, it means the poison has been neutralized. If the leaves taste sweet, it means the poison has not been neutralized. Chew *neem* leaves alongwith salt and black pepper corns.

DOG BITE

Identifying a Bite by a Mad Dog : Knead wheat flour in water and prepare *roti.* Put it unbaked on the spot where the dog has bitten and bandage it. Untie the bandage after fifteen minutes, remove the roti and offer it to some other dog to eat. If the dog does not eat it, it means the patient has been bitten by a mad dog. If the *roti* is eaten by the dog, it implies that the person has not been bitten by a mad dog.

***Gwar-patha* :** Peel the *gwar-patha* on one side and sprinkle rock salt on the soft part. Put it on the spot bitten by a dog and bandage it. Dress the bitten part daily for four days.

Red chilli : Grind red chillies in water and apply it on the part bitten by a dog. It is beneficial. It causes a lot of sweating thus allowing the poisonous saliva of the dog to ooze out.

To know about the use of mango, onions, honey etc. in dog-bite see—'Poisonous Bites' at *pg.334*.

***Chaulai* :** If the patient has gone mad after the bite by a mad dog and begins to pounce on others to bite them, grind 50 to 125 gms. of the root of wild thorny amaranth, mix with water and give it repeatedly to the patient to drink. It will save even a dying man. It neutralizes the poison. Its paste can be applied on all types of poisonous bites.

Soap : Wash the part bitten by a dog with soap and water. It washes off the poison of dog-bite.

Walnut : Grind walnut, onion and salt in equal quantity, mix honey and dress the wound of the dog-bite with the ointment and bandage it. It will neutralize the poison of the dog-bite.

Cumin seeds : Grind 2 tsp. of cumin seeds and 20 corns of black pepper in water and dress the wound of the dog-bite with it. It will neutralize the poison of the dog-bite.

MOSQUITO BITE

Orange : Put some orange peel on live burning coal. The smoke will be bright and fragrant. It will not allow flies and mosquitoes to come near you. If there are bed-bugs, place some orange peel there, bed-bugs will disappear.

Caraway seeds : Grind caraway seeds, mix with equal quantity of mustard oil, smear some pieces of card-board with it and hang them in all the four corners of the room. It will scare away the mosquitoes.

Basil Leaves : Smear your body with the juice of basil leaves. Mosquitoes will not bite you.

Garlic : Put some dried garlic cloves and asafoetida on burning coal. The smoke will scare away flies.

THREAD WORM

Bala (*Naru*) is caused by dirty infected water. Its larvae are found in water. They get into the stomach of a human being when he takes unfiltered infected water. The larvae are fully developed within 8-12 weeks after getting into the stomach. The patient remains unaware of its development. When it is fully developed the female bala can be as long as 1.25 metre and is thin like a thread. While moving inside the body it discharges a poisonous substance which causes burning sensation and a blister appears on that spot with swelling around it. When the blister bursts, the *bala* comes out as a thin and long thread causing great pain to the patient.

When a *bala* patient bathes himself in a river or pond, countless larvae come out of his blister and infect the water. If this infected water is consumed by some one, he catches the diseases.

The best way for prevention is to drink boiled and filtered water. So far no medicine is available for its cure.

Clarified butter : Drinking 50 gms. of heated clarified butter once a day for three days checks the disease.

Brinjal : Roast a round big brinjal, crush and mash it, mix with curd and apply at the blister where from the *bala* is issuing out for ten days.

Asafoetida : Mix asafoetida of the weight of a pea with 30 gms. of *moth* flour, add water, stir well and heat it. When it becomes sticky, use it to dress the blister and then bandage it. It will draw out the thread-like *bala.* Also dissolve 5 gms. of asafoetida in a glass of cool water and drink it twice daily in the morning and evening for four days. It will prevent recurrence of the disease.

Basil : Grind the root of basil plant in a little water and apply it on the blister from where the *bala* will come out by 2-3 inches. Tie it up. Next day repeat the above application. In this way, repeated application will force the *bala* to come out completely. The basil application should continue for some days even after the *bala* has come out for neutralizing the poison in the blister.

Swallow-wort : Heat sesame oil and apply on the blister. Also heat an swallow-wort leaf, smear it with the above oil, heat it and place it on the blister and bandage it. The *bala* will come out.

***Neem* :** Grind *neem* leaves and apply the paste on the blister.

To know more about the virtues of these items, please read the present author's book *Bhojan ke Dwara Chikitsa.*

BURNS

Water : In case of burns, immerse the burnt portions in cold water. Keep them immersed as long as the burning sensation does not disappear. It prevents blistering. If the water gets hot after some time, and the burning sensation starts again, replace the hot water with cold water. But don't stop the cold water treatment so long as the burning sensation is there. Stop it when the pain has disappeared. This treatment brings quick relief and does not leave any scars afterwards. If any portion of the body cannot be immersed in water, use cold water pads replacing them frequently.

Use cold water instead of ointment on burnt parts : Faridabad, 12 Feb., 1994. Pour cold water continuously on the burnt part and start giving milk, curd or water to the patient at short intervals.

It has now been established that pouring cold water on the burnt part is more beneficial than the application of an ointment. If possible keep the burnt part under running water. It reduces the temperature of the skin and the burn wound does not turn severe. Do not wrap the burnt parts in a blanket. It increases the temperature and there is a risk of the wounds becoming deeper.

Harad **:** Burn *harad*, grind it finely, mix it with vaseline and apply on the burnt spot. It will reduce pain and accelerate the healing process.

Mango : Burn mango leaves and sprinkle the ash on the burnt spot. It will help in the healing of burn wounds.

Mustard oil : Application of mustard oil on burns prevents blistering.

Sesame seeds : Grind sesame seeds in a little water into a fine paste and apply a thick layer of it on the burnt spot. It will be beneficial.

Sugar : Dissolve sugar in water and apply the solution on the burnt spots. Mix only a little water so that the solution has a thick consistency. It will relieve burning sensation.

Tea : A part of the body may have been burnt in some manner or it may have been scorched, boil tea leaves in water, allow it to cool down, soak a gauze in the decoction and place it on the burnt spot and bandage it. Keep changing the dressing. It will prevent blistering and will not leave any marks or scars afterwards.

***Gwar-patha* :** It is found in fields. It should be planted in clay pots at home also. In case of burns, cut it and apply its pulp on the burnt portions. It prevents blistering and heals the burns. It is beneficial in relieving burning sensation and pain. There will be no scars after the burn wounds are healed.

Banana : Application of ground banana is beneficial in burns.

Carrots : Application of ground raw carrots on the burnt parts relieves pain and burning and checks pus-formation.

Potato : (1) Application of ground raw potato is beneficial on the burnt parts.

(2) If the skin has been scorched by strong-sun or *loo*, application of raw potato juice on the affected skin brings relief and beautifies the skin.

Salt : Application of a thick solution of salt prevents blistering.

Onion : Grind onions and apply the paste on burn wounds. Continue the treatment as long as healing does not take place. It is beneficial and accelerates the healing process.

Lime : Mix well decanted lime water with linseed oil in equal quantity. Soak a piece of clean cloth in it and dress the burnt spot with it. It will reduce pain and the wound will get healed.

Fenugreek : Grind fenugreek seeds in water and apply the paste on burnt parts to relieve pain. It will prevent blistering.

Wheat : Knead wheat flour in water and apply on the burnt spot. It will be beneficial.

Green gram : Grind green gram in water and apply on the affected part.

Clarified butter : Application of clarified butter on burns is beneficial.

Honey : Application of honey on burns reduces burning sensation. Even if there are wounds, keep applying honey till they heal. After healing white spots appear.

Regular application of honey will remove the white spots also.

Barley : Burn barley and grind it finely in sesame oil. Apply the ointment on burns.

Basil : Mix basil juice with coconut oil and apply on burns. It will relieve pain, prevent blistering and heal wounds.

Glycerine : Anoint the burnt part with glycerine. It will relieve pain and burning and prevent blistering.

Kerosene oil : Application of kerosene oil on burns is beneficial.

Turmeric : Dissolve turmeric powder in water and apply on the burnt spot. Repeat the application when it gets dry. It is useful in burns.

Green chilli : Grind green chillies and apply on burns. It is beneficial.

BLISTERS

Clarified butter : Contact with a spider causes blisters sometimes. Application of clarified butter mixed with salt is beneficial in such a case.

BURNING SENSATION IN THE BODY

Gram : Soak overnight two handfuls of the husk of gram in two glasses of water in a new clay pot. Strain the water next morning and drink it. It will relieve burning sensation.

Millet : Mix millet flour in water and apply on the body. It will relieve burning sensation.

Henna : Those who have a constant burning in the soles during the summer, application of henna is beneficial for them.

Phalsa **:** (1) Drinking *phalsa* syrup relieves burning in the body.

(2) Eating 20 gms. of *phalsa* with sugar relieves burning sensation in the body. If you feel hot or heated up or painful, eat ripe *phalsa* with sugar.

Cucumber : It is beneficial in burning sensation. Drink cucumber juice regularly.

Mulberry : Eating mulberry fruit or taking its juice relieves burning sensation in the body.

Coriander : If you feel a burning sensation in the body :

(1) Soak overnight coriander seeds and rice in water. Heat it in the morning and drink it.

(2) Soak coriander seeds overnight and next morning mix sugar candy, strain and drink it. It is beneficial in case of burning sensation in the body and stomach.

Fenugreek : Grind fenugreek leaves into a fine paste, mix in water and drink it. It is beneficial in case of pain and burning sensation in the body.

Water : If your feet sweat a lot, immerse your feet in hot water for some time, rub them together, then take them out and wipe them well. Take this treatment for a week.

WOUND IN THE GENETICS

Water-melon : If you have a wound in the genetics and feel a burning while passing urine, drink in the morning the juice of the water-melon which has been kept overnight in the open under the sky.

Mix some sugar in the juice. It is beneficial.

IDENTIFICATION OF SYPHILIS

Lemon : Whether a man or woman is syphilitic, to know about it you can apply lemon juice on some part of his/her body. If it is intolerable, it is a case of syphilis.

ALLERGY

Henna : Soak overnight 100 dry leaves of henna in a glass of clean water. Decant in the morning and drink the water. It will have a cooling effect on the body and cleanse the blood. It is a very beneficial treatment for patients of allergy.

PREVENT CHILDREN FROM CRYING

Children who are over-indulged and much doted upon and whose wishes are fulfilled because of their obstinate insistence, do not want to lose easily their 'privilege' and take resort to crying whenever they want their wish to be fulfilled.

Thus, whereas over-indulgence is one of the reasons why a child cries, neglect is another reason for a child to start crying even on unconvincing grounds.

Sometimes a child keeps awake till late in the night and does not get full sleep necessary for him. As a result, he becomes irascible. Parents should be careful about the food-habits of children. Too much of sweets, oily and spicy food makes children obstinate and peevish.

Some children are obstinate. Obstinate children cry a lot. Naughty and obstinate children behave better when they are busy playing in the open air. They give up the habit of obstinacy and become cheerful.

It is absolutely essential to have a tension-free and cheerful atmosphere at home if you want your child to give up his habit of crying. To provide a healthy entertainment to the child, it will be helpful if he is told stories that have a moral.

If the child is grown up and can ask for what he wants, do not give him anything if he takes resort to crying and obstinate persistence. If you give him what he wants because he is crying, it will encourage him to repeat the trick whenever he wants his wish to be fulfilled.

On the other hand, if you do not oblige him despite his crying he will realize his trick cannot succeed and he will possibly give up the habit of crying. But it will take time for him to improve his habit and become normal.

HOW TO CHECK OLD AGE

As you advance in years and you are in the range of 50-60, you begin to feel that you are getting old, the body is getting debilitated. Old age is usually a difficult stage of life. You wonder how old age will affect you. Life becomes insipid as strange thoughts occupy your mind.

What is Old age? Old age is a natural stage in every body's life. After you have lived a long life, wrinkles appear on the skin, it becomes dry, joints become weak, the body becomes stiff and it is difficult to keep the back straight; teeth fall off, the hair turn grey, eyesight becomes weak, knee joints develop pain, bladder control is difficult, arteries are clogged with cholesterol, prostat is enlarged and the presence of excess alkali in the body are indications of old age.

Old age is not measured or known by years. Sometimes a young man spoils his body and is in a worse state than an old man and has less stamina than him. On the other hand, an old man may be more active and agile than a young man. A man is old by his thoughts and not by his body. In old age a man loses all aspirations, is tired all the time, feels debilitated and food seems tasteless, it provides no pleasure. He is pestered day and night by cough and phlegmatic congestion. The definition of old age given above is common knowledge.

The arrival of Old age : Whoever is born will die some day. Today we are young but we will grow old some day. We do not want to grow old, yet old age overtakes the body in due course.

Gradually, there is an accumulation of acidity and toxic matter in the body. These are enemies of health and give birth to disease-causing germs in the body. The gums get swollen because of excess of salts in the body; there is a prickly sensation on the tongue and it becomes whitish, the gums and teeth begin to bleed—all this happens because of excess of filth and salts in the body. The arteries begin to contract and the body loses its agility and power of movement. Blood-cells decrease and old age overtakes us.

Loss of Memory in Old age : Human brain is a mass of nerve tissues. An adult has the same number of nerve tissues as he is born with. The bone and skin cells multiply because of constant cell division but brain cells do not multiply with age, rather their number is reduced by advancing age. The cells that are dead are not replaced by new ones. By the age of 70-80 almost one-fourth of the nerve cells are dead. That is why an old man's hearing is impaired to some extent and loss of memory occurs.

CHOLESTEROL

It is a substance like oxide of calcium which gets deposited in the arteries resulting in their hardening. It causes rigidity and weakness. It destroys agility. The best way to tackle it is to exercise regularly, meditate, massage your body and wipe your body well with a towel after your bath. These little precautions will not make old age a burden and you will not suffer from physical impairment and resulting problems. You will spend your time happily.

The Effect of Old Age on Bones : The joints of bones are of special type. The joints have a flexible white layer of tissues called cartilage and underneath is Synovia, a lubricating fluid secreted in the joints of the bones. There is a continuous friction in the bones which causes wear and tear to the cartilage. The secretion of Synoria lubricant also diminishes gradually and becomes thin. It can be compared to an old machine and useless lubricant. This is why the bones get jammed in the morning for lack of movement during the night. There is pain in the joints if there is excessive movement. The parts most affected are joints of knees, shoulders and backbone. There is a feeling of pain in them. Stooping back is common in old age.

Common Ailments in Old Age : T.B. is caused by weakness and lack of nutrition. Another common disease is cancer. Cancer in any part of the body affects the bones most. Therefore, if you have aching bones, especially the backbone, consult a doctor.

Prevention : Preventive measures such as nutritious food and regular exercise should be taken in order to avoid pain in the bones, weakness of eyesight and debility. Precaution is needed to protect yourself from physical hurt. Bones are made of protein and calcium. The food you eat should, therefore, include protein, calcium and Vitamin-D.

A French scientist maintains that men have the potential to live upto the age of 150 years but because they are ignorant of the laws of nature, they are able to live only half of that age.

Some scientists believe that looking to the new knowledge man has acquired about health and medicine, soon the average life span will be 150 years. But only knowledge about health and medicine is not enough, we will have to control certain other natural factors which are proving a hindrance in the way of longevity. Longevity depends on striking a balance between human knowledge and nature. Improvement in health forms a strong basis for longevity.

Death is a potential risk at every stage of life but once a man has reached seventy, his risk factors are reduced and the possibility of his having a long life increases.

Another scientist, a Russian, says that man has made stupendous progress and it can be assumed that in not too distant a future man's average life span will be between 125-150 years.

Ways to Check Old Age : St. Fort Bennet, Arthur Abplalep and our religious books have enumerated several ways to check old age or to make it happy and peaceful which include regular exercise, proper diet and minimum use of medicines. A healthy body which is the product of exercise does not decay or degenerate easily.

Regular Exercise : Just as we have to eat to live, similarly we have to take regular exercise to keep healthy. Those who do not take exercise begin to show signs of advancing age prematurely, that is, they start looking old early. A healthy body does not deteriorate easily. Life is full of cheer when you are healthy. Hard work gives energy and this energy is automatically recharged if you do not grow lax. To look attractive, keep your backbone straight. Stooping shoulders show signs of old age. Your straight posture and brisk manner of walking add extra charm to your personality.

To ward off old age it is essential to get up early in the morning before sunrise and take exercise or go for a walk. Breathe fresh air in the morning sun. Tiredness comes from lack of exercise.

Improve your appetite. Do not take your meals in a hurry and chew your food well. Lie down on your back and bend forward your head. It will allow your stomach muscles to stretch. When your head falls back, they will resume their normal position. Repeat it several times. It will be beneficial for the veins also. It will also be beneficial to strike your stomach with your fists. Do it gently at first and then gradually increase the force. It will accelerate blood circulation and the digestive system will get strengthened. Afterwards, massage your stomach with both hands upward and then downward. Knead the stomach. The fat accumulated in the stomach will melt down.

To remove constipation you should take such exercises as are good for the intestines. Obesity comes from lack of exercise. With advancing age calcification in the joints hardens up various parts of the body and they lose their flexibility. You can keep yourself fit by regular exercise.

Observing Fast : Fasting increases life span. The body is cleansed and one gets rid of several ailments. One should observe a fast of one's own sweet will. Do not call it a fast if you could not get anything to eat because of certain circumstances. Do not observe fast continuously for days. You can take fruit, milk and water during the fast. Take unsweetened lemon water several times a day. Take plenty of water. Observing a fast once a week keeps diseases off. The body remains healthy.

Food : To ward off old age and live long, no special food is required. Take raw vegetables and fruits alongwith cooked food. Sometimes take only fruits. Because of their cleansing and dissolving effect fruits can check old age. Old age is the result of accumulation of toxins in the body and the resultant deterioration. Fruits do the cleansing job and check deterioration. They help in the regeneration of the body with new cells. If you take only fruits for a month or two, the results will be very much encouraging. Every year, eat only seasonal fruit for a month. It will keep off old age. Toxins, filth and other poisonous substances accumulated in the body are expelled by taking fruits. You can thus cleanse your body of foreign matter. The body will be light, active healthy; and life will be nothing but joy. Our health does not depend on what we eat but on what or how much we digest. We should eat only when we are hungry. Eat only what we want to eat. Always chew your food very well.

Do not over-eat because the food is tasty. You do not get strong by eating too much or eating oil-rich food. You get strength when you eat the minimum required quantity when you are hungry. In fact, over-eating is an enemy of good health and long life. Eating in excess leads to indigestion, obesity, toxins in the entire body and great stress on heart, kidneys and liver. It is, therefore, advisable to eat a little less than your appetite.

If you want to live like a young man ever in old age, have a young spirit. For longevity, looking at green grass, flowing water and the images of God is quite beneficial.

For living a long life, you need to have a fun-loving temper. A slim physique is better than a fat body. Do not smoke. Also do not drink or use intoxicants. Even if your ancestors have been drinking, you should not cultivate this habit. Take light meals in small quantities. Butter milk is good for health. For livelihood, work hard with a sense of dedication and service. Sitting idle is an invitation to diseases. For a few days every year, go for an outing for relaxation or go to a religious or holy places. Consider the joys or sorrows, good things or bad things in your life as something given by God, accept them and live life in a contented manner. Healthy body, healthy mind and healthy intellect are god-given gifts which come to you only when you have faith in God and you follow rules of nature. If you stand facing the rising sun daily in the morning, darkness will never prevail in your life. It is well said, "Early to bed and early to rise, makes a man healthy, wealthy and wise." After the morning exercise take fresh unboiled milk without sugar with three bananas, four dates and a bit of coconut. It will taste wonderful. The coconut will supply the necessary oil to the body. It keeps the bowels clean. Dates are good for the blood. Bananas and milk together make a fine wholesome diet. For lunch, you may take *roti* (60 gms.), rice, cooked vegetable and raw seasonal vegetables, etc. During winter take sugar cane juice and also crush sugarcane with your teeth and suck juice. In the evening take milk and seasonal fruit, such as mango, papaya, pear, melon and dry fruit.

Those above forty years of age should take only milk and fruit in the evening. Those who have been taking this diet, know of its advantages by experience. It keeps a man healthy, does not let him fall sick. He meets death after living a long life by keeping well.

Oil Drops in the Ear : Put two drops each in the ears before going to bed. The symptoms of old age will not appear too soon. It will keep the ears, teeth and eyesight intact.

Sleep : Breathe through the left nostril during the day and the right nostril during the night. While taking rest during the day lie down on the right side and you will breathe through the left nostril. Similarly, sleep on the left side during the night and you will breathe through the right nostril. Breathing in this fashion keeps you healthy.

Avoid Medicines : Medicines do not root out the disease. A disease is in fact not cured because of medicines but because of human body's resistance power. But these days adverse publicity and advertisements have blunted our mind and we do not see the truth.

The person who follows the rules of diet will not need any medicines. Most of the diseases occur because of improper diet. To atone for our mistakes, we should observe weekly fast. What you can achieve through natural food and by following rules of nature, cannot be made possible by law, punishment, threat or sermonizing. Reduce your food intake with advancing age. The intake of salt and spices should be reduced to the minimum.

The habit of taking medicines at the slightest indication of an ailment is not good. As far as possible, medicines should be avoided. The rules of nature do not approve of resorting to medicines and to hope for a long life and strong body with the support of medicines is of no avail. Believe in the rules of nature. Take plenty of water in the morning. Do not check natural pressures. Daily exercise, inhaling of plenty of oxygen and eating raw vegetables as a salad with your meals pave the road to a long life.

Positive thinking—An elixir for a long-life : If you cherish to enjoy life with your grandchildren, you not only need to develop positive thinking, but also need to part with all your despair and passimism. Negative feelings gives birth to problems such as heart attacks, hypertension, high blood pressure etc. Hence, always think positive and thank God for giving such a wonderful life.

Will to Live : It helps if you have a will to live long. Do not entertain thoughts of despair, depression and suicide. Depression leads to suicide and reduces life-expectancy. The attention you pay to the health of the body should be paid to mental health also. To think that you are under the influence of Saturn is fatal. It leads to despair. A man with firm faith and strong will power gets success. Keep yourself mentally and physically occupied. To keep your mind healthy, you should cultivate some hobbies.

Have faith in religion or do not brush away religious thoughts. Be physically and mentally active with zest for life.

Will Power : Know your will power and use it. You can increase or decrease your palpitation by using your will power. Your heart is affected by anger and fear. Fear can even cause death by arresting your heart beat. Fear causes constipation. Through meditation you can direct your blood flow to a particular part of the body or hold it there for some time.

Anger affects salivation. You can control anger by using your will power or you can even totally get rid of it.

Your will power greatly affects your health. With the commencement of old age one loses courage and soon becomes old for want of will power. But a man of strong will power can check old age. A man is as old as he thinks himself to be. Therefore, do not consider yourself old, do not accept the fact that you are old. When you can act like a young man, why to think that you are old. Have faith in yourself, even the impossible can happen. For long life it is essential to keep your thoughts pure. "Old age" has a symptomatic relevance in every respect. For example, getting hurt by sharp words means that you are mentally old. It means that sharp words affect the mind and man becomes unhappy. He does not feel like doing anything. Similarly, if the man feels tired and becomes depressed because of failure, he considers himself old. It is, therefore advisable to keep yourself busy to ward off mental tension. Do not feel lonely, enjoy the beauties of nature and cultivate love for works of art so that despair has no place in your life. You should have a will to learn even in old age and to achieve something extraordinary.

Always consider yourself as young. Let your mind not entertain thoughts of old age. The person who stands facing the sun in the morning, takes exercise daily, eats his meals discreetly, has a sense of equanimity, never becomes old. Always be cheerful. Our present life is built on our past thoughts. Our destiny is determined by our thoughts. Impure thoughts are as terrible as impure deeds. Entertaining divine and good thoughts lead to truth, well-being and joy in life.

COUNTERING OLD AGE

Treatment—Garlic : Regular use of garlic will not let you be a victim of premature old age. Old age means contraction and disease of the arteries. That is why wrinkles appear on an old man's body.

Grind one part garlic and mix in four parts of honey. Take 2 tsp. each in the morning and evening. If you take it for 50 days, you will find that you have a disease-free body and you will look like a young man. Garlic is a fine chemical. If you cannot exert yourself to work out the above recipe, take four cloves of garlic with water or take them boiled in milk. Take two one-clove garlic bulbs before lunch.

If you have grown old and want to become young, observe fast for three days. Spend the three days of fasting in religious thoughts. On the fourth day, squeeze out the juice of four one-clove garlic bulbs, mix in equal quantity of water and drink it. In this way, take garlic juice four times during the day. After an hour of taking the juice, take 2 tsp. butter or clarified butter. Follow this routine for four days. From the eighth day take garlic juice mixed with 2 tsp. of honey for a week. Take it four times a day followed by butter or clarified butter as you were doing earlier. From the sixteenth day, grind four one-clove garlic bulbs with eight large raisins and mix in a glass of water. Take it four times a day for a week. Stop taking butter or clarified butter. From the twenty-fourth day dissolve the ground garlic in the juice of three pieces of *amla* and take it four times a day for a week. Do not take meals during this period. In the following month, take milk and massage your body with garlic oil before taking your bath. To prepare the garlic oil, peel 10 gms. of garlic and boil in 500 ml. of mustard oil. When the garlic gets burnt up, strain the oil and use it for massage. In the third month, grind 8 one-clove garlic bulbs with 2 tsp. of honey, ten large raisins with seeds removed and mixed in ½ cup *amla* juice. Take it for the entire month. In this way, with devoted labour and striving you will shed old age and regain youth. It will be better if your efforts are accompanied by a religious way of life.

If it is not possible for you to do the above exercise, peel seven cloves of garlic, grind and roast in clarified butter and take it once daily in the morning. Or you can grind 5 cloves of garlic with five large raisins and take it daily mixed with 2 tsp. of honey.

Amla **:** In old age, there is an excess of calcium in the body. It hardens the bones, sinews and arteries. The use of *amla* helps you to regain flexibility and ensures proper functioning of various parts of the body. *Amla*, in fact, is a nectar for old age. For longevity, you should use it daily in some form or the other.

Grapes : It plays an important role in the production of blood. Dried grapes, that is, large raisins used regularly will provide in a few days joy and splendour and enhance blood and semen in the body. The use of raisins protects health in old age. The sugar in raisins is easily digested and absorbed in the body.

Salt : According to *Dr. Frederick Morward*, "Salt accelerates the onset of old age." The intake of salt should, therefore, be reduced to the minimum.

Mango : Take two mangoes followed by a glass of milk with 2 tsp. of honey and 1 tsp. of sugar candy after two hours daily for 50 days. It will strengthen the body and postpone old age for some years.

Ginger : Chew a few small pieces of ginger before taking your meals. It is beneficial for health and longevity.

Cashewnuts : It is a nutritious food for old persons. It contains riboflavin which is necessary for preventing the onset of old age.

Clarified butter : Grind 10 corns of black pepper in a tsp. of clarified butter and take it daily in the morning for longevity.

Milk : It is beneficial for long life. Old age does not overpower you. Only 30 per cent of protein of the cereals we take is used by our body but if milk is a part of our meals the body makes use of double the quantity of protein and thus gets greater strength. You may take a glass of milk with 1 tsp. of clarified butter and three tsp. of honey added to it daily. It will delay the onset of old age.

Wheat : (1) Taking the juice of tender wheat grass is very beneficial. To know about the method of preparing the juice, please read *Bhojan ke Dwara Chikitsa.*

(2) Soak overnight a cup of wheat, eat it, by chewing it well in the morning with jaggery. It will remove the symptoms of old age.

Massage : Massaging the body with oil regularly every day makes a weak body strong and increases the weight and wards off old age. Application of honey mixed with lemon juice removes wrinkles from the face and neck.

Curd, Butter milk : Take curd with meals or drink a glass of butter milk after the meals.

Mint leaves : It is a fine wind eliminating substance. Its use improves the appetite. It is, therefore, a beneficial food item for old persons and should be used daily.

Walnut : Eat 8 walnut kernels, 4 almonds and 10 large raisins daily followed by a glass of milk. It provides energy to older persons.

***Harad* :** Soak overnight small *harad* in water. Use only as much water as can be absorbed by *harad.* Fry them in the morning in clarified butter and then store them in a glass jar. Eat one piece each in the morning and evening every day for two months. It will make the body strong. If you suffer from constipation take a tsp. of *harad* powder every day with hot water.

Papaya : Eat papaya every day in the morning for longevity.

Raja Baldev Das Birla's Message for Longevity : Astrologers told Raja Baldev Das Birla that he would die at the age of 50. At this, he moved to Baba Vishwanath's temple situated on the banks of Bhagirathi river in Kashi to spend his last few remaining years in peace. He gave up cereals and began to eat fruit and went for a walk daily. He completed the 50th year of his life and he was still alive despite the prediction of his death by hypocritical astrologers. Even afterwards he maintained his daily routine sincerely.

One day he was out in the sun. An acquaintance asked him why he was out in the sun. Raja Sahib laughed and said, "The body follows its own rules. One of its rules is that hardship ultimately provides relief. But if you are given to comfort and become a slave of the body, it brings pain. Therefore, if you want to be happy don't be afraid of hardships." Those who want to keep healthy should know the implications of Raja Sahib's statement.

One should get up early in the morning and go for a walk. One should not be misled by astrologers who are out to make money by creating all sorts of doubts in one's mind and recommending magical practices, incantations, performance of religious observances and various methods of worship to ward off misfortune. You should know it for certain that, as a principle, the man who talks of omens, harm and evil is not an astrologer in reality and the person who predicts your death must be a total fake. If one can predict death like that, the business of insurance companies would come to an end.

Hard Work : Keep working hard. Hard working persons do not suffer from mental troubles. It is said that a person who has zest for life and is engaged in hard work, will never get old. Instead of sexuality one should give preference to thoughts of purity of life.

Keep Moving : It has been said in an *Upnishad* "Charaiveti Charaiveti", that is, "keep moving, keep moving" and "Charanvai madhu vidanti", that is, "only the one who keeps moving knows the sweetness of life". Those who have lived long also say, "keep moving, keep moving." It means you should remain active and not idle. Those who have lived hundred years and above say on the basis of their experience that they always kept themselves busy and thus they were always active and never dull.

REGULARITY AND PUNCTUALITY

Dr. Vishveshvaraiya lived a long life of 101 years. Once somebody asked him about the secret of his long life. Dr. Vishveshvaraiya said, "I do everything punctually. I am regular in all my works, I eat on time, sleep on time. I go for a walk punctually and take exercise regularly. I am miles away from anger. This is the secret of my longevity."

The Key to Longevity—Keep Yourself Occupied : The author of *History of Hindu Chemistry* and famous Professor of Chemistry, Dr. Prafulchandra Roy was once asked, "What have been the busiest moments in your life?" He replied, "A busy man is never short of time. In fact, my busiest days were when I crossed 60 years of age. Even after 60 I was doing some thing or the other and I kept myself busy."

112 years old Joquin Silva, a resident of Brazil, while telling about the secret of his longevity, said, "I am always doing something or the other. I am active throughout the day. I do not drink alcohol." —*Pragyan Bharti, Jaipur, 16-31 Oct., 1990*

When Shri Morarji Desai, the former Prime Minister of India was ninety-five he was asked how he was self-sufficient and disease-free even at that late stage of life. He replied, "I have total faith in the Geeta. I do my job without expecting anything in return. I regularly use only natural health products. My chief diet is milk. Boiled bitter gourd, dates, fruits, dry fruits provide sufficient energy to me. I have not taken cereals since 1975. I make no difference between what I say and what I do. I have always been an optimist."

Though Sh. Morarji Desai rose to be the Prime Minister of

Inida, he did not own a house. Those were some of the pluses in his life which held the key to his longevity.

—Raj. Patrika, Jaipur, Dated 4-2-1991

The news of the 159th birthday of Shirali Misslimov, an old man of erstwhile Soviet Union, appeared in *Tass.* It was mentioned in the report that he was regular in his morning walk, was never idle, did his job sincerely and kept himself quite occupied. Walk a great deal if you want to live long. Walking is life.

***Satvik* Food—The Basis of Life :** Dr. Verner Macfedan, a Naturopath says that we should not dig our grave with our own teeth. More people die of over-eating than of undernourishment. Keep your appetite under control and do not fill your stomach simply for the sake of your taste-buds. Pure *satvik* food provides vital energy to human body. Over-eating, on the other hand, shortens life.

112 years old Mrs. Katherin Praket, talking about the secret of her longevity, says, "My life style has been the simplest possible but more than that the secret of my long life is my interest in other occupations, anything which can give me joy and engage my attention. I do not do the same job throughout the day."

A 110 years old woman says that whenever she feels sick she takes 125 gms. clarified butter in a glass of hot milk. It relieves her from ailments. She does not take medicines. Such examples as mentioned above are worth following for all those who aspire to live a long and meaningful life.

Conduct : It is necessary for peace and happiness in the family that older persons should offer advice only when it is asked for. When children are grown up and self-sufficient, do not try to exercise control over them. Do not keep brooding over what they do.

Older persons usually have plenty of time at their disposal and little work to do. They can better utilize their time in working for the family, teaching children and offering selfless service to the needy besides taking care of their own health. Do not consider yourself worthless. Read books on health and spiritualism. In the background of your mind you should have the idea that time is approaching near when you will say goodbye to the world. There is no scope for attachment and jealousy at this late stage of life. Contentment lies in detachment.

The feeling that you are old is not good : On the 80th birth anniversary of the famous inventor Thomas Alva Edison somebody advised him to slow down the pace of his work and cultivate a hobby or two for fun and change. "Why don't you start playing golf?" He asked. Edison coolly replied, "I am not that old yet."

The renowned mathematician and philosopher, Bertrand Rusell has this to write about the art of living in old age, "At the age of 86 it is not improper for me to make out a claim that I have certainly acquired some expertise and a technique or two as to how to live in old age. I believe if your interests and sphere of activities are large and varied and you are fully engrossed in them, there is no reason why you should sit idle and count how many years you have already spent and as the years advance, get doubtful about your future."

As far as I know, there are two dangers or risks which require precaution in old age.

The important thing you have to take care of is that you do not remain tied too much to the past. To cry over split milk or rue the past mistakes and be sad about them is not helpful in any way. Instead, concentrate your thoughts on the present. To make the present beautiful it is essential to come out of the depths of the past and work in the present day life with sincerity and diligence. If the present is pleasant, the future will automatically be pleasant.

Get engrossed in your work. Care-free and fun-loving persons live happily.

Children : There are children who serve their old parents sincerely in every respect and feel indebted to them how the parents had brought them up and educated them and made them self-sufficient. They think it their prime duty to serve their parents and make them comfortable when they are old. Such children are blessed ones. The blessings of their parents are always with them and they make progress in life and are happy. Those who have not served their parents, may be very rich but internally they are not happy; their life lacks joy. Serve not only your old parents but also consider it your duty to be of use to any old persons you come across.

MENTAL TENSION

Anxiety leads to mental tension. Several types of worries overtake us in our daily life. How we are affected by anxiety and worries depends on our nature and tolerance. There can be a person who does not worry about even big things but another person worries about petty things and easily loses temper or gets impatient. Whatever the case, we all think that the subject of our worries is apparent to us. But we are mistaken in this regard, because if we think deeply we will find that the root-cause of our worries is altogether different. Try to understand the truth.

The real cause of worries and anxiety is lack of self-confidence and faith in God. If we do something in an anxious state of mind, we will not be able to do it properly because of lack of self-confidence and it will be marked by uncertainty. Our performance and style of functioning will be adversely affected. Moreover, whatever adverse is happening to us because of our disbelief in God will increase our sorrow because we will hold ourselves responsible for it while the fact is that we can do only our duty, our *karma* and have no control over the consequences. Our *karma* should be rewarded as per our own wish is not in our hands otherwise everybody in the world would have got what he wanted. Those who have total, strong and unquestionable faith in God never fall a prey to anxiety in any way because they leave everything to God and accept whatever is given to them. If you do not worry about yourself, almighty God will take care of you, just as parents look after their innocent child and take total care of him in every respect. But when the child grows up and is self-dependent, parents stop worrying about him. You can cultivate the qualities of self-confidence and faith in God by constant practice. You should know that it is necessary to get rid of mental tension caused by anxiety.

How to Relieve Yourself of Mental Tension : Whenever you are overtaken by a problem, anxiety and trouble, do not keep it to yourself. Discuss it and share it with those close to you, because it will prevent you from reaching the stage of frustration. Moreover, your friend may offer some help to relieve you of the problem you are faced with. If not that, atleast a few words of sympathy may bring relief to you mentally.

Do not spend your time alone so that your mind does not become a single track one. Attend musical programmes, go to museums and libraries to pass your time meaningfully. If you do not feel like doing anything, go for a walk or read a newspaper. Divert your attention some how or the other.

If you do not get sleep at night, get up and start reading light short stories. It will relieve the burden on your mind. While going to bed, do not brood over the day's activities or what you are going to do on the following day.

Mental tension is also caused by want and poverty. According to the Psychologist Page, "Happiness is crucial to a successful life. In happiness, he should look at those above him and make efforts to reach their heights. When in sorrow, look at those who are below you. Only then you can feel fully contented."

If you have to reach a place or complete an assignment at a given time, do not do it in haste. You can begin a little early in order to be on time. But do not invite tension which is caused by haste.

It is not proper to interfere in somebody else's work or to

interrupt while he is talking. It is better to listen rather than be over-talkative. Pay greater attention to what is useful and interesting than trivia.

When you are burdened with excess work, do not panic. Rather, take up things in order of priority according to their importance.

If you have learnt to be relaxed, it will be easier to adjust with circumstances in life. Try to change your attitude. Do not pay heed to petty things.

Whenever you feel tired by doing too much of mental work, immediately shift to some physical activity. The change of work will bring mental relief and peace to you. If you are in service, enjoy your week-ends.

Spare some time out of your work to indulge in gossip with the neighbour. Walk a little. It will certainly relieve tension caused by over-work.

When you have leisure time, write letters to friends and relatives because receiving letters is a matter of joy. But do not indulge in too much of letter-writing otherwise it will cause tension if you do not receive back letters.

One of the easier ways of getting rid of tension is to give up your stubborn attitude and ill-will towards others. Have an eye for beauty because a thing of beauty is a joy for ever. It is quite refreshing.

You can certainly succeed in getting rid of mental tension by resorting to the above methods. If in the so-called modern society we are not able to check stress and tension, it may prove fatal for many of us. Therefore, think over the problem without being under stress. Have faith in God.

The Road to a Healthy and Happy Life : Do you want to lead a healthy and happy life? If yes, live intelligently and with determination. Lord Buddha has said, "Understanding is the best treatment of all ailments and problems and lack of it is the root-cause of all troubles."

90% of the patients can recover without the assistance of a medical practitioner because human body is filled with a natural and general immunity system that tends to protect the body from disease and infection. Chanting God's name also induces mental and physical health. Lord Tennyson used to repeat his own name using the beads of a rosary. An author named Cove maintains that a man may not mould himself to his liking by his thoughts but he can do it by his emotions. He should take recourse to auto-suggestion, saying, "I am getting better day by day." It will definitely change him for the better. One should follow the following rules in life to be always healthy and happy in every respect :

1. If somebody sows a thorn for you, sow a flower for him. You will get happiness and he will get pain.
2. Kabir says that you may be living in the neighbourhood of slayers but you need not worry because they will reap as they sow.
3. Whatever has to happen is pre-determined. —*Einstein*
4. God is everywhere and whatever has happened or is happening or will happen must be good.
5. Good men never face sorrow in this world or in the other world. —*Socrates*
6. The essential message of *Vedas* and *Shastras* is—You receive what you give; happiness begets happiness, sorrow begets sorrow.
7. Goodness always brings happiness. Therefore, always be good and do good.

—*Dr. R.N.Verma* on the basis of his study, thinking, experience and application of the above divine qualities.

THE ART OF EATING

Whether we are healthy or sick, proper diet is essential. When you are sick it is more important to pay attention to your diet than medicine.

To keep the body healthy, normal food is required. Energy is consumed when you work hard, tissues are broken or damaged. To replenish them we need special kind of food. Food compensates for the losses in the body. As we advance in years, our food-intake is reduced. We need very little quantity of food. But sometimes to satiate our hunger we eat more than is required.

In wedding parties, social lunches or dinners and on several other occasions we usually over-eat to satisfy our taste-buds but this practice is harmful. If you regularly over-eat, your digestive system will get upset.

The belly and intestines swell; their functioning is impaired and gas-formation creates problems. Fat accumulates in the body, one gets obese and the walls of the stomach which should be strong and flexible become thick and heavy. The stomach should not exceed the waist-line. The best way to avoid all these troubles is to eat sparingly.

How Much Food Should We take? It has been found by experiments that eating in excess or eating simply for taste is a harmful practice. Always eat less than your appetite or what you can eat. Such a quantity will provide sufficient nourishment and energy. In fact, even if we eat in excess, only a little of it gets digested, which provides nourishment and energy. It is, therefore, suggested that you should eat less than your capacity to eat.

Food and Sleep : If you go to sleep immediately after eating you do not get good sleep. The intestines do not relax as much as they should during sleep. Therefore, you should eat three hours before you go to sleep. Eat three times in a day. Do not eat anything during the intervals. Do not eat unless you are quite hungry. Chew your food well. When you are worried or angry, do not eat. Only drink warm water. Be cheerful when you are eating. Your breakfast should mainly consist of starch and lunch of protein. In the evening it will be better to take only fruits, raw vegetables and salad.

Food during Winter : We take food to subsist. If we take food in keeping with seasonal requirements we will get proper energy and will have a strong and sound body.

When cold winds touch our body in winter we feel very cold. To protect ourselves from cold winds we wear warm clothes so that the heat of the body does not escape. If the body remains warm, it is helpful in digesting the food. During winter, nights are long and days are short. Hence, the body gets more rest. As a result, we are able to digest easily even oily, heavy and nourishing food.

When it is very cold, take nourishing and invigorating food alongwith seasonal fruits. Nourishing food includes clarified butter, milk, butter, black gram *daal, halwa, kheer, rabri, jalebi* prepared in pure *ghee* and milk, various dishes made with black gram *daal*, green gram or carrot *halwa*, cashewnuts, pistachio, almonds, walnut, etc.

The seasonal things include *amla*, banana, carrots, guava, honey, ground nut, ripe tomatoes, spinach, fenugreek, etc. They should form a part of your diet.

After meals, do take a glass of sweetened milk after 2-3 hours. You may also take 1 tsp. of clarified butter with it. If you want to take honey in milk, allow the milk to cool down, then add 2 tsp. of honey and drink. Do not take milk in gulps, rather sip it slowly.

During the days of intense cold, you may eat *laddoos* made of sesame seeds and jaggery.

Massage your body with mustard oil. After the winter is over and the spring season starts, eat 15 fresh tender *neem* leaves daily in the morning for a month. It will protect you against blood disorders, skin diseases and fever throughout the year.

Nourishing Dishes in Winter—Almonds-Poppy seeds *Halwa* : Ingredients—Almonds 250 gms., Poppy seeds—125 gms., wheat flour-1 bowl, sugar 250 gms., milk 1 cup, water 2 cups and clarified butter 1 bowl, saffron and cardamom to your requirement.

Method : Soak overnight almonds and poppy seeds in cool water. In the morning grind both the items finely after peeling the almonds. Pour clarified butter in a pan and heat it. Add ground almonds and poppy seeds and roast it well on slow flame till it turns pink. When sweet smell begins to rise, mix wheat flour and continue stirring till clarified butter visibly separates. Boil in a pan one cup of milk mixed with two cups of water. Add this to almonds and poppy seeds *halwa*, put it on high flame and keep stirring. Add sugar. When the consistency is right, remove it from the flame. Also grind saffron and cardamom in a few drops of milk and add to the *halwa* mixing it well. Serve it hot in plates. It is highly nourishing for the mind. It should be definitely taken in winter by students, those who are engaged in mental work and those who have a weak mind.

Almond Powder : Ingredients : Almonds 200 gms., acacia tree gum 50 gms., sugar powder 200 gms.

Method : Soak almonds in water and peel them. Grind them after they are dry. Fry gum in clarified butter and grind it. Mix both the items with sugar powder.

Take 2 tsp. of it daily with a cup of warm milk and take your meals after three hours. For the second dose take only 1 tsp. of it with milk two hours after meals and one hour before going to bed. Take it for two-three months. It is highly beneficial.

During winter, sore throat, cough, tonsillitis and pain in the throat are common complaints. For this, take a glass of warm water, add ½ tsp. each of salt and baking powder and less than ¼ tsp. of alum salt to it and gargle. Do it thrice daily.

SELF-URINE THERAPY

Drinking your own urine and applying it on your body is called Urine Therapy. If it is taken or used in a proper manner, it can cure several diseases.

How to Use it : Early in the morning while passing the first urine, allow the urine to flow out for a moment, then collect it in a clean bottle. In the beginning, drink about 25 ml. of urine, then gradually increase the quantity to two cups (200 ml). You have to take your own urine, not somebody else's. If you cannot digest the idea of drinking urine, at first only rinse your mouth with it and spit it out. After that, gargle with urine. Then one day shut your eyes and take a sip or two. Gradually, you will have no hesitation in drinking urine. You will see its effect in about 15 days. You will overcome the aversion to drinking urine. Those who suffer from Dysuria should not drink urine. It has to be taken only once in the morning.

External Use of Urine : Drinking of urine is to be accompanied by its external application also. It brings prompt relief. The external use means giving a massage to your body with urine, soaking a piece of cloth, cotton, gauze in urine and dressing a part of the body with it and bandaging it or flushing the wounds with it. After a urine massage wash yourself with lukewarm water after an interval of two to three hours. Do not use any soap. For massaging use only fresh urine in the morning.

The apprehension that self-urine is not fit for drinking is baseless. It is not harmful. If you follow the proper method and take wholesome food, self-urine therapy can be beneficial.

Rules to be Followed During Self-Urine Therapy : During self-urine therapy do not use any other system of medicine. If you have been taking some medicine, stop it and start self-urine therapy after a week. If you have taken to it, do it with full interest and sincerity, otherwise don't do it. While undergoing this treatment, do not take any other medicine, tobacco, meat, alcohol, chillies, spices, sugar, saccharin, fried food, polished rice, vegetable *ghee*, canned food, salt, sour food and sweets. One can eat hand-pound rice, jaggery, honey, loaf sugar fresh seasonal fruit, sprouts, fresh *chapattis*, boiled leafy vegetables without spices. Alongwith the above precautions, self-control and abstinence from sex are also necessary.

While following the above rules, you can undergo self-urine

therapy and its external application to rid yourself of any disease. If a healthy person takes up self-urine therapy for the protection of his health, he will grow healthier and will be safe from infectious diseases.

Diseases : Self-urine therapy is beneficial in heart diseases, weakness of heart, high and low blood pressure, the ailments of lungs and bones, cold and cough, asthma, the diseases of the stomach and intestines, head, eyes, ears, piles, diseases of the anus, skin-diseases, disorders of semen, irregularity of periods, etc.

The credit for popularizing self-urine therapy is given to John W. Armstrong, the author of the book **The Water of Life**.

There is a mention of the virtues of urine-therapy in Ayurvedic system of medicine also.

❑❑❑

Glossary of English Medical Terms

Abrotifacient : Causing abortion.

Abscess : Local inflammation of body tissues with deep suppuration caused by bacteria which destroy the cells in the centre of the area and leave a cavity filled with pus.

Acidity : Excess of hydrochloric acid found in the stomach.

Acne : Skin condition, found usually in adolescents, in which glands of skin get infected.

Allergy : Abnormal sensitivity to any substance.

Anemia : A decrease in the volume of blood or some of the normal constituents of blood vessels and induces sleeplessness.

Anesthetic : A substance which produces loss of some from of sensitivity or entire of sensibility.

Anthrax : Disease of man from animals; two forms exist, one of the skin and the other of the lungs.

Appetite-loss : Aversion of food.

Arthritis : An abnormal accumulation of fluid in the peritoneal cavity.

Ascorbic acid : Vitamin C, occurring in fresh fruits.

Asthmatic problems : Periodic attacks of difficulty in breathing.

Bacteria : Single-celled organisms which bring about decay, disease or build up nitrogen compounds in the soil.

Bedsores : Lesions over pressure areas on the body of a bedridden patient.

Bladder : Collecting pouch for urine from kidneys.

Bleeding : Emitting blood. Bleeding can result from a small cut or wound and will usually clot of its own accord.

Blood : Fluid contained in arteries and veins of the body that carries nutrients to and waste away from all tissues. Made up of cells and plasma.

Blood pressure, Low : See Hypotension.

Blood pressure, High : See Hypertension.

Bronchitis : An inflammation of the mucous lining of the bronchial rubes.

Cardiotonic : Tonic for the heart.

Cholera : Epidemic disease with violent vomiting and purging, cramps and collapse, endemic in India and epidemic elsewhere.

Cholesterol : Steroid alcohol present in animal cells and body fluids.

Chronic : A term applied to certain disorders, denoting their slow onset and persistent duration.

Congestion : An abnormal accumulation of blood or lymph in some organ or region of the body.

Constipation : Condition of bowels in which defaecation is irregular and difficult.

Cough : Sudden expiratory movement produced by irritation of the larynx, trachea, bronchi, or pleura.

Dandruff : Condition of the scalp characterized by dry scaling.

Dehydration : Loss of water.

Delirium : A state of more or less clouding of consciousness, dream-like incoherent notions, illusions, and hallucinations, and restlessness or stupor, most common with fever or on a toxic pasis, usually with poor memory of the experience.

Depression : A feeling of melancholy, hopelessness and dejection.

Diabetes : Disease characterized by excessive discharge of glucose-containing urine, with thirst and emaciation, caused by the failure of pancreas to secrete and adequate amount of insulin and the resultant accumulation of glucose in the blood.

Diagnosis : Identification of disease by investigation of symptoms and history.

Digestion : The motor and chemical process by which nutritive substances are ingested, carried along the alimentary tract, and rendered capable of absorption into the blood and lymph.

Dysentery : Disease with inflammation of mucous membrane and glands of large intestine and mucous and bloody evacuations.

Eczema : An itching disease of the skin.

Elephantiasis : Tropical disease in which blocking of the lymph vessels by a parasite leads to great swelling of the tissues, especially in the lower limbs.

Exhaustion : The limiting case of muscular fatigue, in which the stimulus or excitation ceases to elicit any overt motor response whatever.

Flu : (also, Influenza) : Virus infection characterized by fever, inflammation of the nose, larynx and bronchi, neuralgic and muscular pains and gastrointestinal disorder.

Fungus : Mould.

Gall Bladder : Sac beneath the liver which stores bile and secretes mucus.

Gallstones : Stone-like objects composed mainly of calcium, found in gall bladder and its drainage system.

Gastric secretion : Digestive secretion inside the stomach.

Goiter : Enlargement of the thyroid gland.

Gum : The tissues and membranes surrounding the teeth.

Hemoglobin : Red-coloured oxygen carrier in RBC.

Hemophilia : Strong tendency to bleed.

Headache : Pain or ache localized in the head.

Hepatic : A drug that acts on the liver.

Hepatitis : A swelling and soreness of the liver.

Hypertension : High arterial pressure.

Hypotension : Low blood pressure, a fall in blood pressure below the normal range.

Hysteria : A psychoneurosis, resulting from a conflict between the ego and the primitive tendencies of the id, in which the latter tendencies are repressed, and are thus excluded from the direct conscious expression, it being assumed that the unconscious, repressed material finds an indirect physical outlet through conversion, producing the hysterical symptoms.

Intestinal problem : Disorders in the intestine.

Intestine : The membranous tube which extends from the stomach to the anus.

Itch (also itching) : An irritating cutaneous and internal disorder; a sensory experience which involves mild pricking-pain sensations, unpleasantness, and a persistent impulse to scratch.

Jaundice : Increase in bile-pigments in blood.

Kidneys : The vital organs of the human body, which remove waste products from the blood and regulate the amount of water and the delicate balance of chemicals in the body.

Leprosy : Chronic endemic bacterial disease caused by Mycobacterium lepriae. Characterized by thickening and ulceration of the skin with loss of sensation and in severe cases deformity and blindness.

Leukemia : A fatal disease of the organs that manufacture blood, such as the lymph glands and bone marrow.

Lymph : Special functioning fluid that flows through specific vessels, passing through the filtre of the lymph glands before entering the bloods stream.

Malaria : Acute, febrile, infectious disease caused by the presence of parasitic organisms in the red blood cells.

Memory : Recall of past experience.

Metabolism : Energy exchanges in a living organism.

Mucus : A thick, white liquid secreted by mucous glands.

Muscle : The tissue which is responsible for body movement.

Narcotic : A drug which induces narcosis, a condition of stupor, diminished sensitivity to pain, motor paralysis and a tendency towards sleep.

Neuralgia : A painful disorder of one or more nerves. It usually causes sharp fitful pains.

Nervous system : The totality of neurons in the body of any organism.

Neurasthenia : A condition characterized by lack of physical and mental vigour, by abnormal fatigability, and often by the presence of phobias.

Osteo : (Prefix) Bone.

Osteoporosis : A disorder that causes a gradual decrease in both the amount and strength of bone tissues.

Paralysis : Impairment or complete loss of motor function due to some disturbance of the neural or muscular mechanism; impairment or destruction of sensory function.

Peptic ulcer : A non-cancerous crater-like sore in the wall of the stomach or intestine.

Pharmaceutical : Of the use or sale of medicinal drugs.

Piles : Enlarged painful veins in rectum or around anus.

Pimple : Small pointed area on skin, at times filled with infectious material.

Pituitary gland : A small compound endocrine gland, situated at the base of the brain.

Polio (also Poliomyelitis, Infantile Paralysis) : A disease that causes paralysis.

Pyorrhea : Infection of the gums which causes the edges of the tooth sockers to bleed easily when teeth are being brushed.

Rheumatism : Pain, swelling and deformity of joints of unknown cause.

Rubefacient : Causing redness, as of the skin.

Sciatica : Inflammation of or injury to the sciatic nerve in back of thigh.

Sexual : Pertaining to sex.

Skin : Outer covering of body.

Sleeplessness : Lack of sleep.

Stomach : A sac-like enlargement of the ailmentary tract, following the esophagus, in which the preliminary process of digestion takes place.

Therapeutic : That which treats medically curative.

Thyroid : Located below the larynx.

Toxin : Poisonous substance of animal or vegetable origin.

Tumour : A swelling or growth.

Typhoid : An infectious fever caused by the typhoid bacillus, characterized by diarrhoea and other symptoms.

Ulcer : Sores on skin or internal parts of body, caused by various factors.

Urinary bladder inflammation : Inflamation of the bladder.

Vagina : The passage connecting the outer and inner female sex organs.

Vasodilator : Causing relaxation of the blood vessels, thus lowering the blood pressure.

Viruses : Minute organisms that cause diseases such as common cold, measles, mumps, poliomyelitis, chicken-pox, smallpox, etc.

Vomiting : The forcible expulsion of substance from the stomach through the mouth, elicited by intestinal, gastric, cardiac, or pharyngeal irritation.

Wrinkle : Furrow-like crease, depression or ridge in skin.

Whitlow : Infected finger.

Glossary of Non-English Terms

A short glossary of Non-English terms has been given below for ready reference. Few terms have diagrams for support.

Aachar : Pickles.

Aata (Fig.45) **:** A white powder made by crushing grains of wheat, flour.

Agarbattis : Incense sticks generally used while worshipping God.

Agni : Fire digestion; biological fire governing metabolism.

Ajwain : *Trachys permum ammi.* Caraway seeds. A type of herb, the seeds of which are used in cuisine.

Akda (Fig.1) **:** *Calotropis gigantea.* Swallow-wort. A short wild shrub whose stems give white milky substance.

Amla murabba (Fig.2) **:** Jam of *Emblic myrobalan.* Indian gooseberry. A conserve made of whole amla fruits dipped in sugar syrup.

Anar : *Punica granatum.* Pomegranate (fruit).

Anjir : *Ficus carica.* Fig.

Arbi (Fig.3) **:** *Arum calocasia.* Calocasia. Roots of the plant of arum family.

Arhar (Fig.4) **:** *Cajamus indicus.* Pigeon pea. A type of pulse.

Arjun ki chhal (Fig.5) **:** *Terminalia alatagabsa.* The bark of Arjun tree.

Asgandh : *Withania somnifera.* Winter cherry. Ashwagandha.

Bach churan : Powder made from Orris root.

Baheda (Fig.6) **:** *Terminalia bellirica.* Belleric myrobalan.

Bajra (Fig.7) **:** Pearl millet.

Bala : A grub which attacks young wheat and barley.

Banafshah : *Viola odorata.* Sweet violet.

Band-gobhi : *Brassica oleracea.* Cabbage.

Bapchi : A kind of herbal shrub.

Bargad (Fig.8) **:** Banyan tree.

Batasha : Semi-spherical cake which is made of sugar and is very light and spongy.

Bathua (Fig.9) **:** *Chenapodium album.* Pigweed. A wild leafy vegetable.

Batis : A thick bread-cake baked on cinders.

Bel (Fig.10) **:** *Aegle marmelos.* Wood apple tree and its fruit.

Ber (Fig.11) **:** *Ziziphus jujuba.* A Jujube; a plum.

Besan : Flour of gram pulse.

Bhaav-prakash : A 16th-century text on Indian medicines.

Bhang : *Cannabis sativa.* Indian hemp.

Bhindi (Fig.12) **:** *Hibiscus esculentus.* Lady-finger (Okra).

Bidi : A type of cheap cigarette commonly used by villagers.

Boora : Unrefined powdered sugar.

Brahmi : *Bacopa monnieri. Lysimachia monnieri.* Thyme-leaved gratiola.

Cee-cee sound : A hissing sound made by mother to coax an infant to pass urine or stool.

Chameli (Fig.13) **:** *Jasminium grandiflorum.* Jasmine. A fragrant flower plant.

Chameli oil : Jasmine oil.

Chana (Fig.14) **:** *Cicer arietinum.* Gram.

Chandan : *Santalum album.* Sandal.

Chapati (Fig.46) **:** Unleavened thin bread prepared from wheat flour.

Chaulai (Fig.15) **:** *Amaranthus polygamous.* Amaranth tender. A kind of eatable greens.

Cheeku : *Manilkara zapota.* Sapodilla plum.

Chhoti ilayachi : *Elettaria cardamomum.* Cardamom.

Chilgoze : *Pinus gerardiana.* A kind of dry fruit.

Chiraunji : *Buchanania latifolia.* A tree, chironji sapida, its edible nut; dry fruit.

Churan : Powder; a powder made of medicine for improving digestion.

Chutney : Sauce; condiment; a paste added to food to enhance flavour.

Daal : Lentil; Pulse.

Dalchini : *Cinnamomum zeylanicum.* Cinnamon.

Dahi : Curd; Yoghurt.

Desi boora : Unrefined sugar powder.

Desi ghee : See *ghee*.

Desi sugar : Sugar in powder form.

Dhania (Fig.16) **:** *Coriandrum sativum.* Coriander.

Dhatoora : *Datura stramonium.* Thorn apple.

Doob : (also *durva*) *Cynodon dectylon.* Bermuda grass.

Dosha : Bodily humours. The three bodily humours according to Indian system of medicine are: *Vata* (wind or air), *Pitta* (bile) and *Kafa* or *Kapha* (phlegm or water).

Gajar : *Daucus carota.* Carrot.

Ghee : Clarified butter.

Gud : (also *Gur*) Jaggery.

Guggul : *Commiphora wightii.* A germicide gum used as incense.

Gulab : *Rosa centifolia.* Rose.

Gulab jal : Rose-water.

Gulkand (Fig.47) **:** A conserve prepared from rose petals.

Gutka (Fig.48) **:** An intoxicant for chewing prepared from tobacco, betel nuts and other substances, injurious for health.

Gwar (Fig.17) **:** *Cyamopsis tetragonoloba* or *Dolichos fabaeformis.* A plant, the seeds of which are used as pulse; cluster beans.

Gwarpatha (Fig.18) **:** Aloe-vera.

Haldi : *Curcuma longa.* Turmeric.

Halwa : A sweet dish prepared from wheat flour or semolina, sugar, coconut, dry fruits and clarified butter, boiled together; porridge.

Harad (Fig.19) **:** *Terminalia chebula.* Chebulic myrobalan.

Hari Om : Verse of prayer of Hindus.

Heeng : *Ferula asafoetida.* Asafoetida.

Hukka (Fig.49) **:** An oriental tobacco pipe with a long flexible tube which draws smoke through water contained in the bowl at the bottom of the pipe.

Ilaychi (Fig.20) **:** *Elettaria cardamomum.* Cardamom.

Imli : *Tamarindus indica.* Tamarind.

Isabgol : *Plantago ovata.* Fleawort pysillium. A medicinal plant, its seeds.

Jaiphal : *Myristica fragrance.* Nutmeg.

Jal bhangra : *Eclipta prostrata.* A spreading shrub.

Jalebi (Fig.50) **:** An Indian sweet of the shape of lattice, prepared from fine flour-paste fried in clarified butter and dipped in sugar syrup.

Jamikand (Fig.21) **:** Yam.
Jamun (Fig.22) **:** *Syzigium cumini.* The rose apple, Black plum.
Jeera : *Cuminum cyminum.* Cumin seeds.
Jwar (Fig.23) **:** Great millet.
Kabuli : A variety of gram-white.
Kadhi : A frothy dish prepared with curds and spices.
Kadi patta : *Murraya koenigii.* Curry leaves.
Kafa : (also *Kapha*) Phlegm (a watery humour of the body).
Kair : A plant found in desert and its berries.
Kajal : *Collyrium.* Black of lamp for use on eyes as a cosmetic.
Kali mirch : *Piper nigram.* Black pepper.
Kanchali : Camphor layer.
Kanji : A concotion made by fomentation of carrots.
Kapoor : *Cinnamomum comphora.* Camphor.
Karaunda (Fig.24) **:** *Carissa carandus.* A green vegetable.
Karela (Fig.25) **:** *Momordica charantia.* Bitter gourd.
Karma : The sum of good and bad actions in one's life which decide the fate in the next life.
Kateera : *Sterculia urens.* Tragacanth. Its gum is used in medicine.
Kayakalpa : A magical rejuvenation.
Kewra : The fragrant flower, pandamus.
Kesar : *Crocus sativus.* Saffron.
Khus (Fig.26) **:** An aromatic variety of grass.
Khus-khus : *Vetiveria zizanioides.* Vetiver. Poppy seeds.
Kheer : A sweet dish made of rice or anything, milk and sugar boiled together.
Kheera : *Cucumis sativus.* Cucumber.
Khichadi : A rich dish of rice and pulses cooked together.
Khoya : Thickened milk.
Kulthi : *Dolichus biflorus.* A horse bean.
Laddoos : A sweet in the shape of balls of the mixture of fried gram flour, sugar, saffron and other ingredients.
Lajwanti : *Mimosa pudica.* Touch-me-not.
Lal Mirch : Chilli.
Lassi : A drink of diluted, churned and sweetened yoghurt; a cold beverage of curd.
Lauki (Fig.27) **:** *Lagenaria siceraria.* Bottle gourd.
Laung : (also *Lavang*) *Syzygium aromaticum.* Cloves.

Lehsun : *Allium sativum.* Garlic.
Loo : Heat wave blowing during summers.
Lychee (Fig.28) **:** *Seytalia lychee.* The fruit of the tree.
Maand : Rice soup.
Maida : Fine flour.
Malai : Milk cream.
Majuphal : Oak-apple; Gallnut.
Masoor daal : *Lens esculenta.* Lentil.
Mausambi (Fig.29) **:** *Citrus aurantium.* Grapefruit. A variety of orange.
Mawa : Milk thickened by boiling.
Mehndi (Fig.30) **:** *Lqawsonia inermis.* Henna; myrtle.
Methi : *Trigonella foenum-graecum.* Fenugreek.
Mitti : Clay, earth, soil.
Mogra (Fig.31) **:** Double jasmine.
Moong (Fig.32) **:** *Phaseolus aureus.* Green gram.
Moth : *Vigna aconitifoeia.* Kidney bean. A kind of lentil.
Motichur laddoos : See *laddoos.*
Mooli : *Raphanus sativus.* Radish.
Mulathi : *Glycyrrhiza glabra.* Liquorice. Sweet-wood.
Multani mitti : White clay.
Munakka (Fig.33) **:** Large raisins with seed.
Nagarmotha : A tuberous sledge of the genus cyperus.
Namkeen : A kind of Indian snacks or meals.
Neem (Fig.34) **:** *Azadirachta indica.* Margosa.
Nimbu : (also *Nibu*) *Citrus aurantifolium.* Lime.
Paalak (Fig.35) **:** Spinach.
Paan (Fig.36) **:** *Piper betel.* Betel leaf.
Paanwala : Betel vendor.
Paapad : Very thin and crisp cake made of pulse.
Papita : *Carica papaya.* Papaya.
Parwal (Fig.37) **:** *Tricosanthes dioica.* Pointed gourd. A creeper and its cucumber like fruit eaten as a vegetable.
Peeli sarson : Yellow variety of mustard seeds.
Peepal : *Ficus religiosa.* The holy Fig tree.
Petha : *Benincasa hispoda.* Ash gourd. Sweetened gourd, yellow gourd, sweet slices of white gourd-melon–famous in city Agra.
Phalsa : *Grewie asiatica.* A shrub and its berries.

Pippali : *Piper longum.* Long pepper.

Pitta : *Billius humous.* Bile; gall.

Porridge : A hot food made from oat-meal and milk or water, often eaten at breakfast.

Pudina : *Mentha arvensis.* Field-mint.

Pyjama : Loose-fitting trousers.

Raal : *Shorea robusta.* Rasin.

Rabri : Milk thickened by boiling and mixing sugar in it.

Raita : Cucumber or other vegetables chopped and cooked in curds.

Ratan jyot : *Ithospermum vestitum.* A medicinal plant, its roots.

Reetha : *Sapindus amarginatus.* Soap-nut-sapindus, detergents.

Roti : Unleavened bread.

Rudraksha (Fig.38) **:** *Elaeocarpus ganitrus.* A tree and its berries used for rosaries.

Saboodana : Sago.

Sahjan : *Morinbga pterygosperma.* The horse reddish or 'drum-stick' tree or oleifera.

Samudri jhag : Sea-foam.

Sarson : *Sinapis glauca.* Mustard.

Sarson kaali : *Brassica nigra.* Mustard.

Sattu : A meal of parched grain, roasted barley flour.

Satvik food : Endowed with goodness; pure and simple.

Sauf : *Foeniculum vulgare.* Aniseed.

Shahtoot : *Morus alba.* Mulberry.

Shalgam (Fig.39) **:** *Brassica rapa.* Turnip.

Shavasan (Fig. 51) **:** A form of yoga where person lies down like a dead body.

Shikakai : *Acacia concinna.* A prickly climber and its fruit.

Shirshasana : A form of yoga where the head touches the floor and legs are straight towards sky.

Sindoor : Vermilion.

Siras : *Acasia* or *Mimosa* tree and its flowers.

Suji : (also *Sooji*) Semolina.

Supari : Betel nut.

Taramira : *Eruca sativa.* A kind of brassica. Oil extracted from its seeds.

Tarbooj : *Citrullus vulgaris.* Water-melon.

Tawa : A hot plate for the preparation of *Chapatis.*
Tejpatta (Fig.40) **:** *Laurus nobilis.* Cassia leaves.
Thandai : A cooling drink or medicine.
Til (Fig.41) **:** *Sesamum indicum.* Sesame.
Tinda (Fig.42) **:** *Praecitrullus fistulosus.* Indian round gourd. A kind of green vegetable.
Torai : *Luffa acutangula.* Ridged gourd. Cucurbitaceous climber and its fruit.
Triphala churan (Fig.43) **:** Mixture of three kinds of myrobalan powder—harad-baheda-amla—in equal quantities.
Tulsi (Fig.44) **:** *Ocimum sanctum.* Holy basil.
Tundi-ka-shoth : Hindi word for 'Tonsillitis' disease.
Upnishad : Any of the various philosophical works expounding the inner meaning of the *Vedas.*
Urad : *Phaseolus mungo.* Black gram.
Vata : Windy humour.
Wybidang : A kind of medicinal herb.
Yakshma raj : T.B. (Tuberculosis); *YakshmaTapedik.*
Zaitun : *Olea europea.* Olive.

Glossary of English Terms

Amaranth tender : *Amaranthus polygamus.* Chaulai.
Aniseed : *Foeniculum vulgare.* Sauf.
Asafoetida : *Ferula asafoetida.* Heeng.
Basil : *Ocimum sanctum.* Tulsi.
Belleric myrobalan : *Terminalia bellirica.* Baheda.
Bitter gourd : *Momordica charantia.* Karela.
Black gram : *Phaseolus mungo.* Urad.
Black pepper : *Piper nigram.* Kali mirch.
Black plum : (also Rose apple) *Syzigium cumini.* Jamun.
Betel nut : *Areca catechu.* Supari.
Bottle gourd : *Lagenaria siceraria.* Lauki.
Cabbage : *Brassica oleracea.* Bandh-gobhi.
Camphor : *Cinnamomum comphora.* Kapoor.
Cardamom : *Elettaria cardamomum.* Chhoti ilayachi.
Carrot : *Daucus carota.* Gajar.
Cassia leaves : *Laurus nobilis.* Tejpatta.
Chebulic myrobalan : *Terminalia chebula.* Harad.
Chilli : *Capsicum annuum.* Lal mirch.
Cinnamon : *Cinnamomum zeylanicum.* Dalchini.
Cloves : *Syzygium aromaticum.* Laung.
Cluster bean : *Cyamopsis tetragonoloba.* Gwar.
Coriander : *Coriandrum sativum.* Dhania.
Cucumber : *Cucumis sativus.* Kheera.
Cumin seeds : *Cuminum cyminum.* Jeera.
Fenugreek : *Trigonella foenum-graecum.* Methi.
Fennel : *Foeniculum vulgare.* Saunf.
Fleawort pysillium : *Plantago ovata.* Isabgol.
Fig : *Ficus carica.* Anjir.

Gallnut : *Quercus infectoria.* Oak-apple; Majuphal.
Garlic : *Allium sativum.* Lehsun.
Ginger : *Zingiber officinale.* Adrak.
Gram : *Cicer arietinum.* Chana.
Grapefruit : *Citrus aurantium.* Mausambi.
Great millet : Jwar.
Green gram : *Phaseolus aureus.* Moong.
Henna : *Lqawsonia inermis.* Mehndi.
Horse bean : *Dolichus biflorus.* Kulthi.
Indian gooseberry : *Emblic myrobalan.* Amla.
Jasmine : *Jasminium grandiflorum.* Chameli.
Kidney bean : *Vigna aconitifoeia.* Moth.
Lady finger (Okra**) :** *Hibiscus esculentus.* Bhindi.
Large raisins : Munakka (with seed).
Lentil : *Lens esculenta.* Masoor Daal.
Lime : *Citrus aurantifolium.* Nimbu.
Long pepper : *Piper longum.* Pippali.
Margosa : *Azadirachta indica.* Neem.
Mulberry : *Morus alba.* Shahtoot.
Mustard : *Sinapis glauca.* Sarson.
Myrtle : Mehndi; Henna.
Nutmeg : *Myristica fragrance.* Jaiphal.
Olive : *Olea europea.* Zaitun.
Papaya : *Carica papaya.* Papita.
Pearl millet : *Pennisetum glaucum.* Bajra.
Phlegm : Balgam
Pickles : Indian pickle. Aachar.
Pigweed : *Chenapodium album.* Bathua.
Plum : *Ziziphus jujuba.* A jujube. Ber.
Pomegranate : *Punica granatum.* Anar.
Poppy seeds : *Papaver somniferum.* Khus-khus.
Radish : *Raphanus sativus.* Mooli.
Raisins : Dried grapes. Kishmish (seedless)
Ridged gourd : *Luffa acutangula.* Torai.
Rose apple : Jamun, Black plum.
Rose apple stone : Seed (Ghuthali) of Jamun.
Saffron : *Crocus sativus.* Kesar.
Sandal : *Santalum album.* Chandan.

Sesame : *Sesamum indicum.* Til.
Spinach : *Spinacia oleracea.* Paalak.
Swallow-wort : *Calotropis gigantea.* Akda.
Tamarind : *Tamarindus indica.* Imli.
Tragacanth : *Sterculia urens.* Kateera.
Turmeric : *Curcuma longa.* Haldi.
Water-melon : *Citrullus vulgaris.* Tarbooj.
White rock salt : Sendha Namak.
Wood apple : *Aegle marmelos.* Bel.
Yam : Jamikand.
Yellow gourd : Sweetened gourd, Petha.

Diagrammatic Representation

The plants and their parts (roots, rhizomes, bark, leaves, flowers, fruits and seeds) and some other terms used in the book have been given here with diagrams for easy reference.

Fig. 1 : Akda

Fig. 2 : Amla

Fig. 3 : Arbi

Fig. 4 : Arhar

Fig. 5 : Arjun ki chhal

Fig. 6 : Baheda

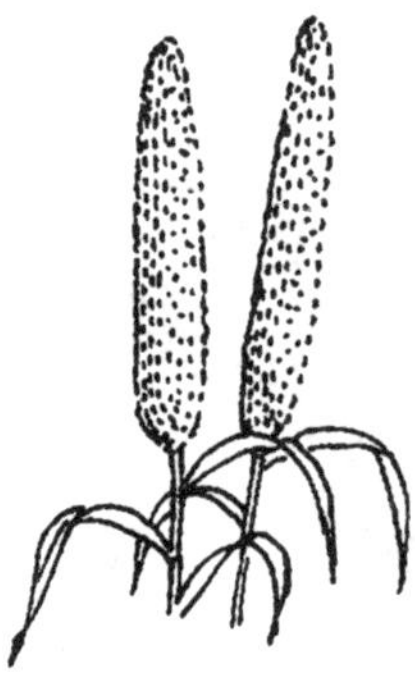

Fig. 7 : Bajra

Fig. 8 : Banyan tree

Fig. 9 : Bathua

Fig. 10 : Bel

Fig. 11 : Ber

Fig. 12 : Bhindi

Fig. 13 : Chameli

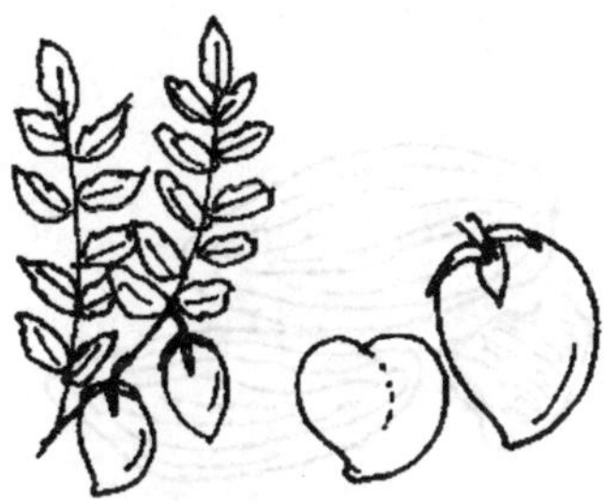

Fig. 14 : Chana

Fig. 15 : Chaulai

Fig. 16 : Dhania

Fig. 17 : Gwar

Fig. 18 : Gwarpatha

Fig. 19 : Harad

Fig. 20 : Ilaychi

Fig. 21 : Jaminkand

Fig. 22 : Jamun

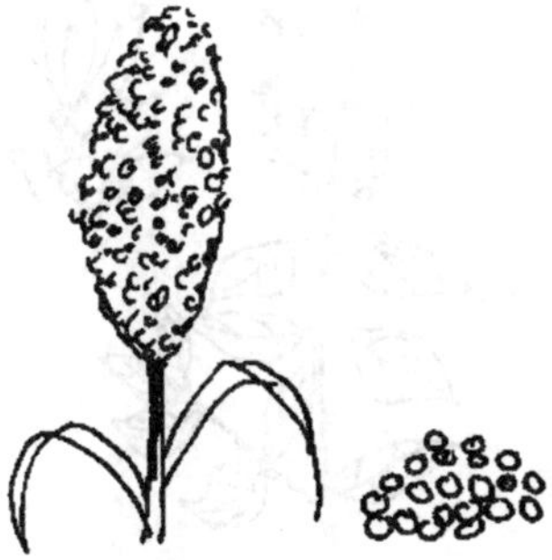

Fig. 23 : Jwar

Fig. 24 : Karaunda

Fig. 25 : Karela

Fig. 26 : Khus

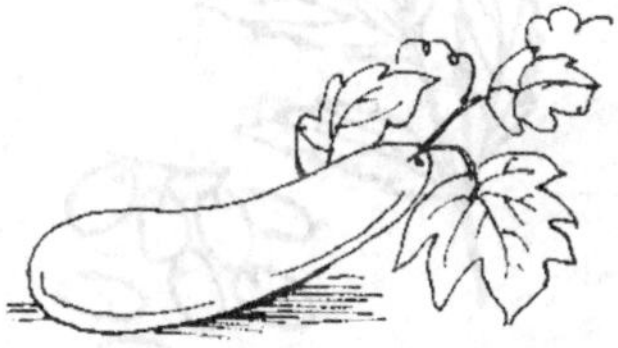

Fig. 27 : Lauki

Fig. 28 : Lichi

Fig. 29 : Mausambi

Fig. 30 : Mehndi

Fig. 31 : Mogra

Fig. 32 : Moong

Fig. 33 : Munaka

Fig. 34 : Neem

Fig. 35 : Paalak

Fig. 36 : Paan

Fig. 37 : Parwal

Fig. 38 : Rudraksh

Fig. 39 : Shalgam

Fig. 40 : Tejpatta

Fig. 41 : Til

Fig. 42 : Tinda

Fig. 43 : Triphala

Fig. 44 : Tulsi

Fig. 45 : Aata

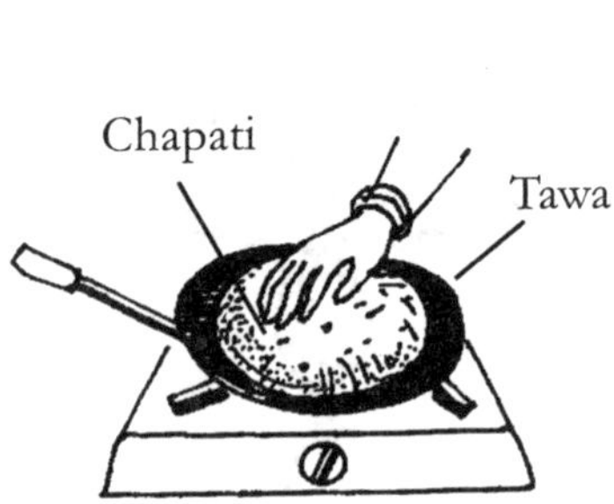

Fig. 46 : Chapati

Fig. 47 : Gulkand

Fig. 48 : Gutka

Fig. 49 : Hukka

Fig. 50 : Jalebi

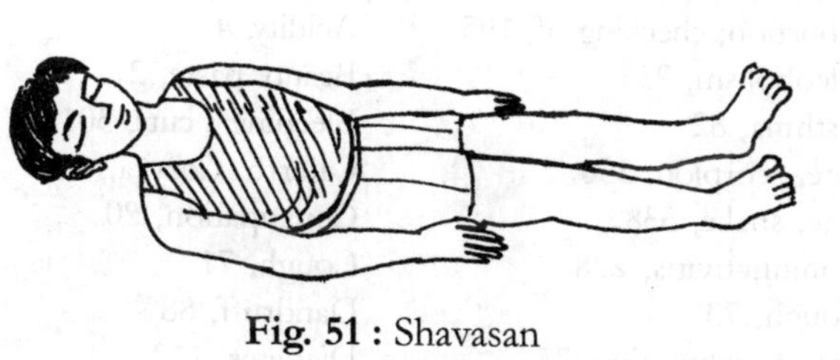

Fig. 51 : Shavasan

Index